Edison with a Commercial electric phonograph. Cornish & Co. of Washington supplied the elaborate organ case on May 17th 1893 for $15.00

Cylinder Phonograph Companion

by
George L. Frow

We ought to envy collectors for they brighten their days with long and peaceable joy
Anatole France 1844-1924

Previous publications by George L. Frow:

A Guide to the Edison Cylinder Phonograph (1970)
The Edison Cylinder Phonographs 1877-1929 (with Albert F. Sefl) (1978)
The Edison Disc Phonographs and the Diamond Discs (1982)

Second Printing 1997
(150 anniversary of the Birth of Thomas Edison)

Published by Stationery X-Press
Post Office Box 207
Woodland Hills, CA 91364 U.S.A.

ISBN 0-9606466-1-4

Also available from Stationery X-Press:

Look for the Dog, an Illustrated Guide to Victor Talking Machines
The Columbia Phonograph Companion, Volume I
The Columbia Phonograph Companion, Volume II
Edison Blue Amberol Recordings, 1912-1914

© 1994 George L. Frow

All rights reserved. Apart from any fair dealing for the purpose of private study, criticism or review, as permitted under the Copyright Act, no portion may be reproduced, stored in a retrieval system, or transmitted in any form by any means, electronic, mechanical, photocopying, recording or otherwise, without the prior permission of the copyright owner.

The Edison Cylinder Phonograph Companion
By George L. Frow

From the Naughty Nineties to the Roaring Twenties the Edison Cylinder Phonographs caught most of the tunes and characters of their day, but were driven into retirement in attics and garden sheds as radio came into their owners' homes. For many years since enthusiasts have been lavishing time and talents on restoring surviving machines and their success is reflected in the growth of Phonograph Societies, books and periodicals, particularly in the English-speaking parts of the world, and a widespread revived interest in early phonographs and their recordings.

In particular the Edison-made instruments respond readily to such care and can be brought back to playing cylinder recordings with a fidelity approaching that reached in the Golden Age of the cylinder record ending in 1914, when Edison's recordings played better than any others. These were the sounds known and enjoyed by great-grandfather; singers, bands, instrumentalists, comedy turns and the voices of the great and infamous of a long-gone age come back to life on these records.

The Edison Cylinder Phonograph Companion traces the careers of the many models of the instruments and follows them through from production committee, early outlines and into manufacture, describing the improvements and accessories as they came along; prices of the day are also shown. The Edison Phonographs were exported as well, sometimes as special models, and an account is given of these rare machines, when known.

Besides being a drawing room entertainer Edison's Phonographs were built into slot machines and formed the first amusement arcades; thousands of offices all over the world took them for recording business letters, some of the first talking dolls were Edison's; phonographs came too with language instruction courses and provided the sound for early Edison talking films.

Appearing originally in 1978 this book has been greatly expanded as a result of years of fresh research with material and illustrations increased by more than half, much of it from kindly correspondents and owners of equipment. It will be a constant identifying source for collectors, libraries and museums and the antique trade and embodies chapters not included earlier.

Ever since acquiring a secondhand red GEM in 1954 George Frow has been attracted both by the quality and the history behind the Edison products and has written several books and articles on them.

Born in South London in the 1920s his first machine was a child's Bing 'Pygmyphone' with five and six inch nursery rhyme records, and he recalls trying to make recordings on this with home-made discs of melted candle wax, without success. In the house there was a piano and parental dislike of "canned music" and not until 1934 did a portable gramophone arrive as a Christmas present, and life changed for the better. A collector friend's early advice to 'specialize' was taken seriously and resulted in a collection of early machines and accessories, and these are now in the possession of the National Sound Archive in London.

Early retirement from a family business gave George Frow the opportunity to research the subject in Britain further, and in America, and to pursue related interests. He is honoured to have been President of the City of London Phonograph and Gramophone Society since 1974, only the third to hold the office since the Society's formation in 1919.

Contents

Introduction		9
Chapter 1	Tinfoil Phonographs	13
Chapter 2	Talking Doll	28
Chapter 3	Electric Phonographs	40
Chapter 4	Treadle and Water Motor Phonographs	65
Chapter 5	Early Spring-Driven Phonographs	70
Chapter 6	HOME Phonograph (CLASS H)	94
Chapter 7	STANDARD Phonograph (CLASS S)	113
Chapter 8	GEM Phonograph	134
Chapter 9	CONCERT Phonograph	151
Chapter 10	CLASS M and CLASS E CONCERT Electric Phonographs	158
Chapter 11	ALVA Phonograph	161
Chapter 12	IDELIA Phonograph	165
Chapter 13	FIRESIDE Phonograph	175
Chapter 14	AMBEROLA Phonographs	181
Chapter 15	PREMIUM Phonograph	226
Chapter 16	OPERA Phonograph	228
Chapter 17	SCHOOL Phonograph	233
Chapter 18	Electric Coin-Slot Phonographs	236
Chapter 19	Multiplex Coin-Operated Phonographs	255
Chapter 20	Electric Coin-Slot CONCERT Phonographs	261
Chapter 21	Spring-Driven Coin-Slot Phonographs	263
Chapter 22	PHONO-KINETOSCOPE 1894-5	271
Chapter 23	KINETOPHONE 1909-1916	275
Chapter 24	Reproducers and Recorders until 1912	288
Chapter 25	Diamond Reproducers	322
Chapter 26	Language Courses	328
Chapter 27	The Polyphone Attachment	335
Chapter 28	Repeating Attachments	339
Chapter 29	The Coming of the Amberols & Combination Phonographs	343
Chapter 30	Horns	351
Chapter 31	Some Notes On Shavers	362
Chapter 32	Batteries	367
Chapter 33	Some Notes on Business Machines	369
Appendix I	First Edison Phonograph Sales, April 1878 to Jan. 1880	381
Appendix II	THE TINFOIL PHONOGRAPH ABROAD	388
Appendix III	THE 1888 GIFT FOR COLONEL GOURAUD	393
Appendix IV	EDISON PHONOGRAPHS and EDISON BELL	400
Appendix V	THE CIRCUMSTANCES OF THE INTRODUCTION OF THE EDISON MODEL C PHONOGRAPHS	407
Appendix VI	CHARLES BATCHELOR'S RECOLLECTIONS OF THE PHONOGRAPH INVENTION	410
Appendix VII	SOME SELECTED POEMS IN PRAISE OF EDISON PHONOGRAPHS	412
Acknowledgments		417
Recommended Reading		419
Springs for Phonographs		421
Some Phonograph Sales 1899-1905		422
The Edison Phonograph Companies		423
Index		427

Introduction

FOR THE READER ......

All Phonograph models registered in Edison catalogues and correspondence are printed in capitals in this book; eg: STANDARD, CONCERT, AMBEROLA etc. and care should be taken to distinguish between model classification of (a) phonographs, and (b) reproducers. These are un-related.

Cylinders quoted in the narrative are as follows:

Standard-	those of 2-minute duration (100 grooves per inch.)
Concert-	large diameter wax cylinders of 2-minute duration
Amberol-	wax, and of 4-minute duration (200 grooves per inch)
Blue Amberol-	similar but made from coloured celluloid

Until 1900 Edison phonographs were given a coding of the initial letter or letters of their type, Class SM for SPRING MOTOR, Class S for STANDARD, and so on, although within the trade they had names like 'the small machine' or 'the Number 2 machine' attached to them. From 1900 the practice of allotting a code word to all Edison machines, attachments and accessories ousted casual names and simplified the sending of cable messages, but in 1901 the phonographs assumed these code names prominently as their titles, but none of the attachments or accessories seemed to have done, except the 'Triton' motor.

From 1901 to 1903 these machine names preceded the term Edison Phonograph in the catalogues eg. STANDARD Edison Phonograph - but after that time it would always be Edison HOME Phonograph etc. for the remainder of the machines' careers.

In anticipation of a possible terminology difficulty, the United States equivalent of the British word 'factor' was 'jobber'; jobbers took the goods from the manufacturer into the wholesale warehouse and distributed them to the dealers, or store/shop keepers.

At some time or other most collectors have been faced by an Edison Phonograph and have needed to put a date on it. Instant identification of the type and model under these circumstances often calls for a little thought and care because many machines are not found in their catalogue state.

Obviously the type of phonograph will normally appear on the banner transfer if there is one, or on the patent plate either in full or as the initial letter in front of the serial number, or in a square of its own, and a reference to these pages should give a guide to its date of manufacture within a year or so either way. Where a patent plate is fitted the last date shown is another indicator, and to be treated with reserve, but early Edison models had no patent plate and origin details are usually scant.

The reasons for these Model-letter designations were two-fold; firstly to show a progressive change such as an improvement in the motor or its suspension, and secondly denoting changes to the upper mechanism, including the position and size of the reproducer carrier-arm. It can be misleading to ascribe a date to a machine solely on its type of horn, presence of a 2 and 4-minute gearing, reproducer and so forth, as these items could be bought and added as extra options years later than the phonograph. Model progressions in the horn phonographs were never for insignificant reasons.

Several variants existed within the early AMBEROLAS that omitted the prefix letter to the (Roman) Model number on the patents plate, in fact the first horn phonographs were not given a Model letter either; succeeding models of that type were not envisaged at the time.

Machines that do not conform to the Model- date pattern derived from company records are sometimes found. These may be 'ends of lines', specials and sports that were allowed to go out and are sometimes found in foreign markets. Foreign copies of Edison phonographs and accessories are also met.

Many of the patentees quoted herein were employees of or contractors to the Edison Company and usually assigned their patents to Edison owned companies such as the New Jersey Patent Company; sometimes Edison himself did this.

The filing date attached to patents in the notes is a useful though not always accurate guide to the state of an invention. It was sometimes Edison practice to file caveats with the U.S. Patent Office for inventions, components or drawings on inventions and if rejected would often be improved and broadened until accepted. In the meantime others working along similar lines would be deterred, knowing the resources and legal talent of the Edison enterprises. At times his attorneys pressed Edison to widen his patent applications abroad, but he waved them aside saying the more he took out abroad the more he lost to infringers and pirates.

In the interests of easier reading several terminology abbreviations will soon become apparent in this book. The Edison company in its several names from 1878 to 1929 is often abbreviated to "the company".

In the same cause and for economy of space the patents quoted have generally been selective, but should be enough to show the way to further investigation if desired.

In the heyday of the Edison phonographs so many options of sale and part exchange surrounded the new accessories for each model as they were issued that these have had to be simplified in the cause of manageable presentation.

Edison's Laboratory at Menlo Park, New Jersey, where the tinfoil phonograph was invented was vacated in 1887 for the one at West Orange, New Jersey, now the Edison National Historic Site, located at Main Street and Lakeside Avenue, and is normally the Laboratory, Factory or Works referred to in these pages.

Today the Edison Site includes the Laboratory, Library, Music Room and Archives and is one of the properties administered by the Eastern National Park and Monument Association, Philadelphia, PA. Most of the Works buildings and the Power House were demolished in the early 'seventies.

●●●●●●●●●●●●●●●

Since the first edition of this book appeared in 1978, passing time has shown the need to bring it up to date with freshly acquired information and amend some errors and shortcomings. It is still not possible, for instance, to reconcile dates of manufacture with the works numbers punched on the machines; this is surely the biggest void in Edison phonograph knowledge. However, a great quantity of internal and outside correspondence relating to the everyday matters of trading and research at the Edison Laboratory has again been helpful, and it may be that one day all the researcher seeks will be instantly unfolded at the touch of a button.

All chapters on the various phonograph types in the earlier book have been expanded, and several new ones added, including material about office phonographs and the early Phono-Kinetoscope and loud-speaking Kinetophone.

The quantity production of phonographs was the first business venture at West Orange from 1888, and it grew to be the largest, and the future of all Edison enterprises came to depend on its success or failure; research on the phonographs took longer and proved very much more costly than ever foreseen, leading to economic problems for Edison who found it difficult to acquire investment to expand his enterprise as a result.

Readers coming to this book for the first time may ask why an all-American invention like the Phonograph has been given some British coverage, but had it not been vigorously promoted by the American Colonel Gouraud in London it might have missed the public fancy and remained in the coin-slot parlors of down-town America, its significance unrealized. Gouraud took Edison's "perfected" Phonograph and by introducing it to a string of eminent and influential personages at his home for letting them amuse themselves after dinner, attracted press publicity that kept the invention highlighted at a critical time and underlined Edison as its creator. Gouraud soon moved out of the scene and others took over promotion in Great Britain, Surviving correspondence with them provides clues to the state of business and mechanical progress that cannot always be found from American trade sources, in fact this aspect is not so apparent from anywhere else in the Edison world of those days.

To quote the earlier edition of this book, no greater tribute can be paid to the Phonograph's inventor and his products than the number that have survived to a century or more, and that can still be restored to playing well and giving pleasure.

George L. Frow
48 Woodfields
Chipstead
Sevenoaks, Kent
TN13 2RB, England

Chapter 1
Tinfoil Phonographs

The story of Edison's invention of the Phonograph has been told many times over the years and is broadly familiar to established collectors. Although fewer inventions are so well served by contemporary documentary material, there are still gaps and inconsistencies, and perhaps continued research will remedy these. There were also some dubious dates put on documents at a vital period to give weight to patent claims. The purpose of this chapter is to relate the experiments that led to the first phonographs emerging from the several Edison concerns, and to fit these to dates. Obviously all the machines in this chapter were fundamental, heavy and far less effective than those that followed some ten years later, but some had equipment or characteristics that appeared on the improved instruments of 1888.

Invention

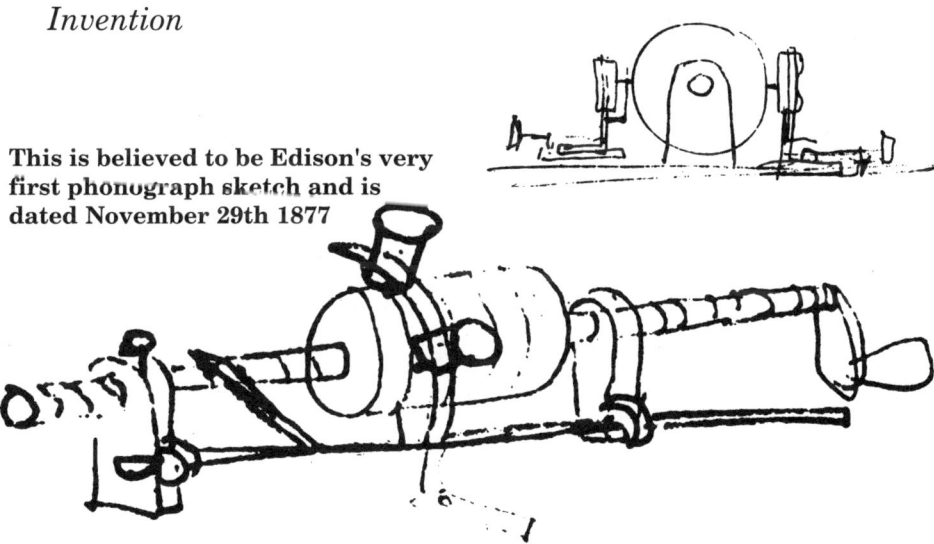

This is believed to be Edison's very first phonograph sketch and is dated November 29th 1877

In the years and months leading to the construction of the first phonograph at the end of 1877, the Edison Laboratory team at Menlo Park, New Jersey, had been concentrating on improving the Automatic Telegraph and indenting dots and dashes on a strip of paper from signals coming in over a line. At the same time the Edison carbon telephone was being developed, an improvement on the work already done by Alexander Graham Bell; in this a diaphragm put varying pressure on a carbon button through vibrations produced by the human voice. Edison reasoned that if a point were put in the centre of the diaphragm and the diaphragm talked to as a strip of waxed paper were drawn along under it, it would be indented and the talking reproduced the next time the paper was pulled through. The laboratory notebook pages of this period are noticeably full of experimental work on such devices, and it is tempting to read phonograph material into many of them; from this distance the discovery of recording and retrieval of the sounds through these instruments seemed inevitable. Earlier trials with the telegraph had provided a ready stock of different thicknesses of wax papers in the laboratory, and Charles Batchelor[1] reported that Edison spoke "Mary had a little Lamb" - a regular testing piece in the laboratory of those days - and that when the paper was again pulled under the stylus it appeared to carry perceptible echoes of the nursery rhyme; the experiment was noted in the laboratory notebook for July 18th 1877. In a footnote Edison wrote "there is no doubt I shall be able to store up and reproduce at any time the human voice perfectly".[2]

The team at the laboratory gave first place to working on the telephone transmitter while the idea of the phonograph seemed to be shelved.[3] It was never very far from Edison's mind and with every confidence in its prospects of success he allowed his press representative E. H. Johnson to write to *Scientific American*, reporting on the earlier experiments of indenting the wax paper strip and reproducing the sounds through a more delicate diaphragm. The letter appeared in the November 17th 1877 issue, preceded by a prophetic editorial headed

A WONDERFUL INVENTION SPEECH CAPABLE OF INDEFINITE RETENTION FROM AUTOMATIC RECORDS.

The first Edison Phonograph, constructed by John Kruesi, from December 4th to 6th 1877

It was possible of course that Edison had done some private and unchronicled work on the idea, but the cat was out of the bag without the protection of a patent application.

At this vital stage of the phonograph's development there is an obscure period in its history as its engineering drawings do not appear in the files. The earliest sketches that survive were made by Edison on a sheet of paper, dated November 29th 1877 and witnessed by Batchelor and John Kruesi. There are two, both of slightly differing machines and the lower one showing a separate recorder and reproducer would be the type engineered some hours later by John Kruesi. His time sheets show more than 60 hours of work on the phonograph from December 1st to 6th[4], and it is now certain that with Edison's hearing impairment Charles Batchelor would have helped with the recording and reproducing phonets, following his long experience with the telephone microphones. The earliest surviving sketch resembling the finished machine reasonably closely is to be found in Batchelor's diary of December 4th alongside a page of description of the phonograph.

Kruesi made the U. S. Patent Office model in wood in ten hours on December 7th, the patent was filed on December 24th and the machine was placed in the Smithsonian Institute, but in 1926 was transferred to the Henry Ford Village at Dearborn, Michigan. Except for December 16th and 17th Kruesi was employed for the whole month to working on the Phonograph.[5] On the day after its construction Batchelor showed the first machine to the editor of the *Scientific American* and reported the event in a letter to his friend George H. Bliss:[6]

> *You probably remember when you were down here about Edison's idea of recording the human voice and afterwards reproducing it. Well, we have done it and today shown it in New York to the Scientific American people who are now sketching the apparatus for a future issue. As a proof that the principle is correct it actually worked the first time we tried it......the Phonograph is going to be a magnificent success!!!!!!* (sic)

Edison's feelings on his new invention and its prospects at this time come through in a letter he wrote on December 12th to "Mac" - James U. Mackenzie, his telegraph mentor:

> *The phonograph is a perfect success and as soon as I have cheapened the mechanism down a little, I want you to take charge of the whole business for this and other countries. But you must think it over well and be ready as we must move quick.*[7] (sic)

Batchelor who had been born in London and brought up in Manchester maintained a connection with *The English Mechanic* through articles and letters, and on December 9th sent in a full description of the new instrument,[8] while *Scientific American* published the account of the Talking Phonograph on December 22nd. Although Batchelor's entry in his diary implied that he alone took the Phonograph to this journal, only Edison's name appeared in the printed account, and is one of the several incongruities that are apparent in this first year of the Phonograph; it is certain that Batchelor and Edison went along together.

The *New York Sun* also printed an early account of the invention on January 2nd 1878.

On the day after Christmas in 1877 Batchelor reported linking the phonograph by telephone to New Brunswick, some hundreds of miles to the north, where it was heard and understood by several people.

The first model made by Kruesi remained at Menlo Park until the end of 1880 when Edison allowed it to be taken to the Patent Office Museum in London - now the Science Museum - after entertaining a visit by the curator, Col. Stuart Wortley. There it stayed until 1928 when it was returned to Edison on the occasion of his receiving the Congressional Medal of Honor on October 20th, and is now at West Orange. Its place at the Science Museum was taken by a replica and several of these exist in museums and in store at West Orange.

Exploitation

> *I've made some machines, but this is my baby and I expect it to grow to be a big feller and support me in my old age.*
> Edison to *Daily Graphic*, April 2nd 1878.

By the end of 1877, only three weeks after the invention, Edison had designed an improved and heavier version of the first model. This too was built by Kruesi and had a flywheel and a larger cylinder to smooth the running. Three or four were then made for experimental purposes and reported in the press as "loud enough to be audible at a distance of 175 ft".[9] It was the type photographed with its inventor in Mathew Brady's studio in Washington before its demonstration to President Hayes and both Houses of Congress on April 18th 1878. These may be regarded as the first production Edison Phonographs and are sometimes known as the Brady models from this association with the well-known photographer. It will be noticed that the lead-screw is now set at the left of the cylinder and that the separate recording and reproducing phonets have been combined with refined adjustment and an improved telephone mouthpiece; light metal or cardboard horns could be used instead of a mouthpiece.

From the end of 1877 Charles Batchelor gave over his day to working on the phonograph - he was not more specific in his diary, but he was moving towards producing practical clockwork machines[10].

Bergmann Phonograph (left) and so-called Brady type of phonograph as shown in Edison's White House demonstration and photographed by Brady in April 1878

With a need for smaller and cheaper models, Edison sketched outlines of the first small tinfoil phonographs on January 8th 1878; these had the combination flywheel and mandrel unit and swinging bracket for the mouthpiece. They and the larger machines were constructed at the laboratory and on one unspecified day in February, Batchelor reported that 9 large machines and 11 small had been made and sent away[11]. Evidence has not been seen at this time of machines being in any numbering system. That there was undoubtedly an interest from institutions and the public to buy the new phonographs is disclosed by the existence of printed cards apologizing for the instruments not being ready[12].

The electrician in Edison is revealed in an experiment of February 2nd 1878 using a magnetized stylus to indent iron foil, but it was found not to work without being made to touch the surface - some years later the inventor worked on similar lines.

As Edison was committed by contract and a salary to Western Union and telephone development, a group of capitalists convened on January 30th to propose forming a company to handle the new invention. They agreed to pay him $10,000 initially with a 20 per cent royalty on every machine sold and a rate for exhibitions; Edison would be vice-president and Gardiner G. Hubbard, father-in-law of Alexander Graham Bell was appointed president.[13] The Edison Speaking Phonograph Company received its Certificate of Incorporation on April 24th, by chance the publication date of Edison's British Patent No. 1644, and until becoming official was calling itself The Phonograph Company.

The new association saw the phonograph as an exhibition novelty, a musical instrument and as a voice for clocks and toys.[14] There now appeared to be a market wide open ahead and Charles Cheever, one of its members, proposed that 500 small sized machines should be made for the concern to handle. On February 8th Batchelor made calls on a number of makers of small engineering products on its behalf with model drawings. Among those he visited was Sigmund Bergmann who had supplied the laboratories with mechanical parts for several years and was reputed for the quality of his work.[15] From March orders were placed with him and with other makers.[16]

At first these machines conformed nearly to the original conception, but improvements began to appear during the year. The early method of fixing the tin-foil with shellac was slow and clumsy and soon a lengthways slot with clamping rod or rubber wedge was made, a half-nut 'throw out' for quick return of the feed screw became a feature of the larger machines; metal diaphragms always prone to rust made way for mica and other materials on more adjustable carrier arms. The stylus and its mounting were improved to give more sensitivity to the hissing consonants such as 's' and 'sh' after trials by Batchelor,[17] and from May 15th the cylinders (or mandrels) altered to having a 'U'

Lightweight Edison tinfoil phonograph of 1878

groove from one with a square bottom. A means of putting a roll of tinfoil inside the cylinder for feeding as needed through the slot was not pursued, as removal of the cylinder end for renewing the foil caused problems.[18] Other metal foils in various gauges were tried; apart from tinfoil copper was most favored but found to stretch, and tinfoil continued to meet the need until the Edison wax record machines appeared in 1887-8. Some machine makers added decoration of leaves and gilt and the prices reflected the proportion of wood, brass and cast iron used in the body and components. There were 'long' and 'short' types according to the size of the mandrel and the smallest machine was the $10.00 PARLOR, the big flywheel demonstration model was the CONCERT, large models sold from round $80.00 to upwards of $200.00, these machines being known in the company private circles as 'big prophet' machines.

Not unexpectedly The Edison Speaking Phonograph Company was stretched in its early days, even by mid-March to fellow directors having to prevail on Edison to resist giving away so many phonographs to friends, scientific institutes and good causes. He was obviously enjoying his invention and the attention it brought him as an interlude before the laboratory took the plunge into the protracted setting-up of the first electric light system, and the Edison Phonograph was put on one side and remained little worked on for years, confined to the limits of its own tinfoil.

There were always plenty of people outside to offer advice, and when they were reasoned Edison often answered these letters himself and sometimes at

Edison demonstration tinfoil phonograph. It bears no markings and lacks the diaphragm and mouthpiece

Edison Concert Phonograph of 1879

Brehmer Salon Phonograph 1878

some length. Being a simple but attractive inspiration it was only a matter of time before amateur engineers started to build their own phonographs. Detailed plans of the first machine had appeared in the supplement to *Scientific American* for July 20th 1878, and Batchelor drew the inventor's attention to this infringement of his first U. S. Phonograph patent (No. 200,521) but the journal refused to retract and Edison was privately told that were he to prosecute, it could cost him his royalties. Several phonographs were marketed unofficially and their perpetrators cautioned rigorously, leading to an official warning circular by E. H. Johnson, acting as agent, that the Company would take every step to protect Edison's phonograph patent.[19]

Demonstrations to the public seem to have started on January 17th 1878 when Batchelor had a phonograph speaking and singing at Cooper's Union American Institute, and an early open hearing was before The Polytechnic Association in New York. In February Edison's agent, Johnson secured rights to exhibit the Musical Phonograph, Musical Telephone and Speaking Telephone across the country, and advertised himself for $100.00 a night, including apparatus and assistant. In spite of pressure from colleagues Edison was reticent in allowing any travelling series of lectures by outsiders to go ahead. He seems to have given approval after mid-April and instruments were made to demonstrate nationally and a number of men taken on and allocated territories.[20] The outcome of Johnson's scheme is not known.

With so much perceptible commitment to the phonograph, it is hard to realize how much a disc version of the tinfoil machine was in the minds of Edison's close staff during these formative weeks. From the early sketch of December 3rd 1877 there is as much prominence given in laboratory notebooks to the disc model as the cylinder machine. The disc method offered a way of preserving the recording that could in theory be replaced on the machine or transferred to a similar model.[21] Once removed from the cylinder phonograph the indentations on the tinfoil were distorted and lost. Edison foresaw duplication of the tinfoil plates using plaster of Paris, and described it as an alternative in his United States patent, and it was mentioned in the December in a letter to a friend.[22] In an article in *Scribner's Magazine* of April 1878 George Scribner described a working model in detail. There was a 10-inch turntable, called a plate, and this was pre-cut by a special groove on both sides, the one below acting as a tracing groove, and driven by a spring motor wound by a ratchet lever and controlled by a butterfly governor. On February 15th 1878 Edison sketched several disc phonographs in cabinets and made for use on tables, and regularly through 1878 mention of plate phonographs was to be found in correspondence; on March 23rd Company notes reported that eight men were kept working on them, trying to stamp out from an electrotype coated with steel. Experiments were still being made towards the end of 1878, and several models were sent to London to W. H. Preece, chief engineer of the Post Office. Despite the numbers clearly being constructed it is strange that none is known to have survived. Two later references to these plate phonographs may be noted. On August 15th 1899 Edison's patent agent Richard Dyer wrote to him about an 1878 survivor:

> *I understand the machine is still about your laboratory. Is that or any other motor tinfoil still in existence?*

John Ott could not find it. On October 4th 1905 a disc tinfoil phonograph with 3 or 4 boxes of discs were reported from Peru and offered to Edison by way of Peter Bacigalupi, the San Francisco dealer. In a reply of October 16th 1906 W. E. Gilmore, president of the National Phonograph Company reported that Edison claimed to have one in his possession, but Gilmore with himself in mind said he

> *would like to obtain a similar outfit if possible, but it is all contingent on what it would cost to get it.*[23]

The outcome is not known and perhaps one lies unrecognised in a storeroom somewhere in the world. Even in the last century as Edison was inventing, those around him began to see the significance of what was being done.

In spite of the requirement of a regulated speed device to ensure that input and output voice pitches were the same, Edison tinfoil phonographs were never adapted to any drive other than manual in the United States except in the smallest numbers.[24] Batchelor was working with a weight drive from January 1878, using pendulums, centrifugal and air governors, and such a machine was illustrated in *Engineering* of March 8th 1878. In a letter of April 16th Batchelor refers to "two clockwork phonographs which I am making", but they were not satisfactory.[25] Three months later he was to write again "it is easy to make a good clockwork, but it is difficult to make it without extra vibrations".[26]

Interestingly, two similar outlines of spring driven tinfoil phonographs survive in laboratory sketches by John Ott. The earlier of March 19th 1878 appears in Edison's British Patent No. 1644 of April 24th 1878, and again as a sketch of the following November 30th noted 'made by John Ott'. The remarkable feature of this machine is that the cylinder and its shaft have no lateral movement, but the reproducer/recorder now traversed, moved by a tracer in a coarse lead-screw, the first appearance of a layout that has become familiar on the wax cylinder electric and TRIUMPH models. There were three additional patent models constructed for Edison for June 7th 1878, one being a spring driven clockwork style, but their fate is unknown.

Further trials with a clockwork mechanism bought from Loriot and Ostrom of New York in 1879 failed to reach expectations and was described by Uriah Painter as 'still a bitch'.[27] Nevertheless, weight and spring driven tinfoil phonographs of other makes do exist and are sometimes seen, but none came within Edison's approval for retailing and most existing in the United States were either imported or privately built.

One last style of tinfoil phonograph must be mentioned although it does not seem to have got further than an idea and the granting of a patent, and is first seen in laboratory sketches on October 6th 1878 and subsequently in more refined forms on October 9th and 11th.[28] Owing something to the disc phonograph this was called the Dictating Cylinder Phonograph and was really a tinfoil cylinder machine set on end and the phonet carrier propelled vertically on a threaded shaft. The sketches offer a spring or electric drive, the first noted instance of the possibility of an electric motor on a phonograph. Although the subject arose on several occasions in letters to Edison, no evidence is known of any tinfoil machines being used in offices.[29]

In the 1880s the Edison Phonograph became neglected, having reached limits of evolution in its current form and no major work was done on it after 1879 for the next eight years. By December 14th 1878 Charles Bailey, treasurer of The Edison Speaking Phonograph Company was reporting a falling-off of sales; he said that interest in a 'mere exhibition' would flag and was hoping to produce something that would excite a new demand.[30] That 'something' was not defined - it was going to be a Talking Doll but that would take 10 years of development - so the firm continued with diminished phonograph sales, and with Edison released from his Agreement with it from January 1879.

Towards the end of 1878 it was realized that through an earlier oversight the final specifications for British Patent No. 1644 had been filed, those for his American Patent No. 200,521 had not. As a United States citizen Edison was required to apply for an American patent first, with the result that his American devices in the British patent were open to all comers in the United States, and later led to much expensive litigation when he returned to his phonograph invention.

The newspapers found they could always get good copy from the inventor, particularly about the phonograph, which in its mysterious simplicity had caught the public's imagination, and from the early weeks of 1878 reporters wore the path to his laboratory door. Their accounts, compared one with another, had truth and fantasy interwoven and were copied and syndicated nationwide. All this must have caused amusement to Edison and his co-workers and a selection of these stories are pasted into their scrapbooks. One, widely circulated, reported the results of turning the crank-handle backwards (something not recommended because it tore the tinfoil), resulting in Edison's voice issuing as:

> *Go to sure was Lamb the*
> *Went Mary that everywhere and*
> *Snow was white was fleece its*
> *Lamb little a had Mary.*

The perpetrator of that yarn is not known.

More seriously *Harper's Weekly* of March 30th 1878 in a famous series of line drawings explained how the tinfoil machine worked and showed a funnel (horn) in use. On April 2nd the New York *Daily Graphic* gave Edison the front page with a series of line drawings, in the next month Frank Leslie's *Budget of Fun* showed 15 cartoons of the possibilities of the phonograph to add something to life. There were concepts of 'the phonograph as a detective', but it was obviously outside its capacity as an under-the-bed recorder. Its use with clocks and watches also proved to be beyond its limits, and in conjunction with Edison's Aerophone,[31] a compressed air or steam amplified megaphone, the phonograph was somewhat extravagantly seen as a station announcer fitted to the head of an approaching locomotive, and after its grand opening in 1885 as the 'voice' of the Statue of Liberty.

The phonograph's success as an exhibition piece having faded due to its limited practical possibilities in tinfoil form, Edison and his associates did little work on it. In a fire at the factory in December 1880 a great number of finished machines were destroyed, and three months later the inventor and his staff left Menlo Park and moved to New York to supervise the installation of the electric light there and the phonograph entered a 'dark age' of its own. It appeared to be still obtainable to order, but not until 1886 did Edison take it up again.

●●●●●●●●●●●●●●●●●●

The question has often been asked that could the sound ever be heard from surviving pieces of recorded tinfoil; this seems unlikely. For one thing the tinfoil has been unwrapped from a cylinder shape and laid out flat and the groove tracks will be distorted beyond retrieval by present day methods. However in these fast moving times it might one day be possible to read these 'in the flat' by some laser or photo-electric cell method yet to be thought of.

The world's oldest recoverable recording claimed so far was found in 1991 on a (Frank) Lambert[32] Phonograph, said by him in a Court case to be made in 1879. The record surface was cut directly into a lead sleeve and announces clock times starting at One o'clock to Twelve o'clock, but oddly omitting Ten o'clock. This phonograph was also equipped with a shaving device - the first surely - and had a separate recorder and reproducer. In Allen Koenigsberg's opinion this may have been made to be combined with a talking clock.

Experimental Graphophone, recording in wax-filled grooves

• • • • • • • • • • • • • • • • •

At the time of his British Patent No. 1644 of 1878, Edison was using the word 'phonograph' to denote the recording head as well as the whole machine, the reproducer or speaker was called a 'phonet', and the cylinder tinfoil message was a 'phonogram', but these expressions were simplified as the machines came into use.

• • • • • • • • • • • • • • • • •

This late tinfoil phonograph with lead screw and lifting button on the speaker arm was a "missing link" between the tinfoil and wax cylinder phonographs

The first full manual for setting-up the tinfoil phonograph was *Instructions for the Management and Operation of Edison's Speaking Phonograph* and was published by The Edison Speaking Phonograph Co. early in 1878 when:

> *this company is prepared to offer to the public only that design or form of apparatus which has been found best adapted to its exhibition as a novelty.*

Evidence points to this manual dating from about April.[33]

Two models were offered, an exhibition instrument grooved to 24 threads per inch, and a drawing-room instrument at 40 threads per inch. Neither was priced but there was a space left for the supplier to write this in.

The first was all made of iron but with a brass cylinder, and was mounted on a white wood box with a drawer for tools and supplies.

The second was all of brass including base and flywheel, and mounted on a rosewood and inlaid box with a drawer for tools and supplies. Each instrument was supplied with the following:

1) Instruction manual
2) 5 lb record foil
3) 1 oil stone

4) 1 oilcan
5) 1 screw driver
6) 1 centering pin
7) 1 funnel (horn)
8) 1 piece rubber cushion
9) 1 piece rubber for wedge
10) 1 piece wax cement
11) 6 prepared styli

Measurement of the instrument in its box:

Length 2 ft. 10 in., width 1 ft. 2 in., depth 1 ft. 2 in.

Total weight of instrument and box 175 lb.

Record foil obtainable from S. Bergmann & Co., 104 Wooster Street, New York

there being 30 sheets to 1 lb., obtainable in 5, 10 and 20 lb. boxes at 45 cents per lb.

Extra styli 15 cents each, diaphragms 10 cents each.

NOTES
1) Charles Batchelor October 12th 1906 "My Recollections of Mr. Edison" - reproduced in Appendix VI - Edison Archive
2) Laboratory Sheet August 17th 1877 - Edison Archive
3) The word 'phonograph' in today's accepted use first appeared in the Edison Notebook of August 12th - Edison Archive
4) Depicted in Petersen's 'Creation of the Original Phonograph' *A.P.C.S. Journal* Summer 1974
5) Petersen *American Phonograph Journal* March 1978
6) General Manager of Edison Electric Pen and Duplicator Company
7) Edison Archive
8) In submissions to this journal he often signed himself 'Asor', an adaptation of his wife's name Rosanna
9) *Scientific American* January 5th 1878
10) The term clockwork was used loosely in laboratory reports and can be confusing, but at this stage usually meant a weight-driven motor
11) Charles Batchelor Notebook PN 78-02-24 - Edison Archive
12) Example dated March 2nd 1878 illustrated in Petersen Article, *A.P.C.S. Journal* Summer 1974
13) Original signatories were Edison, Hubbard, G. S. Bradley, E. S. Converse, Charles A. Cheever, Hilbourne L. Roosevelt, U. H. Painter. Roosevelt, an organ builder, was uncle to Theodore Roosevelt, later President of U.S.A.
14) By January 7th 1878 the phonograph was already earmarked to call the time on clocks and watches, and The Ansonia Clock Company was endeavoring to make a cheap movement. The Edison Toy Manufacturing Company would be formed at the end of 1878. Later in the year Col. Bob Ingersoll, writing in the New York *Daily Graphic* reported a phonograph built into an automaton figure of a Negress at Menlo Park Laboratory.
15) Sigmund Bergmann had arrived from Germany without a word of English, but his technical calibre impressed Edison when Bergmann worked for him. He opened a shop in 1878 in a front room at 104 Wooster Street, New York with one man and two boys, and Edison got him to make small electrical equipment. By 1881 Bergmann had expanded into nos. 108-114 and used letter headings 'By Appointment Manufacturer of Edison's Inventions'. His firm merged with other Edison companies in 1889 to become The Edison General Electric Company. Bergmann eventually left the business with a million dollars in his pocket, returned to Germany and founded one of the largest electrical concerns in Europe.
16) It is known that the following were approached and most contracted to supply machines: Ernst & Co., Tillotsons' Laboratories, Fitch & Messerole, Thaw, Patterson Brothers, E. P. Bullard, all of New York; A. Alex Pool, G & G Greenfield, both of Newark; later, Brehmer Brothers of Philadelphia
17) He tried damping both sides of the diaphragm with rubber, but soon discovered that the best results came from a stylus fastened to the centre of the diaphragm
18) United States Patent No. 227,679 for Phonograph, filed by Edison on March 29th 1879 and granted May 18th 1880 embraces several of these features.
19) Issued August 1st 1878 - Edison Archive
20) The entry charge has been given as 25 cents with the demonstrator receiving a commission. The novelty soon wore off due to the limitations of the machines.
21) The spiral recording was cut on a square piece of tinfoil pinned at each corner to a square turntable; it played from the centre outwards.
22) Letter to Frank Foell of December 22nd 1878, quoted by Petersen in *American Phonograph Journal* March 1878
23) Edison Archive
24) Edison sometimes used a driving belt from steam-driven shafting in the laboratory
25) Letter to James Adams - Edison Archive
26) Letter to Frank McLaughlin July 16th 1878 - Edison Archive
27) Report of July 9th 1879 - Edison Archive
28) U. S. Patent No. 227,679 for Phonograph filed by Edison May 29th 1879 and granted May 18th 1880

29) A predictable sample was from the owner of a large stenographers' business in Philadelphia and dated July 26th 1879 suggesting tinfoil phonographs run by clockwork, able to be stopped, started and set back by the operator would be useful to him. There should also be an attachment to cover the girls' ears. - Edison Archive
30) Edison Archive
31) U. S. Patent No. 201,760 for Speaking Machine filed by Edison on March 4th 1878 and granted March 26th 1878
32) Frank Lambert invented the Typewriter bearing his name and sold by the Gramophone Company Ltd. in London from 1900 to 1904. During these years and until 1907 the name was changed to The Gramophone & Typewriter Co., Ltd. A full account of the early lead cylinder phonograph appeared in an article by Aaron Cramer in A.P.M Vol. X No. 3 in 1992.
33) *APM* Reprint No. 21

The reader's attention is drawn to additional illustrative material in *From Tinfoil to Stereo* (1959 edition), pages 462 - 467

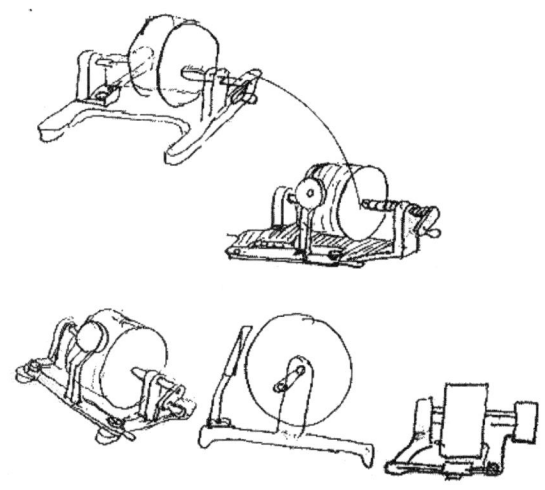

Revised designs for a Tinfoil Phonograph a month after the first had been constructed. Recording and reproducing of the voice were now through the same diaphragm.

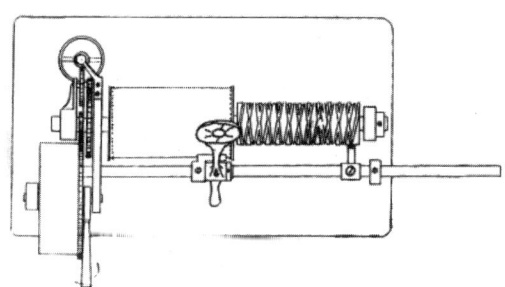

John Ott's model of November 30th 1878 incorporated a spring motor and an early return screw

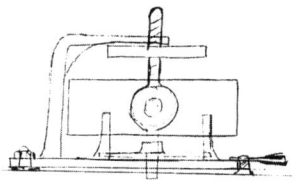

Later concepts of the Tinfoil Phonograph showed it in a vertical mounting

Chapter 2
Talking Doll

Although small compared to the phonographs that followed, the instrument in the talking dolls of Edison's took 12 years to develop, embracing 17 patents on the way, lost a lot of money and generated around itself some shameful practice and much bad feeling. In the end it was in production for a matter of weeks.

The chapter that follows attempts to recount some of the steps leading to its realization without attempting too many details of the setting-up of partnerships and agreements, politics and the capitalization of the companies.*   At the time when the production model of the doll was being achieved in 1888 Edison was perfecting the wax cylinder Phonograph and his Talking Doll adopted its style of speaker and wax cylinder on a more compact scale.

---

*For a fully researched account of the individuals and the business history involved, the reader is directed to R. Wile's paper in *ARSC Journal* Vol. 19, Nos. 2-3 1987, issued February 1989.

The concept of the Edison Talking Doll goes back to the days before the first phonograph had been constructed and shown to work, when Edison expressed his plans:

> *I propose to apply the phonographic principle to make dolls speak, and apply it to all kinds of toys, dogs, animals, fowls, reptiles and human figures to cause them to make various sounds ....*[1]

During January 1878 Charles Batchelor reported taking part in experiments with Edison on speaking clocks at The Ansonia Clock Company in Connecticut, and was able to show miniaturized working phonographs in place of the striking attachments. These assemblies would later feature in his doll mechanisms and even by January 7th he had been promised a royalty of 10 per cent on sales of doll phonographs.[2] On these small machines Batchelor found copper foil would serve well in place of tin, and although in some cases the indented sound could hardly be seen "it came out clearer and louder than ever before"[3]

A machine built by Frank Lambert for Ansonia was for a talking clock, and though not commercially successful the model has survived from 1878 and contains the oldest playable recording engraved on a solid lead cylinder. Batchelor pursued this aspect of the phonograph, experimenting with speaking toys from May 9th, and on July 16th finished an Alphabet Box, a device that spoke letters shown on a box for teaching the young.

By means of a series of agreements starting between Edison and an Oliver D. Russell, the rights to experiment with and to develop talking dolls and other toys passed through several hands and as many transactions – not all straightforward – but producing no marketable results, and after the death of one of its leading figures, Hilbourne Roosevelt in 1886 the rights passed back to Edison.[4]

It was a Bell Telephone researcher William W. Jacques who with a colleague Lowell C. Briggs showed vigour and expertise in the production of a mechanism that could well suit a doll. By incorporating features from the Bell-Tainter Graphophone Jacques was able to claim improvements on any progress that the Edison Laboratory had made, and on October 1st 1887 he and Briggs contracted an agreement with Edison for the manufacturing of the talking dolls with royalty terms for national and overseas sales. In resulting correspondence the inventor allowed his name to be used on the doll and was informed that Jacques and Briggs wished to found The Edison Phonograph Toy Manufacturing Company with an address at 95 Milk Street, Boston, Mass.[5] In the same month Jacques filed his first patent for a phonograph doll.[6] A small phonograph, cranked through the back of the doll emitted sound from perforations in the crown of the head, the head cavity acting as a resonator. A suitable foil for the record was suggested as oroide - a copper-zinc alloy pre-pressed with recorded speech grooves. From its patent illustration the mechanism had a semi-automatic return, but no example is reported to have survived.

Jacques and Briggs saw prospects of a large and immediate market and claimed to have funds for its investment, but the prospects were bogged down by difficulties in getting the mechanism to work reliably.

By February 23rd 1888 Batchelor had returned to working on doll mechanisms and reported using mica and celluloid ivory diaphragms; he also tried a spring drive in his experiments, but this was not used when he reported on March 6th:

> *Made a small phonograph for dolls, etc. with automatic return*

motion, so that you simply turn always in one direction and it says the same thing over and over again.[7]

For the voice recordings Batchelor designed a phonograph to record the doll cylinders with a sleeve of tin that could afterwards be sliced into rings.[8]

Continuing his trials with different diaphragms, foils, sizes of styli and ways of mounting them, he was trying asphalt and carnauba wax mixes instead of foil after April 6th. By April 14th[9] he reported reverting to a semi-automatic return by pressing a button in the front of the doll, and although a note of September 7th reads that "the doll needs 15 winds", his patent application of October 30th 1888 lacked any spring drive and the "winds" were turns of the crank.[10]

In the same month Jacques was granted a very similar patent for a doll mechanism[11] but neither this nor Batchelor's motor in a doll submitted to Jacques and the Toy Manufacturing Co. on August 8th would actually see any production, though hopes of an early start were raised.[12]

Promises, rights and agreements were entered into by Jacques and Briggs, both in and outside the United States, and particularly in Europe. This and other not entirely clear factors caused Edison to take over control of The Edison Phonograph Toy Manufacturing Company from Jacques, presenting Jacques with a grievance he would not forget and installing B. J. Stevens as president of the company in Jacques's place.

Meanwhile, and not for the first time was news of an impending invention allowed to leak prematurely to the press who reported on talking dolls and chattering animals that existed more in the minds of the journalists than in reality; near the Edison works *The Herald* of Orange, New Jersey of December 8th 1888 reported that

> .... *during the past two weeks a large number of workmen (have been) engaged in phonograph factories at the rear of the Laboratory in making the different parts of the talking dolls, and it is expected that within a week or ten days they will be placed on the market in large quantities for the Christmas trade. It is estimated that each doll will cost about $3.50.*

There would be no talking dolls ready for 1888 however, the mechanisms were too unreliable, but during the spring of the next year Edison assembled a small phonograph that seemed to be satisfactory[13] and sample dolls were ready for August 8th 1889.[14] One was taken by Theodore Wangemann to the Paris Universal Exposition where Edison products were well represented. The European market was considered of sufficient importance in November 1889 to appoint an agent D.M. Yeomans to market the foreign rights there on a commission basis as soon as the dolls were ready.

In a statement to stockholders dated October 1st 1889 the Phonograph Toy company claimed that the factory was equipped to make 500 dolls a day,[15] but Christmas came and passed with no saleable quantity or quality of dolls ready. Opinion still wavered as to whether these would be hand turned or spring driven, and the fragile wax cylinders were prone to breaking through shrinkage; this was overcome by wrapping a cloth round the mandrel and reaming to fit, and cylinders were soon given a fabric backing.[16]

Serious production started at the end of January 1890 and weekly output figures were much lower than anticipated. Batchelor reported on February 28th that 425 dolls had been

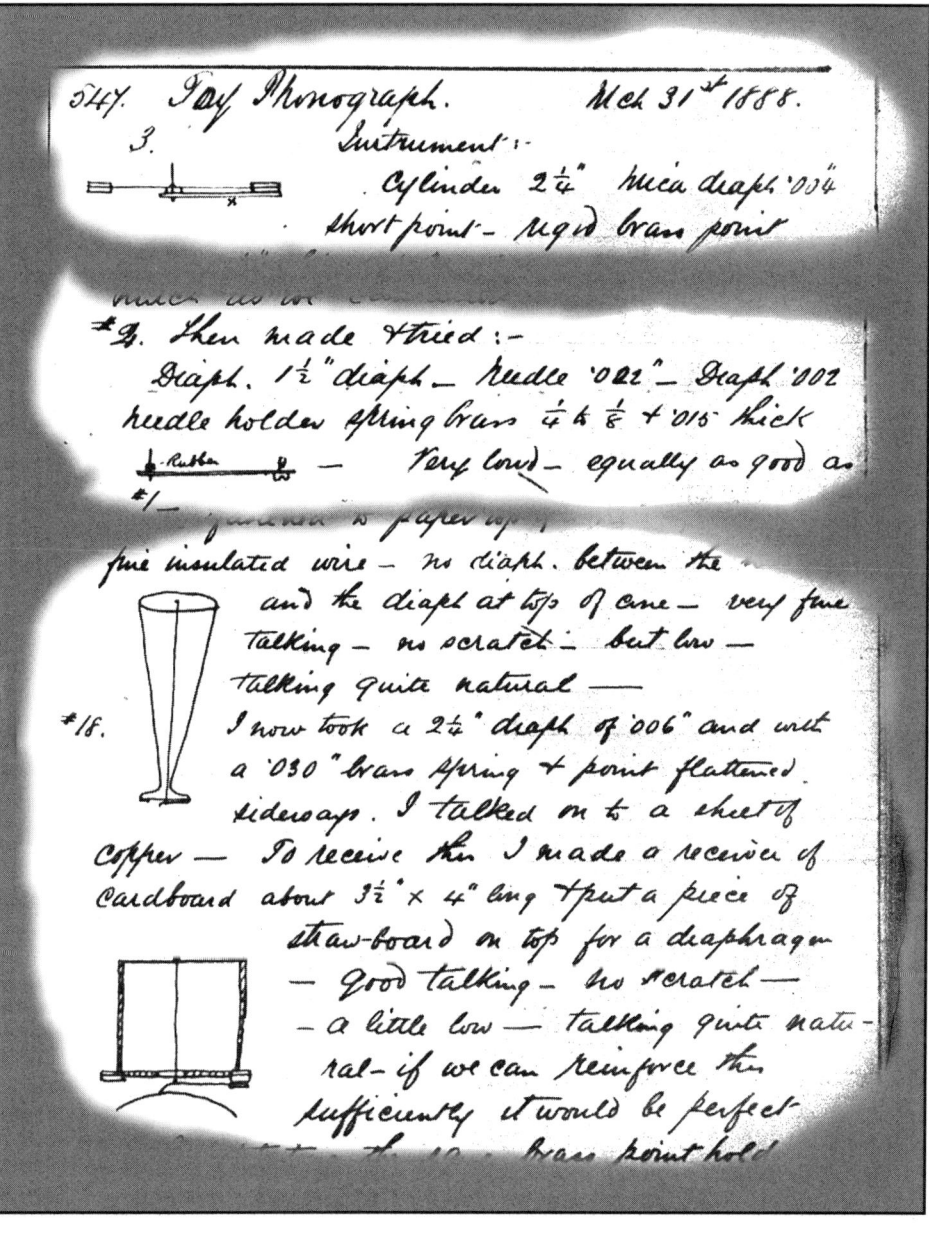

Extracts from Charles Batchelor's diaries for 1888 showing experimental work on diaphragms and styli for the Talking Doll, and contributing greatly to the success of the Perfected Phonograph in the same year

good results.

#20 Talking point - a rigid lever pivoted on its fulcrum 1 which carries a steel knife as shown & which has a front view as 2. The receiving needle bent down as in 4 & drawn into position as in dotted line & held there by a loop of silk shellac'd to diaph. Receiving diaph ...... becomes very bad.

#22 Made a try of one single wheel around which is cut one groove & the words are all put on one turn of the cylinder.

....diaph. back - it is done by pressing a button in front of the doll. A is brass drum on which is cast on half its rim a ring of tin B. A is cut like a screw — Bar C is fastened to the ring that holds the diaphragm & on it is held the knife that engages in the screw & pushes the diaphragm along — E is the talking needle & travels in the record made on the tin B. Very good & practical —

shipped to date with a further 700 ready, and a total of 3,335 had been tested and passed by the end of March.[17]

The dolls were assembled using a body and articulated limbs made from six or more tinplate pieces. Some had hands movable at the wrists, others were rigid. There were two types of bisque head imported from Germany from Simon and Helbig and also from Bahr and Proschild, though the latter may have been made by Simon and Helbig. French Jumeau heads are also known on Edison dolls but the neck fitting was standard and these could be "dolls' hospital" replacements. The dolls also slightly varied in length.

The voices were recorded on cylinder machines by young women in separate booths, and each doll was sold with a numbered card to correspond with its nursery rhyme. The phonographs were inserted into the backs of the finished bodies last, and fixed so that the voice projected forward through a circular cluster of holes just below the doll's neck. The mouth was moulded to be slightly open. The phonograph was turned by hand with the steel speaker stylus coming into play and disengaging at the end of the cylinder by pressing a return lever. The records were 3 in. diameter and ⅝ in. wide with 56 t.p.i., the pitch of the voice depending on how fast it was turned, and the owner was recommended to count 1-2-3-4 for the best results. Edison dolls were never given a spring drive and the mechanism was described at the time as the smallest phonograph made, a claim that could be sustained for the rest of the Phonograph's career.

It is likely from a known example that some of the early Edison dolls had painted bodies and slight variations in motor design, but otherwise remained the same for the run, although a more child-proof model by Edison was granted a patent in July 1891[18] and 50 were reported assembled in dolls for evaluation by The Edison Phonograph Toy Manufacturing Company.[19]

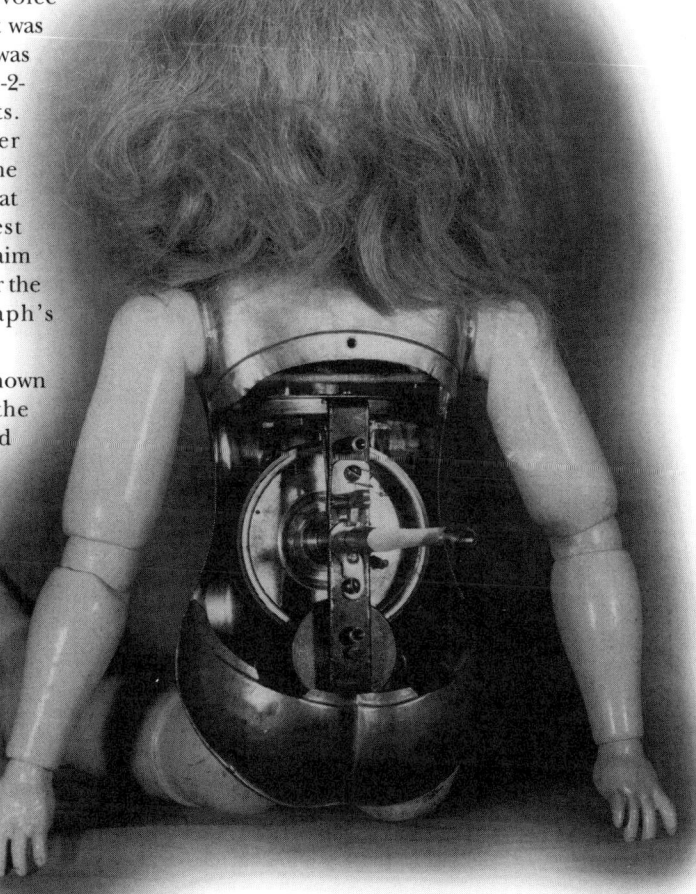

Edison Doll showing back cover removed

There were frequent complaints about the unreliability of the doll mechanism, both from trade and public, and it was withdrawn from sale at the end of April 1890. In spite of some 10,000 being inspected and passed, fewer than 2,500 are thought to have been marketed.[20] Thus the Edison Dolls were withdrawn from business and the phonograph mechanisms were taken out of them and the doll bodies sold cheaply. In a letter to stockholders Edison reported "manufacture is entirely suspended" and called for new management and new money.[21] By February 1892 the Phonograph Toy company had brought a suit against Edison Phonograph Works for breach of contract, and on November 7th Edison's attorney recommended that the remaining doll parts be delivered to a trustee to be sold "at the best available price."[22] It was several years before understanding was achieved between all affected parties, and The Edison Phonograph Toy Manufacturing Co. finally closed up in 1896."[23]

As a talking doll the Edison failed, and once the record wore out the doll was heavy, metallically rigid and un-cuddly and would not have been attractive to children. There is no indication that replacement records could be bought, but in any case the cylinder was not accessible for changing once the motor was assembled. After the dolls were finished Edison is credited with saying ".... the voices of the little monsters (were)

Edison Doll Phonograph

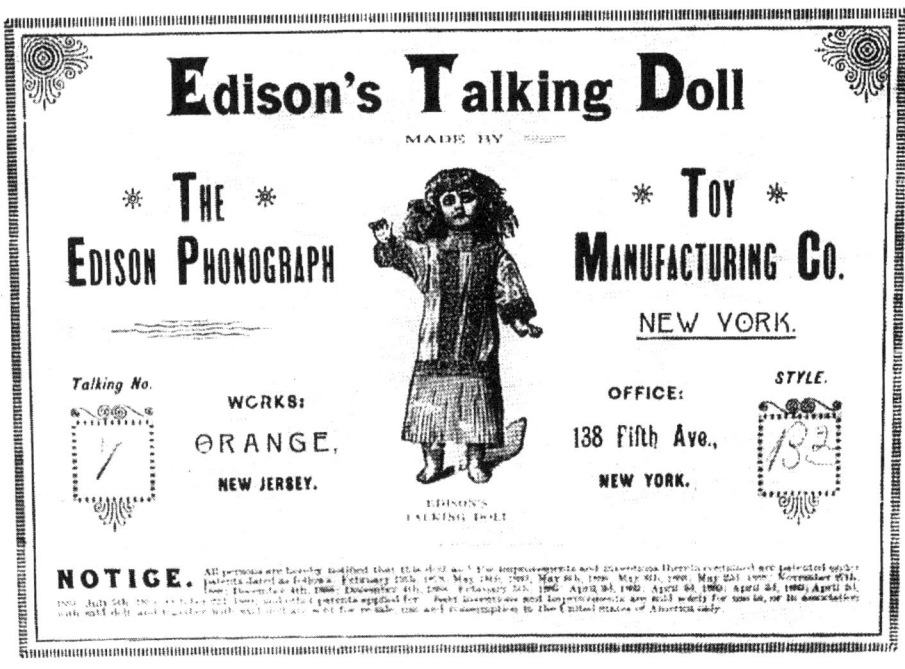

Edison Doll box label

exceedingly unpleasant to hear."[24]

The dolls were 22 in, high, weighed 4 lb. and were sold for $10.00 dressed in a chemise. Most that now survive are found in an elaborate Victorian dress, hat and accessories, and this cost a further $10.00.

On April 26th 1890 with the prospect of a German patent for his doll, Jacques had resigned as a director of The Edison Phonograph Toy Manufacturing Company, giving rise to apprehension that he intended making dolls in Germany. In a letter to B.F. Stevens, its president,[25] he enclosed a copy of his British Patent No. 20,257 of December 17th 1889 for Improvements in Phonographs giving notice of having filed a United States patent on March 7th 1890,[26] and in Germany. This was for a simpler and cheaper doll, and would give him the rights to manufacture and sell in these countries. Shortly after, a further blow came to Edison interests in a letter[27] reporting Kämmer and Reinhart 'Grammophon dolls', patented in Germany as well as in America[28] and selling for 20 D.M., much cheaper than the Edison product.

In view of this competition on the Continent and the brief life of the Edison dolls in America, it is unlikely that any crossed the Atlantic. Consideration had been given to starting trading activities of the Toy Manufacturing company in the United Kingdom in 1890, at the very time when it seemed to be losing its influence in the United States, and The Edison Phonographic Toy and Automaton Company Ltd. was incorporated on July 26th with a capital of £300,000 for application of the phonograph to dolls, toys and automata for continental Europe. Its registered office was in the City of London but threats to sue over licences and rights from The London Stereoscopic Company and Gouraud's Edison United Phonograph Company led to its dissolution in 1895 with no evidence of trading.[29] No advertisements for Edison Talking Dolls have been seen in British journals.

Two years earlier the European press had welcomed Edison's doll understandably with more excess than accuracy. In June 1888 a syndicated report said each doll had a waxen head, the jaw moved with 'the uttered words', the mechanism was started by moving the doll's arm, and that it recited a whole poem for one minute. A further article noticed in the London *St. James's Gazette* of November 8th 1888 erroneously referred to 'this sawdust stuffed doll' and that its records were made by 'silvery voiced children'. In Holland *De Natur* of April 26th 1890,[30] reporting on an article in *Scientific American* alleged that doll owners by speaking into the funnel of the doll phonograph could make their own records, and this could be repeated at will, a notion that would have made the dolls more desirable, had it then been feasible.

The first European phonograph doll was the Frenchman Lioret's 1896 Bébé Jumeau, spring driven and with celluloid cylinders. Two Edison dolls in the United States are reported with Jumeau heads; these may have been late adaptations as the head-neck fitting was congruous.

An unconfirmed report has it that in 1929 the Edison company itself made dolls with celluloid cylinders of the Blue Amberol type and when the phonograph business ceased in 1929 this stock was rumoured to be buried near the laboratory water tower. This may well be related to the doll recordings made at the Columbia Street studios on behalf of a Mr. Rotter. Twelve programmes of nursery rhymes and songs are noted as being recorded by November 25th and a further dozen or so on November 29th.[31] As well as English some of these songs were in German, French and Italian. These cylinders were cut into single records during manufacture, but no further details of the dolls themselves have come to hand.

Though Edison allowed his name to be used on the doll, it is certain that Jacques did the donkey work in the early days, and this was carried on by Charles Batchelor. It was a side-issue to Edison who did not interest himself much in it.

In these days the Edison doll has become overlooked in favour of the more practical and plentiful phonographs, and while they are attractive especially in their Victorian clothing, so very few are complete or will function. They have however, three claims to Edison 'firsts':

1) *The doll contained the first automatic record playing mechanism*
2) *The first phonograph records sold to the public under the name Edison were made for the Talking Doll*
3) *The dolls had pre-recorded cylinders, hence in February 1889 they were the first entertainment cylinders. Wangemann's First Book of Phonograph Records did not start entries until May 24th 1889.*[32]

●●●●●●●●●●●●●●

A version of the doll mechanism of this time was a feature of U. S. Patent No, 470,477 filed by the brothers Criswell of Brooklyn and Washington D.C. in 1891 and should be noted. This was for an artificial crow containing a spring driven mechanism for advertising a cure for corns.

UNITED STATES PHONOGRAPH PATENTS CLAIMED FOR EDISON DOLLS
These are stamped directly into the metal body, on the horn or on a paper label

(incomplete or incorrect dates are found in some pressings)

Date	Number	Description
February 19th 1878	200,521	Original Edison tin-foil phonograph
May 18th 1880	227,679	Edison's second U.S. tinfoil phonograph
May 8th 1888	382,416	Edison's Feed and Return Mechanism for Phonographs filed January 5th 1888
May 8th 1888	382,462	Edison's Phonogram Blank, the tapering bore wax cylinder filed January 5th 1888
May 22nd 1888	383,299	W.W. Jacques's Combined Doll and Phonograph, with sound emitted through top of head; filed October 19th 1887
November 27th 1888	393,640	Gilliland's Phonograph, assigned to Edison and filed June 7th 1888
December 4th 1888	393,966	Edison's Method of Recording & Reproducing Sounds filed June 17th 1888

December 4th 1888	394,106	Edison's Phonograph Reproducer, filed November 26th 1887 and re-applied for March 2nd 1888

The two patents above are representative of five Edison patents granted in this week

February 5th 1889	397,280	Edison's Phonograph Recorder and Reproducer filed September 27th 1888
April 2nd 1889	400,629	Batchelor's Phonograph, filed October 30th 1888 doll type phonograph with spherical sound chamber
April 2nd 1889	400,646	Edison's Phonograph Recorder and Reproducer filed June 7th 1888 - the glass diaphragm
April 2nd 1889	400,647	Edison's Phonograph, filed July 7th 1888 - reproducer point narrower than the groove it has to track
April 2nd 1889	400,851	W.W. Jacques, Phonograph Doll, filed November 30th 1888 and assigned to Edison Phonograph Toy Manufacturing. Co. - hollow doll's head acting as resonator
July 9th 1889	406,569	Edison's Phonogram Blank, filed January 19th 1889 - metallic soap on fabric base

The following patents were not enumerated on the doll or phonograph bodies:

October 22nd 1889	413,282	W.W. Jacques's Phonograph, filed May 16th 1889 - spring driven doll mechanism
March 11th 1890	423,039	Edison's Phonograph for Dolls or other Toys filed July 2nd 1889
July 21st 1891	456,301	Edison's Phonograph Doll, filed July 30th 1890

• • • • • • • • • • • • • • • • • •

Jacques's May 1888 United States patent was the earliest granted for a talking doll. Batchelor's model of 1888 used a wax or metallic soap cylinder, and although an improvement on Jacques's model, the moving parts were not contained within the motor framework and this seemed impractical in a doll, liable to be roughly treated. The sound output emerged in a globular resonating chamber inside the head, a feature that persisted until the Edison production model which had a short conical horn directed at a group of holes at the base of the neck.

Jacques's second mechanism omitted the secondary flywheel shaft and regarded a heavier cylinder as having sufficient inertia. Later he designed a spring driven model.

Edison's Patent No. 423,039 outlined the mechanism used for the dolls. A year later he patented his final and most ingenious doll movement (No. 456,301), using threads of two different cuts in the manual drive and a feeding arm made to engage either. A cam on the inside of the mandrel tripped the arm of the reproducer at the right time. It arrived too late.

Differences in size and placing of holes in the back plates covering the doll motor cavities have been noticed, implying variations of motor construction.

• • • • • • • • • • • • • • • • •

On March 7th 1890 Charles Batchelor drew out nine columns in his notebook to show the number of dolls tested and passed to date, but only the first three columns were ever filled in, as follows:

Doll No:	Title:	Mar. 7	Mar. 20	Mar. 29
1	Mary had a little Lamb	126	143	182
2	Twinkle, twinkle little Star	257	334	300
3	There was a little Girl and she had a little Curl	16	123	401
4	Little Bo-peep	93	183	239
5	Little Tommy Tucker	45	151	242
6	Hickory dickory dock	134	161	233
7	Little Jack Horner	52	94	196
8	Ba-ba black Sheep	12	109	351
9	Jack and Jill	88	138	191
10	Two little Blackbirds	51	218	365
11	Old Mother Hubbard	63	216	398
12	Now I lay me down to Sleep	<u>113</u>	<u>136</u>	<u>237</u>
		1050	2006	3335

NOTES
1) Laboratory Sheet, November 23rd 1877 - Edison Archive
2) Charles Batchelor Papers - Edison Archive
3) Batchelor Notebook, January 29th 1878, p. 53 - Edison Archive
4) Roosevelt, an organ builder, presented the organ in the Menlo Park laboratory
5) Jacques to Edison October 17th and 21st 1887 - Edison Archive. The Company was incorporated for $600,000 of which $400,000 was issued for patents and franchises - W.K.L and A. Dickson *Life and Adventures of Thomas A, Edison.* The Milk Street address was the same as Bell Telephone Company.
6) U.S. Patent No. 383,299
7) Batchelor Record Books - Edison Archive
8) Batchelor Record Book, April 16th 1888 - Edison Archive
9) Batchelor Record Books - Edison Archive
10) U.S. Patent No. 400,629
11) U.S. Patent No. 400,851
12) Letters - Jacques to Edison November 13th 1888, Edison to Jacques November 14th 1888; also Batchelor to Jacques August 8th 1889 - Edison Archive
13) U.S. Patent No, 423,039
14) Edison Archive
15) Correspondence with the late Harold Anderson
16) Batchelor Record Book, January 19th 1890 - Edison Archive
17) Batchelor Record Book, February 28th 1890 - Edison Archive
18) U.S. Patent No. 456,301
19) Edison Phonograph Toy Manufacturing Co. to Edison, July 18th 1890 - Edison Archive
20) R. Wile in *ARSC Journal* Vol. 19 Nos. 2-3 1987 p, 20 (issued February 1989)
21) Letter of October 24th 1890 - Edison Archive
22) 1972 correspondence with A.R. Abel, Archivist Edison Site
23) Letter of March 23rd 1896 from Colie & Swayze, Attorneys, to Edison
24) Public information at Edison Site Museum
25) April 4th 1890 - Edison Archive
26) This patent was not granted
27) May 5th 1890, G. Borgfeldt to E.S. Allien - Edison Archive
28) German Patent No. 45,058 of November 8th 1887. This was Berliner's basic Gramophone patent
29) Frank Andrews, *Talking Machine Review* February 1975
30) Quoted in *Victorian Inventions*, de Vries p. 183, John Murray, London 1971
31) Columbia Street Studio Recording Schedule - Edison Archive
32) Walter Welch, *Hillandale News* June 1971

Chapter 3
Electric Phonographs

Development to 1889

When asked on August 5th 1879 when he would be returning to the Phonograph, Edison said he was busy on the electric light and was not expecting to get back to the Phonograph for a year; in fact it was not until the spring of 1887 that he was free give it his personal attention. During its first year the tinfoil machine had shone brightly as an entertainer, but its limitations soon lost it public regard and it was relegated to the cupboards of technical establishments, a scientific device to demonstrate basic acoustical principles.

On June 27th 1885 Chichester Bell and Sumner Tainter of Alexander Graham Bell's laboratory applied for a patent for Recording and Reproducing Speech and Other Sounds, and were subsequently granted Patent No. 341,214 on May 4th 1886. It was the first phonograph that abandoned metal foil as a recording surface, and used a solid wax or wax-coated disc with a V-shaped groove engraved by a stylus somewhat less rigid than Edison had used on the tinfoil machines. Despite claims bearing a close affinity to Edison's tinfoil patents, this patent was allowed.

Edison was annoyed that while in New York on electric light matters the Graphophone people had "stolen his baby" of 1878 and was determined to humble the interloper with something better of his own.

The first sketches of the new machine were made in April 1886 when Edison was on holiday at Fort Myers, Florida - he first took to visiting there only the year before – and not much imagination is needed to recognize the outline of the future CLASS M and E series.[1] In his sketches Edison also acknowledged that such an instrument should have a constant drive and allowed space for an electric motor.[2]

Meanwhile Bell and Tainter had made further progress with a 6 in. long cylinder comprising a tube of helically wound paper strips covered with ozokerite, a wax-like substance derived from shale.[3] An improved Graphophone mounted on a sewing machine treadle was constructed to play this now transposable record[4] and was in all probability the instrument seen and reported by Charles Batchelor on May 8th 1887 when it was put on display with a typewriter and presented as an office machine.[5] Batchelor noted the paper cylinder had a one-eighth inch thickness of wax on it, and was one and five-sixteenths inches in diameter.

There is no doubt that the appearance of this machine spurred the Edison laboratory into competitive activity and four days later Batchelor was put to making cylinders of various components (plumbago, steatite, resin and paraffin wax), as well as experimenting with points and diaphragms.

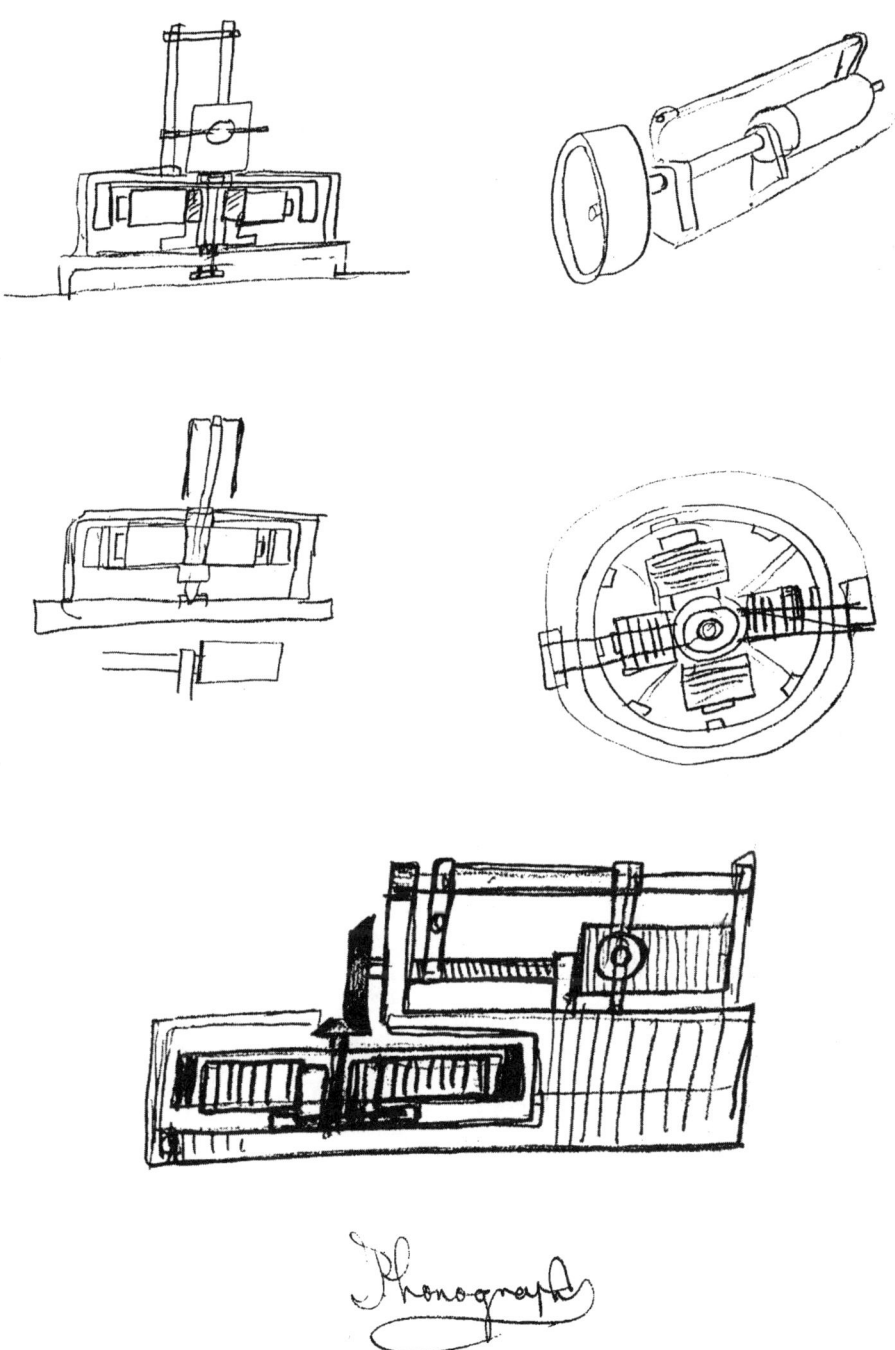

Sketches from Edison's Fort Myers Notebook of April 1886

In these early trials Batchelor's aim was to make a record that would remain malleable under a tinfoil covering, but he also made a removable cylinder and experimented with simple magnetic attraction to indent metal surfaces. It is enlightening to read of his experiments at this critical stage of development. He tried camel-hair points on tinfoil: "makes minimum scratching but difficult to hear", sealskin hair 0.007 in. diameter: "no scratching but talking very low", and he built diaphragm assemblies that are recognizable as such and not far removed from later production types. The diaphragms themselves were of gold-beater's skin, metal or mica.[6]

Gilliland's portable phonograph of October 5th 1886

Ezra T. Gilliland, a colleague from Edison's old telegraph days was drawn in to work with Batchelor in improving the diaphragms, but became ill at this critical period leaving Batchelor to carry the onus of much of their development. By coincidence Batchelor's time too was curtailed by bouts of jury service. Gilliland had been employed since 1886 on occasional work on improving the phonograph, and starting from October 5th of that year had built a portable model capable of being held up to the ear. It was driven by a small electric motor, and its records, cylinder or plate, were to be transposable to an identical model. The cylinder he designed was 1 in. to 1 ½ in. diameter, made of glass and covered with shellac, gum or wax.[7]

The first Edison phonograph for playing interchangeable cylinders was built by Gilliland to Edison's plans in November 1887. (Photograph from Scientific American of December 31st 1887)

This sort of work, though not conclusive, stood Gilliland in good stead, and when the Menlo Park laboratory property was put up for sale on June 25th 1887 and Batchelor drew back from experimental work to supervise the installation of the new laboratory at West Orange, Gilliland moved more into Edison's realm, with a result that from October 28th 1887 he was entrusted with the management of the Edison phonograph.[8] This was a move Edison would soon have cause to regret.[9] For the meantime Gilliland had a workshop and small staff at Bloomfield, New Jersey, and at the beginning of November Edison sent him a wooden model of a wax cylinder electric phonograph for a working copy to be made.

The frame of this phonograph was centrally placed across the large electric motor, with the vertical armature shaft driving the bevelled inner face of the mandrel and ensuring silent contact through a leather-covered arbor pushed up by a compression spring. This instrument saw the first use of the 'spectacle frame' device, usually credited to Gilliland, a pivoted double eye for holding the separate recorder and reproducer side by side, with either brought into use by a sideways turn of the spectacle frame. This machine was described in *Scientific American* for December 31st 1887.[10]

One of these machines was already back at the Laboratory by November 11th 1887, where the Inventor showed it to members of the National Academy of Sciences.

This machine was made in skeletal form mounted on a wooden base, and became known as the 'New' Phonograph, the precursor of a fresh Edison approach to recording and reproducing sound by using an interchangeable 'solid' wax cylinder with ¼ in. thick walls. Its feedscrew was of buttress thread cut to 100 per inch, and several models were constructed,[11] Gilliland having 12 to 15 men available for the work.

From the entries in his notebooks it was Batchelor who continued with the experiments on the recording and reproducing heads, and in the early months of 1888 Edison and Gilliland worked on the electric motor and the important feature of speed control and regulation.

This prototype was soon improved upon by being given a wooden case and in this form it began to be recognizable as an Edison electric phonograph, although it was still fundamental.[12] The phonograph frame and movement were shifted to the right across the electric motor so that the vertical drive now made contact through bevelled faces *at the left end of the feed screw*. There was still no belting or visible governor, the motor was as simple as possible having four pairs of magnets grouped around a brass flywheel with ten iron armatures set equally on its rim. A governor built into the motor maintained uniform rotation through a spring-loaded arm that broke contacts if the motor turned too fast and overcame the pull of the springs. The mandrel shaft ran in bearings at either end of the feedscrew, the end gate was still to come, and there was for the first time an integral automatic return mechanism of Gilliland's design.[13] It seems likely that this model and perhaps others stood around the laboratory while recorders and reproducing phonets and cylinders were being tested. As an indication of the headway made, on February 7th 1888 de Courcy Hamilton demonstrated the machine to four visitors and every word was reported as clear.[14]

The American public heard the new machine for the first time when Edison and Gilliland showed it at a meeting of the Engineers' Club in New York on May 12th 1888, and Gilliland read a paper and gave a further demonstration at the Electric Club there a week later.[15] Recent discovery of a report in a Norwegian newspaper points to the possibility of an earlier public hearing there of the Gilliland instrument in Christiania (now Oslo) at the premises of Heyerdahl & Co., Edison's Norwegian representative. In March it reported "we were given the opportunity to make ourselves familiar with the construction of the apparatus ..... it was not yet assembled and could not work for this reason."[16]

Gillialand built a number if these phonographs at his Bloomfield N.J. machine shop early in 1888. This was the second production wax cylinder phonograph of Edison's.

As well as development of the phonographs much time was given to the composition of the cylinders during 1887, with the laboratory turning away from tinfoil and other metal films over a yielding base; these would never record and reproduce consonants like a wax surface. Wax compounds, either ' solid' or on various bases were tried before the end of the year but were found to give trouble on cooling.[17] For instance, in January 1888 Edison was seeking to patent a method of moulding wax cylinders with a lengthways piece left open at the edge to allow for contraction. The cylinder could then be put on a mandrel, the crack filled with liquid wax and then turned and burnished, a tedious process. The inventor declared that he found carnauba the best hardener of the waxes he was using; this could be combined in such proportions until it made scraping sounds.[18] Experiments led to pre-recorded wax cylinders being plated with lead or tin, then sawn lengthways, the wax melted out and blank cylinders could be rolled on the metal negative for replication. A patent resulted, opening the door for later forms of duplication and moulding.[19]

Jonas W. Aylsworth, Edison's chemist, was a particular help at this time and brought a facility with organic chemicals to the development of the metallic soap cylinders, and the first patent for these was filed on July 30th 1888.[20]

Progress with development of the phonographs continued at the laboratory with a number of experimental models; the bevelled contact drive system gave way to belt and pulleys, a centrifugal ball-governor and speed controller were then added to the deck of the machine while an end gate introduced cone bearings to support the mandrel shaft ends, making for better regulation and more positive shaving and recording.[21]

By June 1888 American Graphophone was already in business with a range of Graphophones made for office use. They were far from reliable and Edison let it be known that he would shortly be perfecting his phonograph. Once again the news was released early to the Press with the purpose of winding up the publicity, and once again reporters beat a path to the inventor's door to find him and his assistants inaccessible, locked in until they had achieved an entirely successful phonograph, one that would pronounce the aspirates (the letter 'h' with full breathing) and the sibilants (the hissing

Thomas A. Edison listening to his improved wax cylinder phonograph after 72 hours of continuous work on the mechanism. This photograph was taken June 16, 1888.

Edison's Phonograph of June 1888

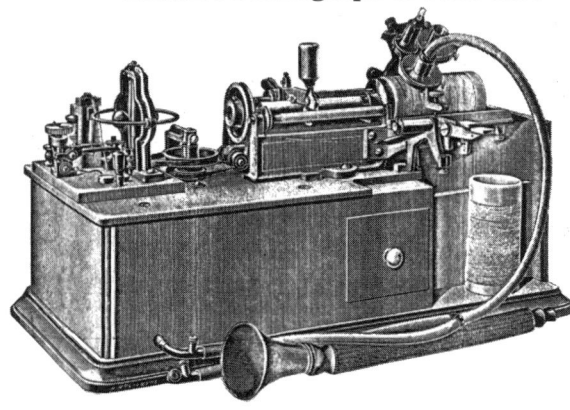

This style of electric phonograph was evolved from Edison's machine of June 16th 1888. The illustration dated from September 14th 1888

letters such as 's'). W. K. L. Dickson was on hand with his camera to photograph Edison at 5am on June 16th in several Napoleon-like poses after a 72 hour stretch of working on the machine. An oil painting was later made from the photograph and one or two other likenesses were taken of Edison with colleagues and friends. The phonograph, a battery-driven machine, was given to Colonel Gouraud.[22] (see Appendix III)

By now the phonograph had begun to assume the recognizable lines of the CLASS M, and after further experiments and a promise of "better things on the way" in September 1888, an intermediate model was produced. A noticeable removal was the solenoid relay near the governor, and a resistance wire under the governor block took its place. This intermediate model was superseded by the CLASS M at the end of 1888. No written date has been seen but in his notebook Charles Batchelor pasted a picture of a CLASS M on the page for December 5th. With this model the electric motor with the vertical armature shaft

The North American Phonograph as shown in the 1889 catalogue of that company

reached its third and final form, one that would endure for 20 years.[23]

From July 14th 1888 until 1894 all Edison Phonographs would be handled through The North American Phonograph Company, formed by Jesse Lippincott through the purchase of Edison and American Graphophone interests.

The wooden cases of the early electric phonographs all stopped short of the inner end of the mandrel and a swarf box shaped to fit under it stood on the baseboard. By 1895 this had been made smaller and became a drawer in the end of a full wooden case.

As with the 'New' Phonograph any temptation to refer to specific models as 'Improved' or 'Perfected' has been resisted. These latter terms were used to some extent and at times without discrimination in Edison literature, and are confusing.

●●●●●●●●●●●●●●●

From pencilled notes by an unknown but authoritative hand found in Edison files the first dates of shipment of early Edison phonographs were declared as follows:

Spectacle types

CLASS M	battery driven	January 24th 1889
T	treadle driven	February 19th 1889
E	electric for DC lighting circuit	July 10th 1889
S	battery driven	August 1890
E	with lamp resistance	December 19th 1891
E	with resistance wire and lamp inside body box	February 20th 1892

Diaphragm models

CLASS M	battery driven	November 22nd 1889
E	electric for DC lighting circuit	November 30th 1889
T	treadle driven	December 3rd 1889
W	water powered	February 19th 1890
C	(commercial) 200 t. p. i. first model	April 7th 1891
C	(commercial) 'latest model'	May 12th 1893
H	(home) version of the above	May 12th 1893

made in 100 t. p. i. form from 1902

All three models having a secondary cell battery rechargeable from DC power sources.

It will be seen that the above include phonographs with a feed of 200 threads per inch.

These were primarily dictation phonographs and were made solely for the United Kingdom where both J. Lewis Young and James Hough of Edison Bell recalled them in interviews.[24] The November 1889 *Tit-Bits* remarked that Edison was experimenting with 200 t.p.i., making a cylinder with 1,000 ft. of track.

• • • • • • • • • • • • • • • • • • • •

Exploitation from 1889

> *"No matter what his private or public utterance may be, his utterances to me and others showed that he and his immediate subordinates had no idea that the phonograph would ever have any use or value beyond that for amusement purposes; he would make the amount of money he calculated on, and then give his attention to something else".*

S. F. Moriarty, Edison European Representative, writing from London about the inventor in 1896.

Work proceeded on the realization of a reliable electric phonograph after the widely publicized success of June 16th 1888 and several intermediate and improving models are known from illustrations, but few if any machines of this era have survived.[25] The earliest portrayal of the perfected electric phonograph in a brochure was during the second half of 1888 when a booklet on the *Phonograph-Graphophone* was put out by The North American Phonograph Company's offices at 160-164 Broadway, New York. This also showed Gilliland-type machines in office settings.

The first CLASS M phonographs to be sent out on January 24th 1889 were destined for office use at the 1889-1890 rental of $40.00 a year; the 'M' probably stood for Motor-power. Shipments were made throughout the United States, and to Mexico, Holland, Denmark, Shanghai, England and France. In early 1889 a first-edition catalogue of 337 parts for the machines was distributed. The hiring-out and sales of spares for these phonographs was through 33 local companies formed during 1889 and spread across American states and regions. These companies were pioneers in fitting coin-slot mechanisms to early Edison electric phonographs, as well as some Graphophones. This type of trade began before the end of 1889 and by August 30th 1890 North American Phonograph was making a variation of the CLASS M, the CLASS S ('S' for Slot) for use in connection with nickel-in-the-slot mechanisms. It was a playing phonograph only with a single eye for the reproducer and the diaphragm lever set parallel to the straight edge of the machine "for the reproduction of music". The Edison company offered a supply of cylinders from May 24th 1889.[26]

A further *Catalogue of Musical Phonograms*[27] from the North American company in 1890 reflected a public interest in electrical phonographs for home use, and was the result of pressure on the company by the local phonograph companies for clearance to sell the instruments outright and not just on hire. North American put out a letter to all these local companies on August 7th 1891 offering 1,000 CLASS M, T and W phonographs for public sale at $150.00 each for those companies that wished to handle them. The offer would last until the end of the year or until 1,000 machines had been sold, if sooner, at a wholesale cost of $95.00 each complete, F.O.B. New York or Orange, and strict financial conditions and settlements were

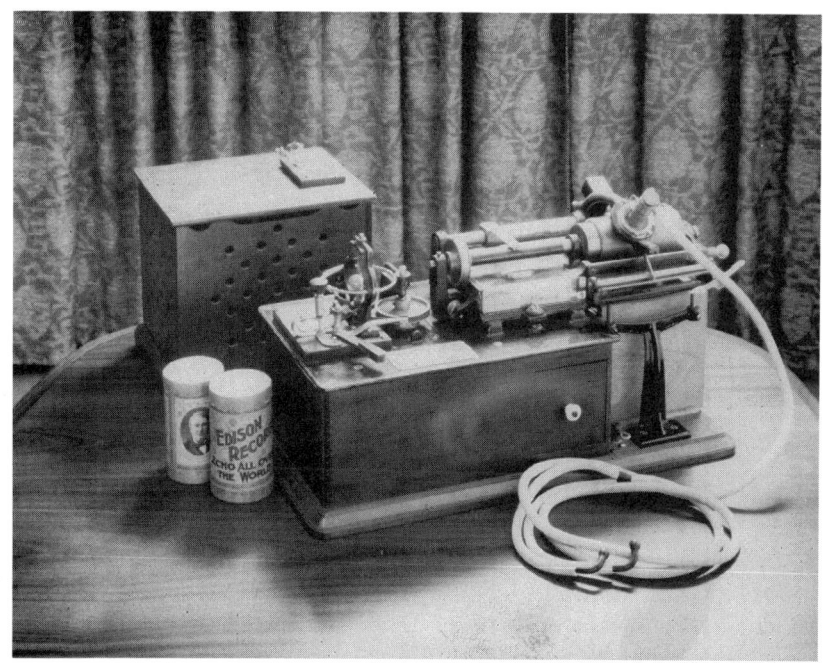

CLASS E mains phonograph showing resistance block fitted with lamps

demanded from participating companies.[28]

The first North American catalogue that was not a component parts list was that of 1891 offering Edison machines 'for Recording, Perpetuating and Reproducing Articulate Speech and Other Sounds', and stressing their uses in different kinds of business offices, so the phonograph's day as a home entertainer had yet to be realized. All the same the catalogue showed several elaborately carved and expensive cabinets in oak or cherrywood 'for parlour use'. There was still no attempt to tailor these cabinets to the metal base-plate of the CLASS M, the instrument just stood in its own case on a chest of drawers and battery cupboard, with a roll top or other cover to keep the dust out. As well as machines and cabinets, this catalogue listed batteries, horns, hearing tubes and cylinder boxes.

By the next year CLASS M and E (and Treadle and Water classes T and W) were described in general as Home Amusement Phonographs and offered as Residence Outfits at prices related to the style of cabinet chosen. There was still a disinclination to separate pleasure from business in the catalogue, and the first wholly-domestic issue was post-September 1893 when Catalogue A was for 'Commercial' and Catalogue B for 'Home Entertainment, Education'.[29] In the same year at the World's Fair a 'Household' CLASS M was on show at the North American company's stand. In 1894, final year of this company the lavish cabinets comprising Residence Outfits had become Domestic Outfits, but still the largest number of domestic CLASS Ms were sold as complete units for standing on a table or sideboard in the home.

Alongside the original CLASS M of 1889 in early photographs sometimes there appears a scaled-down version. Named the MILITARY (or PORTABLE) Phonograph, this instrument was half-size and was presumably conceived for the war reporter to send back on-the-spot

49

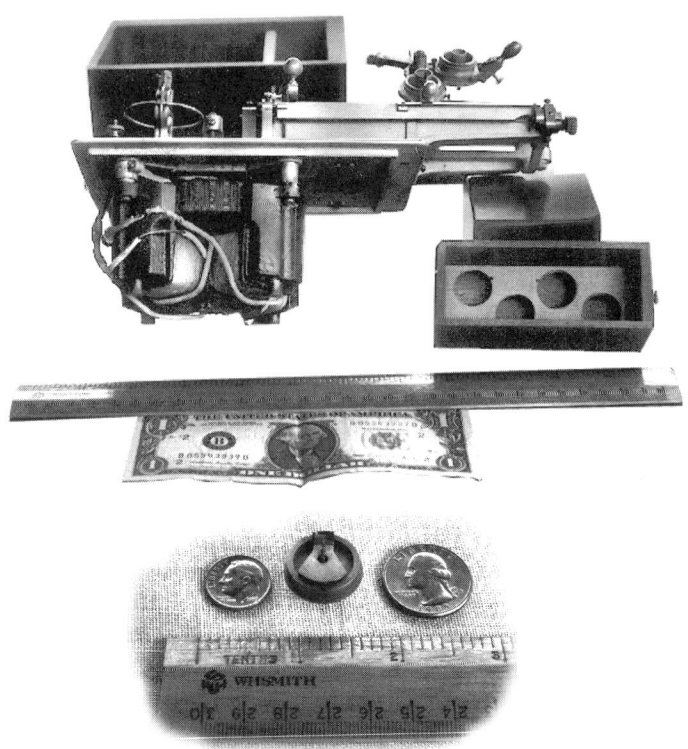

The Edison MILITARY Phonograph was half the size of the CLASS M of the day. No cylinders have been found.

accounts of skirmishes at the front. The cylinders were proportionally small, described in 1890 as no larger than the finger and said to hold as much dictation as the larger ones.[30] Only one MILITARY phonograph is known; it has a recorder and reproducer but there are no cylinders. Nor is there any indication as to how it and the essential batteries would be carried.[31]

Another special class of phonograph user who falls outside the office and domestic fields began flourishing at this time, putting on performances in public halls for an admission charge; these travelled all over the United States and Canada. Another type peddled religion through the phonograph in churches and chapels, using records for the congregation to sing to, and with sermons recorded by noted preachers of the day. These types of showmen normally carried a CLASS M, batteries and an assortment of horns with them. A number went over to spring motors because of weight and problems with the batteries, but spring winding in front of an audience was said "to detract, and should be avoided" (*Edison Phonographic News* March/April 1895). The same journal estimated that a good exhibition at an American seaside resort could make $150.00 a week. These exhibitors flourished for a time over other parts of the world, not all were welcome and individuals were described as being harried in Portugal, driven out of Turkey and put in jail in Morocco.

Portable electric phonograph suitable for an exhibitor

CLASS M in oak cabinet with lid of unknown make

The two distinct styles of casing for these CLASS M and parallel models have been noticed; at no time was a wooden cover provided like the other Edison instruments that came later, although Hawthorne and Sheble advertised a carrying case for them in 1896. That they never gained a more popular acceptance may be blamed on their weight, cost and tedious upkeep of batteries. During their years of production the only innovations were minor and reflected new accessories common to all Edison models and styles, but CLASS M and E acquired name changes. By early 1901 CLASS M was called the VICTOR, and CLASS E CONQUEROR, each from their existing code words used by the trade in ordering by cable. Both words had been in use in

51

1900, but complaints were later made by The Victor Talking Machine Company.[32] The Edison company was reluctant to make any alteration until December 1st 1905 when VICTOR was dropped and BALMORAL adopted,[33] but CONQUEROR lasted the remainder of the machine's existence. Interestingly the names VICTOR and BALMORAL never appeared on the machines' name plates.

In 1907 Edison developed and first offered the ALVA Phonograph. It was designed with a view to using the mechanism, cabinet and many of the parts of the spring driven Model B TRIUMPH; this had come out in mid-1906. When improvements were initiated on the TRIUMPH, so they appeared on the ALVA. Chiefly why the ALVA was advanced was for use with the 110 volt AC electric power that was now finding acceptance in its early years of distribution, but the machine was never a brisk seller. In any case Edison was moving away from the standard vertically mounted motors that had been used for about 20 years and which allegedly contravened patent claims of The New York Phonograph Co. (see Appendix V). It was available until 1912 and was then dropped from production, leaving only spring driven cylinder phonographs in the Edison domestic line.

CLASS M and E Phonograph cabinet of 1890's in Silver Lake finish

•••••••••

Edison Class C and H, Class M and E Electric Phonographs

Class C and H

Although manufactured throughout by Edison, the CLASS C and H in their several manifestations are little known in the United States because they were made for export especially to Edison Bell and allied interests centred in London and revealed in Edison correspondence of May 5th 1899 as 'different to any on the American market'. Despite being seen not infrequently in Great Britain these machines' history in difficult to follow and Edison researchers have been fascinated to come across obscure allusions to the 200 threads per inch cylinders of the 1890s used on them. Only two have been reported, called London Records and space given to the recorded area is quite sparing. A CLASS C is depicted with the inventor in the frontispiece to this book.

The CLASS C stood for 'Commercial', normally a battery-powered machine, but after Capps's spring motor came into use on the SPRING MOTOR (later TRIUMPH) models, the

CLASS C could be bought thus fitted at the same price. There were two models, an 1891 style and a better version for 1893 available until 1905, but the improvements made are not fully known and there is still much to be learned about origins, variations and accessories.

The CLASS H was for home use as a 'Drawing Room' model and was fitted with listening tubes, as was also its 'Exhibition' version for showmen's use. The CLASS H was later available in battery driven or spring motor form.

One CLASS C had its moment of unrewarded importance when Francis Barraud in the 'nineties painted it with the fox-terrier Nipper looking into its black horn and took it along to James Hough of Edisonia, licensees of Edison Bell, but according to Hough's grandson he returned the canvas saying "Dogs don't listen to phonographs".[34] Barraud then painted a Gramophone over the phonograph and in 1899 negotiated with The Gramophone Company for its use as 'His Master's Voice' trademark.

Introduction: First model April 7th 1891, second model May 12th 1893
Class H May 12th 1893

Types: All three models used a 200 t.p.i. cylinder. Only the office machine could shave and record.

CLASS C 'Commercial' for office use, battery powered with speaking and listening tubes, shaving attachment, chip-brush and oilcan. Rubber mandrel for standard cylinder when pulled off exposed a small tapered mandrel for postal cylinders. The main shaft speed for dictation cylinders was 96 r.p.m. and 175 r.p.m. for the postal cylinders. Used a modified Standard speaker.

CLASS H 'Drawing Room' or 'Domestic' for the home, battery powered with 8 listening tubes. No recorder was supplied, records were extra at 5s. 0d. and 6s. 6d. from Edison Bell, and the 'Domestic' lessee was debarred from exhibiting it for money. Its probable speed was 125 r p.m.

The 'Exhibition' for showmen's use was battery powered with 14 listening tubes and 6 free records. Records could not be shaved or recorded and extra music and song records could be bought from Edison Bell for 5s. 0d. and 6s. 6d. each. Again it is believed the speed was 125 r.p.m. and that a modified Automatic reproducer was provided. Two such surviving cylinders are reported to have grooves for only part of their length.

Terms: Rental for the 'Commercial' and 'Drawing Room' was £10 0s. 0d. per annum in advance, the first year's rental to be paid on delivery of the machine. Contracts were for 3 years. Dictation cylinders cost 1s. 0d. each, postal cylinders 9d. each.

For the 'Exhibition' the cost was £50 0s. 0d. royalty (not recoverable) and a rental of £50 0s. 0d. per annum, payable quarterly in advance.

Batteries for all three machines cost £1 7s. 6d. Several years later the 'Commercial' is noticed on a sale basis at £25 4s. 0d.

Edison Bell with a capital of £60,000 was deriving £11,000 a year from the rental of commercial machines in November 1895. There were few amusement phonographs out on hire.

On July 6th 1902 Edison Bell Consolidated Phonograph Co. Ltd. of 39 Charing Cross Road, London sent out a letter to dealers listing all their phonographs and included the CLASS C and H under the 'New' prefix:

Edison Bell 'New Commercial' Phonograph, 200 t. p. i. at 96 and 175 r.p.m. for Standard blanks and postal cylinders
£15 0s. 0d.

.........increasing in 1905, the last year of availability

£17 0s. 0d.

Edison Bell 'New Electric Motor' Phonograph, (the modified 'Drawing Room' model) records, reproduces, shaves, 100 t. p. i., playing Standard records   £15 0s. 0d.

Edison Bell 'New Spring Motor Commercial' Phonograph, 200 t.p.i. at 96 and 175 r.p.m. for Standard blanks and postal cylinders. The electric motor gave way to a Triton spring motor, First noticed April 1st 1898

£15 0s. 0d.

.... increasing in 1905, the last year of availability

£17 0s. 0d.

These machines could have been stockpiled for some time as Edison Bell would be restrained from importing Edison goods from 1903 when Edison set up an office in London. It is not clear which reproducers were supplied with them, but possibly a Standard speaker modified to the fine grooves. The Standard speaker for 2-minute use and probably made by Edison Bell is known.

Dimensions:	Height 13 in., body 17 in. x 10 ¼ in. Overall length 18 in.
Weight:	54 to 58 lb, The amount varies from several sources
Motor:	Edison electric type with vertical armature 2 ½ volts at 2 ampères, the same as used in the CLASS M. The CLASS C and H had a more compact build however, with the motor set more towards the centre of the top works and leaving room for the governor under the left end of the top plate; speed was regulated by contact brushes on the governor. Three belts were used in the drive including one that was sprocketed, and there was no gearing.
Cabinet:	All cabinets seen have been of oak with a metal cover in oak finish.

There was no carrying handle or cover anchorage. The case had a drawer in the right end or at the right end of the front panel, and a metal swarf drawer was provided.

Accessories: A recording tube and listening tubes were standard equipment until the late 1890s when the 'Drawing Room' phonographs were given 14 in. black flared horns. An oilcan and chip-brush also were always listed.

Interesting, if inconclusive figures are noted in the Edison Archive for 1895 and 1896 when Edison Phonograph Works quoted Edison United Phonograph Company (who sometimes shipped to Edison Bell) for the following quantities of CLASS C phonographs:

250 at the rate of 20 per week, each: $42.75
750 " 30 " $40.90
1,000 " 40 " $39.55
1,250 " 50 " $38.45

CLASS M and CLASS E

CLASS M (battery model) became known as the VICTOR in 1901 and BALMORAL in 1905, CLASS E (mains model) became known as the CONQUEROR in 1901.

Introduction: Following the perfection of the electric phonograph on June 16th 1888 the CLASS M emerged at the end of the year as an office machine, and the first were sent out on January 24th 1889, the CLASS E following on July 10th.

Type: 2 - minute

Dimensions: Height 11 ⅛ in., base 20 ¾ in. x 10 in. These figures varied slightly over the years.

Weight: Various quoted from 45 lb. to 65 lb.

Motor: CLASS M, later VICTOR and BALMORAL 2 ½ volt at 2 ampères, increased to 3 ampères after 1906.

CLASS E, later CONQUEROR wound to 110/120 volts DC mains.

Reproducer: The chapter on THE EARLIEST REPRODUCERS 1887-1889 relates the history of these first instruments. In late 1889 the Standard speaker was put into production, having both recording and reproducing styli on the one diaphragm and removing the need for the spectacle device. In 1893 the Automatic speaker was provided with the Edison recorder but did not displace the Standard speaker on these machines until about 1897, the Standard speaker being retained for its recording use. In 1902 the Model C reproducer was included with these phonographs with the New Edison recorder and in 1908 (U.S.) and 1910 (U.K.) when the machines became combination models, the Model H reproducer was included as well as the Model C, for Amberol records. In November 1910 (U.K.) the large carrier arm and Model O reproducer were adopted.

Cabinet: Early models were normally available in mahogany or oak and listed as Cabinet No. 1 for mahogany and Cabinet No. 10 for oak; later, oak would become standard with mahogany an optional extra. Until 1895 the cabinet extended only to the inner end of the mandrel; the space under the mandrel was occupied by a large swarf drawer standing on the baseboard. Then the cabinet was extended over all the baseboard, the accessories drawer enlarged and the swarf drawer made shallow.

By 1893 The North American Phonograph Company was offering a range of heavily decorated sideboard and desk-like furniture for the CLASS M and E to stand on or drop into. These were Residence Outfits, or later Domestic Phonograph Outfits. At this point the catalogue was divided into two, 'A' for Commercial use, 'B' for Domestic use; office machines and amusement machines took the first step towards going their own ways.

March 8th 1893 saw the introduction of a nickel plate with the trade mark design of a tinfoil phonograph with the words: EDISON UNITED PHONOGRAPH CO. surrounding it.[35] Its period of use is unknown.

Accessories and Horns: The earliest illustration seen of a CLASS M type with a small flared horn is in *Harper's Young People* of February 5th 1889, but on the early CLASS M and E a speaking tube, hearing tube/s, chip brush and oilcan were standard accessories. By 1891 horns from 12 in. to 6 ½ ft. could be bought as extras for these phonographs, but by the mid-nineties the 14 in. brass horn became part of the equipment until 1902 when the 14 in. black and brass horn replaced it. In 1906 the option of speaking or hearing tubes in place of the horn was withdrawn and the 14 in. horn became regular equipment.

CONQUEROR mains phonograph

By 1907 the BALMORAL and CONQUEROR were sent out with the polygonal horns with a crane attached to a bracket at the front of the cabinet. In the United States the 12-panel straight TRIUMPH horn was used, while the 8-panel black japanned 19 in. version was standard equipment in the United Kingdom. No evidence has been seen of these phonographs being listed with Cygnet Horn equipment in either the United States or the United Kingdom, but the BALMORAL and CONQUEROR survived just long enough in the United Kingdom for the Cygnet Horn to be bought as an extra. The full range of accessories, repeating and combination attachment options could be used with these machines although a special combination attachment was furnished from October 30th 1908. This was basically TRIUMPH Model A type, with driving pulley of 1 ¾ in. diameter over the belt surface, ½ in. wide with ⅜ in. between flanges and Model C clutch. With this attachment were furnished two GEM idler pulleys, one GEM belt and two idler pulley studs, also a fork lever for operating the clutch.

Features: Electric phonographs of these models never carried the Edison banner transfer, nor the 'Edison' signature emblem and the patent plates always bore the CLASS M and CLASS E designations.

Prices: In their first year or so these machines were sent out on a hire-only basis, but to simplify listing cash prices only are shown:

	CLASS M	CLASS E
from August 1891	$150.00 (without battery)	$170.00
1893	$220.00 (w/battery & records)	$200.00 (with records)
1894 (April)	$100.00 (without battery)	—

1897 (September)	$75.00 (without battery)	$90.00
—	$30.00 (motor complete w/governor, top plate and cabinet)	
1900	$60.00 (without battery)	$75.00
	as VICTOR	as CONQUEROR
1901	$60.00	$75.00
1904	$65.00	$80.00
	as BALMORAL	
1906	$65.00; £13 13s. 0d.	$80.00; £16 16s. 0d.
1907 (October)	$70.00 (w/large straight horn)	$85.00 (w/large straight horn)
1908 (October)	$70.00 (combination type D)	$85.00 (combination type D)
1908 (U.K.)	£14 14s. 0d. (2-minute)	£17 17s. 0d. (2-minute)
1909 (U.K.)	£14 14s. 0d. (comb. type D)	£17 17s 0d. (comb. type D)
	£18 18s. 0d. (mahogany)	£22 0s. 0d. (mahogany)
1910 (Dec. U.K.)	£14 14s. 0d.	not quoted

The last quotation noticed for the BALMORAL in the United States was January 1910. It survived in the United Kingdom until early 1911.

Residence Outfits - some examples from January 1893.

Roll-top cabinet No. 4, antique oak or No. 5, dark cherry
$250.00 (with battery and records) $230.00 (with records)

Double roll-top cabinet No. 6, antique oak or No. 7, dark cherry
$255.00 (with battery and records) $235.00 (with records)

Drop cabinet No. 8, antique oak or No. 9, dark cherry
$250.00 (w/battery and records) $230.00 (with records)

Centre table cabinet No. 15, dark antique oak with French gilt mountings
$315.00 (with battery and records) $295.00 (with records)

•••••••••••••••••••

A New Style cabinet could be bought for a VICTOR or CONQUEROR in 1902 for $3.00.

•••••••••••••••••••

Wholesale prices during this time between Edison Phonograph Works and Edison United Phonograph Company, who handled machines for export were quoted in 1894-5 as follows:

100 CLASS M, each			$45.00
500	"	at 20 per week	$29.60
750	"	30 "	$28.50
1000	"	40 "	$27.65

CLASS M phonograph in gold plated finish presented to the President of the Chase Manhattan Bank of New York in 1893 (Mark Ulano photograph)

Special Finishes

From early days CLASS M and CLASS E were offered in special finishes; these were quite profitable to the Edison company, and not only did the extra decoration bring a talking point to the drawing room, but was useful for enhancing presentation models. Although available outside America, very few of these special finishes have been seen across the Atlantic, but are fairly commonly noticed in essential American collections. Here are a few taken at random:

1893	Extra fancy gilding	$15.00	additional
	Full nickel plated	$25.00	"
	Nickel and gold plated	$100.00	"
1894	Fancy decoration, nickel mandrel and nickel-plated parts	$10.00	"
	Extra gilt finish, Automatic speaker, automatic return mechanism	$45.00	"

Fancy decoration usually meant a floral pattern, while extra gilt finish included a Greek key motif.

In time, less currency was given to these options and by the turn of the century they were relegated to the back of the catalogues with scant details of what could be ordered. From 1905 policies changed and special VICTOR and CONQUEROR equipments were offered in addition to the list prices:

Specially decorated	$10.00;	£2 2s. 0d.
Nickel plated	$25.00;	£5 5s. 0d.
Gold plated	$50.00;	£10 10s. 0d.
Mahogany cabinet	$4.00;	17s. 6d.

•••••••••••

Sales fell away sharply at the turn of the century and it was probably because of the use of electrical phonographs for the coin-slot trade that CLASS M and E lingered in the catalogues long after they had been overtaken by fashion. From the early 1890s several firms and individuals had been promoting spring motors to replace the electric motors in this range of machines. (See chapter on EARLY SPRING DRIVEN PHONOGRAPHS)

Figures of production for the Edison electric phonographs – models unspecified – were 2,906 from 1896 to 1904, 44 in 1900, 66 in 1901 and 4 in 1903, against 340,000 spring motored machines over the same period *(A.P.M.* Vol. 1 No. 3).

•••••••••••

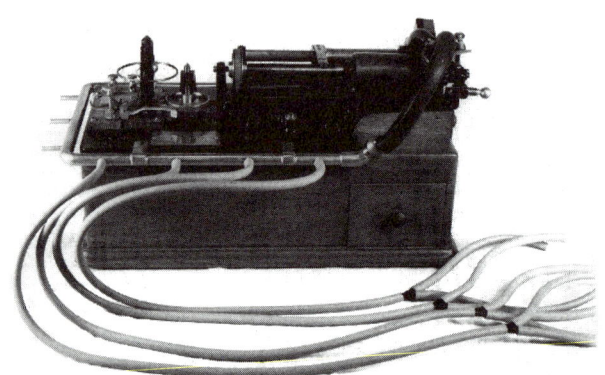

A VICTOR or BALMORAL Phonograph fitted with a gallery for multiple hearing tubes

NOTES
1) Fort Myers Notebook N 86-04-03.3 - Edison Archive
2) The small electric motor was nothing new to the Edison Laboratory. On December 28th 1876 Charles Batchelor wrote to his brother Tom that in the last five years more than fifty applications had been made of "electric engines to small machinery" The first electric motor for a commercial circuit of 110-120 volts was made by Edison in 1879.
3) U.S. Patent No. 374,133 filed April 27th 1887 by Charles S. Tainter and granted November 29th 1887.
4) U.S. Patent No. 375,579 Apparatus for Recording and Reproducing Speech and Other Sounds filed July 7th 1887 by Charles S. Tainter and granted December 27th 1887.
5) Charles Batchelor Papers - Edison Archive
6) Charles Batchelor Notebook June 1st 1887 - Edison Archive
7) E.T. Gilliland in N-86-08-25 October 5th 1886 - Edison Archive
8) Agreement between Edison Phonograph Company and Ezra T. Gilliland - Edison Archive
9) A January 1889 Report of Gilliland's activities from August 1888 with John C. Tomlinson (Attorney of Edison Electric Light Co.) claimed that after Edison perfected the phonograph he told Tomlinson to put it on the market either by getting up a stock company or selling the rights to others. Tomlinson sold the patent rights to Jesse Lippincott ostensibly for $500,000 but in reality $750,000, dividing the difference with Gilliland, and both men departed for Europe. Edison sued them unsuccessfully. In 1938 Alfred O. Tate, Edison's private secretary at the time wrote that the whole matter probably involved nothing more than a breach of ethics, but further speculation is outside this book's purpose.
10) According to this report this phonograph used wax cylinders on a plaster type core, these coming in several lengths from 1 in. upwards. An example of the instrument exists at the Edison Site.
11) U.S. Patent No. 386,974 for Phonograph filed by Edison on November 26th 1887 and patented July 31st 1888. Edison's application for a British patent was through Colonel Gouraud on December 14th 1887, this being granted on October 19th 1888 as No. 17,175.
12) Dimensions: Wood base 18 ½ in. x 12 in. x 1 in. Wood cabinet housing motor 11 in. x 11 in. x 4 in. Overall height 10 in.
13) This differed from Edison's Feed and Return Mechanism for Phonographs patent 382,416 of May 8th 1888, filed January 5th 1888, in that an electromagnet was involved in its operation, but this was not pursued.
14) Batchelor Papers - Edison Archive
15) U.S. Patent No. 393,640 for Phonograph filed June 7th 1888 by Gilliland and granted November 27th 1888.
16) *Norsk Telegraf-Tidende* Vol. 1 Issue I, March 28th 1888 - per Tom Valle
17) U.S. Patent Nos. 382,417 and 382,418 published May 8th 1888. No. 382,418 was originally filed November 26th 1887 and combined Patent No. 382,462 of May 8th 1888, filed January 5th 1888.
18) Letter to Dyer, January 17th 1888 - Edison Archive
19) U.S. Patent No. 382,419 for Process for Duplicating Phonograms filed March 8th 1888 by Edison and granted May 8th 1888.
20) U. S. Patent No. 400,648 for Phonogram Blank filed July 30th 1888 ~ granted to Edison on April 2nd 1889
21) The belt, pulleys and end-gate were featured in U.S. Patent No. 400,647 of April 2nd 1889, filed July 7th 1888
22) This machine somewhat modified was featured in U. S. Patent No. 499,879, filed July 30th 1888 and granted June 20th 1893
23) This model was the subject of Edison's U. S. Patent No. 430,276, applied for January 15th 1889 and granted June 17th 1890. Two examples are known to have survived, one - at time of writing - on display at the American History building at The Smithsonian Institution, Washington, D.C., the other has been in the E.M.I. collection in London and since that was dispersed, is in private hands.
24) *The Proceedings of the 1890 Convention of Local Phonograph Companies* pp 140 and 144 carry references to 200 t.p.i. cylinders. It was reported in the July 1893 *Phonogram*

that these phonographs in Great Britain were the causes of much duping of showmen and exhibitors, No recorder was supplied with the machines and the buyers had to go to the speculator for every 200 t.p.i. entertainment cylinder.

25) Having brought the phonograph to a saleable state, thought was naturally given to bettering its appearance. A bill to Edison of August 27th 1888 survives for 'japanning and ornamenting 21 phonographs at 75 cents each' from Walter M. Conger Jr., Newark, New Jersey. This was for the first batch after Edison's approved model of June 16th 1888.

26) Listed in Koenigsberg's *Edison Cylinder Records* 1889-1912

27) Ibid.

28) Every machine sold had to carry a plate bearing the following: This machine constructed under U.S. Letters Patent as specified thereon, has been sold with the restriction that it is not to be used or exhibited in connection with any coin-slot device; the right to such use is expressly reserved to The North American Phonograph Co. and its assigns, and also with the further restriction that said machine shall be used only within the State of New Jersey.

29) One cabinet manufacturer for these domestic phonographs was Cornish & Co., Washington, New Jersey, who in May 1893 fitted a musical phonograph into an organ case, and two months later supplied cabinets for musical phonographs. The assortment of styles offered from 1893 indicate they were bought in from several sources.

30) Ramsaye in *A Million and One Nights* p. 63 recounts "when the palatial La Burgoyne sailed from New York on August 3rd 1889 Edison stood at the rail ...... clutching a miniature phonograph, delivered at the last minute, under his arm". It was subsequently on show at the Paris Exposition.

31) The machine was built to half size: Baseboard length 10 ½ in., width 5 in. Motor casing 6 ½ in. x 4 ⅜ in. Overall height 6 ½ in. Mandrel length 2 ⅜ in., diameter at smaller end ¹³⁄₁₆ in. Reproducer eye diameter ¾ in. Weight 7 lb.

32) Letters from Horace Pettit on behalf of the Victor Company were dated December 1903, Edison replied on the following March 26th stressing pre-use, and Pettit asked that the name's use should not be extended.- Edison Archive. The Victor name was filed March 12th 1901

33) On instructions from W. E. Gilmore, president of National Phonograph, dated October 16th 1905 - Edison Archive

34) The late Eric Hough to the author

35) Trade Mark No. 22,898 of May 2nd 1893, filed March 23rd 1893

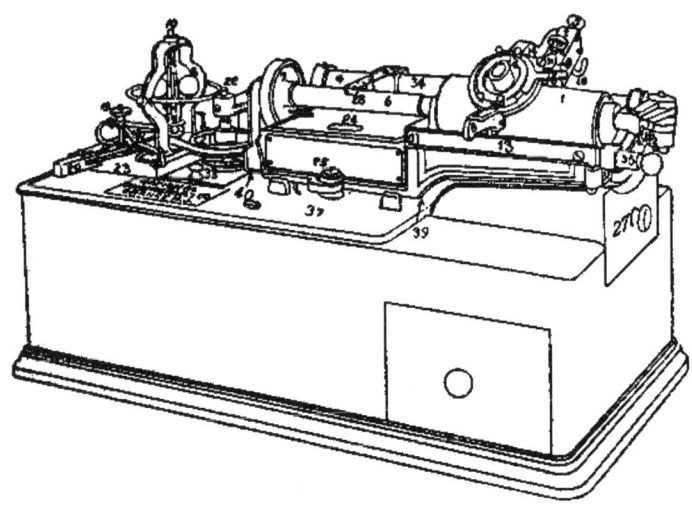

Early North American electric phonograph in elaborate cabinet

Early North American electric phonograph in elaborate cabinet

Chapter 4
Treadle and Water Motor Phonographs

While the tinfoil phonograph needed little more than a crank handle to turn the cylinder at a relatively slow speed, the wax record demanded a steady force to turn it at a higher speed. Electric motors were still costly and needed a power supply when there was yet little mains electricity outside the large towns, and battery cells with these early Edison models were found cumbersome and difficult to contend with. The Edison Spring Motor was still several years away, clockwork with weights was unwieldy, but the sewing machine treadle was an obvious source of steady energy; it was already a workhorse of the garment trade and a piece of furniture familiar to many homes. Moreover it had been in use for Edison magneto driven telegraph instruments certainly since 1878, and shown in brochures of that time.[1] It also had a table surface for standing a phonograph, with room for a typewriter alongside for the office, as well as underhung drawers for accessories.

The situation led to two other curious forms of propulsion for the early Edison machines.

Perhaps the earliest and simplest form of a cranked drive was a digital powered phonograph, with a lever and crank connected to a flywheel and governor and to be pressed intermittently with the finger, just as a leg would operate a treadle. The date of this instrument was late 1888 and was just for use on the laboratory bench, as it also had a grooved pulley for belt connection.[2]

This finger-powered phonograph was depicted in W. K. L. Dickson's *Life of Edison*, but not put into production

The first phonographs built to use on sewing machine treadles were Graphophones[3] and with the uniting of Edison and Bell-Tainter interests by Lippincott in July 1888 treadle-driven Edison machines were an obvious consequence. A message to Colonel Gouraud on October 1st 1888 showed that Edison had completed such a machine by this date.[4] This was the TREADLE Phonograph, later CLASS T, and production models were reported ready for shipping out of West Orange from February 19th 1889. This affinity between Edison phonographs and sewing machines of the day would go on for several years with phonograph accessories such as lids, hoods, handles, catches and enamel finishes all looking like those on sewing machines.

The TREADLE phonograph appeared first in an 1889 North American *Illustrated Catalogue of Parts for the Phonograph*, and as depicted there the phonograph top casting and mechanism did nothing more than replace the sewing machine on its treadle table. Even the letter "H" (for Howe) formed part of the cast-iron stand, and two bobbin drawers were still under the right hand end, Soon after, the "H" gave way to an "E" (for Edison), the two drawers moved over to the left, and the working surface was enlarged with a small swarf drawer under it.

In the North American *Catalogue of Phonographs and Supplies* of 1891 the TREADLE phonograph was listed as the CLASS T and not designated as either an office or entertainment instrument. It sold for $150.00 with accessories.[5] By 1893 it was listed either as an Office Outfit for $140.00, or as a Residence Outfit with musical records for $175.00. The name would soon be changed to Domestic Outfit.

Surprisingly only one of these Edison TREADLE Phonographs is thought to have survived today in complete condition, and is in private hands; it was in its time a personal gift from Edison. The low survival rate of so many of these early phonographs is due largely to the wide hiring-out system of those times. Only when a model was bought outright had it a better chance of being kept and stored away in an attic or shed after it had gone out of use. The CLASS T phonographs were discontinued in 1895, but the treadle continued to be used for shaving machines for several more years.[6] These had the regular CLASS M casting and mandrel with special shaving attachment.

A CLASS T, or North American Treadle Phonograph presented by Edison to his sister in Milan, Ohio, in early 1892

The second curious Edison machine of the time was the WATER Phonograph, completed on January 27th 1890 and introduced on February 19th.[7] Water power had already been used to drive mechanical toys and organs, and harnessed to turn the phonograph through a small turbine or Pelton wheel imparted a smooth regular drive to the mandrel by means of reduction belting. It may have been a visit by J. Lewis Young, the free-lance promoter from London, to Edison in 1889 that brought the idea to the inventor's attention, but he afterwards claimed to have made this proposal because of difficulty in working phonographs in the United Kingdom by public electricity, as this was generally alternating current.[8]

In 1891 the WATER or CLASS W phonograph was offered for $150.00 including accessories,[9] but in 1893 it was described as an Office Outfit for $150.00 or as a Residence Outfit with musical records for $185.00. This would soon be changed to Domestic Outfit. The WATER model was not popular everywhere and was in fact forbidden by the New York Board of Public Works because of its high consumption claimed by that department. The amounts of water needed to run the phonograph were noted on its first day by Charles Batchelor[10], and seemed to be quite moderate:

CLASS W phonograph

Height of water	Speed of phonograph turning off	Time minutes	Water gallons
70 lb. sq. in.	125	5	1
12 ft. 9 in.	80	3	1
29 ft. 10 in.	125	3	1
38 ft. 2 in.	125	3 ¾	1

The CLASS W Phonograph was discontinued in 1895.

Both the TREADLE and WATER phonographs used the essential top works of the electric machines suitably modified. Each was fitted with sturdy 3-ball governors mounted horizontally, but that on the treadle machine had no disc or friction pad and was intended more as a flywheel to control pitch. The governor on the water motor acted conventionally.

The CLASS W phonographs never had more than a wooden baseboard; like the CLASS M series they came without a lid, and a swarf drawer does not feature in any of several models and illustrations seen.

CLASS T PHONOGRAPH

Introduced:	February 1899 (U.S.) It is not known how many were sent abroad
Type:	2 - minute
Dimensions:	Height to table level 26 in. Height overall 35 ¾ in. to cover when closed. Width 36 ½ in., depth 20 ¼ in.
Power:	Foot treadle
Finish:	Early models offered the table top in oak, black walnut and cherry, and were later equipped as Cabinet No. 2 in oak Cabinet No. 3 in cherry
Accessories:	Single hearing tube, speaking tube, chip brush and oilcan
Price:	Hired out by local phonograph companies, but also sold for $150.00 from August 1891. By 1893 it could be bought as an Office Outfit for $140.00 or as a Residence Outfit with musical records for $175.00

CLASS W PHONOGRAPH

Introduced:	February 1890 (U.S.). It is not known how many were sent abroad
Type:	2 - minute
Power:	Hydraulic, usually mains supply
Finish:	Not specified
Accessories:	Single hearing tube, speaking tube, chip brush, oilcan and 10 ft. of connecting pipes
Price:	Hired out at first by local phonograph companies but also on sale for $150.00 from August 1891. By 1893 the CLASS W could be bought as an Office Outfit for $150.00 or as a Residence Outfit with musical records for $185.00.

NOTES

1) Edison Archive
2) First illustrated in W.K.L. and A. Dickson's *Life and Inventions of Thomas A. Edison*
3) U.S. Patent No. 375,579 for Apparatus for Recording and Reproducing Speech and Other Sounds filed by Charles Tainter July 7th 1887 and granted December 27th 1887
4) Edison Archive
5) The North American Phonograph Company in a letter to jobbers of August 7th 1891 offered CLASS T, W (and M) for sale for a trial period until the end of the year. These machines had previously been hired out.
6) Available in Edison catalogues into the 1900s
7) "Water motor tested today" - Batchelor Papers - Edison Archive
8) *The Phonogram* Vol. 1 No. 2, June 1893 p. 30
9) See Note 5
10) Batchelor Papers, January 27th 1890 - Edison Archive

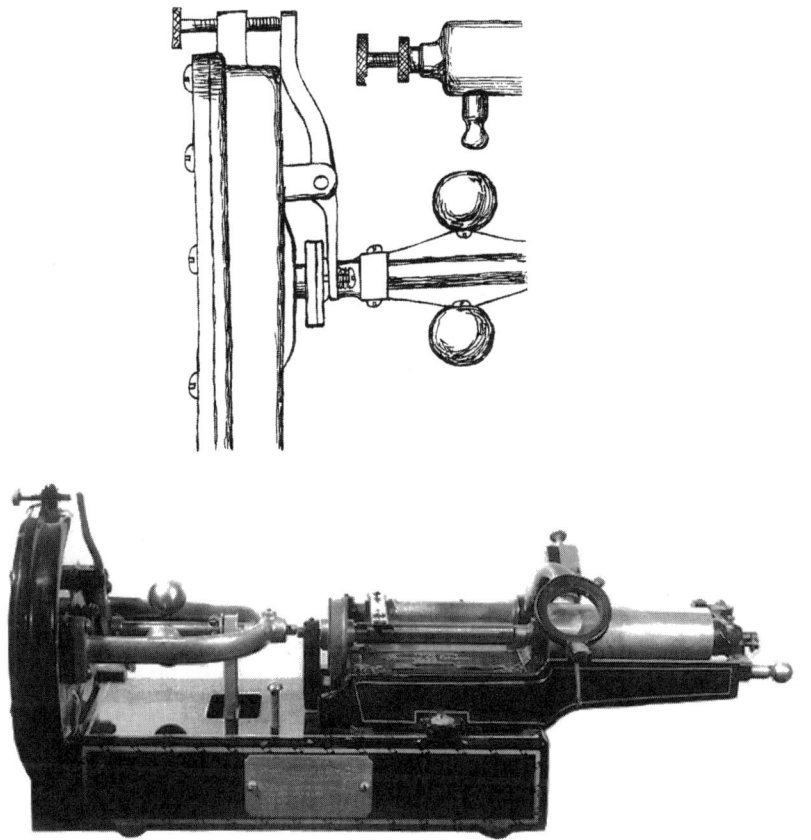

Chapter 5
Early Spring-Driven Phonographs

Although a pioneer of the electric motor, the idea of a spring motor to drive a phonograph was no stranger to Edison from the time of his first tinfoil machine. Several were shown in patent drawings in his Caveat dated February 28th 1878,[1] and two months later in his British Patent No. 1644 of April 24th 1878 for Recording and Reproducing Sounds a handful of tinfoil phonographs were shown having sturdy spring motors. Although none of these has come down to us one firm that produced their versions was The London Stereoscope Company, which also made clockwork (weight) driven tinfoil phonographs besides conventional hand-cranked models. A sight of this Company's catalogue of those days would be illuminating. There are unfortunately insufficient survivors to form any pattern of development of these spring-run tinfoil models and local and laboratory adaptations must have been made. Contemporary pictures of Edison's tinfoil disc phonograph show it as spring-driven; a number were built but none survives.

Certainly any advantages in joining a spring motor to a tinfoil phonograph were not apparent at the time Edison began to work on the later so-called Improved and Perfected Phonographs of 1887 and 1888 when the standard sized wax cylinder was driven by an electric motor, or a little later by treadle and water power if required. The conception of a spring-driven phonograph seemed sensible enough in principle, but no existing spring motor was found to be able to sustain power and was not pursued by Edison or any of his associates when these phonographs were in the development stages, and in consequence the comparatively new electric motors were built into them. At least they were reasonably reliable.

The situation was described in 1888 by Colonel Gouraud with characteristic rhetoric which explained none-the-less why the experts apparently shied away from adapting spring motors to phonographs. He said:

> *"You can't suggest anything that Edison has not already tried. I guess you would have to switch on a small steam engine to wind up a spring strong enough to do the work of driving that machine; besides no man can make a governor that will answer all the variations and fluctuations of the spring".*[2]

The chief difficulty with the spring motor of 100 years ago was to contrive a governor that got away from the clockmaker's narrow perception and was capable of easy regulation.

Two men in particular, working independently and in different countries grappled with these difficulties of spring power and phonographs and overcame them in 1891. The first to file a patent was Edward H. Amet on January 28th 1891, directed at a speed regulator or governor suitable particularly for such a spring motor.³ Amet was a capable general engineer in several electrical and mechanical provinces, and was granted several patents over the years for improvements to Phonographs. His speed regulator comprised a revolving shaft with two opposing cams carrying sliding friction shoes, and when these were thrown out centrifugally met resistance on the inside surface of a friction ring. Speed adjustment was somewhat arbitrary by altering a spring restraint on the friction shoes. Amet's spring motors were not ready until mid-1894 and were used with an Edison CLASS M type top movement as a spring-driven phonograph. It could also be used with a Graphophone movement. Amet motors are usually found with one or two brass-barreled springs, although one quadruple spring Amet motor is known in private hands. The motor was screwed to the bottom of the case and not to the top plate and was accessible through a drop-down door, locked by a key.

The Amet motor phonograph

Amet's motor mounted below the CLASS M top mechanism was marketed by The Chicago Talking Machine Company as an "M" Class Spring Motor Phonograph, and an improved Amet motor called the Peerless was offered also in the same listing. The governor on the Peerless was now a regular 2-ball centrifugal type, using ball bearings for pivot points.

The first Peerless motors bore the name on the frame, but by the end of the machine's short life in late 1896 the name no longer appeared, but the governor was now 3-ball.

The Peerless motor phonograph

The early speed controls were lever operated and a spring cable was later used. The front panel - known as the front lid - continued to be hinged at the bottom, essentially a Graphophone feature and probably due to Amet's association with these instruments, and later cases may be found to be more decorated than the earlier.

A little more is known about Amet's British rival, Joseph Exall Greenhill (1840-1907), a London-based scientist and philosopher who had the benefit of perfect pitch and claimed to have been working on a suitable spring motor for phonographs since 1881.⁴

His first experiments used the striking train from a clock to regulate his mechanism, followed by three years of trials with various governors, then a stage with dual springs and fusees, but all of these brought a flattening of the note to his ear. At first Greenhill used a Bell-

71

Tainter Graphophone, but transferred his experiments to Edison machines after being introduced to Colonel Gouraud by J. Lewis Young when Greenhill demonstrated his motor in 1891. Finally the layout of two mainsprings acting on one pinion and butterfly type of air governor was successful, and led to his application for a joint patent (with Colonel Gouraud) on May 8th 1891; this followed Amet's patent filing date by 14 weeks, and Greenhill's patent was granted on May 7th 1892.[5] Like Amet's, Greenhill's patent was directed solely at speed regulation and he proposed several types of air governors. An unrecorded number of these motors came from the workshop of William Fitch, described as a watchmaker, in the City of London. Years later the unfortunate Fitch was reported as destitute and in the poor-house.

Greenhill motor, 1893, used conjointly with the top-works from an Edison electric phonograph

Two models were offered in the first known advertisements in June 1893, one to play three cylinders for £15, the other eight, for £20.[6] The Greenhill motor sat in its special wooden case alongside the top works of an Edison electric phonograph - not included in the price - and this it drove through a belt. Amet's motor was not in production for a further year.

J. E. Greenhill never made any further patent applications and only one of his £20 models is known to have survived. It is a handsomely constructed motor of large proportions but too elaborate for what Amet's compact design could furnish with reasonable efficiency for the average owner. Amet's motors weighed about 30 lb. and were advertised for $110.00, playing 7-8 cylinders at one winding for the double spring types. The Peerless was claimed to run for 23 minutes and to be noiseless.[7]

A further pioneer patentee whose one invention should be mentioned was Joseph Broich from Brooklyn. He designed a spring motor vertically mounted on the underside of an Edison electric top plate with drive to a vertical governor with conical speed adjustment. The mandrel was driven by a belt. If any were built, none is known to survive.[8]

It is thought that the period of bankruptcy of the (Edison-Graphophone) North American Phonograph Company in mid-1894 until The National Phonograph Company was set up in January 1896 led to phonograph parts being sold off in bulk to traders and individuals prepared to find motors and cases for them, and quickened the need to find reasonably cheap power units.

Another spring driven phonograph, again using the motor plate and upper works from a CLASS M was featured in the January-February 1895 journal *Edison Phonographic News*; this could have been Edison's SPRING MOTOR FOR PHONOGRAPH. An un-numbered SPRING MOTOR type phonograph marked 'United States Phonograph Company, Newark N.J. Patent Applied For' has been reported with no Edison name but with a 3-ball governor and this may have been a subterfuge for Edison to sell machines when he was not supposed to. The same issue of *Edison Phonographic News* featured an announcement from The Ohio Phonograph Company of Cincinnati, offering Edison electric phonograph owners a spring motor in part exchange for their electric motors and batteries, but the designer and maker were not specified.[9]

Likewise Columbia Phonograph in Washington D.C. is on record in October 1894 as offering to fit spring motors to treadle machines, either Edisons or Graphophones. The designer was not specified but they would play from 3 to 4 cylinders, could be bought in an oak or cherrywood box, weighed 31 lb. and cost $50.00. They were 'guaranteed to run regularly'.

A further integral spring motor phonograph was put out by Louis Glass, one-time manager and director of several phonograph companies on the West Coast and a well known character in the trade. Again it used the top works from an Edison electric machine, and was submitted for a patent in February 1894 on the

The Louis Glass motor mounted in conjunction with an Edison upper works. The dial on the right of the bedplate indicates the tension in the spring.

feature of an indicating dial showing the reserve force of the spring.[10] The motor was again set vertically in the case, driving the mandrel through a belt, and the governor pinion directly through a large contrate gear. The governor could be mounted vertically above or below the top plate and still its pinion would mesh with this gear. Unusually, the winding crank emerged from the front, again with the case hinged forward for access to the motor.

Of the spring motors mentioned, Greenhill's was the only one that enveloped the phonograph movement yet could be easily detached. All the other examples were assembled machines as much as the Edison phonographs that followed from 1895-6.

EDISON SPRING MOTOR PHONOGRAPH (CLASS SM), later called the TRIUMPH PHONOGRAPH

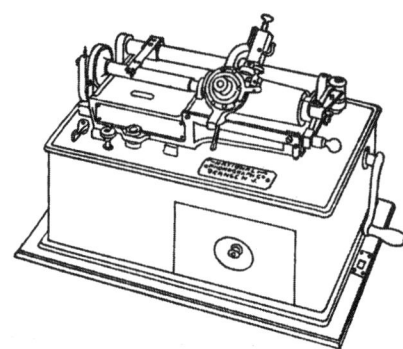

"Ohio (Phonograph Co.) suggested North American Phonograph Company get spring motor but were told Edison believed no spring motor could ever be made with a proper governor to run the phonograph so evenly that musical reproduction could be satisfactorily reproduced. The only spring motors Edison was able to obtain for a year or two were those obtained from Chicago" (Amet)

J.L. Andem in litigation 1907

It happened that The Edison United Phonograph Company in the early 1890s supplied top works of electric machines for others to fit spring motors, drawing George Tewksbury to write of:

"a variety of (non-Edison) spring motors generally bad, has been made for the Phonograph. The common fault is imperfect regulation",

but of the Triton motor he was able to say in 1897 that

(its) "results are no less satisfactory" (than the electric) [11].

The use of a spring motor from the days of the first tinfoil machines had seemed obvious, but proved more difficult than had at first appeared. With the progress of the phonograph at the same time as the small electric motor, the two made a natural combination, but the machines were expensive and cumbersome,

In 1896 Edison started manufacturing and selling the spring-motored phonographs indirectly through The United States Phonograph Company of New Jersey.[12] This was an export distributing company established in 1893, and one of its employees Frank Capps had constructed a robust triple-spring motor capable of giving a firm and prolonged drive to a phonograph, the upper works being from the ubiquitous CLASS M. This was the successful Triton Motor.[13] The first machines were completed in 1895, but did not appear officially until 1896[14] and there were problems with the patent over the sliding disc part of the governor. From 1897, Edison's company as The National Phonograph Company, bought the United States company's output, and the Capps motor in triple and modified single-spring forms would power several other Edison phonograph models.

The first Capps motors used a 3-ball governor, but in a few months the weights were changed for cylindrical types. After a while the CLASS M style of top movement had the guide pulley mountings eliminated from the casting. These CLASS M origins were reluctant to be shaken off, and in 1897 George Tewksbury was still referring to the top movement as being the body of the standard 'M' machine, and the fact that the model was catalogued for five years as the SPRING MOTOR phonograph showed modest promotional direction. Inter-company correspondence and outside letters ponderously spoke of "the 14 to 16-cylinder clock-motor phonograph" as a matter of course. The term 'clock-motor' or 'clock-work' when applied to a phonograph in the first years implied a weight driven machine. The earliest Triton powered SPRING MOTOR machines did not impress everybody; Ludwig Stollwerck, Edison's German agent for a time, wrote offering to get German clockmakers to make better spring motors than the Edison.[15]

The early models carried United States Phonograph's name on a nickel plate. Later, The National Phonograph Company's name appeared and sometimes the enigmatic SPRING MOTOR FOR PHONOGRAPH with its intimation that an earlier motor kit might be involved, but this has not been explained. The next change had the plate marked EDISON SPRING MOTOR PHONOGRAPH. As the treadle phonographs had borrowed heavily from the sewing machine, so did the SPRING MOTOR for its case. The cover enveloped the machine completely and fastened to the baseboard at either end. In early 1901 the SPRING MOTOR phonograph was given the 'New Style' cabinet, adjusting to a general Edison shape and re-named the TRIUMPH.

The Company's literature of this period and later elected to refer to the machines of 1895-1901 as the TRIUMPH Model A, the New Style TRIUMPH of 1901-1904 as the TRIUMPH Model A-1 and the machines from June 1904 to July 1906 with the spring-suspended motor frame as the TRIUMPH Model A-2. But there were still signs of uncertainty at times, because the TRIUMPH setting-up instructions of January 1902 showed the SPRING MOTOR machine with Standard Speaker and speaker clamps.

Owners of the SPRING MOTOR phonograph were advised in the autumn of 1901 that New Style cabinets were now on sale for re-casing their machines in the style of the TRIUMPH models $7.50

SPRING MOTOR Phonograph. Earlier models had reproducer clamping plates with knurled screws.

Introduced:	Mid-1895 (U.S.); its British introduction is not known but it was offered in the 1898 Edisonia price list where it was called the 'Class M Spring Phonograph' and as the 'Type 4 Large Commercial Phonograph' by Edison Bell at about the same time.
Type:	2-minute
Dimensions:	Height 14 in., base 16 ½ in. x 10 ½ in.
Weight:	43 lb.
Motor:	3 spring, and a playing of 14 to 16 records per winding claimed. The black enamelled winding crank was square holed.
Cabinet:	Fully enveloping cover, generally finished in light oak with an accessories drawer in the right front of the body. There were no transfers (decals).
Features:	The top plate was set fully on the cabinet and it had to be lifted bodily for access to the motor. On earlier machines the lugs for holding the idler pulleys of the electric phonograph will be noticed. The shaving device was of the locking plunger type, found only on the heavy range of Edison models.[16] On early machines the straight edge was held by two screws.
Accessories:	Recording tube or 14 inch brass horn or hearing tubes, oilcan and camel hair chip-brush.
Reproducer, recorder and fittings:	Earlier models were sent out with the Edison Standard Speaker, combining recording and reproducing styli, but in 1898 the separate Edison Automatic Reproducer and Edison Recorder took its place. Three styles of speaker clamps are known to have been used; firstly came the twin curved short plates, each held by two knurled screws and with a speaker adjusting screw, then a single crescent lever pivoted at its bottom end to press the left outer edge of the reproducer or recorder into its carrier-arm seating.[17] Then there followed a pair of crescent shaped pivoting levers, and the final knurled screw on the outer periphery of the carrier-arm appeared in 1902. On the early models the reproducer adjusting screw acting on the carrier-arm had both a coarse and fine adjusting thread.[18]

Prices:		
	on introduction:	$100.00
	reducing late 1898	$75.00
	and June 1900	$50.00

In the United Kingdom offered by Edisonia Ltd. extras included record box,
10 records 2 blanks, large japanned horn, hearing and speaker tubes, chip brush,
  screwdriver and oilcan   £27 10s. 0d.

As Edison Bell's Large Commercial Phonograph (Type 4),
  with Automatic Reproducer and with the   £25 4s. 0d.
  Bettini Micro-reproducing Attachment, extra   £7 10s. 0d.

A skeletal form of the SPRING MOTOR Phonograph is known where the top body surfaces have been made with geometric perforations, producing a casting of fragile looking webbing. The reason is not known as any saving of weight is quite small.

Capps's 3-spring motor was called the Triton from its telegraphic code-word; it was a success and remained catalogued for some years "to convert an electric machine into a spring machine with very little trouble".

Price:	1896	$40.00
	September 1897	$30.00
	1900	$25.00 with cabinet and cover
	1903	$17.50, cabinet and cover now extra

The Triton was not advertised separately after 1905 but continued on special order until March 1907, or to the end of 1906 abroad. As fitted to the TRIUMPHS it lasted until 1911, but had a 4-weight governor fitted in its last year to further smooth its running. The 3 and 4-weight governors are not interchangeable. The Triton was used on several non-Edison machines, including the 24-cylinder Multiphone.

The SPRING MOTOR phonograph was also offered with Bettini's Microphonograph Attachments in the years over the turn of the century.

TRIUMPH Model A

From the spring of 1901 the SPRING MOTOR mechanism was re-cased and re-named the TRIUMPH. The new cabinet had the top plate screwed on to a hinged wooden frame, allowing it to be lifted and propped for motor inspection. The cabinet now had corner posts with a recessed front panel where the EDISON TRIUMPH PHONOGRAPH banner was displayed.[19] The cabinet lines were severe but in time the corner posts and mouldings were rounded slightly. The top surfaces had more pronounced gold lining than earlier with rococo corner motifs. There was a patent plate. An interior wooden partition took the place of the earlier drawer.

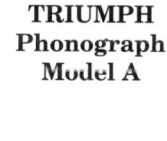

TRIUMPH Phonograph Model A

Introduction:	May 1901 (U.S.) Also available in the United Kingdom after 1903 from Edison's National Phonograph Company.
Type:	2-minute
Dimensions:	Height 14 ⅜ in., base 18 ⅛ in. x 12 ¾ in.
Weight:	49 lb.
Mechanism:	From June 1904 coiled springs replaced the rubber washers holding the motor frame to the top plate; at the same time a belt tightening nut was fitted.[20]
Reproducer:	Initially the Edison Automatic and Edison Recorder, but in 1902 (U.S.) and 1903 (U.K.) the Model C took the place of the Automatic. It is probable that some of the first models had reproducer clamp levers, but were replaced by the knurled clamp screw. The shaving device was retained.
Horn etc.:	The 14 in. brass horn was supplied at the beginning but this was changed to one of the same size but with a black body and brass bell. A speaking tube could be specified instead of the horn. A two-way hearing tube was also supplied.
Accessories:	Oilcan and camel-hair chip brush.
Price:	$50.00; £10 10s. 0d.

From 1902 (U.S.) and 1903 (U.K.) the two-way hearing tubes were no longer supplied with the regular outfit but could be specially ordered in place of the 14 in. horn, as could a speaking tube at the same price.

For several years until 1902 it was possible to buy Phonograph Outfits, the SPRING MOTOR/TRIUMPH with a broader offering of horns, listening tubes, records, spares and tools, and costing up to $112.00.

Specially decorated Edison phonographs were available from 1893 and in its time the SPRING MOTOR could be ordered with gold or nickel plating as an extra ($50.00 and $25.00) and from the early 1900s the options for its successor were more specific:

TRIUMPH

Specially decorated, additional*	$8.00;	£1 13s. 6d.
Nickel plated, additional	$25.00;	£5 5s. 0d.
Gold plated, additional	$50.00;	£10 10s. 0d.
Mahogany cabinet, additional	$10.00;	£2 2s. 0d.

*extra gold lining and applied floral transfers to the top surfaces

The first mahogany cabinets were ready on special order from June 1904 to match the mahogany cylinder cabinets, then in general use.

From June 1904 speed indicator marks of 120, 144 and 160 r.p.m were provided.[21]

Model B

Introduced:	July 1906 (U.S.) and November 1906 (U.K.)
Type:	2-minute
Motor:	3-spring Triton
Weight:	49 lb.
Dimensions:	Height 14 ⅜ in., Base 18 ⅛ in. x 12 ¾ in.

TRIUMPH Model B; this has been fitted with a Combination Attachment

Cabinet:	The green oak case of the Model A gave way to one of antique oak, thought to harmonize better with home furnishings of the day. The corner pillars had gone and the front panel was raised. After a short time the single word 'Edison' replaced the banner decal in the summer of 1906, as the banner had been thought intrusive.[22] The corners of the cabinet were noticeably rounded, otherwise the casework would change little in succeeding models.
Features:	Because of legal objections by Edison Bell (see Appendix IV) the spring-arm locking bolt of earlier models was replaced by a locking latch at the front end of the straight edge.[23] A protective guard that included an adjusting screw was placed over the feednut spring.[24] The winding crank was nickel plated and now screwed to the winding shaft - it was said that the earlier slotted type tended to work loose and could cause rattle. The top casting was screwed to the top plate from below, the holding screw at the back and front of Model A were discarded, as well as the rubber cushions at each of its corners. A shaving device was fitted.
Accessories:	A 14 in. horn and camel-hair chip-brush were supplied, but recording and listening tubes could no longer be exchanged for the horn.
Reproducer:	Model C, with Improved Edison Recorder
Price:	$50.00; £10 10s. 0d.

From October 1907 (U.S.) the new TRIUMPH polygonal horn was offered to boost sales. This was straight, 33 in. long with 12 panels. It had a blue and gold identifying logo, marked TRIUMPH.

TRIUMPH phonograph with new horn equipment	$55.00
horn and crane complete	$ 6.15

Saying they were bowing to public demand, but really in a bid to regain the initiative on the horn business, the Company began to offer horns and cranes separately for affixing to earlier machines from February 1908:

Straight horn (reduced since November)	$2.75
Straight horn, mahogany finish	$6.50
Horn support	$.90

TRIUMPH with mahogany cabinet and mahogany finished horn, available from March 1908 (U.S.) $75.00

Edison machine owners in the United Kingdom were less fortunate with what the Company was offering, and all machines there with the exception of the IDELIA were given 19 in. x 11 in. straight 8-panel polygonal horns in April 1908. These were japanned black with gold decoration, and made in one piece.

TRIUMPH phonograph, complete with this horn	£10 10s. 0d.
horn and crane for fitting to existing machines	11s. 0d.

In February 1908 (U.S.) it was announced that the camel-hair chip-brush would cease to be supplied with machines, but that an oilcan and sample of oil would be supplied instead. This may be seen as a move towards changes to come.

Model C

Introduced:	mid-February 1908 (U.S.), 1909 (U.K.)	
Type:	2-minute	
Features:	Exactly similar to Model B but for three changes; there was no swing-arm, the mandrel being supported on a central bearing,[25] and there was no shaving device. The horn equipment was the same as Model B. Early in 1908 there was a change in governor construction when an additional collar with wire spring attached to the adjoining collar was put on the governor shaft.	
Price:	unchanged at first	$50.00; £10 10s. 0d.
	increasing about April 1908	$55.00; £11 11s. 0d.

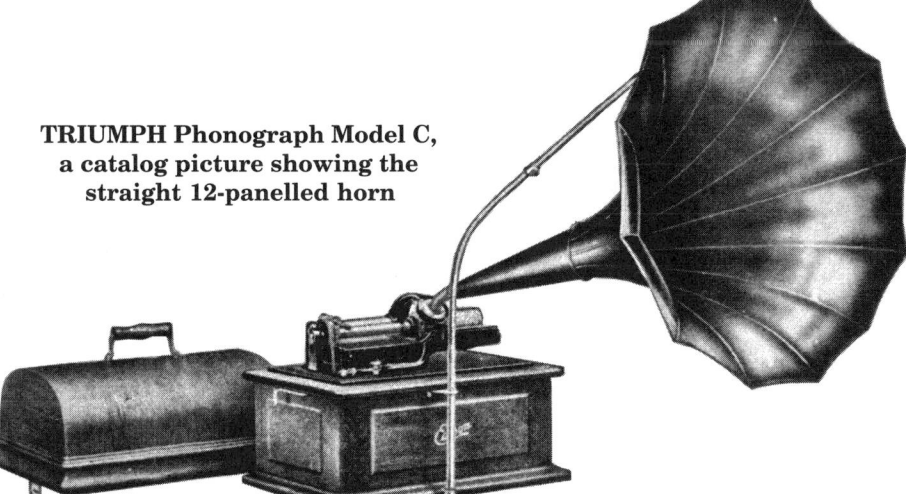

TRIUMPH Phonograph Model C, a catalog picture showing the straight 12-panelled horn

This model was released without official announcement in the United States and for a time was meant for sale only in New York State, Model B still being offered elsewhere. Model C was brought to the United Kingdom during 1909 shortly before the Combination Model D appeared, but had likely been held back until Model B stocks were run down. The reasons given for these mechanical changes will be found in Appendix V. The Edison company tried to make the best of the situation and pushed these changes as improvements, but forced limitations on the machines that were only partly countered as phonograph technology advanced. The absence of the swing arm and mandrel end bearing meant cylinders could no longer be shaved effectively, hence the dropping of the chip-brush and the inclusion of an oilcan for the centre bearing. These phonographs that have been stored for many years will often be found to have this bearing seized up, and it will need expert removal and a new bearing put in.

In April 1908 replacement Model B TRIUMPH cabinets were offered: in oak at $7.50 or mahogany $18.75

To identify readily Models A, B and C from key features:

Model A

Earlier (SPRING MOTOR) style in sewing machine case with drawer
Later (TRIUMPH) style in New Style cabinet

Phonograph body rests on top plate on rubber cushions
Black japanned winding crank with square hole for winding shaft
Shaving device
Swing-arm bolt assembled to the right end of the straight edge
Likely to have single half-nut

Model B

Nickel plated winding crank screws to the end of its shaft
Shaving device
Swing-arm locking lever on right end of straight edge
Phonograph body has no lugs and rests on topplate, being bolted from below
Likely to have twin half-nut

Model C

Likely to have cabinet with raised centre panel
No swing-arm
No shaving device

Some TRIUMPH phonographs of this period, especially in the United Kingdom may be found with a lift pin in the carrier-arm instead of a lift lever. This and other small modifications were made until 1903 to avoid patent infringement.

On July 14th 1908 it was decided that introduction of the Combination Model D TRIUMPH and its accessories would be on October 1st. Manufacture of Model B machines would carry on at the same price but Model D machines would be more expensive. There was a call for them to be re-named, possibly something associated with the Amberol cylinders, but TRIUMPH was confirmed. No new castings would be made for Model B types; when these were exhausted Model C would supersede it. Production was to be as follows:

TRIUMPH Model B	100 per week
C	250 "
Attachments	50 "

This programme was soon altered:

TRIUMPH Model B	50 per week
C	50 "
Combination D	300 "
Attachments	325 "
Model H Repros.	325 "

Pre-production orders received:

TRIUMPH Combination Model D	1784
Attachments	3695

By November 6th 1908 the factory had reached output on all other models, but the TRIUMPH would remain at 300 per week until the order books were cleared and the company was hard pressed to meet the Christmas (1908) demand.

Model D (1)

Introduced:	October 1908 (U.S.), August 1909 (U. K.)
Type:	2 and 4-minute combination
Dimensions:	Height 13 ¼ in., base 18 in. x 12 ⅜ in.
Weight:	50 ½ lb.
Motor:	The Triton motor was modified for this model, having a more substantial 4-weight governor fitted, but earlier machines were sent out with the 3-weight type. With the new governor came a double friction pad on a self-centering stirrup, the motor remaining basically as before, but with a modified frame.
Cabinet:	Antique oak, or mahogany to special order. The case sides were no longer set on a rectangular base, thus slightly reducing the height.
Layout:	Visible mechanical parts very similar to Model C but fitted with a sun and planetary gear motion inside the driving pulley, halving the rotation of the feed screw (and thus the carrier-arm travel) for playing 4-minute cylinders.[26] The helical oil-groove on the back rod was introduced with this model.
Reproducers:	Model C, and Model H for the new Amberols. Improved Edison Recorder included.
Horn:	12 panel straight horn, length 33 in. (U.S.)
	8 panel straight horn, length 19 in. (U.K.)
Price:	$60.00; £14 14s. 0d.
	$80.00 with mahogany cabinet and mahogany finished horn (U.S. only)

When the Combination Model D was placed on sale the Model B was continued for a while, and the Model C until 1910 (U.S.) and for a year longer in the United Kingdom.

In January 1910 to help the trade clear the shelves of earlier TRIUMPHS, they could have Models B and C converted to Combination Model D for $10.00 and $6.50 respectively, carriage to and from the factory at their cost.

The TRIUMPH Combination Attachment for converting 2-minute phonographs to play 2 and 4-minute records was made available in the United States in October 1908 and in the

United Kingdom in the month following, although Model D machines were not publicized there until the following year ....$7.50; £1 11s. 0d.

These Combination Attachments were subject to the return of the old mainshaft and mandrel after the phonograph had been converted.

It was soon found that there were difficulties in fitting the Model A TRIUMPH and earlier SPRING MOTOR machines with the clutch shifting bracket, so Model C clutch castings were continued for all TRIUMPH attachments, the reason being that there were variations in the old Model A body castings. Therefore:

Model A required Model A Outfit with feed screw sleeve 4 $^{21}/_{32}$ in. long
     B   "   B   "   5 in. long
     C   "   C   "   5 ¼ in. long

With Model A and C Attachments no clutch shifting lever was supplied, it being said that there was no room on the body for the clutch to operate freely. All Combination Attachments for the TRIUMPHS included a new wide single feed-nut and spring, and attachments added to TRIUMPHS with Repeating Attachments required a special main-shaft pulley. Attachments for the TRIUMPH and HOME instruments although seemingly similar were said to be incompatible. Despite all these problems one occasionally hears of TRIUMPHS with combination attachments operating well in contravention of these recommendations.

Some Edison owners were never quick enough to change for the Company's liking, and to encourage them to 'Amberolize' their 2-minute phonographs, an added inducement was made in the United States in April 1910 in the form of 10 Special Amberols with the Combination Attachment..... $8.50

The British public had to wait until May 1911 following a proposal from Frank L. Dyer, the Edison Company president, that the Combination Attachment to that country should have 5 Amberols and 5 Standard records with it..... £1 16s. 0d.

As a guide to sales expectations in those times the factory schedule for the TRIUMPH range on January 30th 1909 was as follows:

Model B   to carry 25 in stock

Model C   to carry 10 in stock, 10 in the Testing Dept., and parts sufficient to assemble 100 machines

Model D   to carry 100 in stock, 100 in the Testing Dept. and parts sufficient to assemble 1,000 machines.

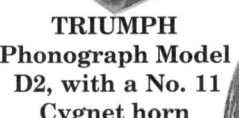

TRIUMPH Phonograph Model D2, with a No. 11 Cygnet horn

The all-metal Cygnet Horn appeared in September 1909 (U.S.), and the No. 11 (11 panels) was supplied for the TRIUMPH. In this form the Combination D TRIUMPH was known as the Model D 2 and sold in the following outfits:

with Cygnet Horn, black with gold decoration	$60.00
with Cygnet Horn, oak finish	$70.00
mahogany cabinet	
with mahogany finish Cygnet Horn	$85.00

At the same time the earlier TRIUMPH Model C was advertised with Cygnet Horn as follows:

with Cygnet Horn, black with gold decoration	$60.00
with Cygnet Horn, oak finish	$65.00
mahogany cabinet	
with Cygnet Horn, mahogany finish	$80.00

In their early months delivery hold-ups of these horns from outside made for delay in getting them to jobbers.

In the following year from August 1910 (U.S.) wooden Music Master Cygnet Horns were offered as part of the equipment with Models C and D TRIUMPHS in the following outfits:

Model C, oak case, oak Music Master horn	$70.00
Model C, mahogany case, mahogany Music Master horn	$85.00
Model D, oak case, oak Music Master horn	$75.00
Model D, mahogany case, mahogany Music Master horn	$90.00
Spruce Music Master horn, additional to above	$5.00
Inlaid pearl Music Master horn, additional to above	$35.00

All this improved horn equipment gave a better tone, was more compact and ousted the earlier 12-panel straight horns, these being no longer listed as TRIUMPH equipment after September 1910, but they could be obtained to special order.

Meanwhile, in Great Britain phonograph owners still had to put up with the 19 in. straight horn, or in desperation had bought horns of other makes. At last in October 1910 the Cygnet Horn was offered in the United Kingdom for phonographs other than the IDELIA and the GEM and the TRIUMPH Model D 2 equipment was listed as follows:

with Cygnet Horn, black with gold decoration	£14 14s. 0d.
with oak or mahogany finish Cygnet Horn	£15 15s. 0d.
with 19 in. polygonal straight horn, as before	£13 0s. 0d.

By now the Model D TRIUMPH had superseded earlier models and these were no longer listed in U.S. or U.K. catalogues.

Model E

Introduced:	September 1910 (U.S.); November 1910 (U. K.)
Type:	2 and 4-minute
Motor:	That of the Model D with a 4-weight governor was continued
Reproducer:	Model O with 2 and 4-minute sapphires was supplied to fit the large carrier-arm; this carried the reproducer along the top of the mandrel. An adapter ring was supplied, providing for a recorder or small-fitting reproducers if desired.
Horn Equipment :	Supplied in several styles as with Model D. In the United States TRIUMPH straight horns were not supplied as equipment after 1910, but in the United Kingdom a special elbow connection to the newly placed reproducer was provided with 19 in. straight horn equipment.
Features:	From February 1911 record cleaning brushes were put on TRIUMPH phonographs.[27]

TRIUMPH Phonograph Model E, with oak Music Master horn

Prices for the Model E follow those quoted for Model D.

The Model O reproducer seems to have caught the public fancy because an internal factory memo of April 1911 reported that to date 13,000 Model O had been put out for the

TRIUMPH alone. About the same time it was estimated that in the United States and Great Britain combined there were more than one million 'un-Amberolized' phonographs still being used for 2-minute cylinders, and with the introduction of the Model R reproducer, the Combination Attachment alternatives increased:

Model R reproducer in place of Model H in TRIUMPH Model D equipment additional $3.00

Model R reproducer supplied with TRIUMPH Combination Attachment, $10.50; £2 5s.0d.

Model R reproducer supplied in place of Model H in TRIUMPH Combination Attachment with 10 Special Amberol cylinders.....additional $1.00

Model R reproducer with TRIUMPH Combination Attachment with 5 Special Amberol and 5 Special Standard cylinders (U.K. only)..... £2 10s. 0d.

TRIUMPH Combination Attachment with 10 Special Hebrew cylinders (L-W) (October 1911 U.S.)....$6.85

 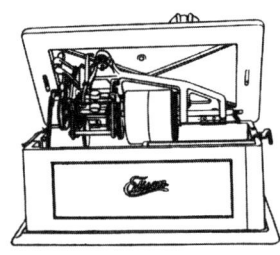

TRIUMPH Phonograph Model F, showing the 2-spring motor

Model F

Introduced:	November 1911 (U.S.); February 1912 (U. K.)
Type:	2 and 4-minute
Motor:	The Triton gave place to one with 2 springs and fitted with a 3-weight governor. The driving springs were the same as AMBEROLA (B) - I and III
Cabinet:	The same as Models D and E. TRIUMPHS have been reported in OPERA cases, but the OPERA was marketed in the same month as

this model and they would have been fitted privately, as the TRIUMPH may be dropped into the OPERA case.

Reproducer: Model O, also Edison recorder with adapter ring

Horn: Oak Music Master

Price: $75.00; £15 15s. 0d.

Some variations in the types of motors supplied with Models D, E and F have been noted.

In October 1912 (U.S.) it was announced that all machines would in future be 4-minute playing only.

In the Edison factory the following quantities of TRIUMPHS were ordered to be on hand for playing the new Blue Amberols from October 1st 1912:

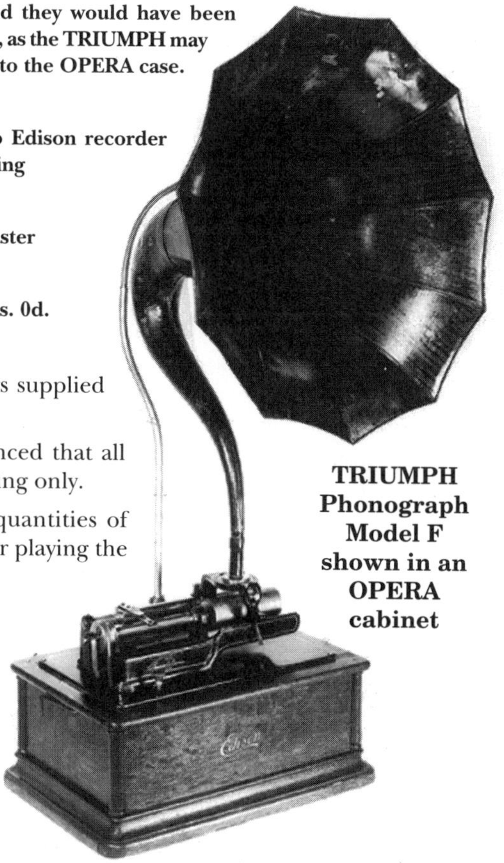

TRIUMPH Phonograph Model F shown in an OPERA cabinet

TRIUMPH Model F with Model O reproducer   25
TRIUMPH 4-minute type (Model G) with Diamond B reproducer   50

The Model G would be the Model F with the 2-minute gearing blocked off and the small 2-4 minute decal effaced.

Model G

Introduced: October 1912 (U.S.); February 1913 (U. K.)

Type: 4-minute

Motor: As Model F

Cabinet: As Model F

89

Reproducer:	Diamond Model B. There was no recorder
Horn:	Oak Music Master
Price:	$75.00; £15 15s. 0d.

This was the final TRIUMPH model.

The assembly schedule for TRIUMPH machines for the next year was fixed on December 30th 1912 at 5 per week.

From the introductory date of the Blue Amberols in October 1912 the public did not get an opportunity to buy a Combination Attachment for the TRIUMPH, together with the 10 Special Blue Amberol Records (A - K) until April 1913 (U.S. and U.K.). The delay was attributed to an insufficient supply of Diamond B reproducers, although an expected daily figure of 250-300 of these was mentioned. Combination Attachments requiring cylinders were still being sent out with sapphire reproducers and wax Amberols until early 1913, and when the Special Blue Amberols were ready some of the old stock of 100,000 wax Amberol boxes were pressed into use.

**TRIUMPH Model G
From the 1912-13 catalogue**

Combination Attachment with Diamond Model B reproducer, carrier-arm and 10 Special Blue Amberols $11.25; £2 10s. 0d.

The trade was directed to adapting earlier models still on their shelves by use of Outfit No. 9, merely a listing of existing parts that should be found in stock.

In March 1913 the weekly shipment of TRIUMPH Combination Attachments averaged 16.

In October 1913 the manufacture of the TRIUMPH was discontinued at West Orange following Company policy to concentrate on the enclosed horn AMBEROLA phonographs.

Sales of the TRIUMPH in its last weeks had been non-existent but continued Edison loyalty towards owners is shown in a Minute of May 1921 ordering 200 Combination Attachments for TRIUMPHS to be assembled at $8.80 each. Such a move also reflected the attachment of owners to Edison products. The last American 2-minute cylinders had reached the shops in October 1912, and 8 ½ years later there were still those who were discovering Blue Amberols. Also parts for "these obsolete models of cylinder phonographs with horns" were still being made in the Twenties.

TRIUMPH recording phonograph, one of several used in the 1920s at Columbia Street Studio, West Orange, Its exact purpose is not known.

TRIUMPH phonograph adapted for making small cylinder recordings, probably for later talking dolls

NOTES:
1) This Caveat is reproduced fully in *New Amberola Graphic* No. 59, Winter 1987
2) Quoted in *The Phonogram* for May 1893, page 6. This was a journal put out by J. Lewis Young in London and was the first British phonograph monthly. Issues of May, June and July 1893 are the only three known to have survived.
3) Amet's U.S. Patent No. 462,228 filed January 28th 1891 for Speed Regulator for Motors was granted November 3rd 1891. Edward Hill Amet was an inventor whose workshop was at the back of the Chicago Scale Works, Waukegan, Illinois. One of his inventions was the automatic platform scale with the printed weight ticket.
4) Greenhill's experiments were described in *The Phonogram* of June 1893.
5) British Patent No. 7962 applied for May 8th 1891 for Apparatus for Controlling the Speed of Clockwork Mechanism and Other Machinery. The U.S. Patent No. 494,633 filed March 25th 1892 was awarded to Greenhill on April 4th 1893, with one half assigned to Gouraud.
6) In *The Phonogram* and the motor was first depicted in the July issue.
7) *Edison Phonographic News* January-February 1895
8) U.S. Patent No. 532,718 for Phonograph filed December 13th 1893 and granted January 15th 1895
9) *The Antique Phonograph Monthly* Vol. I Nos. 1 & 3, Vol. II No. 2, Vol. V No. 7 contain material on these early spring motors
10) U.S. Patent No. 535,445 for Operating Mechanism for Phonograph filed February 16th 1894 and granted March 12th 1895. Examples of two types of these machines may be seen at the Edison Museum at Fort Myers, Florida.
11) From Tewksbury's *Complete Manual of the Edison Phonograph*
12) *The Electrical Engineer* of April 1st 1896 forecast an Edison spring motor and it was reported four days later in *New York Times*. In that column Edison promised the opera 'Norma' on 5 cylinders.
13) U.S. Patent No. 570,378 for Spring Motor for Phonographs filed December 20th 1895, granted October 27th 1896 and assigned to United States Phonograph Company. Capps was also assigned a Design Patent No. 26,491 for the motor frame. On February 1st 1898 the new assignees of National Phonograph filed a Disclaimer on 4 sections of Capps's patent 570,378; these involved the sliding governor and followed a lawsuit against Edison by American Graphophone.
14) There is evidence that the SPRING MOTOR phonograph had been in restricted circulation earlier, perhaps as samples, because two works orders for this model give varying dates of October 18th and 25th 1895. Capps had not applied for his patent at this time.
15) Letter of August 6th 1896 to S.F. Moriarty of Edison United Phonograph Company.
16) U.S. Patent No. 465,972 filed by Edison on November 18th 1889 and granted December 29th 1891 embodied several improvements including the large shaving knife and swarf chute.
17) U.S. Patent No. 567,738 for Diaphragm Clamp for Phonograph was filed by Victor Emerson on December 20th 1895 and granted September 15th 1896. Emerson, an Edison employee, later left to run his own record company
18) Edison Patent No. 453,741 filed July 30th 1890 and granted June 9th 1891 shows details of the carrier-arms of SPRING MOTOR and electric phonographs, especially with regard to the working of the Standard speaker.
19) The word TRIUMPH in the banner form of display was Edison Registered Trade Mark No. 6,679 of August 29th 1905.
20) U.S. Patent No. 798,478 for Means of Sustaining Phonograph Motors filed by Edward L. Aiken on June 20th 1904 and granted August 29th 1905
21) U.S. Patent No. 811,010 for Governor Speed Index filed by Peter Weber on June 29th 1904 and granted January 30th 1906. It was an arrow pointer on the shaft of the speed regulator.
22) U.S. Trade Mark No. 33,236 of July 18th 1899 was for the word 'Edison' in characteristic autographic script; filed May 27th 1899.
23) U. S. Patent No. 878,032 for Phonograph filed by Aiken on August 3rd 1905 and granted February 4th 1908.
24) U.S. Patent No. 821,071 for Phonograph filed by Peter Weber on October 21st 1905 and granted May 22nd 1906.
25) U.S. Patent No. 1,046,188 for Phonograph filed by Charles L. Hibberd on July 31st 1909 and granted December 3rd 1912.
26) U.S. Patent No. 942,475 for Phonograph filed by Peter Weber on April 8th 1908 and granted December 7th 1909 was for the hollow feed screw and an optional gear engagement for 2 and

4-minute playing, but the full combination capacity as Edison owners would recognize is in Patent No. 955,424 filed by Henry T. Oliver on September 15th 1908 and granted April 19th 1910. Not only did this use the hollow feed-screw but the main pulley with enclosed sun and planetary gearing.

27) The Edison use of a record cleaning brush was founded on three patents assigned to or granted to J. N. Blackman, an Edison salesman and manager of a distributing firm in Kansas City, Missouri: U.S. No. 831,987 of September 25th 1906; 832,249 of October 2nd 1906; 865,674 of September 10th 1907 and Edison paid Blackman an annual royalty of $100.00.

Chapter 6
HOME Phonograph (CLASS H)

The 'Clockwork' Home

(This) new machine conforms in a general way to the older type, but it has two decided elements of novelty. One is that it is operated by a spring motor and the other that it is to be sold for about $40.00, thus placing the instrument within the reach of everybody as a formidable rival to the limited music box. Mr. Edison has found that many people are unable to avail themselves of street current for the dearer (electric) phonograph, or else are very averse to bothering with primary batteries, which few of them understand.

Electrical Review New York, April 8th 1896

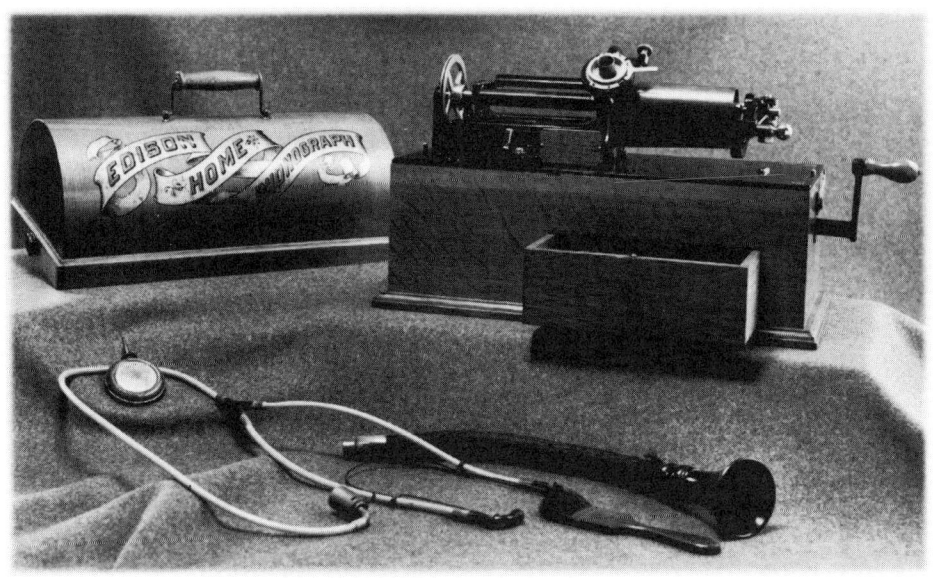

Clockwork HOME phonograph No. 138, last patent date June 3rd 1893
(Mark Ulano photograph)

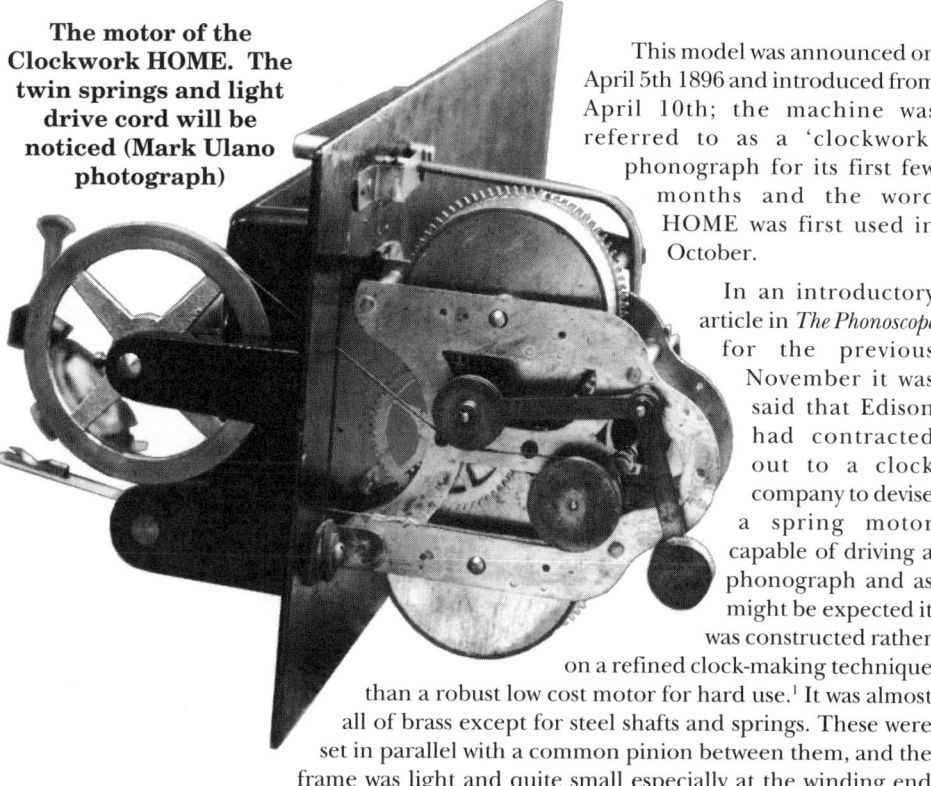

The motor of the Clockwork HOME. The twin springs and light drive cord will be noticed (Mark Ulano photograph)

This model was announced on April 5th 1896 and introduced from April 10th; the machine was referred to as a 'clockwork' phonograph for its first few months and the word HOME was first used in October.

In an introductory article in *The Phonoscope* for the previous November it was said that Edison had contracted out to a clock company to devise a spring motor capable of driving a phonograph and as might be expected it was constructed rather on a refined clock-making technique than a robust low cost motor for hard use.¹ It was almost all of brass except for steel shafts and springs. These were set in parallel with a common pinion between them, and the frame was light and quite small especially at the winding end where there was room for a drawer in the case. In the planned design the drawer was central but moved towards the crank end when put into production.

The governor ball-weights were about the size of large peas. Speed regulation was haphazard, there being no regulator as such, but the on/off lever was stiff and could be parked in any position at the operator's whim. It should be remembered that cylinder speeds were not fixed at this time and often turned at a speed to fit the material on them.

The flat belt and usual flanged pulleys were absent from this machine, the pulleys were V-grooved and a driving cord was kept taut by a weighted idler. The lower pulley was but half the diameter of the upper, but in spite of this power endeavour the motor had no reserves, nor could it shave effectively. It was said to play 2 cylinders per wind, even 2 ½ in some publicity! The gate end bearing for the mandrel shaft did not yet carry tension screws.

The HOME was provided with a Standard speaker, held in the carrier-arm by two crescent clamps, each secured by a pair of screws, such as were used on the SPRING MOTOR phonograph of the day. A small roller supported the carrier-arm along the straight edge. A speaking tube, oilcan and chip-brush were also provided and there was a shaver. The machine weighed 19 lb. and retailed for $40.00.

The single example known is finished in light oak with the red and gold EDISON HOME PHONOGRAPH banner across the front of the cover (Reg. No. 47,117); the top plate and casting were black japanned and lightly lined. A nickel patents plate was fitted near the straight edge and two cover catches of a hook type peculiar to this model were on the ends of the case.

At first the Clockwork HOME was sold only through Edison United Phonograph, and carried a nickel plate with the name of United States Phonograph, even appearing on the crank handles, this being changed later to National Phonograph Company. Production life of this machine was short; it had been and gone within eight months.

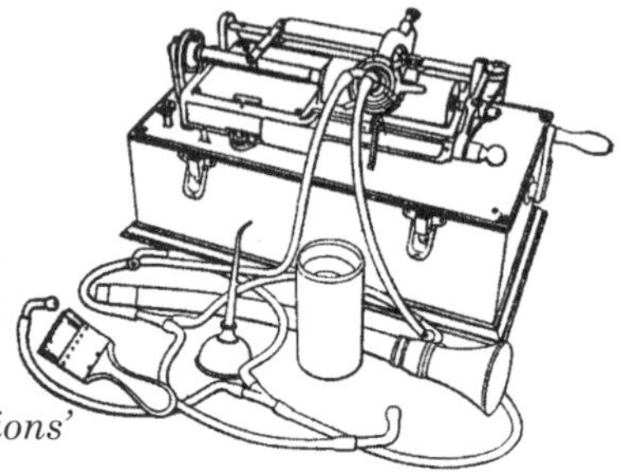

HOME Model A - the early style

An advance advertisement in *The Phonoscope* for November 1896 proclaimed the newly-designed HOME

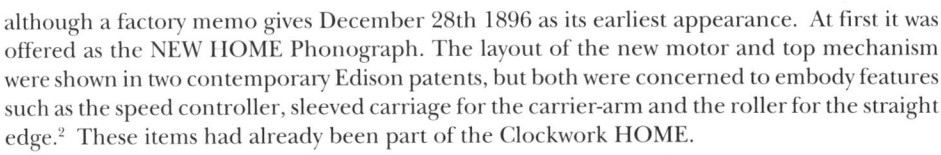

'The very latest, a machine for the millions'

although a factory memo gives December 28th 1896 as its earliest appearance. At first it was offered as the NEW HOME Phonograph. The layout of the new motor and top mechanism were shown in two contemporary Edison patents, but both were concerned to embody features such as the speed controller, sleeved carriage for the carrier-arm and the roller for the straight edge.[2] These items had already been part of the Clockwork HOME.

The motors were now driven by a single spring but the first springs were not satisfactory and were made wider from February 1897. So hastily were the new motors substituted for the clockwork types that the motor frames were ground out where the top works bolted on so as to clear the bolt ends. The first governor pads were double on a swinging yoke, the stop lever being applied to the side of the yoke, but this upset the governor so the stop arm was extended with its own brake pad. The shaving device was continued until 1904, but the motor was never strong enough for this to work really efficiently. Several reproducer clamping devices were used, the crescent-shaped clamps held by knurled screws, then the lever types, and finally the knurled clamp screw that came in with the 'New Style' HOME in 1901; with the last the speaker adjusting screw was discontinued. This had acted on the lever of the early reproducers and recorders for fine adjustment of the stylus. A normal belt drive took the place of the cord and V-pulleys.

HOME Model A, the 'suitcase' HOME, so called from its cover fastenings

96

Weighted feed nut depicted on HOME phonograph H 968

Introduced:	December 1896 (U.S.), October 1897 (U.K. by Edisonia Ltd.)
Type:	2 - minute
Dimensions:	Height 12 in; base 16 ½ in. x 8 in.
Weight:	25 lb.
Motor and Mechanism:	Capps type single-spring with speed control operated from above the top plate and playing 6 cylinders per wind. In the early models there was no stop-start lever and the feed-nut was weighted. The winding crank was slotted and finished in black enamel. A ball-headed bolt secured the swing-arm at the end of the straight edge.
Cabinet:	The drawer had departed with the 2-spring model and until 1901 an oak case was provided, its cover secured by suitcase clips, two at the front, two at the rear of the machine, giving it the name of the 'Suitcase' HOME among collectors today. The banner transfer in red and gold still appeared on the cover. The metal top-plate rested on and extended to the edges of the case, being aligned on pins at two corners. The patents plate on the early models was on the front with the machine's number stamped on to a hump in the top casting.

Accessories:	Edison Standard Speaker and Edison Recorder. By 1899 the Automatic Reproducer was provided in place of the Standard. A 14 inch brass horn, 2-way hearing tubes, oil can and camel-hair chip-brush were supplied, and if desired a speaking tube could be taken in place of the horn.
Price:	$40.00, reducing August 1897 to $30.00
	£15 0s. 0d. as outfit with 6 records (U.K. through Edisonia Ltd.) reducing to £10 10s. 0d. for machine only. In the U.K. the HOME was marked as Type 3 when handled by Edisonia.

By the end of November 1897 HOME production at West Orange was noted as not less than 10 per day with a capacity for 20 if needed. Edison United was buying HOMES from Edison Phonograph Works at this stage for $17.90.

HOME Model A - the new style

Early in 1901 the HOME was housed in the New Style cabinet; because of its generous length this became known as the 'Long Case' HOME. The motor on its top plate now fitted on to a wooden frame that lifted back on hinges with a stay support for inspection. The cabinet was finished in green oak with the gold and red banner now displayed on its front. Owners of the earlier 'Suitcase' HOMES were advised in the autumn of 1901 that New Style cabinets could now be had for re-casing their machines to the pattern of the current selling models....... Price: $3.50

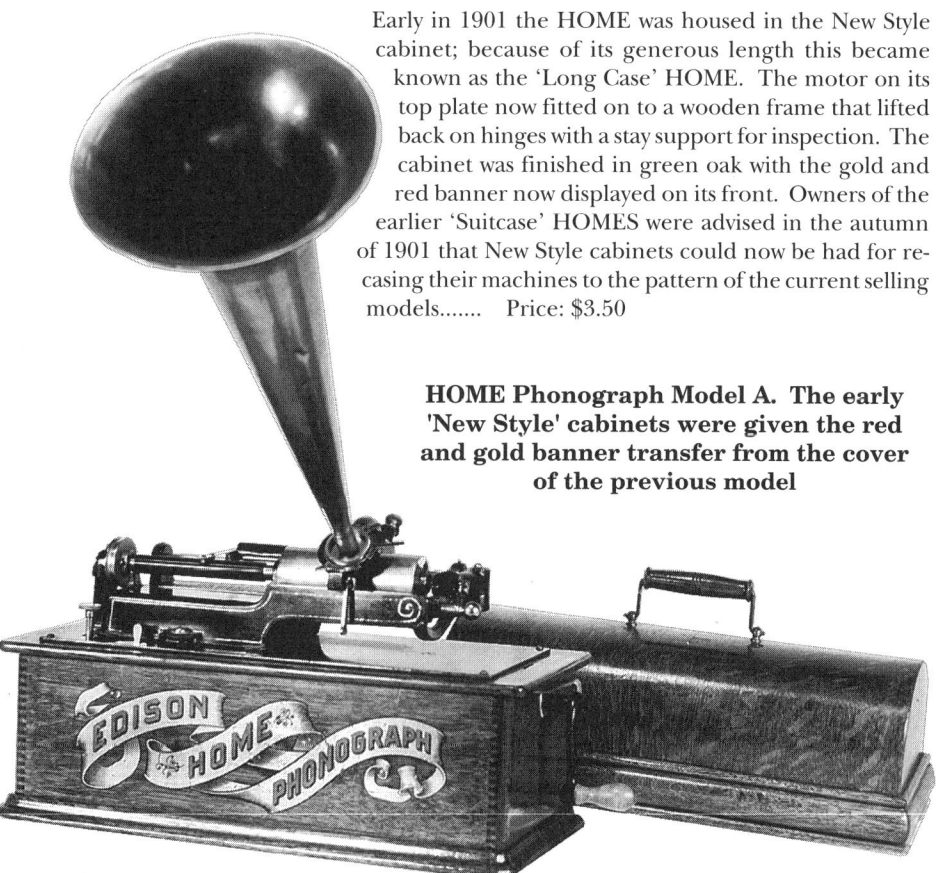

HOME Phonograph Model A. The early 'New Style' cabinets were given the red and gold banner transfer from the cover of the previous model

Dimensions:	Height 12 1/8 in; base 18 in. x 9 in.
Weight:	28 lb.
Accessories:	Offered with the Automatic Reproducer and Edison Recorder, 14 in. horn and camel-hair chip-brush, with the option of a speaking tube instead of the 14 in. horn. In 1902 (U.S.) and 1903 (U.K.) the HOME was supplied with a Model C Reproducer instead of the Automatic, and the reproducer clamps made way for the knurled clamp screw. An extension horn crane could be ordered as an extra ($1.50), fitting a socket and sleeve at the back of the machine; this also hinged for adjustment and supported a horn of up to 30 in. long without overbalancing the phonograph. A shaver was fitted.
Price:	$30.00 (U.S.), £7 10s. 0d. (U.K. through Edison Bell) reducing to £6 6s. 0d. (U.K. c. 1903 through Edison's National Phonograph Co.)

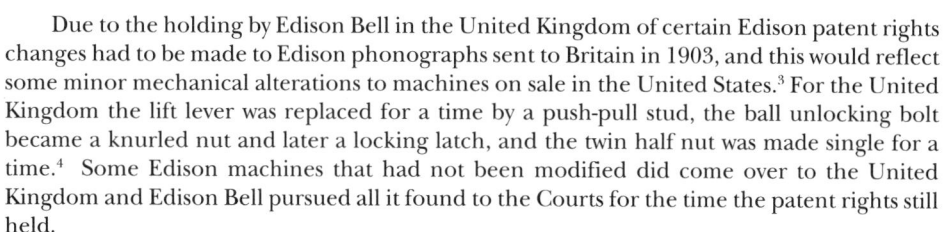

HOME Phonograph Model A shown in its third and last style with the modified banner transfer

Due to the holding by Edison Bell in the United Kingdom of certain Edison patent rights changes had to be made to Edison phonographs sent to Britain in 1903, and this would reflect some minor mechanical alterations to machines on sale in the United States.[3] For the United Kingdom the lift lever was replaced for a time by a push-pull stud, the ball unlocking bolt became a knurled nut and later a locking latch, and the twin half nut was made single for a time.[4] Some Edison machines that had not been modified did come over to the United Kingdom and Edison Bell pursued all it found to the Courts for the time the patent rights still held.

From June 1904 the HOME motor suspension had coiled springs fitted between the frame and top plate instead of rubber washers; this was to inhibit governor whirr.[5] Adjustment by a knurled nut altered the tightness of the belt and did away with the belt tensioner. At about the same time the banner transfer on the case was changed from red and gold to black and gold.[6]

A Hilton Speed Indicator

The first Repeating Attachment suitable for the HOME was available from September 1903, followed in the next autumn by the improved Model D, and this lasted until 1912. Price: $15.00 (earlier type); $7.50; £1 11s. 6d. (Model D)

HOME phonographs of this period have been reported with a slot in the front for a coin, but no coin mechanism. For several years until 1902 it was possible to buy Phonograph Outfits, the HOME with a broader offering of horns, listening tubes, records, record cases, spares and tools from $39.00 to $89.00. Specially finished HOMES too could be bought at extra cost, gold plated at $50.00 and nickel plated at $25.00, and in 1904 the options were widened to the following:

Specially decorated, additional*	$8.00;	£1 13s. 0d.
Nickel plated, additional	$25.00;	£5 5s. 0d.
Gold plated, additional	$50.00;	£10 10s. 0d.
Mahogany cabinets	$5.00;	£1 1s. 0d.

*extra gold lining and applied floral transfers to the top works

The first mahogany cabinets were available to special order from June 1904. They were produced to match the mahogany record cabinets, then in widespread use.

Model B

Introduced:	October-December 1905 (U.S. and U.K.)
	Catalogue changes were not made until after this time to help dealers clear earlier models.
Type:	2-minute
Dimensions:	Height 12 ⅛ in; base 6 ½ in. x 9 in.
Weight:	28 lb.
Motor and Mechanism:	Movement layout similar to Model A, but the winding shaft was shortened and its supporting frame modified. The earlier motor chassis gave way to a more compact type with a three-point suspension from the top plate. The top plate was cut back from the mandrel end to little more than half the previous area, the remaining portion

becoming an integral part of the top casting at the feed-screw end; at the same time its left edge was shortened by nearly an inch. What had now become the top plate screwed directly to a wooden floor hinged at the back for inspection. Thus the front and back holding screws, together with the rubber cushions at each corner of the top casting were no longer needed and the motor was spring-suspended through the wooden floor. The mechanism now had a longer and wider spring.

Cabinet: Finished in antique oak instead of green oak. During the summer of 1906 the black and gold banner decal gave way to the single word 'Edison'.[7] Blue lining as well as gold decoration appeared on the top works of the Model B, but gold only is reported on some models.

Features: The earlier speed adjusting screw was removed from above the top plate and located within the case where it could not be shifted by accident. The swing arm locking bolt was changed to a locking latch or lever, or on some machines a knurled knob, and this helped towards shortening the cabinet. A protective guard that included an adjusting screw was placed over the feed-nut spring.[8] The winding crank was now nickel plated and being screwed to the winding shaft was less likely to cause vibration by touching the thimble hole of the cabinet. Speed marks 1 6/10 in. were cut on the back rod and represented one minute's running at 160 r.p.m. The shaving knife was omitted.

Accessories: 14 in. horn, camel-hair chip-brush. Until the end of 1906 (U.S. and U.K.) a recording and hearing tube could be substituted for the horn when a machine was purchased, but after that date these items were obtainable only as extras.

HOME Phonograph Model B

Reproducer: Model C and Edison Improved Recorder

Price: $30.00; £6 6s. 0d.

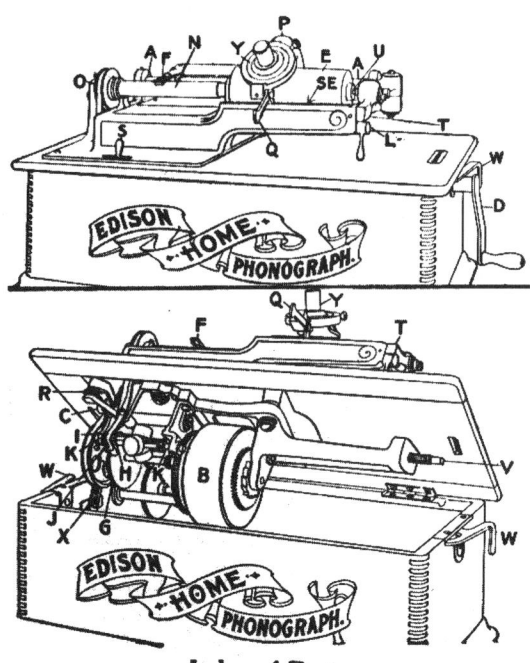

Index of Parts

A.	Back Rod.	O.	Main Shaft Center.
B.	Barrel.	P.	Reproducer Arm.
C.	Belt Tightening Pulley.	Q.	Reproducer Arm Lift Lever.
D.	Crank.	R.	Speed Adjusting Screw.
E.	Cylinder.	S.	Starting Lever.
F.	Feed Nut.	SE.	Straight Edge.
G.	Fourth Gear.	T.	Swing Arm.
H.	Friction Felt.	U.	Swing Arm Center.
I.	Governor Pinion.	V.	Winding Shaft.
J.	Governor Disc.	W.	Catch Lever.
K.	Governor Shaft Pivot	X.	Supporting Link.
L.	Locking Lever.	Y.	Reproducer.
N.	Main Shaft.		

In ordering parts give NAME and NUMBER of Phonograph

Some HOME phonographs are reported with an automatic start/stop mechanism built on to the Model B. This worked by closing the locking lever, the machine starting by way of a rod passing directly to the governor below and there was no regular starting lever. The terms of this fitting are not clear, whether it was standard for a while or an optional extra through the dealer.[9]

From October 1907 (U.S.) new horn equipment became available for all models in an effort to boost sales. That for the HOME was polygonal with 11 panels, straight and 32 in. long with a bell diameter of 21 ½ in; it was black with gold decoration and had a blue and gold identifying logo. The crane stood at the front of the machine and was screwed to the bottom and braced to the cabinet face and had a stabilizing shoe. All HOME phonographs were now sold thus, as follows:

HOME, complete with new horn and crane	$35.00
Horn available separately $5.00, reducing Nov. 1907	$3.90
Crane extra	$1.50

Horns and cranes were not interchangeable with other horn types, but in March 1908 (U.S.) the TRIUMPH type of horn crane was adopted for the HOME (and STANDARD) and the HOME could also be bought in a mahogany cabinet with mahogany finished horn.

Price: $47.50

In the United Kingdom things were a little simpler since in April 1908 the 14 in. self-supporting horn was discarded in favour of a one-piece straight polygonal horn of 8 panels, length 19 in., bell diameter 11 in. black with gold decoration. The HOME now cost £7 7s. 0d. The crane mounting for this horn was fitted to the face of the HOME, and to equip existing cabinets a slot 1 ⁵⁄₆₄ in. wide and ¹⁄₁₆ in. deep was cut on the top edge of the case with the centre of the slot 6 ¹⁄₁₆ in. from the inner left edge of the case. The larger 11 panel HOME straight horn was never put in the British catalogue.

Model C

Issued some time after mid-February 1908 and sold initially only in the State of New York (see Appendix V), the Model C was not dissimilar to Model B in motor design, but above the top plate the swing-arm was no longer fitted and the mandrel was supported on a central bearing. A push button lift was fitted to the carrier-arm. During early 1909 the Model C was imported into the United Kingdom, there was no price increase in either country for machine or horn equipment, and this was the same as had been offered with HOME Model B. Early in 1908 there was a small modification to governor construction when an additional collar with wire spring attached to the adjoining collar was put on the governor shaft.

From April 1908 HOME phonograph cabinets were available separately: in oak $3.50, in mahogany $8.75. The mahogany cabinets had a new wide moulding from July 1908.

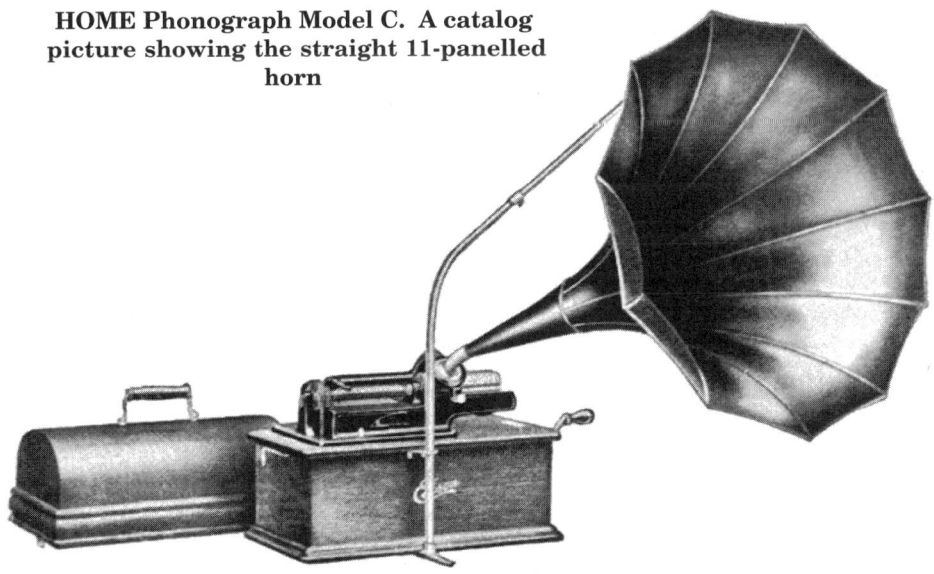

HOME Phonograph Model C. A catalog picture showing the straight 11-panelled horn

To identify readily HOME Models A, B and C from key features

Model A

First types have 4 suitcase clips, banner transfer on lid and top plate extending to edge of cabinet plinth.

Second types have full length top plates mounted on lifting wooden frame, black japanned slotted winding crank, swing arm locking bolt and many have shaving device.

Model B

Half length metal top plate, nickel plated screwed winding crank, swing arm locking lever, no shaving device.

Model C

Similar to Model B but no swing arm end gate.

On July 14th 1908 it was decided to introduce the Model D HOME and its accessories on October 1st. As well as the new machine Model B would be continued at the same price but Model D would be dearer. Attachments would be produced to convert existing machines to 2 and 4-minute playing. There was discussion on re-naming the new combination range but this was not pursued. The horn cranes would be simplified so that the brace would fit the STANDARD as well. Stocks of the new and existing models were put in hand, with output being noted on August 11th as follows:

HOME Model D	2,500	per week
Model C	100	"
Model B	1,000	"
2 & 4-minute attachments	5,250	"
Model H repros. (for HOMES)	2,500	"
Model H repros. (for attachments)	5,250	"

Orders received for Model D HOMES grossed 13,361 by Sept. 19th and attachments 25,555.

Model D

In October 1908 4-minute Amberol cylinders were introduced both into the United States and the United Kingdom and combination Model D HOME became available from that date but did not reach the U.K. until August 1909.[10]

Type:	**2 and 4-minute combination**
Dimensions:	**Height 11 ¼ in; base 16 ⅜ in. x 9 ⅛ in.**
Weight:	**30 lb.**
Reproducers:	**Models C and H**

HOME Phonograph Model D, with Cygnet horn

Horn:	Straight 11 panel (U.S.), straight 8 panel (U.K.)
Cabinet:	The standard finish was oak; from this model onwards the cabinets were constructed rather differently with the sides no longer standing on a solid baseboard, reducing the height fractionally. More pronounced moulding round the base gave the machine a more stocky look.
Price:	$40.00; £8 8s. 0d. $52.50 with mahogany case and mahogany finished horn.

By November 19th a rough total stock of 1,000 Model B HOMES was reported with a further 2,500 body castings in hand. Model C would be allowed to supersede this model, being almost the same as Model D except for taking the old type feed screw.

As a guide to sales expectations at this time the factory schedule for the HOME range on January 30th 1909 was as follows:

> Model B To carry 150 in stock, 100 in test department and sufficient parts to assemble 1,000 machines
>
> Model C To carry 25 in stock, 25 in test department, and parts sufficient to assemble 250 machines
>
> Model D To carry 1,000 in stock, 1,000 in testing department, and parts sufficient to assemble 5,000 machines.

Combination Attachments could be bought to convert Models A, B and C to playing 2 and 4-minute cylinders. Due to the small mechanical differences in the models, the proper attachment for each was necessary:

Price: $7.50; £1 11s. 0d., subject to the return of displaced mainshaft and mandrel to the dealer.

Combination Attachments for HOMES already fitted with Repeating Attachments were also available.

The 10-panel Cygnet Horn was introduced in September 1909 (U.S.) and October 1910 (U.K.) as part of the following HOME equipment:

Model C HOME with black Cygnet Horn	$40.00	
Model C HOME no longer available in the U.K.		
Model C HOME with oak finish Cygnet Horn	$45.00	
with mahogany case and mahogany finish Cygnet Horn	$53.00	
Combination Model D HOME		
with black Cygnet Horn	$45.00;	£9 9s. 0d.
with oak finish Cygnet Horn	$50.00;	£10 10s. 0d.
with mahogany case and mahogany finish Cygnet Horn	$58.00;	£12 0s. 0d.

As an inducement to convert to 4-minute equipment, a special set of cylinders was offered with Combination Attachments, as follows:

HOME Combination Attachment with 10 Special Amberol cylinders (A- K) .... $8.50 in April 1910 (U.S.)

and with 10 Special Hebrew Amberol cylinders (L- W) .... $6.85 in October 1911 (U.S.)

HOME Combination attachment with 5 Special Amberols and 5 Standard cylinders ..... £1 16s. 0d. in May 1911 (U.K.)

None of the above cylinders could be bought separately.

In August 1910 (U. S.) the wooden Music Master horn was offered with the HOME machine in the following equipments:

HOME Model C, oak cabinet, oak Music Master horn	$50.00
mahogany cabinet, mahogany Music Master horn	$58.00
Combination Model D HOME	
oak cabinet, oak Music Master horn	$55.00
mahogany cabinet, mahogany Music Master horn	$63.00
spruce Music Master horn, add to above	$5.00
inlaid pearl Music Master horn, add to above	$35.00

On January 18th 1911 a decision was taken to equip the HOME with Model O reproducers and larger carrier-arms, and an initial 5,000 were ordered from the shop.

Model E

Introduced:	March 1911 (U.S.), July 1911 (U. K.)
Type:	2 and 4-minute
Dimensions and Weight:	as Combination Model D

HOME Phonograph Model E, with Cygnet horn

Features:	This machine was similar to Model D except that it was fitted with the large carrier-arm to take the Model O reproducer set horizontally. This reproducer would be part of the machine's equipment, and a special E-type Cygnet Horn came with the Model E HOME to allow for the extra height of the carrier-arm. Record brushes were put on all HOMES with Cygnet Horn and Model O reproducer. A recorder and adapter ring were included.
Price:	$45.00; £9 9s. 0d.

At the same time as the HOME Model E was marketed, the Model R reproducer appeared, resulting in a complex number of combination attachments and reproducer options open to the HOME owner, and these are summarized as follows:

HOME Combination Attachment with Model O reproducer $15.50; £3 3s. 0d.
(allowance of $2.00 for return of Model C, mandrel and mainshaft)

Model O for HOMES already with Combination Attachment $10.00; £2 2s. 0d.
(allowance of $4.00 for return of Models C & H and carrier-arm)

HOME Combination Attachment with Model R reproducer $10.50
    same with 10 Special Amberol records $11.50
    same in U.K. with 5 Special Amberols and
      5 Special Standard records   £2 10s. 0d.

In November 1911 the Combination Model D with black Cygnet Horn was discontinued and in its place the Model E was given an oak finish Cygnet Horn, and retained the Model O reproducer.... $50.00

From September 16th 1912 1,000 HOMES for 4-minute playing only were ordered, for sending out with a Diamond B reproducer from October 1st.

Model F

Introduced:	October 1912 (U.S.); February 1913 (U.K.)
Type:	4-minute
Dimensions and Weight:	As Combination Models D and E

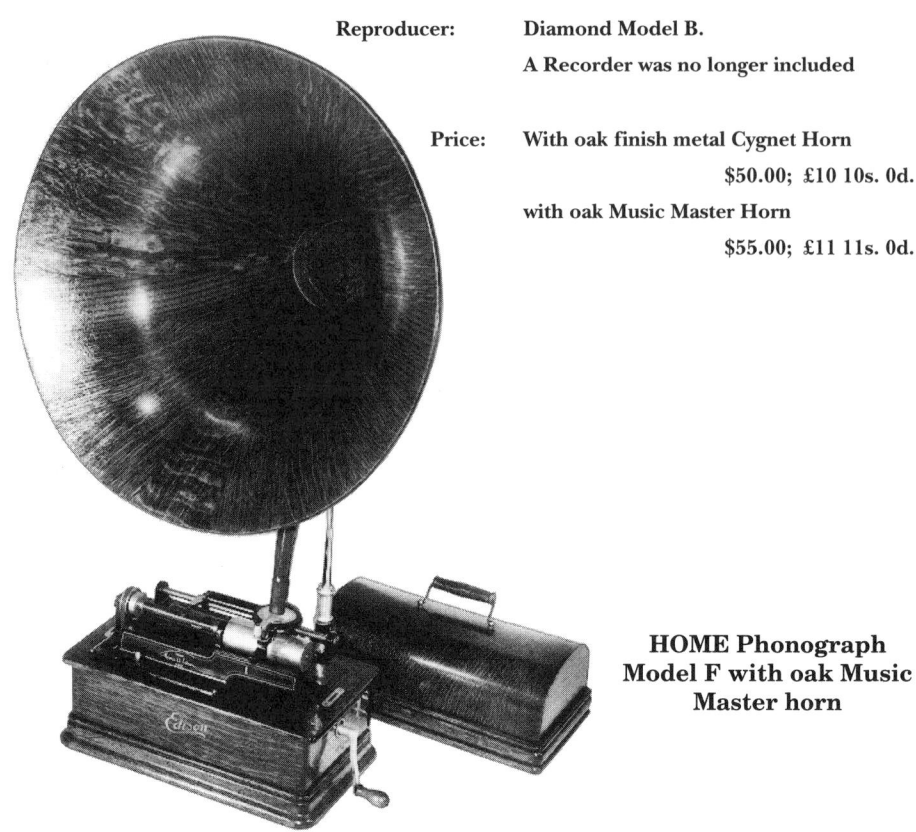

Reproducer: Diamond Model B.
A Recorder was no longer included

Price: With oak finish metal Cygnet Horn
$50.00; £10 10s. 0d.
with oak Music Master Horn
$55.00; £11 11s. 0d.

HOME Phonograph Model F with oak Music Master horn

The Model F was really a Model E with the 2-minute gear blanked off. This was the final HOME model, although the TRIUMPH and STANDARD ran to Model G. A 4-minute HOME had been discussed in January 1911 when it had been hoped to withdraw earlier straight horn styles, but the 2-minute recording facility kept these earlier machines available until mid-1912 when the 4-minute recording equipment was introduced.

HOME orders in hand on October 5th 1912 are noticed as 258 with production at the end of December at 120 per week.

When the Model F was marketed all the existing range of accessory options that were making confusion for the trade were swept away and from now cylinder policies were centred on the 4-minute record.

Jobbers and dealers holding supplies of earlier HOME models were told to make these play Blue Amberols by altering the carrier-arm and adding a Diamond B reproducer from spares they should have in stock. The final styles of HOME Combination Attachment Outfits were still offered to owners of earlier 2-minute machines, as follows:

Complete with Diamond B reproducer and large carrier-arm
$9.75;   £2 2s. 0d.

Diamond B reproducer, large carrier-arm, adapter ring and

10 Special Blue Amberol cylinders (A- K) (April 1913 U.S.& U.K.)
$11.25;   £2 10s. 0d.

Combination Attachments as well as other spares are noted as still being made for the HOME in May 1921 when 1,000 sets were ordered to be made. In October 1913 production of the HOME was discontinued as a result of the policy of concentrating on enclosed horn models. Much of the HOME motor was used in the small run of AMBEROLA IVs in October 1913. Earlier, it had been used on the 'H' Coin-slot Phonograph of 1898.

HOME Model A with Bettini reproducer and horn

Notes:

1) A.P.M. Vol, 1 No. 6 states however that these motors were made by The United States Phonograph Company of New Jersey. The springs were clockmakers' from Waterbury, Conn.
2) U.S. Patent No. 604,740 Governor for Motors filed by T. A. Edison on January 27th 1897, published May 31st 1898 features a knurled screw through the top plate and acts on a spring-loaded friction lever with double friction points on a swivelled yoke. U.S. Patent No. 607,588 for Phonograph, filed by Edison on January 27th 1897 and granted July 19th 1898 outlines the layout of the HOME top mechanism in a less cluttered form and introduces a sleeved carrier-arm carriage and roller for the straight edge. The roller was dropped later as 'presenting unnecessary complications'.
3) Vide Appendix IV on the relationship between Edison Company and Edison Bell in the United Kingdom
4) U.S. Patent No. 878,032 for Phonograph filed by Edward L. Aiken on August 3rd 1905 and published February 4th 1908 embodied the locking latch
5) U.S. Patent No. 798,478 Means for Sustaining Phonograph Motors filed by Edward L. Aiken June 20th 1904 and granted August 29th 1905
6) The word HOME on the black and gold banner was filed as a Trade Mark on May 24th 1905 and granted on August 29th 1905 as No. 6,677
7) U.S. Trade Mark No. 33,236 of July 18th 1899 was for 'Thomas A. Edison' or 'Edison' in characteristic autographic script. Filed May 29th 1899
8) U.S. Patent No. 821,071 for Phonograph filed by Peter Weber on October 21st 1905 and granted May 22nd 1906
9) U.S. Patent No. 1,002,479 for Phonograph filed by Edward L. Aiken on June 28th 1905 and granted September 5th 1911. Patent No. 1,041,922 by Peter Weber was an improvement
10) U.S. Patent No. 955,424 for Phonograph filed by Henry T. Oliver on September 15th 1908 and granted April 19th 1910. It featured the main pulley containing the sun and planetary gearing, and the hollow feed screw.

Chapter 7
STANDARD Phonograph (CLASS S)

EDISON STANDARD PHONOGRAPH CLASS S

The STANDARD was in the forefront of the Edison company's plans in early 1897 and a reference appears in an Edison Phonograph Works internal letter of July 27th when it was projected as a $25.00 machine. It became known as 'the small machine' and then 'the Number 2 machine', and this appellation remained in the trade until April 15th 1898 - and for some time after - the day it officially became the STANDARD. In these times it was also called the New STANDARD.

The Edison company proposed to sell it for $25.00 with Standard speaker and shaving device and for the same machine with Automatic reproducer and without shaving device or recorder for $20.00 and the trade was assured on September 28th 1897 that:

Edison will not make a cheaper machine than the No. 2 type.

The GEM was of course still two years ahead.

Early sample models ran into difficulties often through badly formed parts, and one, due to be sent to S.F. Moriarty in London was held back for this reason. This machine brought in an early order dated February 8th 1898 from Edison Bell for 10,000 in 6 months at $10.00 each at 250 per week and 100 to German Edison, but the Works order for production of these machines did not go ahead until the end of March, and the first shipment to London was not made until April 29th. The first STANDARDS reached the American trade in mid-February 1899 but many were defective.

These early days of production showed up faults especially in the motor frames and 50% of finished models were rejected in subsequent weeks and months. Failures were blamed on ground settlement causing machinery to distort in the new factory extension where the parts were made. Things had improved by the beginning of the next year but STANDARDS were still being sent out uninspected although HOMES were checked. Complaints of broken and defective motor frames and noisy gears and pinions would dog the STANDARD for a long time.

Once into satisfactory production the STANDARD ran the full octave to Model G as did the TRIUMPH, and proved successful and popular. It started at $20.00 but as the accessories

**Top view of early STANDARD No. S 4.
The first models had no gear guard**

became better, so its price climbed and was about double this figure when in 1909 a companion model, the FIRESIDE was introduced; it was hoped this would retail for $20.00 and overtake the STANDARD, but the basic FIRESIDE started at $22.00 and appeared not to affect sales of the STANDARD to any extent although probably a better machine, and the STANDARD stayed in production until the end of the external horn phonographs.

The STANDARD was the first step towards compactness in Edison phonographs with its mandrel no longer an extension of the feed screw, as both were now in parallel positions with a connecting gear train. This layout was not patented by Edison, being anticipated by other makers and used by Columbia since 1894. The Models A to G of the STANDARDS showed more variations than other contemporary Edison models.

Model A

Introduced:	February 1898 (U.S.), soon after in U.K.
Type:	2-minute
Dimensions:	Height 9 ½ in.
	base 12 in. x 9 in.
Weight:	17 lb.
Motor:	Single spring playing 2 to 3 cylinders at one winding. The spring was strengthened shortly after the machine's introduction. This early motor could not be interchanged with the later Model A. The knurled knob speed controller was above the top plate and was similar to that on the TRIUMPH and HOME machines.[1] These early STANDARDS had brass gears.
Cabinet:	The early STANDARD case may be recognized readily from its square corners and flat-topped cover secured by suitcase clips, either with the earlier layout of one at each end, or by 1900 two on the front and two on the back. With either variation this style has moved into the language of Edison owners as the 'square-top STANDARD'. The motor plate fitted on ledges within the top and could be turned upside down and worked on.

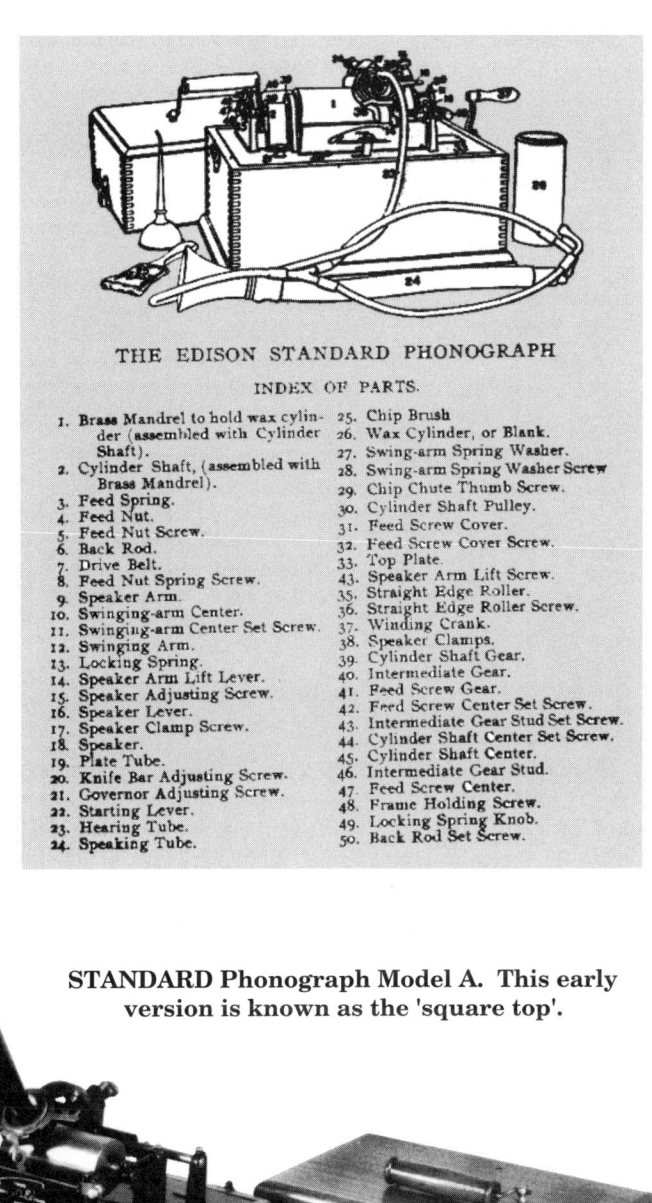

THE EDISON STANDARD PHONOGRAPH

INDEX OF PARTS.

1. Brass Mandrel to hold wax cylinder (assembled with Cylinder Shaft).
2. Cylinder Shaft, (assembled with Brass Mandrel).
3. Feed Spring.
4. Feed Nut.
5. Feed Nut Screw.
6. Back Rod.
7. Drive Belt.
8. Feed Nut Spring Screw.
9. Speaker Arm.
10. Swinging-arm Center.
11. Swinging-arm Center Set Screw.
12. Swinging Arm.
13. Locking Spring.
14. Speaker Arm Lift Lever.
15. Speaker Adjusting Screw.
16. Speaker Lever.
17. Speaker Clamp Screw.
18. Speaker.
19. Plate Tube.
20. Knife Bar Adjusting Screw.
21. Governor Adjusting Screw.
22. Starting Lever.
23. Hearing Tube.
24. Speaking Tube.
25. Chip Brush
26. Wax Cylinder, or Blank.
27. Swing-arm Spring Washer.
28. Swing-arm Spring Washer Screw
29. Chip Chute Thumb Screw.
30. Cylinder Shaft Pulley.
31. Feed Screw Cover.
32. Feed Screw Cover Screw.
33. Top Plate.
43. Speaker Arm Lift Screw.
35. Straight Edge Roller.
36. Straight Edge Roller Screw.
37. Winding Crank.
38. Speaker Clamps.
39. Cylinder Shaft Gear.
40. Intermediate Gear.
41. Feed Screw Gear.
42. Feed Screw Center Set Screw.
43. Intermediate Gear Stud Set Screw.
44. Cylinder Shaft Center Set Screw.
45. Cylinder Shaft Center.
46. Intermediate Gear Stud.
47. Feed Screw Center.
48. Frame Holding Screw.
49. Locking Spring Knob.
50. Back Rod Set Screw.

STANDARD Phonograph Model A. This early version is known as the 'square top'.

Features:	The end of the mandrel shaft was supported in these early models by a straight swing arm but later machines had the mandrel and upper works raised and the swing arm was angled. The carrier-arm was supported at the front by a small roller along the straight edge and this persisted into the New Style models of 1901. The centre-pivoted lift lever on the carrier-arm was peculiar to this model. The early models had neither gear cover nor screw holes for fitting one. The STANDARD had a plain black enamel finish at this period but was the first model to display the 'Thomas A. Edison' signature.[2] Early models had the nickelled patent plate below the swing arm but in time this moved inwards and towards the back of the top plate. Several types of speaker clamps are known on the square-top STANDARD, usually the pair of levers held by two screws, but the first models had one pivot retaining screw to each lever. The crank handle was black japanned with a slotted end.
Accessories:	This model was supplied from the start with a Standard speaker and Edison recorder, shaving device and 2-way hearing tube, 14 in brass horn, camel-hair chip-brush and oilcan. If desired a speaking tube could be substituted for the brass horn. In the United States the Automatic reproducer replaced the Standard speaker in the machines' equipment, probably in February 1899.
Price:	$20.00; £4 4s. 0d.[3] approx.

By 1901 the STANDARD was given a smart New Style cabinet in oak, with a rounded cover. The motor was unchanged, but the top plate now screwed on to a wooden frame that hinged back for inspection and the working parts on top had a more 'set up' look. This new style of case carried the full EDISON STANDARD PHONOGRAPH banner on the front, but 'Standard' never became a registered trade mark. Its moulding and corners were now rounded and from the autumn of 1901 owners of older STANDARDS could buy this for $3.00 to give their machines a new look. The accessories with the new STANDARD were similar to those of the earlier machine but by 1902 (U.S.) and 1903 (U.K.) the Automatic reproducer had given place to the Model C. In 1902 the Edison recorder became an optional extra, price: $3.00 or 12s. 6d. The 14 in. brass horn was discontinued after 1901 and a similar one with black body and brass bell substituted.

Dimensions:	Height 10 ¾ in; base 12 ¾ in x 8 ¾ in.
Weight:	20 lb.
Features:	The shaving device was left off in 1904 as the motor was just not strong enough to shave effectively. The metal parts were finished in black enamel with the gold lining being more plentiful than earlier. The swing arm was now angled down just below the mandrel shaft bearing to clip round the end of the straight edge casting. From

October 1901 for a time the carrier-arm lift lever was replaced by a push-button stud. From November 1st 1903 a recorder was no longer supplied with the STANDARD on account of cost, but was listed extra at $3.00.

Price: $20.00; £4 4s. 0d.

The STANDARD could be specially finished, either gold or nickel plated almost from the outset, and in the early 1900s the options were:

Specially decorated, additional	$4.00;	17s. 0d.
Nickel plated, additional	$25.00;	£5 5s. 0d.
Gold plated, additional	$50.00;	£10 10s. 0d.
Mahogany cabinets, additional	$4.50;	19s. 0d.

For several years until 1902 Phonograph Outfits were available, the STANDARD with a broader offering of horns, listening tubes, records, spares and tools for $29.00 and $49.00.

STANDARD Phonograph Model A in 'new style' cabinet

Model B

Introduced:	October-December 1905 (U.S. and U.K.)
Type:	2-minute
Dimensions:	Height 11 ¾ in. base 13 in. x 9 ½ in.
Weight:	20 lb.
Motor:	Single spring playing four 2-minute records at one winding. The spring was now wider and thicker than the STANDARD Model A and was the same as used in the HOME. The nickel plated winding crank now screwed on the shaft.

STANDARD Model B Phonograph - the 'Tall Standard' in its earlier banner transfer

Features and Accessories: A principal difference to its predecessor was that the motor was suspended from the underside of the top plate on cushion springs, causing the body of the case to be ½ in. deeper.[4] This meant that the Model B - and the later Model C - stood higher than the Model A, and is sometimes called 'the tall STANDARD'. The case had an antique oak finish, replacing the green oak that did not suit furniture of the period. The earlier models still carried the banner transfer but during the summer of 1906 it was replaced by the decal with the single word 'Edison' in characteristic script. The speed control knob was now set underneath the top plate where it could not be altered by mischance. In 1906 speed test marks were cut on the back rod 1 $^{6}/_{10}$ in. apart, so if the motor were run at 160 r.p.m. the carrier-arm would move from mark to mark in one minute. The gold lining on earlier Model B STANDARDS usually includes 'tufts of grass' at the corners and these gave way to scrollwork in the later examples. The Model C reproducer, 14 in. horn and camel-hair chip-brush were given with this model, with a recorder for $3.00 extra. A recording tube or listening tubes could be obtained as a substitute for the horn with the machine for $21.00; £4 4s. 0d., but by the end of 1906 this exchange was cancelled. The Model B still had the swing arm.

The beginning of 1907 brought complaints about the STANDARDS, broken mainsprings, bad governor springs and noisy pinions, despite a big demand for them in the United States. A report from the chairman in London, J. R. Schermerhorn said the early STANDARDS shipped to Edison Bell in 1898 were still playing much better than any then being made, but he seemed to have forgotten the trouble those models had given.[5] The Edison trade in Great Britain was in a poor way with Edison Bell's new range and cheap German machines.[6]

In October 1907 (U.S.) and April 1908 (U.K.) larger horns were offered as part of the equipment with all machines and the 14 in. black and brass horn was discontinued except with the STANDARD phonograph for I.C.S. Language Study.

STANDARD complete with suspended straight 10 panel polygonal horn, length 30 in., diameter at mouth 19 in., black with gold lining	$25.00
Horn and support only for fitting to existing machines	$5.00

These horns were marked with the STANDARD logo.

In November 1907 (U.S.) the camel-hair chip-brush was omitted from the STANDARD equipment, but an oilcan and bottle of oil provided instead. There had been no shaving device for several years so the brush was no longer needed and the oilcan was a more practical accessory.

By March 1908 (U. S.) the STANDARD phonograph was also offered with mahogany cabinet and mahogany finished 10-panel straight horn $36.50

In April 1908 (U. K.) the STANDARD was fitted with a polygonal horn and crane. This horn was black with gold lining, 19 in. long, diameter at bell 11 in., and with 8 panels and was in one piece.

STANDARD, complete with this horn	£4 15s. 0d.
with mahogany cabinet and mahogany-finished horn	£7 10s. 0d.
horn and light crane for fitting to existing machines	11s. 0d.

Straight polygonal horns larger than 8 panels were never officially introduced into the United Kingdom with the rare exception of the 12-panel horn for the IDELIA. In spite of this, advertisements in Great Britain made up from American printing blocks showed examples of 10, 11 and 12-panelled straight horns on Edison phonographs; this made for confusion and resentment among dealers and owners, and on several occasions drew from the British company denials that these larger horns were contemplated.

American STANDARD owners with the 10-panel horn were advised that to position the support on the phonograph correctly, it should be fitted to the cabinet by cutting a slot in the left of the top edge $1/16$ in. deep and $1\,5/64$ in. wide, the centre of the slot to be 2 in. from the left inner edge of the cabinet.

German-made phonographs closely resembling the STANDARDS have been seen, the top works particularly being Edison-like, but the frame carrying the motor hinged at the front rather than the back. A double spring motor version is known. An Edison Model B STANDARD has also been seen with a back bracket and tone arm conversion kit, also originating in Germany.

Model C

Introduced:	mid-February 1908 (U.S.) and for a while was sold only in the State of New York, Model B still being offered elsewhere. (see Appendix V)
Type:	2-minute
Features:	Exactly similar to Model B but for two things. There was no swing arm, the mandrel being supported on a centre bearing, The horn equipment remained the same as Model B in both U.S. and U.K. Early in 1908 an additional collar with a wire spring attached to the adjoining collar was put on the governor shaft.
Price:	$25.00

The mandrel support bearing was of die-cast metal. This is often found seized up but can be replaced by a good mechanic. A few appeared that were factory fitted with a self-aligning steel bearing, and these do not normally give trouble.

The Model C was announced for the United Kingdom in June 1909, only 2 months before the Combination Model D appeared; there are signs of it being available before then and the delay in distribution was to help the trade to clear old stocks. Price £4 15s. 0d.

In April 1908 (U.S.) replacement STANDARD cabinets were offered in oak at $3.00 or mahogany $7.50. The latter was a new venture and from July 1908 was given a special wide moulding.

STANDARD Phonograph Model C with Morning Glory and added combination attachment

Townley's Patent Speed Indicator fitted to a Model A STANDARD

To identify readily Models A, B and C from key features:

Model A

Earlier style in square-top oak cabinet, the later in New Style cabinet, usually in green oak with banner transfer. Both types had black japanned winding crank with slot and there was a swing arm. The shaving device was omitted from 1904. The speed regulator for these models was above the top plate

Model B

The 'tall STANDARD', early models having the banner transfer, the later with the 'Edison' signature decal on the front. Swing arm fitted, no shaving device. The nickel plated crank screws on. The speed regulator is found under the top plate on this and subsequent models.

Model C

As Model B but there was no swing arm.

On July 14th 1908 the Phonograph Committee decided to introduce a Combination STANDARD. There would be 2 and 4-minute gearing and a reproducer for the 4-minute

Amberol cylinders. The cabinets would have the same base moulding as the new mahogany STANDARD, the same width as the HOME so that the horn brace would fit both HOME and STANDARD machines. There was discussion on bringing in a fresh name for the new model, but this did not happen and the new machine became the Model D STANDARD. Based on the existing Model C construction, both machines would have much in common so that the earlier could be converted to combination state readily at the factory as needed. From July 20th the Edison works started an 11 hour day with 5 hours on Saturday mornings to produce 1,000 Model B and 2,000 Models C/D per week. When Model B castings were all used up, Model C would take its place.

By August 11th the schedule stood at:

Model D	4,000	per week
C	100	"
B	2,000	"
Attachments, various	7,300	"
Model H reproducers	4,000	"
for attachments	7,300	"

By September 19th orders received for Model D totalled 21,879, 12,004 immediate and 9,875 for the future. While 2,034 had been sent out to date, orders received for Attachments for STANDARD Model B and C were 35,446, 24,874 immediate and 10,572 for the future.

Model D

Introduced:	October 1908 (U.S.), August 1909 (U.K.)
Type:	2 and 4-minute combination
Dimensions:	Height 11 ¾ in; base 13 ⅛ in. x 9 ½ in.
Weight:	21 ½ lb.
Motor:	Single spring. The gear train from the mandrel to the feed screw incorporated a second ratio that halved the speed of the feed screw for playing the 200 t.p.i. Amberol cylinders. This gear change was operated by a push-pull button.[7]
Features:	The case of the Model D was re-designed with the sides no longer standing on a solid rectangular base, as in earlier models. Molding was applied round the lower sides and seemed to reduce the apparent height of the two predecessors. The cabinets remained unaltered through succeeding models.

STANDARD
Phonograph
Model D shown
with and without
Morning Glory
horn

Horns, Reproducers and Finishes:

In the United States with a straight horn of 10 panels, Models C and H reproducers, in antique oak cabinet $30.00.

In mahogany cabinet with mahogany finished horn, $41.50. In the U.K. with 8 panelled straight horn, Models C and H reproducers, in antique oak cabinet   £5 15s. 0d.

As a consequence of the new gear train the Model D STANDARD was given a <u>left hand</u> feed screw thread, whereas Models A, B and C had a <u>right hand</u> feed screw thread. Feed nuts were cut accordingly and stamped with the appropriate model letter and were permanently fixed to the spring on this model.

On both sides of the Atlantic the Model C phonographs were still offered alongside the new Model D machines for about two years until the wax Amberol became established in the minds of Edison buyers. Those possessing the earlier models were advised to fit a Combination Attachment to enable their machines to play 4-minute cylinders. These attachments were announced for issue on October 1st 1908 (U.S.) for fitting to STANDARD Models A, B and C, and on the same date in the United Kingdom for Models A and B. It was emphasized that Models B and C Combination Attachments could be fitted only to their respective machines and were not interchangeable. These outfits consisted of the necessary gears, gear cover and Model H reproducer: $5.00; £1 1s. 0d.

By January 1910 the Company, anxious for the trade to alter as soon as possible to 2 and 4-minute models, offered jobbers a conversion service at the Works for older stock:

Model B STANDARD to Model	D	$5.00
C "	D	$4.00, both carriage extra

The Model A, B or C machine with STANDARD Combination Attachment fitted may be distinguished readily from Combination Model D as gear covers of the Combination Attachment <u>outfits</u> slope towards the rear of the phonograph, while those on Model D and later have level tops.

A skilfully contrived attachment was manufactured by a British firm to convert the STANDARD to 2 and 4-minute playing. It consisted of a train of 4 integral gears mounted on a plate pivoted on the feed screw shaft, and carrying the drive from the mandrel shaft to the feed screw gear, and by lifting or lowering the plate fractionally at the mandrel shaft end, engaged one or other gear and determined the speed of the feed screw. The Edison intermediate gear was eliminated, and an eccentric device substituted on its pivot fixed the setting of either gear.[8] An example of this ingenious attachment has been seen on a STANDARD, but it is not known whether it was ever adapted to a GEM.

The schedule for STANDARDS for January 1909 was issued to Peter Weber, General Superintendent at the Edison factory:

Model C	Carry 500 in stock and 500 in testing department and parts sufficient to assemble 2,000 machines
Model D	Carry 1,000 in stock and 1,000 in testing department and parts sufficient to assemble 5,000 machines.

Cygnet Horn No. 10 (10 panels) was offered with the STANDARD Model D phonograph in the United States in September 1909 and in the United Kingdom in October 1910 to make the following Model D2 arrangements:

STANDARD Model D2 with black Cygnet Horn	$35.00;	£7 0s. 0d.
with oak finish Cygnet Horn	$40.00;	£8 0s. 0d.
with mahogany cabinet and mahogany finish Cygnet Horn	$47.00	

Although the Model D with Cygnet Horn was listed as D 2 the same model with straight horn was rarely shown as D 1.

The following models still remained available in the United States:

STANDARD Model C with black Cygnet Horn	$30.00
with oak finish Cygnet Horn	$35.00
with mahogany cabinet and mahogany finish Cygnet Horn	$42.00

and in the United Kingdom the following remained in the catalogue until 1912:

STANDARD Combination Model D with straight polygonal horn	£5 15s. 0d.

The Cygnet Horn was sold separately for converting existing STANDARDS, with crane, socket and flexible connection:

in black with gold decoration	$7.50;	£1 15s. 0d.
oak or mahogany finish	$12.50;	£3 0s. 0d.

A Cygnet Horn (No. 11) finished in original blue and marked 'Standard' is reported.

After 18 months of selling Amberol cylinders it was obvious that many owners had not converted their machines from 2-minute playing, and as a further inducement the STANDARD Combination Attachment was offered with 10 Special Amberol cylinders (A- K) in April 1910 (U.S.) $6.00, and a similar offer was made in the United Kingdom in May 1911, but included instead 5 Special Amberol records and 5 Standard records: £1 16s. 0d.

In October 1911 (U.S.) the STANDARD Combination Attachment was offered with 10 Special Hebrew cylinders (L-W): $4.35

Wooden Music Master horns were announced in August 1910 (U.S.) and further variations of the STANDARD equipments were listed as follows:

STANDARD Model C with oak cabinet, oak Music Master horn	$40.00
mahogany cabinet, mahogany Music Master horn	$47.00
STANDARD Model D with oak cabinet, oak Music Master horn	$45.00
mahogany cabinet, mahogany Music Master horn	$52.00

with spruce Music Master horn, additional	$5.00
inlaid pearl Music Master horn, additional	$35.00

In March 1911 (U.S.) and in July 1911 (U.K.) the Model R reproducer was introduced and could be taken with STANDARD Model D, if specified, in place of Model H at extra $3.00; 12s. 6d.

if supplied with STANDARD Combination Attachment	$8.00
if supplied in place of Model H reproducer with the STANDARD Combination Attachment and 10 Special Amberols, extra	$1.00
or in the United Kingdom this equipment with 5 Special Amberols and 5 Standard cylinders:	£2 0s. 0d.

In a number of respects the STANDARD was treated a little differently from its contemporaries and when at this time most of the rest of the Edison range could be fitted with the Model O reproducer and its 'on-top' carrier-arm with the large eye, the STANDARD had to wait until the arrival of the Blue Amberols in late 1912 before it was allowed to adopt this feature. At a meeting of the Amusement Phonograph Committee on January 10th 1911 the Model O reproducer for the STANDARD (and HOME) was deemed "of the utmost importance" as an extra item with its carrier-arm for the trade to sell, but when this equipment became available for the HOME in March 1911 the Company had other plans for the STANDARD later in the year.

Model E

Introduced:	November 1911 (U.S.)
Type:	4-minute
Reproducer:	Model N, requiring the large carrier-arm set in the side position. A recorder was not included.
Horn:	Straight with 10 panels, coloured blue with chrysanthemum decoration and Edison STANDARD decal near the crane hook. Horn available separately $2.75. There were no horn options with this model.
Cabinet:	Antique oak finish only. The horn was supported by a socket on the front of the case
Price:	$30.00

STANDARD Phonograph Model E, shown with and without Special Flower Decorated Horn. The connector between horn and reproducer is a ball-jointed swivel (not Edison) with a volume control.

There is no evidence of this machine ever being available in the United Kingdom. It was devised following correspondence with Babson Brothers of Chicago, one of Edison's largest jobbers, who wanted a machine for their mail-order business and Edison put this model out as a concession to the whole trade generally.[9] When the equipment for the Model E was first determined in August 1911, a Model R reproducer was going to be offered, but a special large carrier-arm was made for the Model N.

Model F

Introduced:	November 1911 (U.S.); January 1912 (U.K.)
Type:	2 and 4-minute
Dimensions:	Height 11 ¾ in. base 13 ⅛ in. x 9 ½ in.
Weight:	21 ½ lb.
Reproducer:	Model S 2 and 4-minute swivel type in the United States. Models C and H were still included in the United Kingdom equipment however. The recorder was extra at $3.00
Horn:	Black Cygnet with gilt lining.
Features:	A unique model in the Edison range of domestic machines, having a small reproducer eye set in the 'on-top' position, and suited to Models R and S reproducers.
Price:	$35.00; £6 16s. 0d.
	with oak finish Cygnet Horn, additional $5.00
	oak Music Master horn, additional $10.00
	spruce Music Master horn, additional $15.00
	inlaid pearl Music Master horn, additional $45.00

On its introduction to the United Kingdom in February 1912 the Music Master horn was offered in oak with the Model F STANDARD outfit £8 18s. 0d.

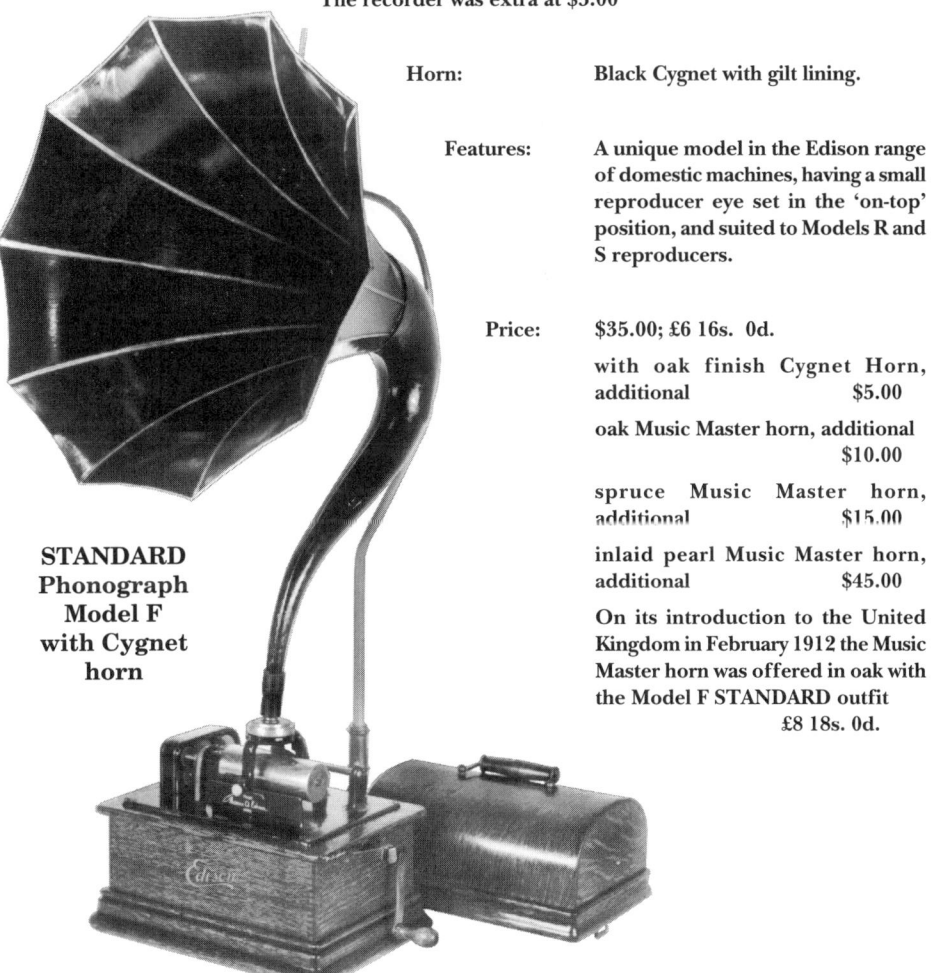

STANDARD Phonograph Model F with Cygnet horn

November 1911 was a clearing-up month in the United States when many confusing combinations of phonograph kits and accessories were weeded out and the catalogue simplified. The Model D STANDARD with straight horn and Models C and H reproducers were now dropped, but Model E with the flowered horn was retained.

In preparation for the arrival of the Blue Amberols in October 1912 (U.S.) orders from the factory went out on September 16th that all Model F STANDARDS surplus to 200 be converted into Model E machines with Diamond Model B reproducer but with no horn. 10,000 carrier-arms for the STANDARDS were ordered to be ready by October 1st and all machines would be 4-minute only from this date. Whereas the Model E had been the Combination Model D with the 2-minute gearing blocked off and the transfer effaced, the Model G was a re-geared phonograph to play only 4-minute records. Despite the impending Blue Amberols, factory orders went out that the Model N reproducer would be regular equipment with the new model STANDARD where a diamond reproducer was not specified. The reason for this was probably commercial as the $5.00 extra the Diamond Model B reproducer would cost may have been too much of a sales deterrent.

To prepare them for the new recordings, jobbers were all to receive 3 Blue Amberols and one Diamond B reproducer by September 30th.

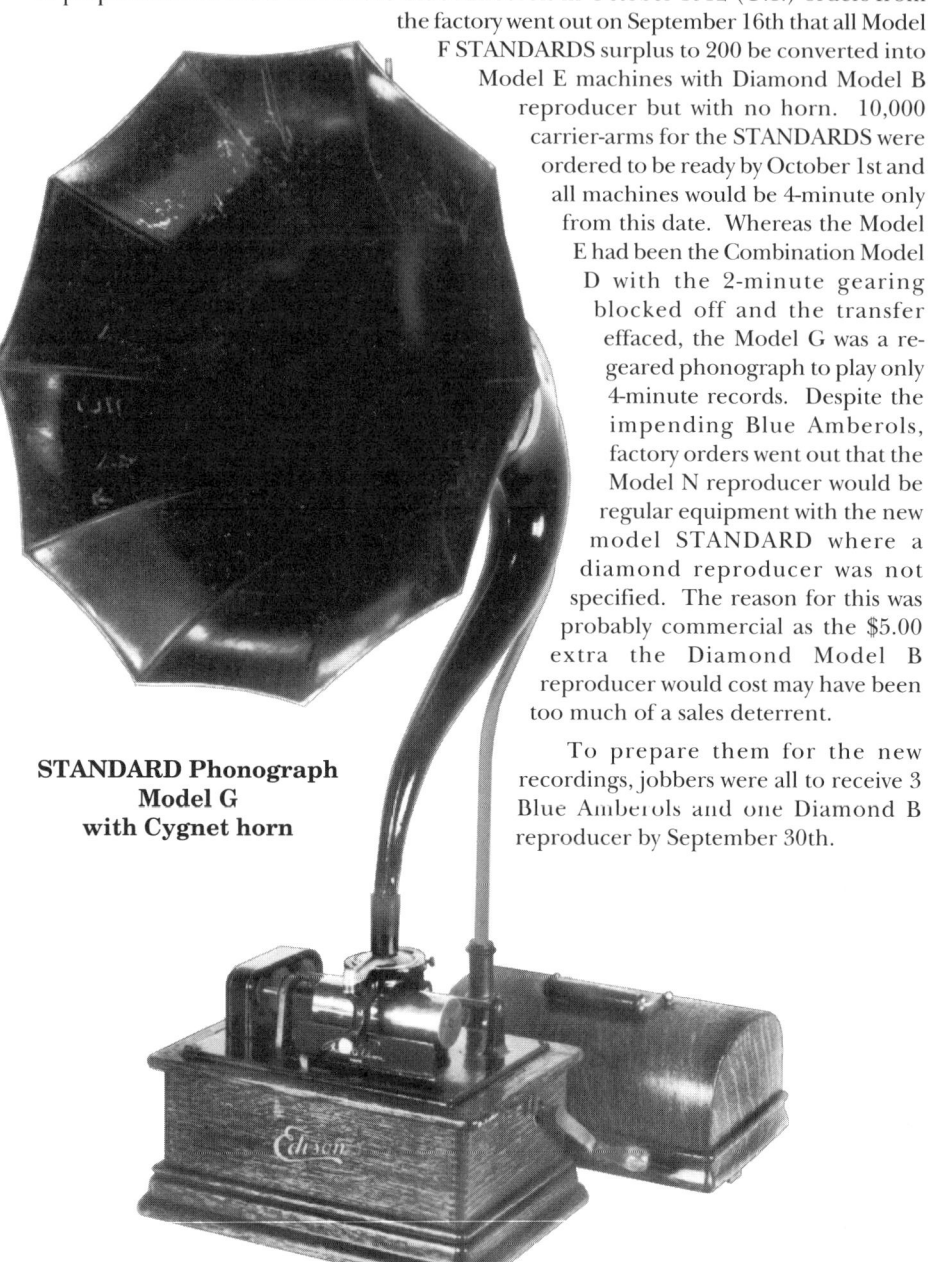

STANDARD Phonograph Model G with Cygnet horn

130

Model G

Introduced:	October 1912 (U.S.) and February 1913 (U.K.), both at the same time as the Blue Amberol cylinders. In the United Kingdom it seems likely that stocks of earlier models such as the F were sold as the Model G for a time and that substantial shipments of the authentic Model G may not have arrived before horn phonographs ceased to be listed in October 1913. A sample consignment of STANDARDS, as well as Diamond B reproducers and numbers of Blue Amberol cylinders were sent over to Great Britain in September 1912 to prepare the trade.
Type:	4-minute

The Model G was similar in appearance and dimensions - apart from the carrier-arm - to Models D, E and F and was offered in the following outfits:

with Cygnet Horn, Model N reproducer	$35.00;	£7 7s. 0d.
Cygnet Horn, Diamond Model B reproducer	$40.00;	£8 8s. 0d.
oak Music Master horn, Diamond Model B reproducer	$50.00;	£10 10s. 0d.
flowered horn, Diamond Model B reproducer	$35.00	—

No recorder was included with this model.

By October 5th 1912 orders for 595 STANDARDS with Diamond Model B reproducer had been received by the factory and there was a waiting stock of over 2,000.

From April 1913 the STANDARD Combination Attachment (average weekly shipment of 250) was sent out with the Diamond Model B reproducer ($8.40) and in April 1913 (U.S. and U.K.) the same attachment and reproducer with 10 Special Blue Amberol cylinders (A - K) cost $10.00 or £2 2s. 0d. This outfit included a large carrier-arm and adapter ring and straight or Cygnet Horn fitting as required, and had been delayed from September 1912 due to a shortage of Diamond B reproducers.

In January 1913 (U.S.) the Model N reproducer was reduced to help jobbers and dealers to clear old type STANDARDS (and FIRESIDES) from their shelves $3.00

It was announced in October 1913 that horn phonographs would no longer be made at West Orange following the company policy of concentrating on the AMBEROLA range, but output of the STANDARD continued into early 1914, being survived only by the FIRESIDE and GEM whose motors were put to use in some of the AMBEROLAS.

Production of parts for "obsolete models of cylinder phonographs with horns" was still possible in May 1921 and at that date 1,926 Combination Attachments for STANDARDS were ordered to be put in hand at $6.35 each.

NOTES

1) The Speed Controller was part of Edison's U.S. Patent No. 604,740 for Governor for Motors, filed January 27th 1897 and granted May 31st 1898
2) 'Thomas A. Edison' in characteristic autographic script was U.S. Trade Mark No. 33,236 of July 18th 1899, having been used since December 15th 1897. The Trade Mark was re-registered on December 15th 1903 and subsequently.
3) The U.K. introduction is unclear and complex, Edison Bell/Edisonia offering it initially as the Standard Commercial Phonograph for £5. 0s. 0d., then again at £6 6s. 0d. and as the Type 2 Phonograph perhaps at £6 0s. 0d. After 1903 Edison handled its own machines in the U.K. and Edison Bell put out its own version of the STANDARD for £5 5s. 0d. On June 2nd 1898 Edisonia opened in the Strand, London and listed the STANDARD with 8 records and 2 blanks for £9 9s. 0d., a high figure.
4) U. S. Patent No. 798,478 Means for Sustaining Phonograph Motors filed by Edward L. Aiken on June 20th 1904 and granted August 29th 1905.
5) Letter of January 11th 1907 - Edison Archive
6) Gilmore to Edison April 10th 1907 - Edison Archive
7) U. S. Patent No. 932,200 for Phonograph, filed by Peter Weber on January 20th 1908 and granted August 24th 1909
8) British Patent No. 2196, dated January 29th 1909 and awarded to Premier Manufacturing Company Ltd., and F. W. Pleasance
9) Fred Babson was a friend of Edison's and had been known to order phonographs and records by the train-load. This gave him 'pull' with the Company and from the time of the 1899 Polyphone he had radical ideas of promoting Edison phonographs and records within the restraints of the fixed price agreement that would have brought censure or worse to lesser factors. Babson's sold Edison phonographs and records with their own branded accessories as 'outfits' especially for the mail-order business and featured the STANDARDS in Parlor Grand outfits. That for 1908 featured the Model B with 14 Gold Moulded cylinders and was offered on approval for $34.50. A feature was the non-Edison Parlor Grand straight horn with floral decoration. This had 12 panels with convex ends. The outfit also had the Fosler automatic stop, tripped when the carrier-arm reached the end of the record, automatic (record cleaning) brush, oil and oilcan and Parlor Grand tone modifier in the neck of the horn. Height including horn 3ft. 6in.

STANDARD Phonograph with Bettini reproducer and horn

Chapter 8
GEM Phonograph

The GEM was the baby of the Edison phonographs and was brought out in 1899 to compete with other small phonographs then on the market. By a coincidence the CONCERT appeared the same month; this was the largest Edison domestic machine. Collectors will find that the GEM is still the smallest practical phonograph for regular use as it does not suffer the disadvantages of the floating reproducer and may be adjusted within reasonable limits to play well, although most found have noisy motors. It ranged through five separate models from a sturdy utilitarian two-minute machine to one playing only the four-minute cylinders, and with a pleasing maroon finish, the only Edison phonograph to be so coloured. Utility models always attract improvers, and various makers offered items to go with the early GEM such as cases and horns and later, speed changers, and the Edison company having produced a good cheap machine for the lowliest home must have been reluctant to follow by offering the GEM with extra equipment and finish at a higher price, and the last models retailed at more than double the cost of the first.

For such a small machine much variation is found, particularly in the early ones.

A. F. Sefl in the *A.P.S. Journal Vol. V No. 1* reports 29 variants in the Model A alone and more over the other models may reasonably be expected.

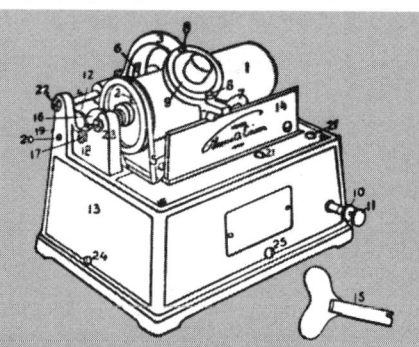

THE EDISON GEM PHONOGRAPH.

INDEX OF PARTS.

1. Mandrel (to hold Wax Cylinder), assembled with Cylinder Shaft.
2. Cylinder Pulley (assembled with gear).
3. Speaker Arm.
4. Back Rod.
5. Drive Belt.
6. Feed Nut Spring Screw.
7. Speaker Arm Lift Lever.
8. "   Clamp Screws.
9. Tube Plate, under which is the Speaker.
10. Speed Adjusting Screw.
11. Starting Knob.
12. Feed Screw Gear.
13. Body.
14. Straight Edge.
15. Winding Key.
16. Intermediate Gear.
17. Intermediate Gear Stud.
18. "   "   "   Nut.
19. Cylinder Shaft Center Set Screw.
20. Feed Screw Center.
21. Frame Holding Screws.
22. Back Rod Nut.
23. Cylinder Rod Nut.
24. Drip Pan Screw.
25. Gov. Brake Angle-piece Screw.

When in September 1897 Edison let it be known that he was not interested in making a cheaper machine than the STANDARD, preliminary work at his factory was already well forward with the GEM, although at this stage it was still called the Type 3 and was going to be an answer to the Graphophone Eagle. This had appeared on the market a few weeks earlier and had rattled the Edison United Phonograph Company whose Secretary G. N. Morison wrote to the London branch on August 27th:

> *Type 3 machine is not completed and I cannot find out when it will be .....but we ought to have a cheap phonograph at once*

A week later Morison wrote again to S.F. Moriarty in London:

> *We can get little or no information about this type. It is said not to be ready and we don't know whether it is being pushed or not.....*

Progress was indeed slow, the GEM was still nearly 18 months away and the Phonograph Works had plenty on its hands with the STANDARD, and although the Graphophone was known to be doing 'great business',[1] Edison would not:

> *(build) the cheapest machine until he saw business in others (of his own). He (thought he) might even be able to cheapen the No. 2 (STANDARD).*[2]

Almost as if in answer Graphophone brought out the five-dollar Model Q.

Inter-departmental notes continued to remark on the progress of the 'small machine' for the rest of the year; an early view of it appeared as a line drawing in *The Phonoscope* of January 1899, to sell for $7.50.

The early uncased Model A GEM is sometimes call 'the drip-pan GEM' because of the protective metal plate under the motor. The reproducer is one of the later types for this model. This machine was imported into the United Kingdom in 1899-1900.

135

Perhaps its official unveiling was on February 3rd, when the GEM trade mark was first seen.[3] In the first month only 25 were made, although 'expected to sell like hot cakes'.[4]

Yet again the earliest sales records seem to be for Europe where in April 1899 GEMS in lots of 2,500 at $3.85 each and 5,000 at $3.75 were quoted Edison Bell in London who ordered one or other quantity - which is not clear - and some more went to France where The Edison Phonorama Company had been formed in 1897 for the exploitation of Edison Phonographs and Columbia Graphophones. In France the GEM soon met opposition from Pathé who marketed a close copy called the Gaulois, selling from $4.95 to $5.20.[5] The GEM never enjoyed successful sales in France, but years later London was taking from 70-80% of the Works output of these machines.

In general appearance the Model A GEM stands in two classes, the earlier without a wooden cabinet or case, the later supplied with a wooden base and rounded cover. It had basically three types of reproducer and its motor and drive were altered drastically. No GEM ever had a spring barrel and could not be wound up while playing, neither was a shaving knife ever fitted.

The un-cased Model A GEM had the drive taken from the governor and its own speed control arrangements

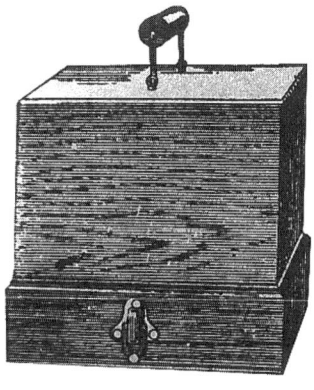

This non-Edison case for the early GEM is believed to have been from Hawthorne and Sheble

Model A (uncased)

Introduced:	February 1899 (U.S.)
Type:	2-minute
Dimensions:	Base 7 ¾ in. x 5 ⅞ in.
Weight:	7 ½ lb.
Motor:	Single spring playing two 2-minute cylinders per wind; after the early months a slightly more robust spring was fitted and the spooling washer omitted. The earliest were given a wooden mandrel but were soon converted to metal.
Horn:	Model A GEMS were supplied with a 10 inch black japanned conical horn, not supplied with any other type of Edison machine. It is believed that the very earliest GEMS were provided with an 11 in. black japanned horn with a brass bell.

Edison GEM Model A with branded case and GEM reproducer. This dropped into the carrier-arm, turned a little to the right and was held by the two knurled screws. This machine was one that had been imported into the United Kingdom by Edison Bell.

Reproducer:	This was fixed to and pivoted from the carrier-arm and had the weight and stylus of the Automatic reproducer. The upper portion, or tube plate was secured by two screws, removable for access and for tension adjustment. Later tube plates had a larger diameter than the earlier ones and this helped gasket tension.
Accessories:	Camel-hair chip-brush and oilcan provided.
Features:	Access to the motor was gained by removing the metal drip-pan underneath; there are two retaining screws. Viewed from below with the machine resting on its back the driving mechanism is to the right; the drive runs from the spring and main gear through two gear shafts to the governor shaft, at the far end of which is a small belt pulley.

The governor seems larger than might be expected, but is to compliment the combination of this small pulley and the solid one on the mandrel shaft; this is noticeably larger than the mandrel. The motor winds in a clockwise direction by a slotted shanked key, fitting two pins on the winding shaft and is controlled by a speed adjusting screw - a starting knob passing through the centre of this - and located on the right front of the body. It is likely that the nickel-plated brass patent plate appeared on the front of all uncased GEMS and this model did not have a swing arm. The guide rod was secured at one end by a nut.

The body of the GEM was japanned black with gold lining and carried the 'Thomas A. Edison' signature.[6] Several manufacturers offered cases for this GEM; one such was Hawthorne and Sheble of Chicago who advertised it for $2.50.

Price:	$7.50; £2 2s. 0d., reducing to £1 10s. 0d.

Model A (cased)

Introduced:	May 1900 (U.S.) and September 1900 (U.K.)
Type:	2-minute

GEM Phonograph Model A, with branded case, special GEM reproducer and all-brass GEM horn of 1901

Dimensions:	Height 8 ¾ in. base 9 ⅜ in. x 7 ⅜ in.
Weight:	13 lb.
Motor:	Single spring, playing two 2-minute cylinders. The motor was relocated and simplified and the spring strengthened, but the key-wind was now counter-clockwise. Earlier models had a cast-iron drive pulley with spokes, this was later die-cast with 4 round holes.
Horn:	10 in. black japanned conical horn with gold band and known in the Works as the 'b and g'. From October 15th 1904 in the United Kingdom the GEM was sent out with a 10 ½ in. x 8 in. spun aluminium horn.
Reproducer:	Although the fixed reproducer may have lingered into the earliest cased models, a special lightly made GEM reproducer was sold with the cased machine from 1900, modelled on the Automatic. The carrier-arm eye was smaller than standard and the new reproducer was dropped in, turned to the right and locked by two knurled screws. During the same period a recorder, very similar in appearance, was included. From 1902 a standard diameter carrier-arm was fitted and until October 1st 1905 a Model B reproducer supplied to the machine. A standard recorder became an optional extra for $3.00. From June 1902 after protests Model C reproducer became regular issue with GEMS sold in the U.K.

**GEM Phonograph Model A
in banner transfer case and
with Model B reproducer**

139

Accessories:	Camel-hair chip-brush and oilcan provided.
Cabinet and Finish:	The New Style cabinet first appeared with a distinctive EDISON GEM PHONOGRAPH branded on the cover; this method of marking was not used on any other Edison machine and by the end of 1902 was replaced by the familiar banner transfer.[7] The earliest cases seem to have been finished in medium oak, changed to green oak when given the banner transfer, and changed again to antique oak in line with the larger instruments. The earliest banner case used a spring catch at either end, but these soon gave way to knurled screws that tightened into the metal body of the machine. The body was black with gold lining and the word GEM in capitals adorned the body front. The patents plate was now fixed at the back. From 1901 the New Style cabinet was available for the earlier GEMS, price $2.00.
Features:	From 1900 the motor was re-sited and the over-size mandrel pulley - now diecast - reduced in diameter. The front speed adjusting screw and stop-start button were moved to the left end of the body and combined in a knurled screw that was pushed or pulled to start or stop, and turned to adjust the speed. This GEM had a large end-gate that pivoted from near the end of the straight edge and clipped to the back of the right-hand guide rod stanchion. This proved to be unnecessarily large, cylinders were easily scored while being changed and it was shortened just to give support to the mandrel shaft and was called a swing arm. The guide rods of this period were held at one end by a nut, but changed to being secured by grub screws in the stanchions.
	In 1901 the motor was moved to the left of the body of the machine as viewed from below, and the movement inside the motor frame reversed. The winding shaft was now longer to meet the shanked and slotted key, but after two years it was itself slotted and hollowed and the key became flat. The motor now wound in a clockwise manner, the drive being taken off the outer end of the second gear shaft by a large belt pulley. A similarly large gear on the other end of this shaft drove the governor, now much shortened. An idler pulley on a spring-loaded arm kept the belt under tension. Some GEMS of this model are known with cranks, and may have been unofficial accessories.
Prices:	$10.00; £2 2s. 0d. through Edison Bell in 1900 £2 15s. 0d. " 1902-3 £2 2s. 0d. from Edison in 1903

Its United Kingdom introduction in September 1900 was through The Edison Bell Consolidated Phonograph Company Ltd. or its subsidiary Edisonia Ltd. of London, who being licensees of Edison patents controlled all cylinder phonograph sales in the country. In an early advertisement in the issue of February 16th 1901 of *The Illustrated London News* Edison Bell offered the 'New Gem'. This was the Edison GEM with branded cabinet and shanked key and cost three guineas, but this price was quickly reduced. Soon after this date Edison Bell

**The later Model A GEM had the motor re-sited and
the drive no longer came from the governor**

marked its machines 'Type 1 Gem'. Because of legal difficulties with Edison Bell, a lift button was substituted for the lift lever on some GEMS from October 22nd 1901.

What the Edison (National Phonograph) Company said about its inability to handle its own machines in Great Britain may be imagined, but with the expiry of the patent in November 1903 Edison was all ready for business there in its own products. National Phonograph soon took steps to stop Edison products being sold by Edison Bell, forcing that company into production of its own range of phonographs but owing nearly everything to Edison design. Such is the origin of Edison Bell GEMS and STANDARDS.

A curved steel rod capable of supporting a 24 in. horn could be bought in 1900-1. It included an adjustable socket for screwing to the body of the GEM   Price 25 cents.

Special finishes for the GEM could be had to order from the phonograph's introduction, consisting of either gold or nickel plating, but between 1904 and 1911 the options were widened to the following:

Specially decorated, additional	$4.00;	17s. 6d.
Nickel plated, additional	$15.00;	£3 3s. 0d.
Gold plated, additional	$25.00;	£5 5s. 0d.
Mahogany cabinets, additional	$2.00 until 1908	

Model B

Introduced:	October/December 1905 (U.S. and U.K.)
Type:	2-minute
Dimensions:	Height 8 in; base 10 in x 7 ¾ in.
Weight:	13 lb.
Motor:	As in the later Model A. The key wind gave way to a crank winding clockwise by the addition of two extra gears separating the winding shaft. Therefore the winding shaft had to be pushed in to engage, so it no longer revolved as the motor unwound. The crank was threaded to the winding shaft and could be detached if needed. Some of the early winding shaft assemblies gave trouble with the ratchet and pawl and the pawls were re-designed. Early governor pinions of this model proved noisy and fibre gears were tried but not adopted.

**GEM Phonograph Model B
with straight one-piece horn**

Horn:	The black and gold 10 inch conical horn was supplied in the United States and the spun aluminum type in the United Kingdom. From October 1907 (U.S.) and April 1908 (U.K.) this model was equipped with the 8-panel one-piece polygonal horn 19 in. long and 11 in. diameter in black Japan finish with gold decoration. The Model B was now sold with a 3/16 in. socket to the left of the straight edge to take the horn crane, but this was soon enlarged to 1/4 in. From September 1906 the option of receiving a speaking tube or hearing tube in place of the horn was withdrawn.
Reproducer:	Model C, recorder extra $3.00; 12s. 6d.
Cabinet:	The cover in this and following models was slotted to fit over the winding crank and bore for some months the banner transfer, but this became the 'Edison' signature decal during the summer of 1906.[6] The cabinet was finished in antique oak, the body of the phonograph in black with gold lining and the word GEM continued to appear on its front. The letter 'M' of GEM now reverted to Romanesque style.
Features:	The starting button was now on the right end of the body. Instead of pushing and pulling to start, a coarsely knurled button working on a cam embodied the speed adjustment.[8] The trade found difficulty in getting accustomed to this, complaining to the Works that it was impossible to regulate the speed of the machine and many new GEMS were returned for re-setting. The swing arm of the later Model A continued.

Prices:

with small horn	$10.00;	£2 2s. 0d.
with polygonal horn and crane	$12.50;	£2 12s. 6d.
with mahogany cabinet and mahogany finished horn		
	$16.50;	£3 10s. 0d.

In October 1905 following criticism in France that the GEM looked like a Beatrice oil stove and that about 1400 were lying unsold, France, and possibly Belgium were promised specially finished GEMS. They had oak cabinets of truncated pyramid shape and the conventional round topped cover fitted on with end clips similarly to the larger machines. Where these were made is not known.

Despite good sales of the GEMS their problems at this time drove Edison's London Chairman of Directors to report in confidence that he preferred Edison Bell's version of the GEM.[9]

The specially cased GEM made for the French market in 1906. This was No. 76 (J-P Agnard photo)

Model C

Introduced:	Mid-February 1908 (U.S.); early 1909 (U.K.) The circumstances of the introduction of the Edison Model C Phonographs are related in Appendix V
Type:	2-minute
Dimensions:	as Model B
Cabinet:	as Model B
Motor:	as Model B. Early in 1908 there was a modification to the governor construction when an additional collar with wire spring attached to the adjoining collar was added to the governor shaft to take up shocks.
Horn:	8-panel polygonal, as with the later Model B
Features:	Similar in appearance to the later Model B, but there was no swing arm.
Price:	$12.50; £2 12s. 0d. reducing in August 1909 to £2 6s. 0d.
	With mahogany cabinet and mahogany finished horn $16.50; £3 10s. 0d.

GEM Phonograph Model C with straight one-piece horn

From February 1908 the camel-hair chip-brush was omitted from the GEM outfits but the oilcan continued.

To identify readily Models A, B, and C from key features

Model A (uncased)
- There was no wooden base or lid
- Reproducer built into the carrier-arm
- Oversize mandrel pulley
- No swing arm end gate
- Stop-start and speed control knob on the front of the body
- Motor winds clockwise by shanked and slotted key

Model A (early cased)
- Wooden case has name branded on lid
- Swing arm fitted
- Special small GEM recorder and reproducer
- Motor winds anti-clockwise by a shanked and slotted key
- Stop-start and speed control knob on left-end of the body

Model A (later cased)
- Case lid has banner transfer EDISON GEM PHONOGRAPH
- Swing arm made with hole in it for flat key storage
- Motor winds anti-clockwise with a flat key
- Model B or C reproducer

Model B
- Decal 'Edison' on lid of case
- Horn crane socket cast in left end of straight edge
- Control knob in right end of body
- Swing arm fitted

Model C
- No swing arm
- More elaborate gold lining on body with decoration in corners

All these models had black bodies with gold lining

As each model was developed the changes did not occur all at the same time, and fringe variations of the above may be noticed. Also parts of the machines may have been substituted or cabinets updated.

With the arrival of the 4-minute Amberol cylinders in October 1908 (U.S. and U.K.) at the same time as the TRIUMPH, HOME, and STANDARD 2 and 4-minute Model D Phonographs to play them, GEM owners had a further year to wait for a similar GEM and nine months for Combination attachments to convert their Models A, B and C machines to dual playing. One attachment would fit any of the three models. Although the GEM was advertised as playing two 2-minute cylinders the imposition of up to 4 ½ minutes of playing and the extra gearing meant that it was touch-and-go, and the GEM could not be wound while playing. This accounts for the Edison reticence in introducing the new equipment (July 1909 U.S. and U.K.). It comprised a longer back rod to replace the old one, change-gear bracket with gears assembled, new intermediate gear stud with intermediate gear assembled; Model H reproducer........ price complete $4.00; 15s. 0d.

While waiting for the Edison Combination Attachments it is worth mentioning several non-American attempts to make kits to convert the GEM to 2- and 4-minute playing. One of the more noteworthy and ingenious was by Arthur Walshaw of Otley, England, who sent his invention to West Orange for evaluation early in 1909 where it was said to be substantially similar to one invented there by John Ott, and for which a U.S. patent had been applied for. This was not strictly true because John Ott's patent was for the train of gears that became the GEM Combination Attachment. Walshaw's invention worked on a similar principle to Herman Wolke's already applied for on Edison's behalf,[10] but was more compact and would readily allow the GEM lid to go over it. Walshaw's device consisted of a brass gear in the place of the half nut on the feedscrew and contiguous to a gear of larger radius, this meshing with a nonrotating threaded rod parallel to the feedscrew and retarding the carrier-arm movement by half. It was the Edison opinion that this device was too flimsy and liable to wear but this was doubtless a deliberate hindrance as Walshaw's persistence probably damaged any goodwill towards him at West Orange. Although he did not go ahead with a patent application Walshaw put his mechanism on the market as "The Variol Attachment", and examples survive.

    Price: 18s 6d. post free or 15s. 0d. on approval

                  GEM ~with Variol Attachment already fitted £3 10s. 6d. (March 1909)

To accompany his attachment Walshaw applied for a British Patent (No. 2332 of February 1st 1909, but not granted) for a turnover button type sapphire and mounting with options of 2 or 4-minute styli faces on opposite sides of the stylus bar; when produced this took the form of two different sized sapphires on a common mounting that could be rotated 180°. This has been seen but price and availability are not known.

A further British Combination Attachment for the GEM was put on sale by The Premier Manufacturing Company Ltd.[11] This company made Clarion cylinders. Other combination attachments for the GEM were said to be the British-made Murdoch and Formband, and the German Lindström and Excelsior.

A special GEM Model C was offered for The International Correspondence School, taking the place of the STANDARD in February 1910 (U.S.).

Model D

Introduced:	October 1909 (U.S. and U.K.) An internal memo showed it to be under test in the laboratory in March 1909
Type:	2 and 4-minute, the only GEM expressly designed to play both types of record, and normally designated The Combination GEM.
Dimensions:	Height 8 in.; base 10 in. x 7 ¾ in.
Weight:	14 ½ lb.
Motor:	Spring thickened to improve performance duration. Apart from minor variations it closely resembled Models B and C, but both motor and mandrel were moved a little to the right to accommodate the gear-change mechanism, with a shorter governor shaft resulting.
Cabinet and Finish:	The cabinet was a little longer than earlier models and was finished in antique oak, and the metal body was more stocky and finished in maroon with gold and black lining on sides and top. The decal 'Edison' replaced GEM on the body front.
Reproducer:	Model K
Horn:	The straight maroon horn provided with the Model D, and with the later Model E differed from the earlier 19 in. black horn because it was made in two parts and screwed together. It may be found marked 'Fireside' as the horn was sold also with that machine.

GEM Phonograph Model D. The part floral decoration is by an earlier owner.

Price: $15.00; £3 0s. 0d.

with mahogany cabinet and mahogany finished horn $34.00; £7 0s. 0d.

It will be noted that the GEM, basically conceived as a utility phonograph to compete with Graphophones and cheaply-made European machines had in ten years doubled in price. None the less the company was pleased with the success of the FIRESIDE, put on sale three months earlier, and with the Combination GEM was able to offer a slightly smaller phonograph for $7.00 less but employing the same horn and the same Model K reproducer.

As part of a policy of weaning Edison owners away from 2-minute cylinders and on to 4-minute Amberols, in May 1911 (U.S.) and June 1911 (U.K.) the Model R reproducer was offered with the GEM at extra cost instead of the Model K, but to play Standard cylinders a Model C reproducer would have to be bought..... $5.00; £1 1s. 0d. This arrangement was reversed in 1911 when the Model D GEM was again offered with Model K reproducer only, but with Model R offered as a separate accessory. The reason for these 'second thoughts' is not clear.

In April 1910 (U.S.) and July 1911 (U.K.) the GEM Combination Attachment was offered with Model R reproducer in place of the Model H .... . $7.00; £1 10s. 0d.

Simultaneously the GEM Combination Attachment Outfit was made available with 10 Special Amberol records.... $5.00,

or with Model R reproducer in place of Model H. $6.00

In May 1911 (U.K.) a similar offer of records with the GEM Combination Attachment Outfit was made, but it consisted of 5 Special Amberols and 5 Standard cylinders....... £1 0s. 0d.

People were slow to take up these attachment offers, leading in October 1911 (U.K.) to a reduction in these prices. In October 1911 (U.S.) the GEM Combination Attachment was offered with 10 special Hebrew Amberol cylinders (L-W).... $5.00

In anticipation of the new Blue Amberols the following quantities of GEMS were ordered to be prepared by October 1st 1912:

Model D with K reproducer... 200

Model E with Diamond B reproducer ...500

Of a stock of 450 Model D GEMS in hand 250 were to be changed to 4-minute only and equipped with Diamond Model B reproducer.

The Diamond Model B set in a carrier-arm in the 'on-top' position was a certainty for this model GEM until the very last moment.[12] The phonograph would have cost $20.00, but after tests until the eleventh hour it was realized that there was no way of getting this heavier reproducer to play a Blue Amberol through satisfactorily in its entirety. Thus it was given the lighter Model N.

Model E

Introduced:	October 1912 (U.S.); December 1912 (U.K.)
Type:	4-minute
Dimensions:	Height 8 in; base 10 in. x 8 ¾ in.
Motor and mechanism:	The motor was as Combination Model D. The reproducer carrier-arm was of the large type set on the side position.
Cabinet and Finish:	Similar to the Model D and with the maroon finish of that model.
Reproducer:	Model N
Horn:	Two-piece maroon horn, as with Model D
Price:	$15.00; £3 3s. 0d.

In July 1913 (U.S. and U.K.) the GEM Combination Attachment Outfit included 10 Special Blue Amberol records, Model N reproducer and special carrier-arm...$4.75; £1 0s. 0d. This had been held up together with outfits for the other Edison machines because of their demand for Diamond Model B reproducers.

In October 1913 (U.S.) in common with all other horn phonographs except the SCHOOL Model it was announced that manufacture of the GEM would be discontinued, but works figures show it still

The GEM Phonograph Model E, showing the Model N reproducer and large carrier-arm

149

being assembled at West Orange at the beginning of 1914 with orders in hand, and GEM motor parts were used in the AMBEROLA X. In December 1913, in a circular to the United Kingdom trade, the Edison company announced that manufacture and listing of the GEM (and FIRESIDE) would be continued, and these may have been imported into the outbreak of the Great War in August of the following year.

The GEM had never been given a shaving device, for which its motor was not suited, nor a diamond reproducer nor horn larger than the straight 19 in. polygonal, if the short-lived and disproportionate brass 24-inch type at the turn of the century is disregarded. The numbers sold and those that have survived are indicators of its success.

NOTES

1) Letter of G. N. Morison to S.F. Moriarty March 1898
2) Ibid April 5th 1899
3) U.S. Trade Mark No. 33,015 of June 6th 1899, the word GEM as it appeared on the front of Models A, B and C. Claimed as used since February 3rd 1899. Until 1907 the letter 'M' of GEM was patterned with its legs slightly astride.
4) G.N. Morison to S.F. Moriarty March 14th 1899
5) C. E. Stevens to W. E. Gilmore January 19th 1900
6) U.S. Trade Mark No. 33,236 of July 18th 1889 was for 'Thomas A. Edison' or 'Edison' in characteristic autographic script. In use since December 1897. The trade mark was re-registered on December 15th 1903 and subsequently
7) U. S. Trade Mark No. 6,674 of August 29th 1905, filed May 24th 1905. This was for the word GEM in the form it appeared on the banner transfer.
8) U. S. Patent No. 842,042 for Speed Regulator of January 22nd 1907, filed by Peter Weber on September 27th 1905
9) Letter from J. R. Schermerhorn of January 1907
10) U.S. Patent No. 936,264 for Gearing of October 5th 1909, filed by Herman Wolke on September 12th 1907
11) British Patent No. 2196/09 granted to F. W. Plaisance and Premier Manufacturing Company January 29th 1909
12) Note of October 16th 1912 from G. E. Wilson to Peter Weber who had been keeping Edison advised: ".... hold on GEMS so far as equipping with new arm and diamond repro. until advised"

(all Letters from Edison Archive)

Chapter 9
CONCERT Phonograph

The Edison CONCERT Phonograph was anticipated by several months by its cylinders, and perhaps longer, as these were used regularly in the Works as masters for dubbing Standard brown wax cylinders.[1]

It was Thomas Macdonald of Columbia who first demonstrated the machine to play such large cylinders, the Graphophone Grand witnessed on December 16th 1898 by G. N. Morison of Edison United Phonograph who described 'this new Graphophone with large cylinder as big as your head'.[2] In a further letter two months later he foresaw that the (Edison) 'big one to compete with the big Graphophone will be out soon', so it would have acquired its CONCERT name just around this date, although a month later this forgetful correspondent was writing about the Edison Grand machine.[3]

The earliest advertisement traced for the CONCERT was in February 1899 (U.S.) when it was offered for $125.00, but it had come down to $100.00 by the September and reducing in June 1900 to $75.00 and a United Kingdom price of £15 15s. 0d. by 1903. The U.K. had been quoted $50.00 each in quantities of 50.

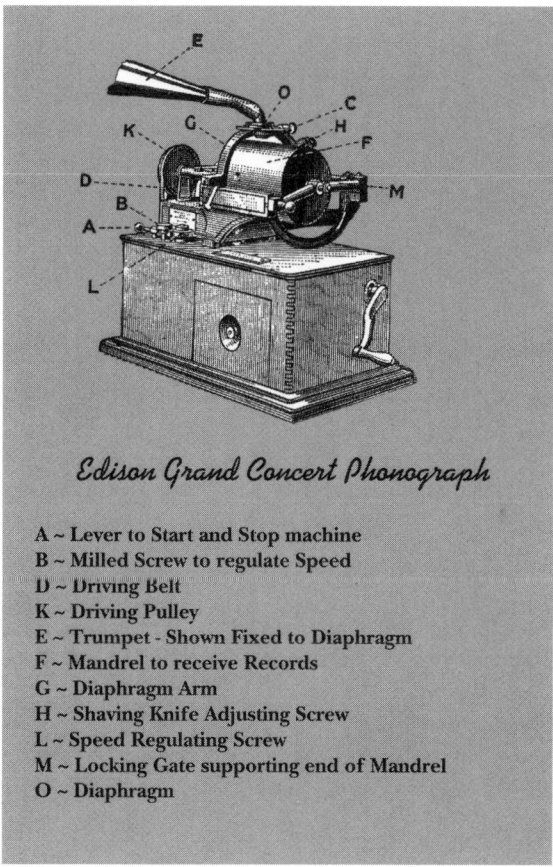

Edison Grand Concert Phonograph

A ~ Lever to Start and Stop machine
B ~ Milled Screw to regulate Speed
D ~ Driving Belt
K ~ Driving Pulley
E ~ Trumpet - Shown Fixed to Diaphragm
F ~ Mandrel to receive Records
G ~ Diaphragm Arm
H ~ Shaving Knife Adjusting Screw
L ~ Speed Regulating Screw
M ~ Locking Gate supporting end of Mandrel
O ~ Diaphragm

An interesting aspect of this List of Parts is the use of the word 'Grand', usually applied to the large Graphophone of the day

The designation CONCERT was one of the most overworked words in the talking machine industry, being universally applied to horns, sound boxes, machines and records by several makers. Edison had been the first to use it for the large demonstration tinfoil phonographs in 1878, but had failed to get a trade mark for it in 1901. After it was bestowed on this 1899 phonograph and its 5 in. cylinder the name was substituted for the OPERA in 1912 because of pressures from the owners of this trade mark.[4] At times the large AMBEROLA Is were alluded to as Concert AMBEROLAS and there were Concert Blue Amberol cylinders featuring better class music.

A drawback of the early phonograph had been its inability to yield much sound from a groove on a small soft wax cylinder, but the Concert cylinder with a deeper cut and higher linear speed went a long way towards more volume, though this record was never offered by the Edison company in anything but a brown wax composition. The large cylinder equipment was also adapted to other Edison models of that time, the OPERA and ORATORIO electric machines and on several coin-slot phonographs. Chief objections to the large cylinder of course were its fragility and size, and it imposed great bulk on the machine made to play it, not least those of Edison origins. These Concert cylinders were made by mechanical duplication from electroplated masters and featured in catalogues until August 1907 (U.S.) and May 1908 (U.K.) but were still available later. At first they were given their own catalogue numbers prefixed by the letter 'B' but after March 1901 were made to special order, prefixed with the letter 'C' and numbered to their Standard equivalents. While Edison's large cylinders were always Concert, Columbia's were Grand Records and Edison Bell combined the two into Grand Concert. Similar records were marketed by Pathé, and some of Lambert's were made of celluloid material.

In retrospect it is perplexing to understand why after the introduction of the superior hard-wax Edison moulded cylinders from January 1902, Concert cylinders still lingered in the catalogue for the die-hards who preferred the large cylinder, while at the same time a conversion kit for changing the CONCERT machine to playing Standard records could be bought by those turning their backs on Concert cylinders.

The earliest style of the CONCERT phonograph resembled an enlarged SPRING MOTOR machine

There was only one model CONCERT Phonograph and this underwent only slight mechanical changes, but its case appeared in three styles.

Motor and Layout:	The 3-spring Triton motor used in the SPRING MOTOR/TRIUMPH models was the drive for the CONCERT phonograph. This played 6 to 8 CONCERT cylinders at one winding. The springs in the CONCERT version of the motor are said to have been given a $^{13}/_{16}$ in. hole, not the TRIUMPH spring with $^{7}/_{8}$ in. hole, but TRIUMPH springs will do for replacement. The layout too was similar although the top casting, end gate etc. were enlarged to accommodate the larger mandrel. The end pulley was 2 in. diameter on most models but 3 in. on some versions. The carrier-arm was set for the reproducer to move horizontally along the top of the cylinder. The cabinets though were as follows:

1899 Model: An oak case with all-enveloping cover, the body of the case being easily recognized by its square corners and front drawer and lack of any decal. The top plate rested on the top edge of the case and was not hinged but could be lifted out bodily for inspection. On most machines an engraved nickel plate on the top read 'Edison Spring Motor for Phonograph'.

Dimensions:	Height 17 in; base 17 in. x 12 in.
Weight:	51 lb.

The number produced reached 3,000 by May 1900

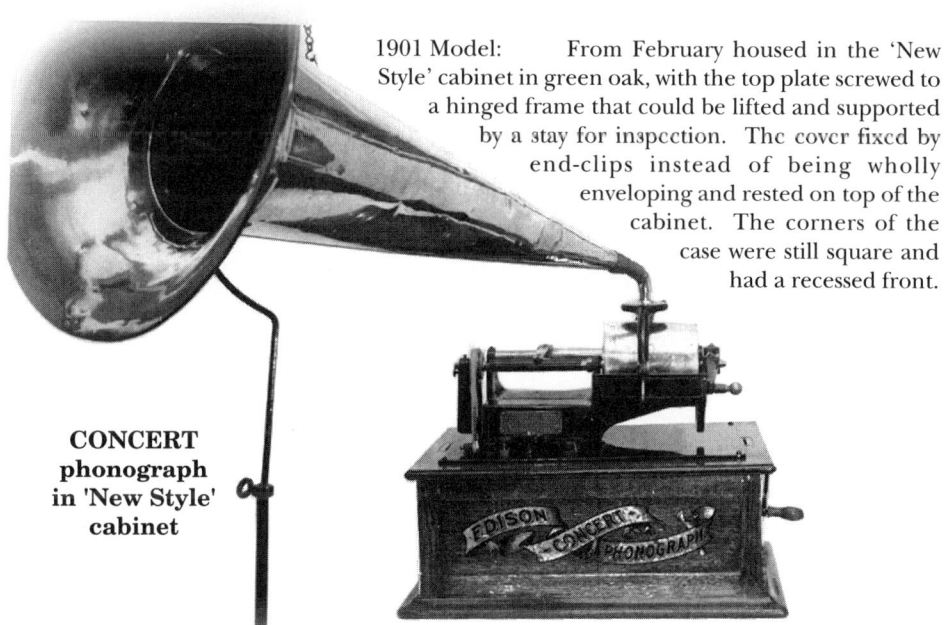

1901 Model: From February housed in the 'New Style' cabinet in green oak, with the top plate screwed to a hinged frame that could be lifted and supported by a stay for inspection. The cover fixed by end-clips instead of being wholly enveloping and rested on top of the cabinet. The corners of the case were still square and had a recessed front.

CONCERT phonograph in 'New Style' cabinet

The metal parts had a more pronounced lining and decoration. On the carrier-arm the speaker clamps made way for a knurled screw. Full EDISON CONCERT PHONOGRAPH banner appeared on the case front.[5]

Motor:	This was spring-suspended and incorporated a belt tightener from June 1904. A speed indicator regulated from 120 to 160 r.p.m.[6]
Dimensions:	Height 16 ⅜ in; base 18 ⅛ in. x 12 ¾ in.
Weight:	59 lb.

Owners of the CONCERT phonograph were advised in 1901 that New Style cabinets were now available for re-casing their machines like current selling models: $10.00

Sport versions are sometimes found among Edison models, and an unusual 1901-6 CONCERT phonograph has been reported. The top casting is more pronouncedly curved when viewed from above and the Triton motor has its governor set at right angles to the gear train.

1906 Model: From about July the CONCERT was housed in the TRIUMPH Model B pattern of case, in antique oak. The front panel of this design was raised and the single word 'Edison' was displayed thereon from September.[7] The case corners were fully rounded.

Motor:	Basically still the same as the 1901 model with 1904 suspension.
Dimensions and Weight:	as the previous model

CONCERT in Model B style of case. This example has a Combination Attachment fitted as well as a slip-on Concert mandrel.

The 1906 model was catalogued only for a matter of months, there being little residual interest in the large cylinders, and it must be rarely found today.

With all these CONCERT phonographs the winding crank and its shaft remained square fitting, and the swing arm locking bolt was fitted. The shaving device also went through from the earliest to late models, but may have been omitted from the last machines.

Horn:	The CONCERT was always supplied with a 24 in. horn, the earlier ones being all-brass and the later black enamel bodied with brass flare from 1905. A floor horn stand was supplied, until with the 1906 casing a horn crane was attached to the rear of the machine.
Reproducer:	Until 1902 the Edison Automatic Reproducer was supplied, and after, the Model D. Also supplied were the Edison recorder and chip-brush and until 1902 a speaking tube and oilcan were included.

A Repeating Attachment was offered from 1900 for $15.00, reducing in 1904 to $7.50 with the coming of the Model D repeater, and withdrawn after July 1907.

From its introduction the CONCERT could be bought in the following special finishes:

Gold plated, additional	$50.00;	£10 10s. 0d.
Nickel plated, additional	$25.00;	£ 5 5s. 0d.
Specially decorated, additional, (from 1904)	$10.00;	£ 2 2s. 0d.
Mahogany cabinet, additional (from 1904)	$13.00;	£ 2 15s. 0d.

Following the introduction of moulded cylinders a conversion kit to change the CONCERT Phonograph to playing Standard cylinders was announced in March 1904, consisting of a new carrier-arm, mainshaft and mandrel: $7.95; £1 13s. 6d.

When the Amberols arrived in 1908 provision was made for CONCERT owners to play the three types of cylinders extant. In November 1908 (U.S.) and February 1909 (U.K.) Amberol attachments were announced for the CONCERT, consisting of the regular TRIUMPH attachment with special Model J reproducer and diaphragm arm (the extension tube). These would be available from mid-December (U.S.)... $7.50; £1 11s. 0d.

Owners who had not converted their CONCERT machines to play even Standard cylinders would need an attachment: $9.75; £2 0s. 0d.

In March 1911 (U.S.) and July 1911 (U.K.) the Model O reproducer was offered separately for CONCERT Phonographs already converted to playing Amberols, with adapter ring and special carrier-arm necessary: $10.00; £2 2s. 0d. The Models D or J reproducers were not returnable, being already obsolete.

For CONCERT phonographs not equipped for playing Amberols, the Model O Reproducer and Combination Attachment with larger carrier-arm and adapter ring for the recorder were offered: $15.50; £3 5s. 0d.

All these sizes and options are confusing but indicate how the Edison company looked after its customers by supplying outfits to enable them to convert to the latest developments. One would have thought that the most obdurate CONCERT owner would have long gone over to Amberol playing or thrown his machine out by July 1913 (U.S.), but by this date Combination Attachment outfits were still being offered, but now with Diamond B reproducer, carrier-arm and 10 Special Blue Amberols: $13.75; £2 17s. 3d.

In June 1907 it was announced that the CONCERT and the other large cylinder Edison models would appear no longer in the American catalogues; however these have been seen quoted in literature of September 29th 1908, so this was a fade-out and not an instant withdrawal. Records would still be on sale as follows:

U.S.		U.K.	
Oct. 1907 to Oct. 1911	75 ¢ each	December 1908	3s. 0d.
		" 1909	4s. 0d.
		" 1910	4s. 0d.

CONCERT Phonograph with standard mandrel and special carrier-arm supplied from 1902 to convert the machine to playing Gold Moulded cylinders

NOTES
1) U.S. Patent No. 648,645 for Apparatus for Duplicating Phonograph Records was filed by Edison on October 28th 1899 and granted May 8th 1900
2) Letter from G.N. Morison to S.F. Moriarty, London, of December 16th 1898
3) Ibid. February 16th 1899 and March 17th 1899
4) United States Phonograph Company
5) The word CONCERT in the style of the banner decal was the subject of U.S. Trade Mark No. 6,676 filed May 24th 1905 and granted August 29th 1905
6) U.S. Patent No. 811,010 for Phonograph Speed Index filed by Peter Weber on June 29th 1904 and granted January 30th 1906
7) U. S. Trade Mark No. 33,236 of July 18th 1899 was for the word 'Edison' in characteristic autographic script. Filed May 27th 1899

Letters and production figures from Edison Archive

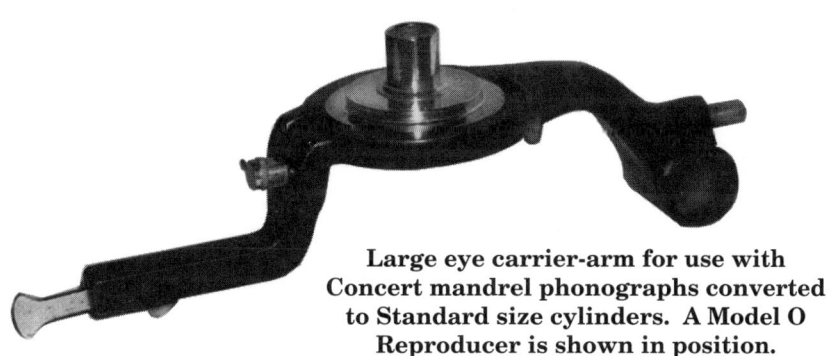

Large eye carrier-arm for use with Concert mandrel phonographs converted to Standard size cylinders. A Model O Reproducer is shown in position.

Chapter 10
CLASS M and CLASS E
CONCERT
Electric Phonographs

It was only to be expected after the Edison company was involved with the large Concert cylinders in 1898-9 that electrically driven as well as spring motored phonographs should be devised to play them. The former were always ungainly hybrids combining the CLASS M and CLASS E motors with the top mechanism of the CONCERT and creating an instrument of some weight and near unportability for the average household. These great machines never became very popular and today are not often found. There are reasons for believing the CLASS M preceded the CLASS E by a few months; both were dropped from the catalogue after July 1907 when the spring motored CONCERT was also withdrawn. At first they were listed as 'M' CONCERT and 'E' CONCERT Phonographs, but by 1901 had adopted their telegraphic code names of OPERA and ORATORIO, respectively.

Type:	2-minute Concert cylinders
Dimensions:	Height 13 ¾ in; base 21 in. x 10 in.
Weight	73 lb.
Motor:	Standard electric of the CLASS M (battery) and CLASS E (mains) models, with exposed vertical ball governor. The CLASS M was 2 ½ volts. 2 ampères, later 3 ampères, the CLASS E 110-120 volts DC.
Cabinet:	Antique oak as designed and constructed for the standard CLASS M and CLASS E models, but on a larger scale. These never had a cover or a lid, nor were modified in the 1901 'New Style' and were never marked with the 'Edison' decal. There were the usual accessory and swarf drawers, although the latter could not fit closely under the CONCERT size top casting.
Mechanism:	The upper works were those of the regular CONCERT unit, driven from the motor armature by belt and secured to the top plate by the usual screws and rubber cushioning. No modification of this suspension, such as took place to the main models in 1904, has been

	reported. All models had a shaving attachment.
Horn:	A 24 in. all-brass horn and stand were regular equipment until after 1903 when a similar size black and brass horn took its place. Until September 1906 there was an option to take speaking or hearing tubes in place of the horn. In the machines' last year a horn crane was adopted, fixing to the back of the phonographs' bodies.
Features:	The patent plate carried the words CLASS M or CLASS E to denote the type of operating voltage.
Reproducers:	Early models were sent out with the Automatic reproducer and Edison recorder, but in 1902 the Model D reproducer replaced the Automatic until the end of the machine's time. Later the Improved Edison recorder was supplied.
Accessories:	Camel-hair chip-brush and oilcan. Several types of batteries could be bought for playing the CLASS M/OPERA Phonograph. All accessories and attachments offered with the spring-wound CONCERT could be fitted to these machines.
Price:	CLASS M CONCERT, later OPERA $85.00; £17 17s. 0d, excluding battery
	CLASS E CONCERT, later ORATORIO $100.00; £21 0s. 0d. United Kingdom availability until 1907.

Electric
OPERA
Phonograph
of 1899-1907

From introduction these machines could be had in special gold or nickel finishes but in time these options were widened to the following, all additional to the list prices:

Specially decorated	$10.00;	£2 2s. 0d.
Gold plated	$50.00;	£10 10s. 0d.
Nickel plated	$25.00;	£5 5s. 0d.
Mahogany cabinets	$4.00;	17s. 0d.

Chapter 11
ALVA
Phonograph

In 1906 there was a move towards bettering Edison electric phonographs, especially those installed in coin-slot machines. These had remained basically unchanged since the improved machines of 1888 with the large vertically mounted motor and open governor on the top plate. Another influence was pressure exerted by the New York Phonograph Company's claim to patents disallowing the use of vertically mounted electric motors in phonographs sold in New York state.

Smaller and more efficient motors were coming into general use and wider access to AC mains electricity in towns made these machines more attractive, although the Edison company could never envisage large sales but felt the new instrument would commend itself to a certain class of customer".

The ALVA was first announced by C. H. Wilson, Assistant General Manager of National Phonograph on May 16th 1907, to sell for $80.00.

It used the case and much of the mechanism of the TRIUMPH and passed through the several

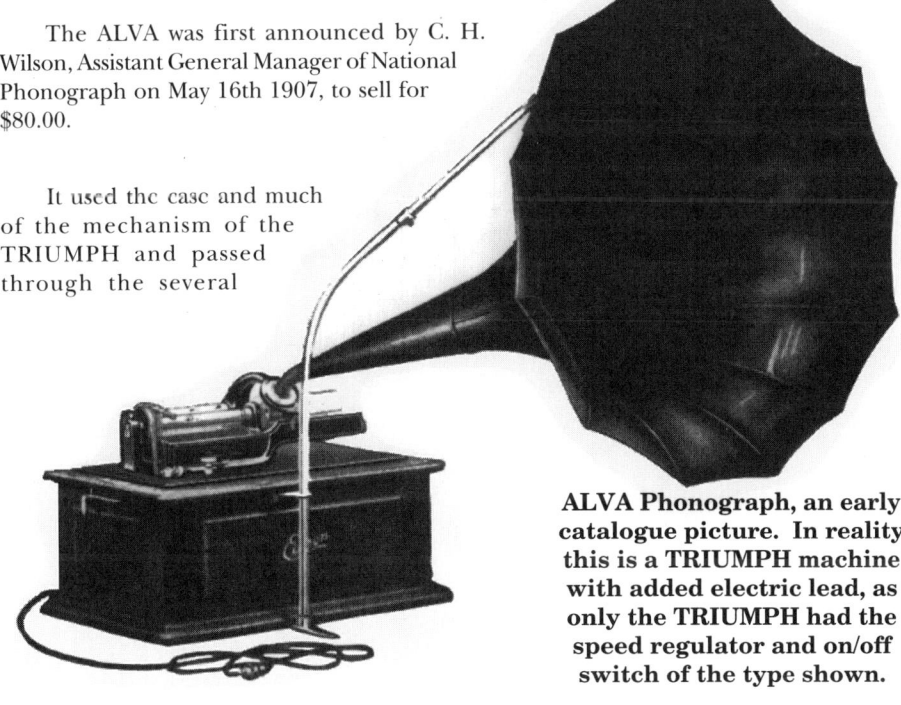

ALVA Phonograph, an early catalogue picture. In reality this is a TRIUMPH machine with added electric lead, as only the TRIUMPH had the speed regulator and on/off switch of the type shown.

161

models (B, C, D & E) of that machine from its introduction until 1912 and parallel reference should be made to the TRIUMPH for accessories, attachments, horn equipment and so on, as these were supplied similarly for both machines.

The ALVA motor and mechanism were also introduced into a coin-slot phonograph and given the name. Many of the motors were made by The Burke Electrical Company of Erie, Pennsylvania.

ALVA Phonograph Model D, fitted with Model D Repeating Attachment

Introduction:	July 1907 (U.S.); September 1907 (U.K.)
Type:	Initially 2-minute, combination models being available from October 1908 (U.S.) and 1909 (U.K.)
Dimensions:	Height 14 ⅜ in., base 18 ⅛ in. x 12 ¾ in.
Weight:	43 lb.

162

Motor:	At first this machine was fitted with a 104-115 volt 60 cycle AC electric motor, but soon after its introduction was given a universal motor to run on either 110 volts AC or DC. This model had three binding posts at the rear for selection of type of current being used, there being one common post and one each for AC and DC. Other voltages and frequencies were available to special order, but due to the problems of getting a range of motors this offer was withdrawn from December 1907. ALVA governors appeared in two versions, the earlier on Model B offset from the motor shaft and belt driven with normal friction pads, the later on subsequent models was on the extended shaft of the motor and also of the friction pad type. As with the TRIUMPH, access to the motor was by lifting its wooden mounting frame and tilting back.
Cabinet:	Antique Oak and identical to the TRIUMPH with lid securing catches at each end and carrying handle on the cover. The casing had the raised panels with the 'Edison' decal on the front. The patent plate was labelled ALVA
Reproducer:	At first the machine was issued with the Model C reproducer and Improved recorder, but on the introduction of Amberol records in 1908 the Model H was added. The Model O in the larger horizontal carrier-arm came in September 1910 (U.S.) and November 1910 (U.K.)
Horn:	Starting with the 14 in. black horn with brass bell, the horn equipment followed the same changes as the TRIUMPH Model B and following models.
Accessories:	Camel-hair chip-brush and oilcan. In the United States the current attaching plug was for fitting to the Edison (ES) socket. The plug type for elsewhere not ascertained. From October 30th 1908 the ALVA took the regular TRIUMPH Model D Combination Attachment except for the mainshaft pulley with a 2 ¼ in. diameter over flanges and $\frac{1}{32}$ in. smaller width of belt surface than on the existing pulley.
Features:	Early models had a shaver and end gate, but as the Model C came into production in 1908 these were omitted and the mandrel shaft supported by a central bearing. The shaving device was now left off.

Prices for all ALVA models:

July 1907	$80.00	
Aug. 1907	$85.00;	£17 17s. 0d. with new straight horn equipment
Oct. 1908	$85.00;	£17 17s. 0d. combination Model D type
		£22 0s. 0d. in mahogany cabinet with mahogany finished horn
		£23 2s. 0d. in mahogany cabinet and mahogany finished Cygnet Horn
Oct. 1910		$90.00 with Cygnet Horn and Model O reproducer
		$110.00 in mahogany cabinet and mahogany finished Cygnet horn
Dec. 1910		£17 17s. 0d. with straight horn
		£18 18s. 0d. with Cygnet Horn
		£19 19s. 0d. with oak finish Cygnet Horn
Oct. 1911		$100.00 with Music Master horn and Model O reproducer.

It was withdrawn shortly after this date

Further permutations on these prices were available in the United States with spruce and mother-of-pearl Music Master horns.

Special Equipments were available for the ALVA as follows:

Specially decorated, additional	$8.00;	£1 13s. 6d.
Nickel plated, additional	$25.00;	£5 5s. 0d.
Gold plated, additional	$50.00;	£10 10s. 0d.
Mahogany cabinet, additional	$10.00;	£2 2s. 0d.

Chapter 12
IDELIA
Phonograph

The IDELIA[1] was announced simultaneously in the United States and United Kingdom in October 1907 for sale the following month as a luxury phonograph designed to be acceptable in the more opulently furnished home of the time. It occupied this position until superseded in 1911 by the OPERA. For much of its existence the exposed metal parts were finished in oxidized bronze, and as they were made available all accessories, combination attachments, etc, were sold thus, albeit at a higher price. Similarly the metal horns were mahogany finished to tone with the cabinet.

IDEAL Phonograph, from a late 1907 catalogue. This had a similar mechanical layout to the TRIUMPH Model B. From January 1908 the IDEAL name was changed to IDELIA

At first the IDELIA was called the IDEAL for two months, but the name was changed from January 21st 1908 on the grounds of dictionary words being difficult to register in foreign countries, but there was an obstacle with prior use of the name by others, an error uncharacteristic of the Edison company with its watchful legal officials.

When it arrived on the phonograph scene in 1907 the IDELIA mechanism was the same as that of the TRIUMPH which by then had reached Model B, and from there it followed through to Model E, but always with the richly furnished cabinet, mechanism and accessories. The normal practice of giving Model letters to machines in the Edison catalogues was not extended to the IDELIA, although this phonograph went through parallel changes and improvements of its fellows; gate-less 2-minute IDELIAS have been reported with the letter 'C' as suffix to the serial number.

It is thought that production of the IDELIA was quite low when compared to other Edison phonographs, although perhaps the inflated numbering system of this model was meant to let us think otherwise. Until more is known about all Edison machine numbering, it would be injudicious to comment on the IDELIA system.

The IDELIA cabinet was like no other in the Edison phonograph range; the heavy moulding, square corner pillars and absence of cover securing latches will be noticed, although the baseboard was always given slots.

(Model B type)

Introduced:	November 1907 (U.S. and U.K.)
Type:	2-minute
Dimensions:	Height 14 ⅜ in; base 18 ⅛ in. x 12 ¾ in.
Weight:	53 lb.
Motor:	Triple spring Triton motor of the TRIUMPH of that time, belt-driven to the upper mechanism; this was essentially the same assembly as the TRIUMPH
Cabinet:	Mahogany, piano finish with pronounced moulding on the upper and lower parts of the casing, adding much to the top and base area. The corner pillars were square and reeded and there were end carrying handles. The cover rested on top of the case in the usual manner but without securing clips for lifting the machine. Edison sources claimed the heavier cabinet was contributory to steadier cylinder reproduction.
Features and Accessories:	The first model of the IDELIA conformed to the layout of Model B of the TRIUMPH and included the new feed nut spring, protector and adjuster[2], and the locking latch at the front of the straight edge[3] and a shaving device. The decal 'Edison' appeared on the front panel of the case.[4] The top casting, reproducer carrier-arm, handles and winding crank were finished in oxidized bronze as were the horn crane and socket. Supplied with a camel-hair chip brush.
Reproducer:	Model C, Improved Edison recorder, both in oxidized bronze finish.
Horn:	Polygonal straight horn of 12 panels, mahogany finish with gilt decoration, 33 in. long, 24 in. diameter, supported by a swinging crane. The horn was marked IDELIA (earlier ones were IDEAL) on a black and gold logo on the horn.
Price:	$125.00; £26 5s. 0d.

From May 1908 (U.S.) and June 1908 (U.K.) oxidized reproducers and recorders were available separately as follows:

Model C $6.00; £1 5s. 0d. Recorder $4.00; 16s. 6d.

(Model C type)

In the early months of 1908 (U.S.) the IDELIA was issued without a swing arm and the mandrel shaft supported on a central bearing, again in a similar style to the Model C TRIUMPH. The shaving device was no longer fitted, but a recorder continued to be included, and the price was unchanged. (See Appendix V)

For those desiring a superior finish the IDELIA could be bought with visible metal parts gold plated from July 1908 (U.S.) and September 1908 (U.K.) for an additional $10.00 or £2 2s. 0d. If a Repeating Attachment were required, this would be supplied in gold plating at no extra charge.

The regular Repeating Attachment in oxidized bronze was $12.50; £2 12s. 6d.

With the announcement of the 4-minute Amberol cylinders in October 1908 a Combination Attachment for the IDELIA was made available from November 1908 (U.S. and U.K.). This included a Model H reproducer and parts to convert the 2-minute machine to play 2 and 4-minute cylinders. Price $7.50; £1 11s. 0d.

Those IDELIAS already fitted with Repeating Attachments required a special Combination Attachment containing a suitable mainshaft pulley, November 1908 (U.S.) and February 1909 (U.K.). Price $7.50; £1 11s. 0d.

The Company, disturbed about the number of 2-minute phonographs not converted to 2 and 4-minute playing, offered 10 Special Amberol Records with each Combination Attachment in the United States in April 1910 for $8.50, and 5 Special Amberol and 5 Special Standard cylinders with each Combination Attachment in the United Kingdom in May 1911, price £1 16s. 0d.

From July 1909 half nuts were fixed to the spring by two screws. This allowed for adjustment or replacement.

Model D(1)

Introduced:	September 1908 (U.S.) and August 1909 (U.K.)
Type:	2 and 4-minute[5]
Dimensions:	Height 13 ¼ in., base 18 in. x 12 ⅜ in.
Weight:	53 lb.

Motor:	Triple spring Triton though with slightly modified frame for the 4-weight governor instead of the 3-weight type. To steady the running further a self-aligning brake was fitted
Cabinet and Finish:	Similar to earlier models, though a change to the joinery at the bottom of the case reduced its height by a little.
Reproducer:	Models C and H, also recorder
Horn:	The polygonal straight horn in mahogany finish continued to be supplied
Price:	$125.00; £26 5s. 0d.

**IDELIA Phonograph Model D 1
with straight Morning Glory horn**

Model D 2

The Cygnet Horn appeared in September 1909 (U.S.) and December 1909 (U.K.) and the IDELIA was given the No. 11 size (11 panels) at no extra cost. In this form it was known as the model D 2 IDELIA. However in the United Kingdom the IDELIA was the only phonograph sold with the Cygnet Horn until the October 1910 catalogue when it was generally available.

In the United States the IDELIA straight horn was discontinued as there had always been complaints of it occupying too much room space, but it was still on offer until the end of 1909 in the United Kingdom where it was also offered separately for £2 5s. 0d.

In June 1910 it was reported that Pope Pius X had been presented at a Vatican ceremony with an IDELIA Phonograph and a selection of records. This was instigated by Signor Bocchi, managing director of Aston and Mitchell's Royal Agency, Bond Street, London, on direct orders from Edison, acting on a recommendation from Thomas Graf, his London manager. The IDELIA was specially decorated, finished in white and gold, and emblazoned with the Papal monogram. It is reported that his Holiness expressed his pleasure and asked to have this conveyed to the inventor, and he presented Bocchi with a Papal Order of Knighthood, who was henceforth known as The Chevalier Arrigo Bocchi. The Pope was said to have been charmed by the recital and was attracted particularly to the self-recording feature of the machine to facilitate correspondence, and ordered further records to be sent a year later.

IDELIA
Phonograph
Model D 2 with
No. 11 Cygnet
horn

Model E

Introduced:	September 1910 (U.S.)
Type:	2 and 4-minute
Dimensions and weight:	As models D 1 and D 2
Cabinet:	Mahogany, piano finish, as before

IDELIA Phonograph Model E with Music Master horn

Reproducer:	Model O fitting the large carrier-arm. A recorder and adapter ring were included
Horn:	Cygnet, mahogany finish, with the longer crane to raise the horn to the horizontal carrier-arm fitting.
Finish:	As this model was only the Model D with the large carrier-arm in the 'on-top' position added, the earliest had the oxidized bronze finish, but after October 1st 1910 the exposed metal parts were enamelled in maroon to compliment the cabinet. The mandrel and horn crane were now nickel plated and the machine reduced in price to $100.00. Existing oxidized-finished machines were still available from stock at the old price of $125.00; £26 5s. 0d. There is no evidence that the maroon enamelled IDELIA was ever available in the United Kingdom and the few surviving IDELIAS there indicate low sales for an expensive machine.

In August 1910 (U.S.) Music Master Cygnet Horns were introduced and offered instead of metal Cygnet Horns, as follows:

IDELIA with mahogany Music Master horn, additional	$10.00
with spruce Music Master horn, additional	$15.00
with inlaid mother-of-pearl Music Master horn, additional	$45.00

Four years of an owner's improvements are evident on this 1908 Model B IDELIA (above and facing page). This 2 and 4-minute gear change date from 1908, the large carrier-arm from September 1910, the Music Master horn and crane from August 1910 and the Diamond B reproducer from 1912. All nickel surfaces have since been finished in oxidized copper.

Music Master horns were available in the United Kingdom from February 1912 and offered as extras, with cranes at additional cost. As the IDELIA was discontinued there in the same month, these wooden horns were never offered as part of its equipment. The later IDELIAS had a helical groove cut in the back rod like the TRIUMPH, and from February 1911 (U.S.) a record brush was put on all IDELIAS with Cygnet Horns and Model O reproducers.[6]

In a Report of January 17th 1911 the Edison Amusement Phonograph Committee commented that the IDELIA was not selling in any quantity and this resulted in an entirely new horn phonograph design by Peter Weber, to take its place. This was ready for inspection by August 17th 1911, and 12 days later its name - the OPERA - was privately decided and that its price would be $90.00.

Edison sources show model lettering of the IDELIA up to F, but there is an inconsistency if one remembers that the 2-spring TRIUMPH Model F - and the IDELIA Models ran parallel to those of the TRIUMPH - appeared in November 1911 (U.S.). This was the same month as the OPERA, the IDELIA'S successor. In the same way the IDELIA was discontinued in the United Kingdom when the OPERA was introduced in 1912, but foreign catalogues of Edison Phonographs have been seen where the IDELIA and OPERA were offered on adjoining pages.

NOTES

1) U.S. Trade mark No. 69,914 of July 14th 1908 for use on phonographs and horns etc. Filed March 24th 1908 and in use since January 21st 1908
2) U.S. Patent No. 821,071 for Phonograph filed by Peter Weber on October 21st 1905 and granted May 22nd 1906
3) U.S. Patent No. 878,032 of February 4th 1898 for Phonograph, filed by Edward L. Aiken on August 3rd 1905
4) U.S. Trade Mark No. 33,236 of July 18th 1899 was for 'Thomas A. Edison' and 'Edison' in characteristic autographic script. Filed May 27th 1899 and in use since December 15th 1897
5) The 2 and 4-minute capability of this type of combination phonograph was the subject of U.S. Patent No. 955,424, filed by Henry T. Oliver on September 15th 1908 and granted April 19th 1910. Its feature was the main pulley containing the sun and planetary gearing and the hollow feed screw
6) Edison use of a record cleaning brush was based on three patents:

   U.S. No.
   831,987 of September 25th 1906, assigned to J. N. Blackman
   832,249 of October 2nd 1906, granted to J. N. Blackman
   865,674 of September 10th 1907, granted to J. N. Blackman. The Company paid an annual royalty of $100.00 to Blackman, an Edison salesman and manager of a distributing firm in Kansas City, Missouri

Chapter 13
FIRESIDE
Phonograph

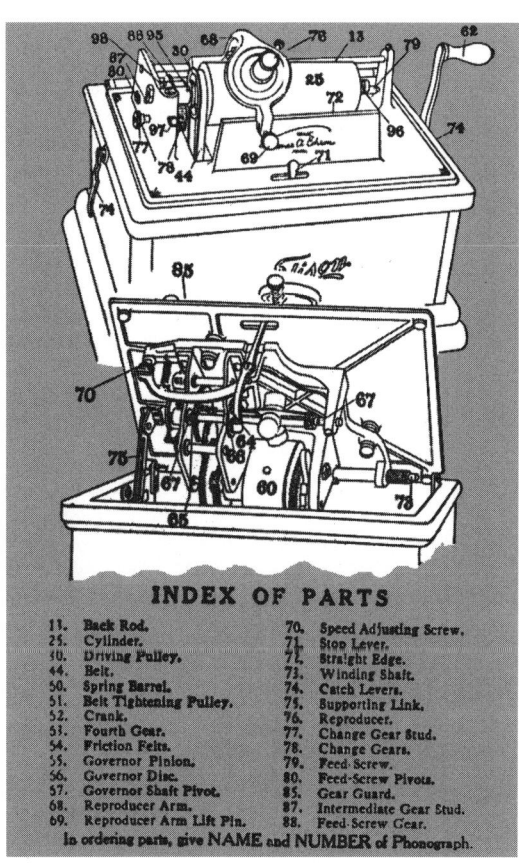

INDEX OF PARTS

11.	Back Rod.	70.	Speed Adjusting Screw.
25.	Cylinder.	71.	Stop Lever.
30.	Driving Pulley.	72.	Straight Edge.
44.	Belt.	73.	Winding Shaft.
50.	Spring Barrel.	74.	Catch Levers.
51.	Belt Tightening Pulley.	75.	Supporting Link.
52.	Crank.	76.	Reproducer.
53.	Fourth Gear.	77.	Change Gear Stud.
54.	Friction Felts.	78.	Change Gears.
55.	Governor Pinion.	79.	Feed Screw.
56.	Governor Disc.	80.	Feed-Screw Pivots.
57.	Governor Shaft Pivot.	85.	Gear Guard.
68.	Reproducer Arm.	87.	Intermediate Gear Stud.
69.	Reproducer Arm Lift Pin.	88.	Feed-Screw Gear.

In ordering parts, give NAME and NUMBER of Phonograph.

The FIRESIDE[1] was a combination type phonograph introduced in 1909 to fill the place left by the increase in price of the STANDARD, now with combination gearing incorporated. It had been hoped to market the FIRESIDE in the United States as a twenty dollar phonograph, but production within that figure was not possible.

Looking back from this distance, it is a little difficult to see why it failed to oust the STANDARD entirely, some of the parts were interchangeable, the FIRESIDE was more compact and had several improved features, including built-in 2 and 4-minute working for the first model and 4-minute only for the second; there was no necessity for combination attachments with the FIRESIDE. The motor was identical to that on the contemporary STANDARD with the exception of the second gear with the first pinion, the barrel gear and the mainspring[2]. This motor would soon be used for some of the AMBEROLAS. A new type of securing clip for the wooden cover was peculiar to the FIRESIDE, making it readily recognizable.

Perhaps the FIRESIDE never displaced the STANDARD because the STANDARD was there first and was an established best-seller of the Edison range, and people were inclined to buy what had been proved in use and what their friends owned.

There were just two models but a number of options with horns and finishes.

175

Model A

Introduced:	July 1909 (U.S.) and August 1909 (U.K.)
Type:	2 and 4-minute combination
Dimensions:	Height 11 in; base 11 ¾ in. x 9 ¼ in.
Weight:	18 lb.
Cabinet:	Antique oak with rounded top cover secured by special end clips. An 'Edison' decal appeared on the case front;[3] the FIRESIDE arrived several years after the banner transfer.
Motor:	Single spring with belt drive mandrel. There was no swing arm or shaving device. A push-pull button shifted gears in the upper train to make 2 and 4-minute selection by varying the speed of the feed screw.[4] The top plate was pivoted at both back corners and could be lifted back and stayed for inspection of the motor.
Reproducer:	Model K, recorder supplied extra for $3.00 or 12s. 6d.
Horn:	Polygonal straight horn in maroon with gold decoration. The earliest FIRESIDES may have been sent out with blue or black japanned horns, as available, and green horns are known. This FIRESIDE horn was an adaptation of that supplied to the Models B and C GEM, and in the United Kingdom to the TRIUMPH, HOME and STANDARD. These had been made in one piece, the FIRESIDE horn was in two parts that screwed together, and just above the suspension ring was a black and gold decal incorporating the word 'Fireside'. This horn was 19 in. long with a bell diameter of 11 in. and had 8 panels. A nickel 2-piece crane fitted a socket molded in the top casing.

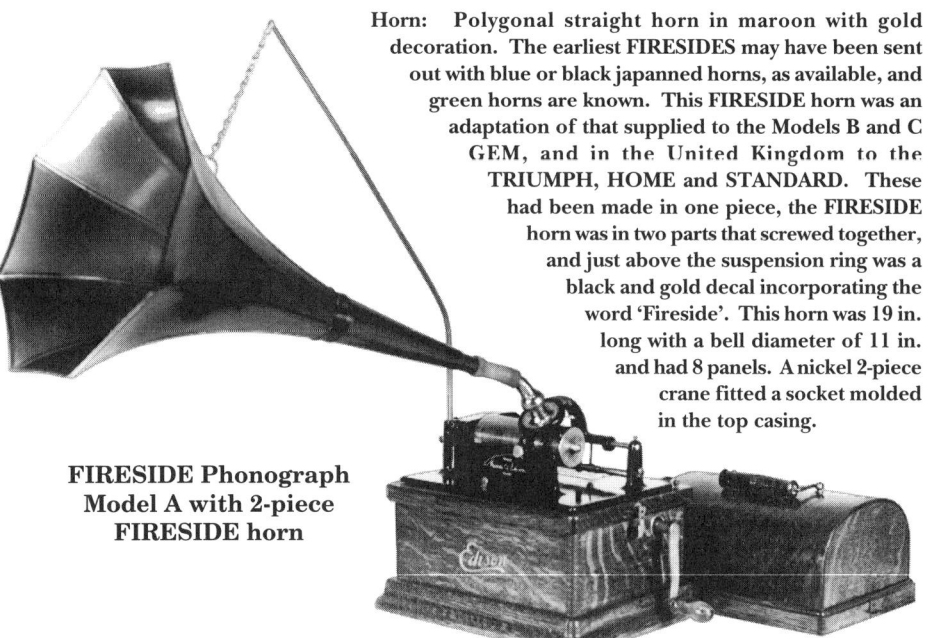

FIRESIDE Phonograph Model A with 2-piece FIRESIDE horn

Price: $22.00; £4 4s. 0d.

The following FIRESIDE finishes were offered from 1909 to 1911:

Specially decorated, additional	$4.00;	17s. 6d.
Nickel plated, additional	$25.00;	£5 5s. 0d.
Gold plated, additional	$50.00;	£10 10s. 0d.

From September 1909 (U.S. and U.K.) the FIRESIDE was available with mahogany cabinet and mahogany finished horn $39.00; £6 6s. 0d.

and in the United States with mahogany cabinet and black horn $27.00

or with oak cabinet and oak finished horn $32.00

On the introduction of the Music Master Cygnet Horn in the United States in August 1910, FIRESIDE equipment was offered as follows:

with oak cabinet and oak Music Master horn	$37.00
with mahogany cabinet and mahogany Music Master horn	$44.00
spruce Music Master horn, additional	$5.00
inlaid pearl Music Master horn, additional	$35.00

Matters in the United Kingdom moved a little more slowly and in September 1910 the equipment for the FIRESIDE was modified on the introduction of the metal Cygnet Horn, as follows:

with regular polygonal straight horn, as before	£4 4s. 0d.
with black Cygnet Horn	£5 5s. 0d.
with oak or mahogany finished Cygnet Horn	£6 6s. 0d.

In May 1911 (U.S.) and July 1911 (U.K.) the new Model R reproducer became available in place of Model K at extra cost, and the 2-minute Model C would be extra:$2.50; 10s. 6d.

By this time the options on equipment had indeed become complicated, and in November 1911 (U.S.) and February 1912 (U.K.) were standardized as follows:

FIRESIDE with polygonal straight horn and Model K reproducer	$22.00;	£4 4s. 0d.
with oak finish Cygnet Horn	$32.00	
with black Cygnet Horn and Model K reproducer	$27.00;	£5 5s. 0d.
with oak Music Master horn and Model K reproducer	$37.00;	£7 7s. 0d.
with spruce Music Master horn	$42.00;	
with inlaid pearl Music Master horn	$72.00	

With Blue Amberols coming on the market on October 1st 1912, plans were made for the FIRESIDE from July 18th. The Model B FIRESIDE would be a 4-minute only machine. 2,500 carrier-arms for the large reproducer were ordered, but the new model FIRESIDE would be sent out with the Model N unless the Diamond B reproducer were specified; this would cost an extra $5.00. The following numbers of finished models were ordered to be stocked for October 1st:

FIRESIDE	
Model A with Model K reproducer	200
Model B with Diamond Model B reproducer	2,000

Model B

Introduced: October 1912 (U.S.); February 1913 (U.K.)

Dimensions, Weight and Motor: In all respects similar to Model A, except the machine was geared to playing 4-minute only by the locking of the gear shift into 4-minute position and omitting the second gear from the mandrel shaft. All models had the large carrier-arm with reproducer traversing the top of the mandrel.

Price: FIRESIDE, with Model N Reproducer and:

maroon FIRESIDE horn	$22.00;	£4 12s. 4d.
black Cygnet Horn	$27.00;	£5 13s. 3d.
oak Music Master horn	$37.00	£7 15s. 3d.
blue japanned decorated straight horn	$24.50;	£5 2s. 10d.
Diamond Model B Repro., extra to above	$5.00;	£1 1s. 0d.

The blue japanned decorated horn was an added incentive to mail-order business. None has been reported in the United Kingdom.

By October 5th orders for the FIRESIDE with Diamond B reproducer totalled 2,555.

Within three weeks of the Model B's introduction Babson Brothers, the large mail-order firm in Chicago approached the Edison company for the FIRESIDE to be put in a special cabinet which they would promote. In reply Edison said that this would not be fair to other dealers and profit margins would not allow such a move and in any case the development of the Disc Phonographs was occupying too much time at the moment.

By December 30th 1912 the demand for FIRESIDES had settled at about 100 per day or 600 a week.

In March 1913 the company felt that although the FIRESIDE was unaffected by the larger AMBEROLAS, once the $30.00 and $40.00 concealed horn models were introduced, these would kill it, but as history turned out it was these small AMBEROLAS that led to its production for a further two years.

By midsummer 1913 the FIRESIDE (and GEM) were topping sales of Edison open-horn phonographs, the FIRESIDE'S output for instance showing 250 a week against the STANDARD'S 50, and demand for the dearer models of the old horn range shrunk to a thin trickle; with the order books for the smaller AMBEROLAS growing healthily, the time was coming to concentrate the factory solely on AMBEROLA production, and in October 1913 (U.S.) the Edison company announced that manufacture of all horn phonographs would cease with the exception of the SCHOOL model. This message however, did not cross the Atlantic in its entirety, where in an Edison circular to the British trade in December 1913, it was announced that apart from the AMBEROLA range, the open-horn FIRESIDE and GEM would still be continued; thus they are shown in a 1914 British catalogue, and were presumably offered into the Great War of August 1914 until supplies ran out. They were still priced at £5 13s. 3d. with Cygnet Horn or £4 12s. 4d. with 19 in. straight horn.

FIRESIDE Phonograph Model B with Cygnet horn

At the factory however, the continuation of the FIRESIDE (and GEM) was in part due to their motors being incorporated in the smaller AMBEROLAS, and to the company having sizeable orders for small horn machines on its books, in fact at the end of November 1913 there were well over a total of a thousand FIRESIDE, GEM and STANDARD machines to ship; these figures were maintained into early 1914, so the decision of October 1913 was gradual rather than sudden, and production returns of this time do in fact show that very few large models were still being despatched to jobbers, even being made up in ones and twos as needed.

That the FIRESIDE lingered into 1915 in the United States is shown by an internal factory memo of March 31st, noting that stocks of black Cygnet Horns were now exhausted, but that there were some in oak finish and these would be shipped with the phonographs at no extra charge. This was the ultimate clear-out of horn phonographs, jobbers were told to regard these as obsolete machines that could be offered to dealers and the public at reduced prices; this was a radical step for the Edison company to even think of a year or two earlier.

1) FIRESIDE for use on phonographs, horns etc. is United States Trade Mark No. 75,512 dated October 12th 1909, filed June 22nd 1909, in use since May 7th 1909
2) The spring in fact was the same as used on the STANDARD Model A
3) United States Trade Mark No. 33,236 of July 18th 1899 was for 'Thomas A. Edison' and 'Edison' in characteristic autographic script. Filed May 27th 1899
4) United States Patent No. 932,200 for Phonograph, filed by Peter Weber on January 20th 1908 and granted August 24th 1909.

Production figures are from the Edison Archive

Chapter 14
AMBEROLA
Phonographs

From its first appearance the AMBEROLA I was known simply as the AMBEROLA[1]. When the 4-minute only version came out in 1911 this was listed briefly as the AMBEROLA B but soon reverted to AMBEROLA as the earlier model was phased out. On the appearance of the pedestal model in 1912, known as the AMBEROLA III, the existing model became AMBEROLA I. There was no AMBEROLA II.

On May 12th 1909 at a meeting between Edison and the Company Executive Committee and attended by Jonas Aylsworth and Edward L. Aiken, it was agreed that a hornless phonograph should be designed for playing the Standard and Amberol records and Walter Miller was instructed to get the work in hand as soon as possible.[2]

Such an instrument had been in consideration for some time, the cabinet Victrolas and similar makes were popular and Edison owners - and especially their womenfolk - were calling for something more attractive, compact and easier for housework than the current range of phonographs with their projecting horns, cranes and floor stands. In any case the Company had decided to develop a line of cabinet machines to play the planned Edison Disc Records that arrived eventually late in 1912.

It was resolved to offer something of quality to compete with the Victrola, and would of necessity be an expensive instrument.

A major obstacle was that Victor held a number of patents for cabinet phonographs, but by careful design and by offering such a machine as a cylinder phonograph, a number of Victor objections might be overcome with the minimum number of lawsuits. Work was started right away and a prototype cylinder phonograph was put in the Committee Room for examination by Delos Holden, the Company's patent adviser, for an estimation of its chances.

He reported on July 2nd that it had many features of the cabinet similar to Victor design patents, in particular the hood and carved front corner posts. By cutting off these corners and making it octagonal, would it not fit better into the corner of a room, a good selling point because Victor would find this difficult to compete with commercially?

By radically modifying the cabinet's internal features, about two-thirds of the claims of a Victor-Miller re-issue patent of May 1909 might be avoided and the Edison Company would have to rely on its own earlier patents for dolls and other devices containing phonographs when it came to the enclosed horn.

Holden recommended that there should be only one compartment housing both motor and horn, the latter curving under the motor. This motor would be fixed to mounting brackets and kept clear of the cabinet walls with easily removable falsework laid around it to prevent small articles falling through.

Preferably the horn should not be sectional but extend in one piece from the sound-box to the mouth, and should not be fixed to the opening of the cabinet, and it should have no movement. The stylus should be moved out of engagement with the record by a device for lifting the floating weight, and the motor should not be cased.

Holden felt that subject to these points being met and laying stress on the single compartment, he was of the opinion that there were not more than five claims on which the Company could expect to stand suit and defend on the grounds of non-invention, and these were largely concerned with the situation of the horn within the cabinet.

From these recommendations of over 80 years ago, the owners of the AMBEROLA I can understand how it acquired some of its characteristics.

Experimental cabinet having a panelled horn, possibly the AMBEROLA I prototype examined by Delos Holden in July 1909

In spite of Holden's advice, the corner posts and Victrola type of hood would remain and the octagonal shape did not materialize, but the difficulties in the way of the design may have inspired Edison in August 1909 to submit a patent for a phonograph in a grand piano shaped cabinet with a straight horn on the same level as the motor, but separated from it by a partition, slotted to allow horn movement.[3] This patent was not allowed until January 1913.

It was agreed to accept a quotation on September 1st 1909 for 1,000 cabinets from The Herzog Art Furniture Co. of Saginaw, Michigan, at a figure of $28.85 apiece. The cost of the Edison motor and horn were estimated at $30.00, jobbers would pay just under $100.00 and the public would be asked $200.00. These were the earliest AMBEROLA cabinets and the first 500 had the lyre grilles.[4]

So as to get the new models promoted in time for Christmas, the trade was apprised in October 1909 of a $500,000 advertising campaign that was promised for the winter season and involving 450 newspapers and 25 magazines, many with 2-page spreads stressing the culture of the Amberols, and the instruments that were going to trounce all competition were to start going out in November for sale on December 1st. The advertising had an early response because 'up to noon' on October 26th there were orders on file for 1242 AMBEROLAS while the November issue of *Music Trade Review* was reporting 'immense Amberola demand'. By the end of November only 30 cabinets had come through from Herzog and the first (train) carload arrived by December 7th. Not only did the delays cause concern but so did the quality of the workmanship, and all Herzog cabinets were held back as not good enough to send out to the jobbers until corrected by the Edison works staff.

To relieve the situation the Edison plant was constructing and sending out similar cabinets to provide one demonstration sample to every jobber by Christmas, and in December embarrassed circulars to the trade apologized for the delay, promising early deliveries:

"We feel sure that if the trade knew the extremes to which we have resorted in order to provide immediate relief they would show their appreciation by a corresponding degree of patience"

The Company claimed to have been working from 7am on Monday morning to midnight on Saturday throughout February to try and get the AMBEROLA I into production.

In early December 1909 The Pooley Furniture Company of Philadelphia was approached and on the assurances of first deliveries in February and completion by March 1st, an order of 500 mahogany cabinets was placed. F. Pooley, its president, also submitted three sample cabinets to Edison "far superior to anything the Herzog people have turned out and they cannot be mentioned in the same breath". These samples were really intended for the planned Disc Phonographs, but the first cabinet was similar in most features to the model draughted by Peter Weber.[5]

As contracted, the advertising began in January 1910 and continued in reducing format through the year.

The phonograph trade and public had to wait until the Spring before there began to be sufficient cabinets to satisfy demand. Edison never used Herzog again and charged him up with having to correct the inadequacies of the cabinets. All concerned at West Orange felt humiliated at the let-down on top of all the publicity, and with the failure to capture some of the opposition's trade at Christmas.

The first to hear the new AMBEROLA outside the factory staff was Peter Bacigalupi, the jobber from San Francisco, who expressed himself in enthusiastic terms.

FIRST PRODUCTION FIGURES OF AMBEROLA Is for 1910

	February				March			April	
Week ending:	<u>5</u>	<u>12</u>	<u>19</u>	<u>26</u>	<u>5</u>	<u>12</u>	<u>19</u>	<u>26</u>	<u>2</u>	<u>13</u>
Shipments:	67	95	98	91	12	20	137	122	109	64
Unfilled orders:	1008	953	873	835	863	870	741	672	582	540
Orders received:	95	55	32	54	52	27	26	54	57	22

These survive in production reports sent to Edison on holiday in Florida.

The first Victrola had been a luxury instrument and had cost $200.00, so did the first AMBEROLA, and Edison in June 1910 offered a version in the current luxury Circassian walnut finish for $250.00, to show the AMBEROLA was "to appeal to people of means and refined taste".[6] The first AMBEROLA recitals by dealers are reported in August 1910, indicating a move towards the formation of early phonograph societies.

The restrictions of other companies' patents imposed several new features to the AMBEROLA Is, most prominent being the stationary reproducer and traversing mandrel, and there was a lever that raised and lowered the reproducer as well as starting the motor and engaging the feed-screw; there was an automatic stop.[7] No AMBEROLAS, in fact no Edison phonographs could have single or twin sound-controlling doors over the horn aperture until the Edisonic Disc Phonographs of the late Twenties. The motor was a developed Triton spring motor, but with two large spring barrels and a 4-weight governor. The AMBEROLA (A)-I had a belt drive and the (B)-I model was gear driven and played only 4-minute cylinders, and was also used in the later OPERA horn model.

On August 3rd 1911 it was decided that 2,000 cabinets be fitted out as AMBEROLA (B) - Is for entering the market on October 1st 1911, and that the trade be given every opportunity to clear stocks of the Model (A) - I; this would be regarded as an obsolete type but still obtainable from the works for a time on special order. By doing this, jobbers and dealers would be given an opportunity to divest themselves of the old models.

The future policy with the AMBEROLAS was debated in January 1911. It was now realized that the existing style was not popular and could not be made more saleable, a fact admitted among Company principals. The cabinets were inferior to Victor's, they were 'crude things' and did not appeal to the women.[8] It was no secret that cylinder sales were falling back, and a decision was made to respond to the trade and public's demands for smaller and less expensive hornless models, and in a tidying-up of the whole range straight horned phonographs were discontinued from this date. Not until February 12th of the next year was a decision made to put the 4-minute motor of the AMBEROLA (B) - I into the Number 3 Disc Phonograph cabinet, and one was assembled for Edison's approval; the new model was announced two weeks later as the AMBEROLA III. This would sell for $125.00, and 100 were to be prepared in piano finish mahogany immediately. There were the now customary delays but 250 mahogany and 50 each of golden and mission oak were prepared for July 1st 1912 and placed on sale in the next month.

There was an early pointer towards getting rid of the horn phonographs one day when the dealers had a shock in December 1912 to find their 40% discount on the AMBEROLAS I and III reduced to 35%.

Further new AMBEROLAS were outlined by Peter Weber incorporating a stationary mandrel, gear drive, new swivel structure for the horn, silent winding and automatic stop, and shown to the Amusement Phonograph Committee on April 11th 1912. It was decided that these should form two table models, the AMBEROLAS V[9] and VI, and would be put on sale from October 1st at $80.00 and $60.00, but mechanical difficulties and the works' occupation with the Disc Phonographs caused many months of delay[10]. Initial quantities of 5,000 and 10,000 respectively were to be put in hand, and would be the first Edison machines to be sent out with the new diamond reproducers.[11]

These two AMBEROLAS achieved a further 'first' by not being fitted with black silk behind the grille to hide the horn, and on December 30th 1912 it was agreed that similar silk masking on the AMBEROLA I and III be discontinued as soon as the horns in them could be painted to match the cabinets.

In spite of difficulties with the AMBEROLA VI motors the Committee pressed on in March 1913 with ideas for two further concealed horn table machines to sell at $40.00 and $25.00, incorporating the STANDARD/FIRESIDE and GEM motors. The problems with the AMBEROLA VI began to get in the way of future cylinder phonograph policy, especially relating to horn machines, and it was hoped that AMBEROLAS would replace all these at an early date. The motor was still very noisy and besides there was a fear that if marketed, the VI would inhibit sales of the comparatively successful and dearer AMBEROLA V. There were far too many rejections at test, and eventually modifications led to two variants being released.[12] In July 1913 Edison decided to have no more to do with the motor, and the remaining cabinets eventually had FIRESIDE and the (later) AMBEROLA 50 motors installed to clear them.[13]

In the early part of 1913 the new AMBEROLAS VIII and X were being tested, and hope was expressed that the playing time of the former could be extended to a full two cylinders. Both were put on sale in the October, not at $40.00 and $25.00 as planned, but at $45.00 and $30.00.[14] The AMBEROLA VIII ran to two variations although the differences were slight, hence there was no Model IX in the series, and the AMBEROLA X ran to four.

The only AMBEROLA not so far noticed was the model IV of October 1913. It owed something to the Mission or Arts & Crafts style of the day with a robust appearance and simplicity, and was out of character with anything else that had come out of the phonograph works. It was the only Edison machine to have a flap lid. An adapted HOME motor with STANDARD top plate was installed, but only 100 models were ever assembled and few of these were ever sold at full price.[15]

December 1913 saw an important policy revolution when the Edison Company announced after Christmas that all horn phonographs except the FIRESIDE and GEM would be discontinued and resources concentrated on AMBEROLAS in the future. It was the factory fire of December 9th 1914 that sealed the fate of the first range of AMBEROLAS. Plans for a new and simplified range had been agreed at a meeting exactly a month earlier when the Chief Engineer, John P. Constable outlined in a report an entirely fresh design to sell at $25.00, $50.00 and $75.00, with mechanisms and horns standardized as far as possible.[16] Five days after the fire it was decided to clear out what remained of the AMBEROLAS I - X.

The first to go would be the AMBEROLA Xs, and a start would be made on a $30.00, or AMBEROLA 30 in their place.[17] This was first disclosed in a letter to Edison's friend and loyal jobber Fred Babson of Chicago, in fact Babson was promised the bulk of the first production. At the factory a start was made on tooling up for the new model.

Of some of the model range at West Orange only one or two had survived the fire, with others there were hundreds of cabinets in stock or on contract with manufacturers, and in a report dated February 4th 1915 instructions were given to abandon the whole series except for the AMBEROLA V and VI, and that these should be fitted with the new motors, accounting for these hybrid models being offered alongside the AMBEROLA 30, 50 and 75 for many months.

SALES OF AMBEROLAS OVER 6 MONTHS FROM AUGUST 1913 TO JANUARY 31st 1914
showing orders Received (R) and Shipped (S)

Week ending	30/8/13		27/9/13		1/11/13		29/11/13		3/1/14		31/1/14	
AMBEROLAS	R	S	R	S	R	S	R	S	R	S	R	S
I	2	1	2	2	9	2	2	2	3	3	6	2
III	12	2	1	6	12	9	5	3	1	1	2	3
IV			23	-	3	9					1	1
V	101	42	120	63	115	136	75	98	28	31	53	32
VI	178	162	208	316	143	75	159	120	129	161	75	51
VIII	1416	-	322	820	230	348	82	162	14	38	51	15
X	2127	-	367		1237	265	312	1057	747	8	181	3080	1075

NOTES
1) The word AMBEROLA became a Registered Edison Trade Mark from March 1910 (No. 77,134) and was stated to have been in use from November 11th 1909. Interestingly it was renewed in March 1930.
2) At the time of this decision a further cylinder machine was authorized for playing a standard record and one of larger diameter. A catalogue of 25 master records was commissioned, all to be of high quality and to contain pieces by Beethoven, Bach, Handel, Wagner and others, and a listing of 56 proposed names for this machine was prepared. Further work on the proposed large records and the phonograph was held up by Edison on September 11th 1909.
3) U. S. Patent No. 1,050,355
4) The cabinets were made to Peter Weber's U.S. Design Patent No. 40,347 of November 9th 1909, filed September 11th 1909.
5) E. F. Pooley's U. S. Design Patent No. 41,732 of August 29th 1911, filed June 3rd 1911 and assigned to T.A. Edison Inc. Most noticeably the lyre grille was replaced by the more general rococo design. Pooley had designed original Victrola cabinets and went on in the late 1920s to design Atwater Kent radio cabinets.
6) 100 of these were ordered from Pooley in December 1909
7) U.S. Patent No. 1,220,480 for Phonograph filed by Peter Weber on August 6th 1910 and granted March 27th 1917. Peter Weber had in fact designed the mechanism as well. This was the first talking machine produced since the tin-foil models where the record moved under a stationary reproducer, a feature not unknown on recording machines. It was a design revolutionary for its day and conformed largely to Delos Holden's requirements.
8) Internal factory letter from F. K. Dolbeer, sales manager, to Frank L. Dyer, the president. (Edison Archive)
9) Joseph Rubino's U. S. Design Patent No. 43,896 of April 22nd 1913, filed January 22nd 1913 and assigned to T. A. Edison Inc.
10) Advertising layouts for the AMBEROLA VI were planned for March 21st 1913 but were delayed due to the high rejection rate of the AMBEROLA VI motors. Output of these machines was intended to be 25 mahogany and 5 oak per day. After tests running to 330 hours Edison decided on July 16th to discard the AMBEROLA VI and to put the AMBEROLA V in its place in a different cabinet.
11) To play 4-minute wax Amberols on the AMBEROLAS V and VI it was necessary to design a special Model N reproducer called the N-56, and having a special V - shaped weight.
12) These were AMBEROLAS VI A and VI B; for this reason there was no Model VII assigned.
13) These were AMBEROLA VI C and VI D
14) Several ways of making up machines to meet the planned figures were tried, but the small size imposed a power limitation and some patents to be avoided.
15) U.S. Design Patent No. 45,048 of December 16th 1913 of Frank D. Lewis, assigned to New Jersey Patent Co. and filed September 29th 1913
16) U. S. Patent No. 1,265,179 for Phonograph or Talking Machine filed June 21st 1915 by Constable and granted May 7th 1918 covers these AMBEROLAS. Two further Constable patents for features of these machines were No. 1,359,966 for the reproducer support and 1,425,177 for the spring shock absorber inside the mandrel
17) The policy of giving the Disc Phonographs a Model Number representing the price in dollars was also applied to this new AMBEROLA series.

AMBEROLA I

There were two models, the 2-speed AMBEROLA A with the belt drive, and the AMBEROLA B which followed, this having a 4-minute gear drive motor that was simultaneously put into the OPERA Phonograph. These large AMBEROLAS were sometimes referred to as the 200 and 250 models, but this was really an unofficial dealers' code for the selling figure in dollars, a practice encouraged by the company who would number the Disc Phonographs in a similar way, and also the later 1915 series of AMBEROLAS. Both AMBEROLA I models were also sometimes referred to as Concert AMBEROLAS.

The AMBEROLA Is were undoubtedly the most luxurious cylinder phonographs ever put on sale and the Edison company was proud of them in their early years. With a greater concern for publicity than grammar, Edison literature of the day called them"..........the most perfect of the Edison machines".

The AMBEROLA (A)- I had several cabinet variations of Peter Weber's basic design, depending perhaps on particular whims of the manufacturer and skills and materials available. The earliest were built by Herzog and thought to have numbered 1,000. The first 500 had the elliptical lyre grille, the second 500 are likely to have the first rococo grille* the front pillars having a bulge at the cornice, three cords and lightly decorated feet. The door had a wavy bottom and the hood exterior swept up in an unbroken curve. At the time that the contract was with Herzog, the works at West Orange were building cabinets to augment output, and variations then started to appear. When the cabinet-maker Pooley came into production in the spring of 1910 the rococo grille was modified to incorporate an urn or fountain motif at lower centre, and this pattern persisted until AMBEROLA Is were abandoned.

Soon the wavy-bottomed door of Weber's design and Herzog's making gave way to a rectangular door with the underside of the lower stretchers having a flattened cantilever; there was more decoration on the front corner posts although this seemed to vary from batch to batch, and hooved front feet also featured on some cabinets. In due course the hoods were given a stepped sweep and the cornice heightened and notched to ease record changing. Variations will be noticed in the lengths and positioning of the three vertical sound louvres at either side of the horn chamber.

With the Edison Diamond Discs in prospect some early AMBEROLA cabinets were modified by Charles Schiffl, an Edison designer and carpenter, to try and make them economically adaptable either as Disc or Cylinder phonographs. Cupboards for Disc storage were substituted for the Cylinder drawers, but Committee indecision meant final approval was withheld for some months as the first Disc mechanisms were far from ready. These equivocal policies of the time may have led to the height variation of two inches being found in some AMBEROLA (A) - Is.

---

*The first rectangular rococo grille had small scrolls at each corner joined by a margin, whole along the bottom, partially broken at the sides and wholly broken across the top. Within this marginal frame are two larger scrolls, centre right and left with two smaller scrolls at lower right and left.

A few general words about the AMBEROLA I may be helpful. The earliest lyre grilles were hinged on the left side for access to the horn, and held closed by a ball catch. A back door, also with a ball catch opened on the space behind the motor where accessories could be stored, but was ideal as a hiding place for valuables, or as a secret wine cupboard, a feature of some disc talking machines of the day. The rococo types of grilles lifted out of grooves in the upper and lower edges of the horn aperture, but some of the first are reported as being secured at the bottom edge by woodscrews.

The AMBEROLA I horn mouth was made of a fibrous material back to where it was fitted to the metal neck by a similar socket fitting as the Cygnet Horns; this metal neck tapered in three sections to the reproducer carrier bracket. The grille had a black silk backing on earlier models, but it was done away with in 1912 and the mouth of the horn was always painted to match the cabinet.

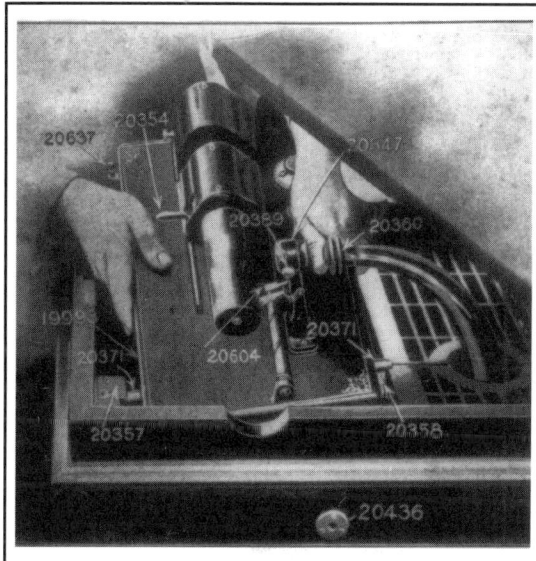

Index of Reference Parts

19993	Top Plate	20371	Supporting Bar
20347	Reproducer Bracket	20389	Set Screw
20354	Controlling Lever	20436	Thimble Hole
20357	Metal Bracket	20604	Reproducer Weight Lifting Leve
20358	Metal Bracket	20637	Governor Stop-Lever
20360	Screw Connection		

The Company's attitude to the AMBEROLA I reproducers is difficult to understand. It originally sent out the AMBEROLA (A) - I with the sapphire Model L for playing 4-minute Amberols, while offering no compatible reproducer for playing the standard 2-minute cylinders the instrument was also geared to play. One to be designated Model N was promised, but the 'N' never materialized in this form and owners had to wait until May 1910 for the 2 and 4-minute turnover sapphire Model M, although this was first mentioned in January, 1910 as being passed for sending out as soon as parts could be got ready.

The Model L was not entirely successful and tended to be too rigid and wearing, but this flaw was modified by March 1910 for all who cared to return their reproducers and the Model L could be exchanged for Model M in August 1910. The Model L reproducer was also sent out with the 4-minute AMBEROLA (B) - I on its introduction in November 1911

189

and when the Blue Amberol cylinders arrived in the next year, a Diamond Model A Reproducer was supplied and the Model L became an optional extra at the reduced price of $4.75.

A down-grading in quality, especially of cabinet finishes is reported by owners of the AMBEROLA (B) - Is. The maroon enamel motor bedplate coloured to harmonize with the mahogany cabinet, was sometimes sent out in brown finish.

Two styles of cabinet key are known, the earlier displayed a pair of dolphins and was of the flat type, the second was shanked and incorporated an Edison 'E'.

MOTOR OF AMBEROLA PHONOGRAPH

Index of Amberola Motor Parts

2132	Friction (Felt)	10713	Second Shaft
2729	Governor Shaft Bushing	10715-F	Driving Pulley
2732	Third Gear and Hub	10718-F	Speed Adjusting Lever Shaft
2733	Fourth Gear and Hub	10719-P	Motor Frame Screw
2783	Winding Ratchet Pawl	10721-P	Belt Tightening Screw
2792	Second Gear	10722-F	Belt Tightening Screw Nut
3258	Friction Holder	10730	First Shaft
3270	Second Pinion	19897-S	Secondary Spring Barrel
10701-S	Motor Frame	20338-F	Bell Crank Shaft Bearing
10702	Spring Barrel Retaining Washer	20340-F	Bell Crank Fork
		20341-F	Bell Crank Shaft
10703-S	Main Spring Barrel	20342-F	Bell Crank Lever
10705	First Pinion	20367-F	Change Gear Link
10706	Winding Shaft	20373-F	Change Gear Crank
10707	Spring Barrel Gear	20490-S	Governor Stop Lever Shaft
10710	Winding Gear	20637-E	Governor Stop Lever
10711	Winding Ratchet		

The first AMBEROLA I had a lyre-shaped grille. This factory photograph shows a very early, or perhaps even prototype, model. Note that the cornice is low and un-notched. The slots on the side of the cabinet differ from the usually seen graduated configuration.

Model (A)-1

Introduced:	December 1909 (U. S. and U.K.). This instrument was not featured in early 1910 U.K. catalogues
Type:	2 and 4-minute combination
Dimensions:	Height 42 in; base 21 in. x 22 in. The height may vary
Reproducer:	Initially Model L (4-minute only), but Model M supplied from mid-1910
Horn:	Internal, fibre mouth with metal neck
Motor:	New type double-spring, unique to this model, driving a traversing mandrel through a belt, and using some of the gears and basic parts of the TRIUMPH in a special frame. Its speed was controlled by a four-ball brake type governor, and an automatic stop was fitted. On this model only the starting and lowering of the reproducer point on to the cylinder was regulated through one controlling lever on the carriage. A master governor brake was situated on the left corner of the top plate. The AMBEROLA (A)-I and Disc motor for the A-250 had similar origins, but ended up with only three major items common to both, crank handle, spring barrel gear and barrel cover.
Cabinet and Finish:	Upright cabinet, floor standing on patent roller casters, four drawers each holding 25 cylinder boxes in clamps. The cabinet was offered in either piano finish mahogany or mission oak, but options to special order of dull or satin finish mahogany or golden oak. From July 1910 Circassian walnut finish was offered. Metal parts such as door knobs, winding crank and control knobs were gilt finished, while upper motor parts were in maroon enamel and oxidized bronze for mahogany and Circassian walnut, and brown enamel and gun metal for oak cabinets; variations of these combinations have been noted. An ornate decal in the lid stated it was an 'Edison Amberola Phonograph'. Cleaning brush and oilcan were provided.
Price:	Mahogany and oak $200.00; £42 0s. 0d. Circassian walnut $250.00; £52 10s. 0d.

The first rococo grille of early 1910 AMBEROLA

The second rococo or 'urn' grille on a late 1910 AMBEROLA.

AMBEROLA (A) -I phonograph in oak

Model (B) - I

Introduced:	November 1911 (U.S.); December 1912 (U.K.)
Type:	4-minute
Dimensions:	Height 42 in; base 21 in. x 22 in. The height may vary
Reproducer:	Initially Model L, but Diamond Model A from October 1912 (U.S.) and December 1912 (U.K.) If Blue Amberols did not arrive officially in the United Kingdom until February 1913, some samples would have been on hand for the Christmas trade and the new AMBEROLA

Horn: As on AMBEROLA (A) - I

Motor: Double spring driving a traversing mandrel through a gear train.
The 3-weight brake type governor was driven by a worm gear from a pinion below the motor plate. Only 4-minute cylinders could be played, and a similar motor was put into the OPERA; this was released at the same time as this AMBEROLA. Fitted with an automatic brake. *

Cabinet and Finish: While dimensions and prices remained as before, there were slight variations in finishes offered. In addition to Circassian walnut there was mahogany in dull finish and oak, weathered, fumed or golden. In late 1913 this was simplified to Circassian walnut, semi-gloss mahogany and quartered golden oak. A cleaning brush and oilcan were provided.

Price: As (A) - I

*U.S. Patent No. 1,187,115 for Stop Device filed December 7th 1911 by Peter Weber and granted June 13th 1916.

AMBEROLA (B) - I This model was now equipped with the OPERA motor

AMBEROLA II

No such machine was ever advertised, to avoid confusion with the two AMBEROLA I types

AMBEROLA III

Introduced:	August 1912 (U.S.); September 1912 (U.K.)
Type:	4-minute
Dimensions:	Height 44 ½ in; base 20 ¼ in. x 20 ¼ in.

AMBEROLA III phonograph

Motor and Mechanism: Identical to that of AMBEROLA (B) - I and OPERA

Reproducer: Model L, later Diamond Model A, on the introduction of Blue Amberols when Model L became optional

Horn: Internal grained sheet metal to match cabinet finish

Cabinet and Finish: Pedestal type on four thin legs with lower shelf. There were spells on three sides to retain albums for cylinder records; three such albums could be accommodated, each holding thirty cylinders and costing $2.00 apiece. The legs had chair glides. Originally the upper mechanism was in maroon enamel with gilt and blue ornamentation, the mandrel in gun metal finish, but in its 18 months of production it veered towards the OPERA finish of brown enamel and oxidized copper for standardization of production. Cabinets were offered firstly in piano or dull finished mahogany, or weathered, fumed or golden oak. In late 1913 finishes were simplified to mahogany in semi-gloss finish or quartered golden oak. The ornate 'Edison Amberola Phonograph' decal of the AMBEROLA I was retained inside the lid. An oilcan and cleaning brush were provided. The cabinet was designed by Edward F. Pooley, who in August 1911 was awarded three U.S. Design Patents for cabinets. The second (No. 41733 filed June 1911) was for an upright model with shelf. 100 were built before being modified, and in February 1912 after consultation between C.H. Wilson, Peter Weber and Joseph Rubino, Pooley's designs were changed to become Model A-150 (Edison) disc phonograph and the AMBEROLA III cylinder machine.

Price: $125.00; £26 5s. 0d.

A Recording Outfit for AMBEROLAS I and III was available for making records at home at a basic price of $8.00 or £1 13s. 4d. with a special recording arm and recording horn extra.

The AMBEROLAS I and III faded away reluctantly following the February 1915 Report on the works fire of the previous December 9th. In the *Edison Phonograph Monthly* of June 1915 several old-style AMBEROLAS were offered at full price and on easy terms. These were Models I and III (and VI and X) and may have been the five AMBEROLA Is and seven AMBEROLA IIIs reported in April as "urgently required to dispose", or the stock of a jobber disinclined to order the new range until the old was cleared.

AMBEROLA IV

Introduced: October 1913 (U.S.), December 1913 (U.K.), but almost certainly in circulation before those dates. Although allotted the number IV, this model was released out of numerical order. The reason for this is not clear, but it may have been decided to hold it back and put forward less expensive AMBEROLAS on the market.

Type: 4-minute

Dimensions: Height 41 ½ in; base 21 ¼ in. x 22 ¼ in.

Motor and Mechanism: A HOME Model F motor was fitted below a STANDARD Model G top movement, which was belt-driven; the lower pulley was noticeably larger than that found on the normal HOME motor. A hole was drilled in the base plate to allow a speed control thumbscrew to come through. The edges of this plate were ground square to fit against the cabinet surround. Of those top movements seen, all have been in dark brown enamel with gilt finish, nickelled mandrel etc. The winding crank was of the HOME type.

Reproducer: Diamond Model B, sapphire Model N optional extra

Horn: Internal, oak finish

Top view of the AMBEROLA IV motor. The motor was a HOME suspended from the bedplate and top works of a STANDARD. The STANDARD gear change was used with the 2-minute gear blocked off.

AMBEROLA IV phonograph

Cabinet and Finish: 'Craftsman' designed, standing on four legs with shelf for albums. Flap lid hinged three-quarters of the way back. Offered in quartered oak, mission design, fumed finish.

This machine's appearance made it distinctive among all the AMBEROLAS; it was different to anything that Edison put out either for cylinders or discs, and its severe appearance made it unpopular. Those who wanted the AMBEROLA would not have Mission style. A cleaning brush and oilcan were provided.

Price: $100.00; £21 0s. 0d.

In the February 1915 Report of the fire, it is clear that only 100 IVs had ever been built, 29 remaining in stock, with most of the 71 still in the hands of Jobbers and Dealers, the public being reluctant to buy at $100.00. It was decided to reduce the price to Jobbers and licence them to clear these to Dealers at whatever price they cared to. The breaking of the tight Edison Agreement on fixed prices was said to be justified as this was an obsolete machine.

197

AMBEROLA V

Despite its numbering this was the third model AMBEROLA in the series and it was presented as "the first medium-priced AMBEROLA with a concealed horn", and being a table model was recommended for use on private yachts, church parlors, colleges or seminaries. The instrument was the result of two years' study in acoustics, it was claimed.

Introduction: March 1913 (U.S.), but examples are known to have been ready for an exhibition in the preceding August. It was then shown as due out by September 30th 1912. In mid-1913 1,200 had been shipped out from the works, then at the rate of 50 per day. It was listed in both U.S. and U.K. Christmas catalogues for 1912.

Type: 4-minute

Dimensions: Height 16 ½ in; base 16 ¾ in. x 22 in.

Reproducer: Diamond Model B. On the appearance of the AMBEROLA V the Model N Reproducer was recommended for playing wax Amberols, but it was found not to function on this machine and the modified N-56 reproducer could be used instead.

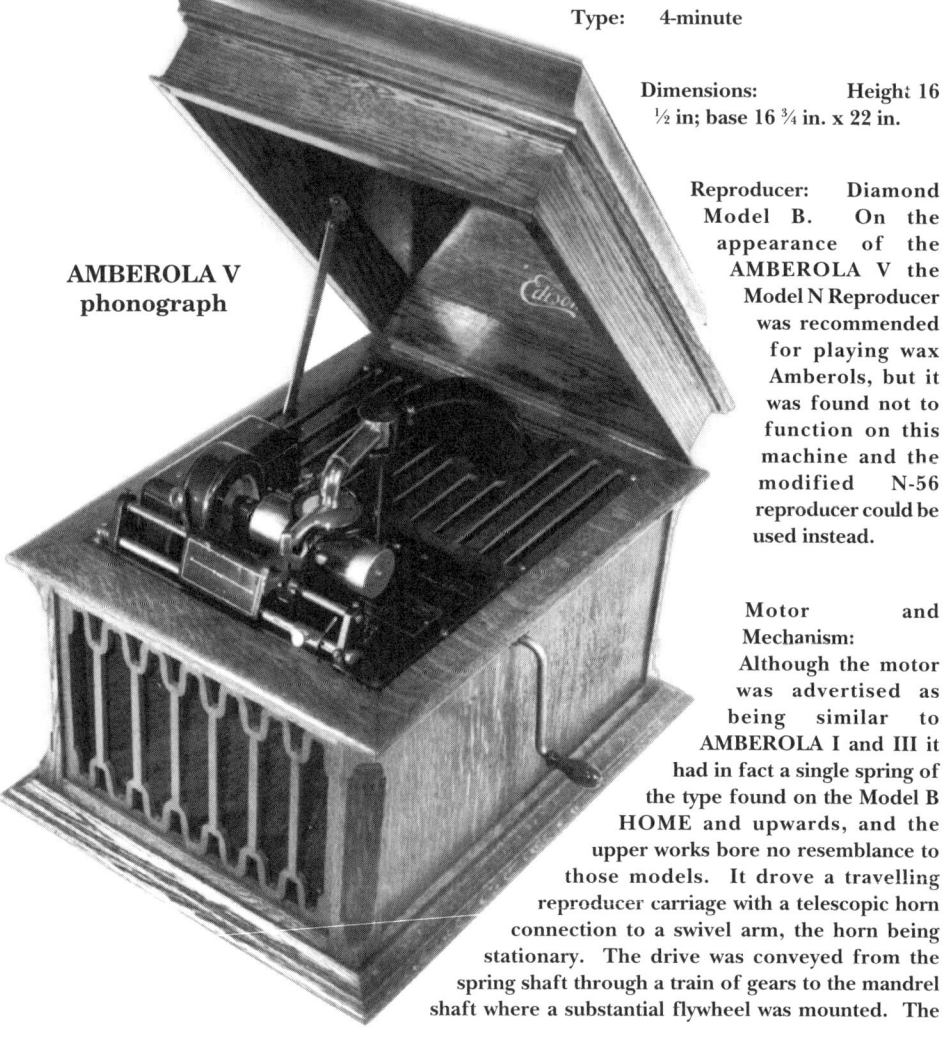

AMBEROLA V phonograph

Motor and Mechanism: Although the motor was advertised as being similar to AMBEROLA I and III it had in fact a single spring of the type found on the Model B HOME and upwards, and the upper works bore no resemblance to those models. It drove a travelling reproducer carriage with a telescopic horn connection to a swivel arm, the horn being stationary. The drive was conveyed from the spring shaft through a train of gears to the mandrel shaft where a substantial flywheel was mounted. The governor was worm driven. The spring, gears, winding crank, etc. were all set in stanchions extending below and were indeed part of the top plate. The carrier arm was supported by twin guide rods set in front of the mandrel and had automatic stop cams. The act of disengaging the feed screw also lifted the weight under the reproducer, clearing the stylus from the cylinder, and this movement made the design of the N-56 reproducer necessary.

Cabinet and Finish: Table model, finished in piano or dull mahogany or golden oak. In late 1913 the options were changed to mahogany, semi-gloss finish or quartered golden oak. The top plate and castings were enamelled in dark brown and parts of the mechanism nickel plated, with a male crank handle of bent rod. All four corner pillars were heavily bevelled, the hood was deep and had pronounced moulding. The wooden grille had six pillars, but at some time, perhaps later in 1914 but before the December fire, this model was sent out with a pressed steel grille with fitting grooves in the style of several of its contemporaries. Its wooden top grille was not changed.

A cleaning brush and oilcan were provided.

Price: $80.00; £16 16s. 0d., reducing April 1915 to $60.00; £12 12s. 0d.

In August 1913 Edison decided the AMBEROLA V motor should be put into AMBEROLA I and III cabinets, saying this would be a decided improvement, but none of these has been reported. A number of similar red herrings exist in Edison history.

AMBEROLA B - V

After the fire of December 1914 the stock situation showed that 33 AMBEROLA Vs had escaped, but that 859 cabinets were expected from the cabinet-maker; these would have to be accepted under contract, making a total of 892 AMBEROLA Vs for disposal. The cheaper AMBEROLA 75 mechanism was put into the 859 cabinets and they were shipped out starting in May 1915, at about the time the first AMBEROLA 75 started to move.

Price: $65.00, reducing December 1915 to $60.00

AMBEROLA VI

There were three forms of the AMBEROLA VI Phonograph until the factory fire of December 1914, being styled the AMBEROLA VI, B-VI and C-VI, and listed retrospectively as AMBEROLA A-VI, B-VI and C-VI, but a further hybrid model D-VI was put on the market early in 1915 to absorb surviving stocks of cabinets, and clear the way for launching the AMBEROLA 50.

There was difficulty with the motor from the start with a humming noise while playing. This was traced to a brass gear, but an aluminium substitute was found to wear out quickly. Four machines on early test developed 'drunken' governors and the mainsprings gave trouble. After 330 hours of testing it was decided to discard the phonograph in this form, but to use up stocks of cabinets Edison specified several changes. These included a new governor with a larger disc and hardened pinion, rounded governor balls weighed in sets for balance, and curved governor springs. The aluminium gear was proposed at the same time. There were also voices in favour of the AMBEROLA V in a different cabinet to take the place of the AMBEROLA VI, but there is no evidence that this was taken further.

Introduced:	Officially in the U.S. in July 1913, but examples were already in existence in August 1912 for an exhibition, and the intended date of issue was September 30th 1912. Listed in both U.S. and U.K. Christmas catalogues for that year.
Type:	4-minute
Dimensions:	Height 16 in; base 17 in. x 21 ¾ in.
Weight:	42 lb.
Reproducer:	Diamond Model B, sapphire Model N-56 as optional extra

AMBEROLA (A) - VI phonograph, close up view

AMBEROLA (A) - VI phonograph

Motor and Mechanism:
Single spring, much of this being set above the motor plate, and in this respect unique among Edison phonographs. Removing the gear cover exposed most of the spring barrel and the gear train that drove the mandrel. As in the AMBEROLA V there was no familiar frame for the motor, the movement being mounted in stanchions forming part of the top-plate casting. As in the AMBEROLA V the carrier-arm was fixed to double rods set in front of the mandrel and the sound carried to the horn through a sliding tube pivoted to the horn neck. The act of disengaging the feed screw of the travelling carrier-arm lifted the weight on the reproducer and cleared the stylus, a peculiarity of movement that required the use of the sapphire Model N-56 reproducer when playing wax Amberol records.

The mandrel was independently mounted on a hollow support shaft connected to an aluminium gear through a spring connection, and unusually the mandrel was cast and acted as flywheel to eliminate 'flutter'. Owners of this model have reported noisy motors attributable to wear on the aluminium gear in the main drive, and spare aluminium gears have been found with the machines.

The male crank handle was of bent rod and had a long shaft to reach the mechanism.

Cabinet: Table model, finished in piano or dull mahogany, or golden oak. The motor plate and upper parts were finished in brown enamel and nickel plate. The hood was deep and the corner pillars square and the side panels recessed. The wooden grille had six pillars. Late in 1913 the cabinet finishes were reduced to semi-gloss mahogany or quartered golden oak.

Model B -VI

Introduced:	December 1913 (U.S.)
Motor:	Single spring FIRESIDE type with conventional belt drive and upper works. The lower belt pulley was larger than that normally found on the FIRESIDE. 'Flat' type of FIRESIDE crank supplied.
Reproducer:	Diamond Model B, with sapphire Model N an optional extra
Features:	The dimensions and cabinet details were identical to AMBEROLA A-VI, but the upper parts of the mechanism were finished in black enamel. The pivoted tone-arm of the Model A-VI was changed to a ball joint and a perforated metal plate filled the space between the motor top-plate and the front sill of the cabinet. In the casting of the FIRESIDE top works of these machines the horn crane socket was omitted.

AMBEROLA (B) - VI phonograph, from a catalogue photograph

Model C-VI

Introduced: 1914

Motor: Single spring FIRESIDE, identical to AMBEROLA B-VI. 'Flat' crank handle.

Reproducer: Diamond Model B, with sapphire Model N an optional extra.

Features: The dimensions and cabinet finishes are identical to preceding AMBEROLA VI models, but the upper parts were finished in brown. The chief difference between this and the B-VI was that the FIRESIDE motor top plate was displaced by one of greater area, making the top grilles of the B-VI no longer necessary

Price: All these AMBEROLA VI models cost $60.00; £12 12s. 0d.

AMBEROLA (C) - VI phonograph

Model D - VI

The Report of the fire of December 1914 showed there to be seven completed AMBEROLA VIs in stock, of the A-VI type. There were 204 cabinets surviving or awaited from manufacturers and these were fitted with AMBEROLA 50 mechanisms. All 211 machines of both types were cleared out in May 1915 at a special price of $50.00.

AMBEROLA VII

No such machine was ever announced

AMBEROLA VIII

A further step towards producing a cheap AMBEROLA using a well-tried motor. In its early days a retail price of $40.00 was hoped for, but this was not to be.

Introduced:	October 1913 (U.S.). At or after this date in the U.K.
Type:	4-minute
Dimensions:	Height 15 ¼ in; base 13 ⅞ in. x 16 ⅞ in.

Reproducer: Diamond Model B; sapphire Model N optional extra

Motor and Mechanism: Single spring belt drive FIRESIDE or STANDARD Model D types with travelling carrier-arm connected to the horn by a swivel arm. The lower pulley was larger than that usually found on these motors and a minimum playing of two records to each wind was expected of this model.

Cabinet: Table type in plain golden oak, dull finish. Elaborate ogee lid capping an otherwise rather plain machine. Pressed metal grilles were set in front of and behind the motor top-plate, and the wooden fret had six pillars.

AMBEROLA VIII phonograph

Form No. 533—11-1-04.

ANTIQUE CYLINDER and DISC PHONOGRAPHS
Bought, Sold and Repaired
MORNING GLORY, BELL HORNS
CYLINDER RECORDS
OLD POPULAR SHEET MUSIC

AL. GERICHTEN

23 Waldo Ave.
Bloomfield, N. J. 07003

(201) 748-8046

Directions for
Setting Up and Operating the
EDISON TRIUMPH Phonograph.

NOTICE.

Every Edison Phonograph and every Edison Record and Blank is sold by the NATIONAL PHONOGRAPH COMPANY under restrictions as to the persons to whom and the prices at which such Phonographs, Records and Blanks are to be sold, and as to the removal or change in whole or in part of the serial numbers on such Phonographs. Any violation of such restrictions terminates the license to use and vend such Phonographs, Records and Blanks implied from the sale thereof, and any subsequent use or sale of such Phonographs, Records or Blanks is an infringement of the Edison patents.

**National Phonograph Co.,
Orange, N. J., U. S. A.**

The Edison TRIUMPH Phonograph

Same Instructions Apply to the Edison Concert Phonograph

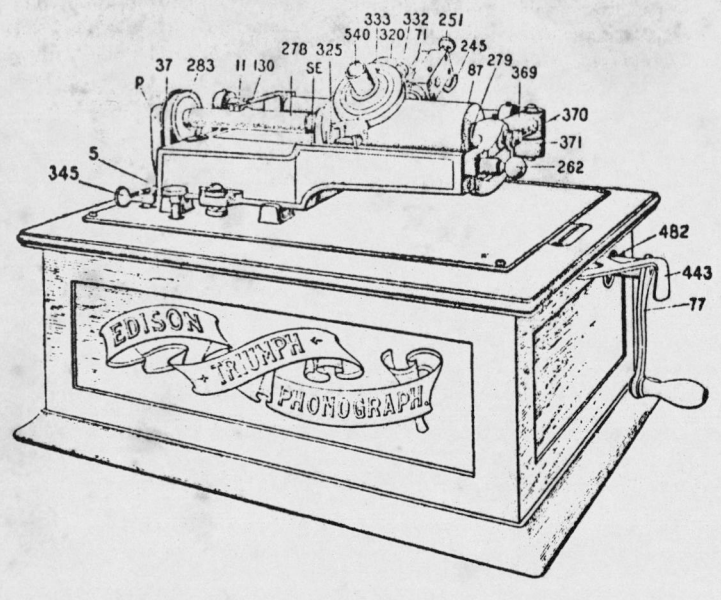

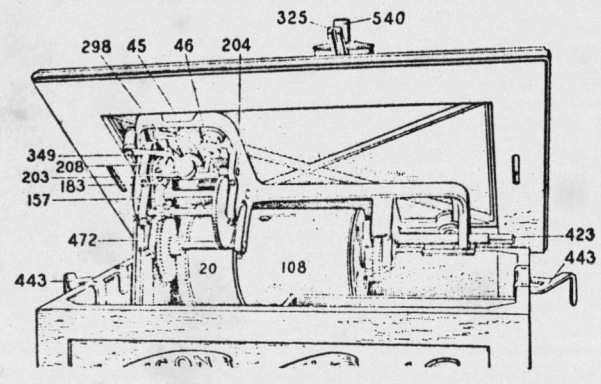

INDEX OF PARTS.

- 5. Speed Adjusting Screw.
- 11. Back Rod.
- 20. Single Barrel.
- 37. Belt.
- 45. Belt Tightening Screw.
- 46. Belt Tightening Nut.
- 71. Chip Chute.
- 77. Crank.
- 87. Taper Cylinder.
- 108. Double Barrel.
- 130. Feed Nut.
- 157. Fourth Gear.
- 183. Friction Felt.
- 203. Governor Shaft.
- 204. Governor Shaft Bearing.
- 208. Governor Disc.
- 238. Shaving Knife Knob.
- 245. Shaving Knife Lever.
- 262. Lock Bolt Knob.
- 278. Main Shaft.
- 279. Main Shaft Center.
- 280. Main Shaft Pulley.
- 298. Friction Rocker.
- 320. Reproducer Arm.
- 325. Lift Lever.
- 332. Reproducer Clamp Screw.
- 333. Reproducer Locating Pin.
- 345. Starting Lever.
- 349. Starting Lever Spring.
- 369. Swing Arm.
- 370. Swing Arm Center.
- 371. Swing Arm Center Adjusting Screw.
- 423. Winding Shaft.
- 443. Catch Lever.
- 472. Supporting Link.
- 482. Crank Hole Thimble.
- 540. Reproducer Cup.

State name and number of your Phonograph when ordering supplies.

DIRECTIONS FOR OPERATING.
Read these directions before operating the instrument.

1. Unpack the case carefully.
2. Pull out catch lever (443) on each side of the cabinet and lift off the top.
3. Remove carefully all fastenings and paper that hold the different parts during transportation, especially the rubber band which holds the reproducer weight.
4. Get access to the inside of lower case by raising table (upon which the machine rests) at the front high enough to allow the supporting link (472) at the inner and left hand side to drop into the catch
5. Take out the padding under spring barrel (108) and while motor and gears are exposed in full view apply a drop of Phonograph oil to friction felt (183) which comes in contact with brass governor disc (208) and to each center of the governor shaft (203) and other bearings Be sure that there is no excelsior between the teeth of the gears especially between the teeth of the fine g vernor pinion and large gear (157) that engages the governor pinion. A little vaseline applied to these fine gears is beneficial
6. Before closing the lid of table set the machine in motion by pushing starting lever (345) toward the left and observe if the motor is running smoothly Close the lid of table by holding it up at the front with right hand and push supporting link (472) off the catch pin with the left hand. Lower it gently.
7. Clean off with soft cloth all the upper parts of the machine and wipe off back rod (11) and top of straight edge (SE). Apply now and occasionally afterward a few drops of Phonograph oil to the back rod (11) and straight edge (SE) but first always wipe off dust and gum The threads of the main shaft (278) and both main shaft centers (279) require oil occasionally.
8. Raise lift lever (325) and slide reproducer arm (320) to the left as far as it will go. Lift lever should always be up when the machine is not in operation. Push catch levers (443) into place against side of case. Insert crank (77) through thimble hole (482) on right side of case Turn crank to the right as long as it can be turned, then attach horn to tube or reproducer (540) and machine is ready for reproducing.
9. Push down the lock bolt knob (262), pull the swing arm (369) wide open and place Record on taper cylinder (87), (bevel end first) push it on as far as it will go with a slight pressure Next close swing arm (369) and pull up the knob (262). Start motor by pushing starting lever (345) to the left as far as it will go and slide reproducer arm (320) to the point where the Record seems to begin and turn down lift lever (325) This engages feed nut (130) with thread of main shaft and also brings the sapphire point on reproducer in contact with surface of Record. When reproducer has traveled to the end of the Record raise up lift lever (325) and stop machine by pushing the starting lever (345) to the right. Then slide reproducer arm (320) to about the center of the cylinder and with three fingers of the left hand loosen the Record from the cylinder by pushing it toward the right. Then open swing arm (369) and take off Record with right hand. To play another Record repeat the above operations.

SPEED OF CYLINDER, 160 REVOLUTIONS PER MINUTE.

All master Records, from which Edison Gold Moulded Records are made, are recorded at a speed of 160 revolutions per minute. To reproduce these Records perfectly it is absolutely necessary that the Phonograph cylinder should run at the same speed (160 revolutions per minute), no more, no less.

Every Phonograph is adjusted to run 160 revolutions per minute, but after a machine leaves the inspector's hands, the speed adjusting screw (5) may be inadvertently turned, thereby changing the speed.

The announcement at the beginning of the Record should sound perfectly natural; if not, the speed is either too fast or too slow and is to be regulated by the speed adjusting screw (5). A more correct way to adjust the speed of the machine is to start the machine running, drop lift lever (325) (so as to apply the same friction as when the machine is reproducing), rest thumb of left hand against top of post (P) at the left of machine and with the forefinger lightly touch set screw of the main shaft pulley (283) as it revolves; take watch in right hand and count the revolutions. The set screw should strike finger between 26 and 27 times in ten seconds. If set screw strikes finger more or less than 26 or 27 times the speed is not correct and is to be regulated by speed adjusting screw (5). If once adjusted for correct speed there should be no occasion for changing it unless it is desired to reproduce a special Record which has been recorded at a different speed.

If a large horn is used, requiring a horn crane or horn stand, the crane or stand should be adjusted so that the small chain from which the horn is suspended hangs in a vertical position.

Sometimes the machine may repeat or tremble; this may be caused by the Record being loose on the cylinder, in which case a light push at the end of the Record will fasten it; or the reproducer weight may be caught; in this case raise lift lever (325) and drop it again gently. This also happens when the machine is set on a table or other surface which is not perfectly level, which allows the reproducer weight to lean toward the lower side. It is therefore important that the machine should set on a level surface.

If the machine should not run freely, apply a drop of oil to centers and thread of main shaft; back rod (11) and straight edge (SE) should also be cleaned and oiled; also look at belt (37), as it may have run on the flange of the pulley, which would retard the motion. After a time the belt may become too long or loose, so that it will slip on the main shaft pulley (283), in which case it should be tightened by turning the knurled nut (16) on belt tightening screw (45) to the left slightly.

If gears become noisy, put a few drops of oil on the teeth. Above all, keep the machine clean, as the mechanism will not work properly unless free from grit.

Always keep the cabinet top on the machine when not in operation to prevent dust from accumulating on the working parts.

HANDLING CYLINDERS.

The high speed Edison Gold Moulded Records are made of an entirely new composition, much harder than the ordinary wax Record. They may be handled without fear of spoiling the surface with finger marks; they are not, however, indestructible.

Cylinders should be kept in boxes or cabinets made for the purpose, which have perpendicular pegs at fixed distances to prevent cylinders from coming in contact with each other.

Do not leave the cylinder upon the mandrel (87) of the Phonograph for any length of time when the machine is not in use.

AMBEROLA B - VIII

Introduced:	1914
Dimensions:	As Model VIII
Reproducer:	Diamond Model B, sapphire Model N optional extra
Motor and Mechanism:	as Model VIII
Features:	Instead of the two pressed metal grilles in front of and behind the motor plate, a longer top plate was cast that filled the top of the cabinet area and the double metal grilles were no longer necessary.
Price:	Both AMBEROLA VIII models cost $45.00; £9 9s. 0d. each

AMBEROLA (B) - VIII phonograph

Factory-made record cabinets could be bought to support these AMBEROLA VIIIs, but the maker or cost are not known. There were three drawers each holding 30 Blue Amberols and plinth and phonograph stood slightly smaller than the later AMBEROLA 75.

All stocks of AMBEROLA VIIIs were destroyed in the December 1914 factory fire and the model was discontinued. The forthcoming AMBEROLA 50 would take its place.

AMBEROLA IX

No such machine was ever announced.

AMBEROLA X

It took the Company four attempts to make this a wholly successful machine, the first three using the small GEM motor or elements of it, and resorting to the FIRESIDE in the fourth. Quite simply the diamond reproducer was too heavy and the machine fell short of a minimum playing of 1 ½ records to one winding. The GEM springs were much tested and modified and various bearings were tried including the Arguta wood compound, vegetable ivory and boxwood. The governor was improved by making the balls lighter.

No evidence has been seen of any enumerating of these machines other than Models X and D-X; the modified models in between seem to have been sent out unheralded. It was not until after their discontinuance and the Model D-X mutated to the AMBEROLA 30 that Edison literature made reference to the (A) - X, (B) - X and (C) - X, but the D- X was a contemporary appellation.

**AMBEROLA X
phonograph**

Model (A) - X

Introduced: October 1913 (U.S.). At or after this date in the U.K.

Motor: Single spring belt drive with travelling carrier-arm connected to the horn by a swivel arm. The GEM Model D and E motor was used, but with a wider mechanism (or motor frame), using fractionally longer spacers and shafts to accommodate a spring $^3/_{16}$ in. wider. Rod type push-to-wind crank handle.

Model (B) - X

Introduced: November 1913 (U.S,)

Motor: The GEM Model D and E was still used, but in September 1913 the side-members were thickened and the pulley shaft diameter was recommended to be increased from $^1/_8$ in, to $^3/_{16}$ in. A heavier ball-governor was suggested and the belt-idler moved from the slack side to the driving side of the belt. It is not clear to what extent these modifications were carried into effect. The spring was made longer and wider.

Model (C) - X

Introduced: To be determined

Motor: The GEM type motor was discontinued and the end-frames re-modelled, requiring the re-positioning of the winding shaft, and this was still provided with a push-to-wind crank handle. This new frame directed the unwinding open spring outwards from the motor rather than downwards towards the horn neck, as had happened on the two previous models.

Model D - X

Introduced: July 1914

Motor: FIRESIDE type motor with FIRESIDE type of crank set through an escutcheon plate. The earlier push-in cranks used a ferrule.

The history behind these four models is not well-defined and would benefit from further researching.

The following details were applicable to all four models :

Type:	4-minute
Dimensions:	Height 13 ⅜ in; base 12 ¾ in. x 15 ½ in.
Weight:	22 lb.
Reproducer:	Diamond Model B, sapphire Model N optional extra
Features:	The hood was deeply recessed and moulded, ogee style. The horn grille was of a metal stamping with oak grain finish. The front edge of the motor plate to the sill of the cabinet was filled by a stamped metal grille, with a shaped metal grille at the back of the motor top-plate.

Price: $30.00; £6 6s. 0d.

Plain belts were used instead of stitched ones on belted AMBEROLAS from November 1913.

On December 14th 1914, a few days after the fire at the Works, an internal memo was circulated, reading:

"Decided to build no more AMBEROLA X. Will go ahead with new type AMBEROLA X (AMBEROLA 30)"

This is described in the following pages

AMBEROLA D-X phonograph

THE LATER AMBEROLAS

It was either a strange coincidence or perhaps an arrangement sprung by an insider that brought a letter to the Edison company from one of its jobbers, W.A. Kipp of Indianapolis dated January 9th 1915, asking for a new range of AMBEROLAS to sell at $30, $50 and $75, the first two to be table models, the third floor-standing with record space underneath it. With the Disc Phonographs then starting at $100 this would make a well-balanced line. Since Constable's report in the preceding November had almost exactly outlined these models, this was one of the rare occasions when it seemed the company would rise to furnishing machines the trade was asking for.[1] Constable's report on this New Model Amberola opted for simplification of tools and mechanisms with a standard motor that would accept either one or two springs and two sizes of horn and an entirely new Diamond Model C reproducer. At first it was intended that both the $30 and $50 models would be single spring with the $75 model having two, but something caused a change of mind and the $30 became the baby of the three with a single spring and small horn. It was claimed the double spring motor would play through 3 ½ records.[2]

Six machines, two of each type were built on the premises for approval.

A starting quantity of 6,000 of the AMBEROLA 30 was ordered, and by January 2nd 1915 Edison gave instructions for the tools to be started, but the new model was pushed aside to allow priority to the Disc Phonographs. On January 13th a production schedule of 100 per day was ordered "at the earliest possible moment". The February *Edison Phonograph Monthly* forecast a shipment date of February 5th, but the following month's issue gave February 15th as the day when the first machines were ready. The chief beneficiaries of the earliest production were Babson Brothers of Chicago who got most of the first month's output. Babsons' even advertised a custom-built oak cabinet for an AMBEROLA 30 to be dropped into.

The Models 50 and 75 followed over the early summer months.[3] It was intended that the AMBEROLA 50 should occupy the former niche of the AMBEROLA VIII, all stocks having been lost in the Fire, and the Model 50 was first quoted to jobbers in a price list dated April 1st 1915, and by June production had settled down to 20 per day. The early days of the AMBEROLA 75 are not well defined, as its release was held back in February 1915 until more of the old AMBEROLA Vs could be cleared out. It was certainly being assembled in the May, and in June production was noted as 15 per day, and in July the first 400 were sent out to jobbers. No. 55 is dated June 7th 1915.

Judging from the Company reports, sales of the three new AMBEROLAS were profitable from the start and reached high figures in their first year. From October 1915, in line with the trend in the Edison Disc business, these phonographs were referred to as Edison Diamond Amberolas (and the cylinders just as Amberols), and this style lasted for several years. The brisk business called for the following numbers of cabinets for the first six months of 1917:

> Instructions for Unpacking, Setting Up and Operating Edison Cylinder Phonographs.
>
> ## AMBEROLA TYPES
>
> ### FOREWORD
>
> We will esteem it a great favor if you will follow these instructions carefully, and check off each successive operation as completed.
>
> THOMAS A. EDISON, INC.
>
>
>
> ### UNPACKING
>
> 1. Read the packing slip found with these instructions and check off the parts and accessories listed thereon when found.
> 2. Carefully remove all packing material, such as cords, cardboard, etc., from the various parts of phonograph, including the horn.
> 3. Cut all cords, as the phonograph may be injured if you attempt to break them.
> 4. Make sure that all packing material is removed before playing phonograph. Sometimes such material allowed to remain within cabinet will prevent phonograph from playing satisfactorily.
>
> ### OILING
>
> NOTE.—Use only Edison Diamond Oil.
> 1. Oil the phonograph when received, and occasionally (about once a month) when in use.
> 2. To oil phonograph, remove the top grille (T.G.) and apply oil at all the points listed below:
>   (a) All bearings in mechanism beneath the top plate (T.P.).
>   (b) The two oil-holes in top of gear cover (G.C.).
>   (c) Along reproducer feed screw, directly beneath cylinder (C).
>   (d) Along reproducer carriage slide rod (S.R.).
> 3. Replace the top grille.
> 4. To put in the front grille (F.G.), insert one edge of grille into upper slot at front opening of cabinet, push grille as far as it will go and allow lower edge to drop into its slot.
> NOTE.—The illustration herein shows the Amberola 30 cylinder phonograph, but those parts referred to in these instructions will be found similarly located in the other Amberola models.
>
> ### TO PLAY PHONOGRAPH
> 1. Attach the winding crank (W.C.), as shown, and wind phonograph fully.
> 2. Raise the reproducer by means of the lift lever (L.L.) and slide the reproducer carriage (R.C.) to extreme left.
> 3. Slide record (title end out) onto cylinder (C.) until it fits tightly.
> 4. Start phonograph by pushing to left the operating lever (O.L.).
> 5. Slide reproducer (R.) to right until the diamond point comes just within the left end of the grooved or playing area of the record.
> 6. Lower reproducer onto record by turning down the reproducer lift-lever. Be sure that the lever is down as far as it will go, or the phonograph may repeat.
> 7. When record is finished, raise reproducer and stop phonograph, by pushing lever (O.L.) to right.
> 8. Slide reproducer about half way toward left end of cylinder and remove record by pushing gently but firmly against its inside end.
> 9. To play another record, rewind phonograph and proceed as above.
> 10. Rewinding after each record is not necessary, but will be found more convenient than to allow phonograph to run down before rewinding.
>
> **These setting-up instructions may be applied to the 30, 50 and 75 AMBEROLAS**

AMBEROLA 30 18,000

AMBEROLA 50 1,900

AMBEROLA 75 1,400

and there was still a shortfall reported.

In November 1916 consideration was given to increasing the price of the AMBEROLA 30, in spite of a booming trade and the fact that the cabinets in numbers of 15,000 cost only $2.60. The entry of the United States into the European war brought the first increase to all three models from October 25th 1917 when a small War Tax was imposed and selling prices remained above the $30, $50 and $75 rate for several years. This rise caused the AMBEROLA model numbers to be changed to match prices as they went up (eg. AMBEROLA 31, 51 and 76 from October 1917), but this practice was not followed very much in the Works and must have been confusing whenever prices were raised. The AMBEROLAS were also offered with cylinders as Outfits and some of these were numbered in line with their dollar cost. The September 1918 increase was to cover expected diminished production and sales during 1919, the Company intending that there should be no drop in turnover figures.

Unlike the ARMY & NAVY Disc Phonograph the AMBEROLAS could not claim any part in winning the war. The AMBEROLA 50 was quoted on May 26th 1917 to the Depot Quartermaster for the Army in New York for $50, but he chose the ARMY & NAVY instead, and a Red Cross AMBEROLA 30 put forward for consideration on January 30th 1918 was not followed up. These would cost $12.89 to make against the regular AMBEROLA 30's $12.87, with a painted white wood finish.

In December 1919 John Constable prepared a report on the state of all disc and cylinder phonographs since the fire of five years earlier, and was critical of the later AMBEROLAS. They were too expensive and not as reliable as earlier types, particularly the AMBEROLA V, nor did they run as quietly or as steadily. In their original designs they had a better finish and reproduced records better in spite of a number of modifications. He blamed standardization of parts and cost savings for the deterioration in efficiency, tone quality and appearance. Constable's name disappears from Company memos at this time; perhaps he was tired of his advice being ignored. At any rate a further attempt to cheapen the AMBEROLAS came in the summer of 1920 when the cabinets were made lighter and simpler and other alterations proposed.

In November 1920 a proposal to put the single spring motor into all three AMBEROLAS met with Edison's approval but was not carried out, it would seem due to the matter of stocks and remaining parts. Despite this drive for economy, prosperity ruled at this time. A dividend of $400,000 was declared by the directors on January 6th 1920, being the estimated earnings of December 1919, while W. Maxwell, vice-president and manager of T.A. Edison Inc. forecast a turnover of $30 million for 1920 for the Musical Phonograph Division.

It is not possible to ascribe any cheapening of the 1920 AMBEROLAS to a slight fall in turnover in 1921 but there was great alarm at 1922 when the Board of Directors was faced with figures showing a drop of more than 90 per cent in turnover of the AMBEROLAS, and serious consideration was given to closing down the cylinder business altogether, but the Board was anxious not to cause losses among the jobbers and dealers.[4] From this time the cylinder business was allowed to contract naturally, with effort being directed to the Disc Phonographs and Diamond Discs which were also facing hard times. Old and loyal jobbers, their trade diminished, considered the time had come to retire from stocking cylinder phonographs. In December 1924 both The Kansas City Phonograph Company and Harger and Blish of Des Moines, Iowa ceased to handle Edison goods and in the next months Schultz Brothers of Omaha, Nebraska withdrew. In June 1925, after a year's consideration, Fred Babson wrote to Charles Edison reporting that he could do little more to promote cylinder machines, but he could still sell Blue Amberols, even though some customers had given up their machines. Charles Edison replied that so long as the Disc Phonograph had been prosperous it had propped up the Blue Amberols, but as discs were now making a loss, Amberol losses had assumed critical importance. Ironically the three AMBEROLAS had been recognized by the company as having a market among the poor in the south-west farming district, and now even their support was failing in face of radio and the automobile.

In March 1926 both The Buehn Phonograph Company of Pittsburgh and R.S. Williams & Sons of Toronto gave up Edison business.

In spite of this falling popularity the cylinder trade continued for over four more years, but there are few references to AMBEROLAS. The lack of profitable Disc Phonograph business meant that the company had thousands of cabinets on hand, and from 1926 some London No. 1 cabinets were given double spring AMBEROLA motors and put on sale as the AMBEROLA 60.

Stock sheets of phonographs over the latter half of 1926 and the first months of 1927 indicate sales of the AMBEROLA range of one or two a week, some finishes did not move at all. In August 1927 the Heppelwhite Disc Phonograph cabinet was advertised as the AMBEROLA Special Filing Cabinet. Without its cover the AMBEROLA 30 could be stood in the space normally taken by the Disc Phonograph motor and horn, and the cupboard housed 84 cylinder records. Its price was $24.00.

In February 1928 the AMBEROLA range was extended by the Model 80, made up of a double spring motor in the Sheraton Sans Inlay Disc Phonograph cabinet.

This was the last Edison Cylinder Phonograph in the amusement range, and all cylinder production ceased by October 1929. The AMBEROLA 30, 50 and 75 series were not advertised any longer although could almost certainly have been obtained from the Edison works if specially requested, and at the time of closing, phonograph repairs and spare parts services were still obtainable from West Orange.

An enclosed horn cylinder phonograph was reported as built at the Ford factory in 1916; it aroused little enthusiasm and further details are lacking, but was probably Henry Ford's way of showing his friend (and one-time employer) Thomas Edison what the phonograph should look like.

The motors of these later AMBEROLA phonographs were made for simplicity of assembly and economy of parts, the lower and upper works combining to make a compact mechanical unit. An extended winding handle bracket screwed under the top plate and its end stanchion acted as bearing for one end of the shorter arbor of the single spring, while in the double spring version the arbor was of course longer and needed a shorter winding handle bracket; it was a comparatively simple idea.

A new style of carrier-arm travelled along the cylinder and the small lever that turned to engage the feedscrew also lowered the stylus on the record. The power from spring to mandrel was through several large silent-running gears and the small two-ball governor ran directly off the mandrel shaft. The mandrel itself had an integral balance wheel.

The neck of the horn pivoted on the reproducer collar as it traversed the cylinder and was loosely pinned to the cabinet floor near the horn opening, and in addition lightly suspended from the motor frame by a spring.[5] This made for a rolling movement in the case, a system meant to give as much freedom to the horn as had been possible with the exposed Cygnet types, but perhaps an aesthetic improvement; being small however, the sound output was not so great. These horns were made at West Orange.

There is a noticeable falling off in the cabinets of this series and they do not measure up to the robust cabinetry of the AMBEROLA I - X models.

The early models had silk-covered grilles.

The AMBEROLA 30, 50 and 75 underwent the following adjustments and modifications:

May 1915	Top plates for all models simplified, two coats of japan black, no gilt except trade mark.
September 1915	Trouble reported with brittle springs. Tensile strength to be altered from 250,000 to 275,000 lb. sq. in.. Makers were American Steel and Wire Company of Worcester. Recommended lubricant dry graphite only.
September 1915	Two set screws fitted to hold reproducer instead of one.
September 1915	Spiral groove cut in end of mandrel shaft to accept collar and to allow adjustment.
January 1916	New style double threaded governor shaft first appearing on AMBEROLA 30 No. 55517 AMBEROLA 50 No. 6421 AMBEROLA 75 No. 3270
January 1916	Oil cup fitted to spring sleeve on all models
March 1916	1,200 spring barrels supplied to works found to be $\frac{1}{32}$ in. too shallow. These were dished before being assembled to accommodate the spring.
March 1916	Reproducer weight modified to allow more swing for limit pin. A smaller ($\frac{3}{32}$ in.) steel disc substituted for $\frac{1}{8}$ in. brass governor disc.
August 1918	Cost saving in Models 50 and 75 by new top plate construction and mechanism suspension.
Summer 1920	The motor was mounted on the body top frame with woodscrews instead of the three interior brackets with bolt and nut fastening; a ferrule replaced the winding crank escutcheon. Thinner stock was used on the cover moulding and cover panel made of 3-ply instead of 5-ply. Base moulding and cabinet contour was simplified to allow mechanical sanding, the lower grille rail was eliminated and base moulding was held to body with 5 instead of 8 wood screws. The side and rear panels were down-graded from 5-ply to 3-ply.
c. 1923	Governor with non-twisting device fitted; this inhibited the whirr of the governor springs.

In general several small variations to the AMBEROLAS 30, 50 and 75 are noticed; these may be grouped roughly as follows:

1) The first motors have the speed adjustment passing through the governor guard. Model and number plate riveted to the rear of the main top plate.
2) The next motors had fully enclosed speed adjustment, the governor guard having to be removed for access.
3) The next type had a bullet-end mandrel and the name plate screwed inside the lid.
4) The last and most commonly found type had the name-plate inside the lid or body and a return to the flat-ended mandrel. The name plates started as brass but in time became anodized aluminium, perhaps from March 1916.

AMBEROLA 30

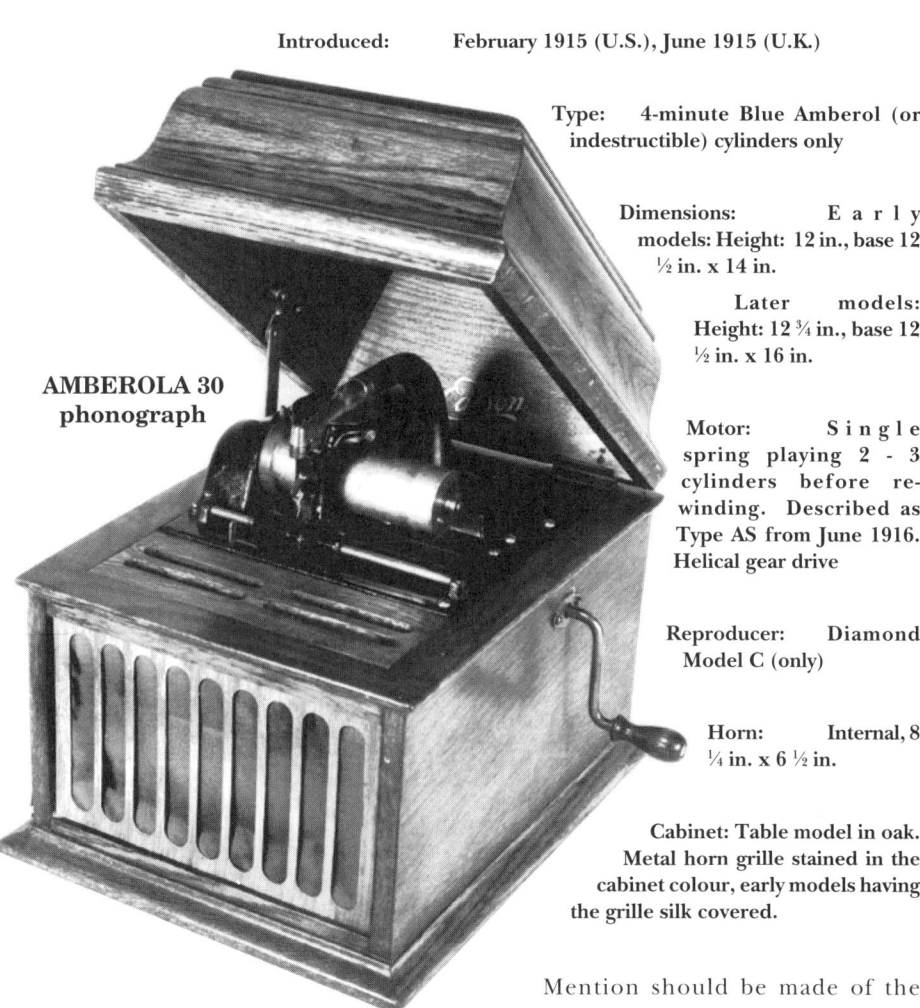

AMBEROLA 30 phonograph

Introduced: February 1915 (U.S.), June 1915 (U.K.)

Type: 4-minute Blue Amberol (or indestructible) cylinders only

Dimensions: Early models: Height: 12 in., base 12 ½ in. x 14 in.

Later models: Height: 12 ¾ in., base 12 ½ in. x 16 in.

Motor: Single spring playing 2 - 3 cylinders before re-winding. Described as Type AS from June 1916. Helical gear drive

Reproducer: Diamond Model C (only)

Horn: Internal, 8 ¼ in. x 6 ½ in.

Cabinet: Table model in oak. Metal horn grille stained in the cabinet colour, early models having the grille silk covered.

Mention should be made of the

AMBEROLA 30 in portable form as made in New Zealand, standing alongside an AMBEROLA D-X

Woledge portable AMBEROLA peculiar to New Zealand but existing in numbers sufficient to be included. None of Edison's smaller AMBEROLAS could be regarded as truly portable, the AMBEROLA 30 being governed by the size of its horn. Mr. Woledge reasoned that by reducing this and retaining the small motor, a compact portable model could be built. Constructing one himself in the 1920s he offered to send this to West Orange, but although Edison's company asked to see it and were impressed, there was little interest shown in marketing it.

Ultimately, after Woledge's request for half a gross of motors and reproducers, the company sent three dozen of each saying the matter was being considered. Woledge had three dozen cabinets and horns made, making the tone arm himself, and about half these machines were fitted with a clip-on box to carry twelve cylinders. Not hearing any further encouragement for his adaptation from Edison, he put the matter of the portable AMBEROLA on one side, but in the meantime (in 1929) the Edison company marketed needle-cut portables and discs for them, and there the matter stopped.

Of the original number of the Woledge AMBEROLAS sent out, about 29 were later accounted for, of which about six were actually found.[6]

AMBEROLA 50

Introduced:	June 1915 (U.S.), probably 1915 (U.K.)
Type:	4-minute Blue Amberols (or indestructible) cylinders only
Dimensions:	Height 15 ⅜ in., base 15 in. x 19 ¾ in.
Motor:	Double spring, playing up to 5 cylinders before re-winding. Described as Type ADS from June 1916. Helical gear drive.
Reproducer:	Diamond Model C (only)
Horn:	Internal, 10 in. x 8 in.

Cabinet: Table model, mahogany or golden or fumed oak finish. Early models had cloth louvres. A neat matching stand for the AMBEROLA 50 with a shelf 1 ft. from the floor was available, but details are not known.

AMBEROLA 50 phonograph in mahogany, and showing original cloth louvres

AMBEROLA 75

Introduced:	July 1915 (U.S.), probably 1915 (U.K.)
Type:	4-minute Blue Amberols (or indestructible) cylinders only
Dimensions:	Height 41 in., base 16 in. x 19 ¼ in.
Motor:	Double spring as in the AMBEROLA 50. Described as Type ADS from June 1916. Helical gear drive.

Reproducer:	Diamond Model C (only)
Horn:	Internal 10 in. x 8 in.
Cabinet:	Floor standing upright in mahogany, weathered or golden or fumed oak finish. Mahogany was more popular than all the oak finishes combined. A cupboard housed three sliding trays, each holding 28 cylinders stored in their boxes.

The distribution dates of these three models in the United Kingdom has not been fully determined. The Great War started in Europe in August 1914, some nine months before this range was put on the market, and priority for essential cargo coming from the United States would have been expected, especially with losses from U-boat attacks. It is not known how many were received in the United Kingdom before the total British Government embargo on the importation of musical instruments in April 1916. Certainly the London *Talking Machine News* had a regular (Murdoch) advertisement until March 1916 boasting EDISON GOODS STILL ARRIVING. The two table AMBEROLAS are found frequently in the United Kingdom, the Model 75 less often.

The next two AMBEROLAS were the last two Edison domestic phonographs and were made available in an attempt to use up some of the large numbers of Disc Phonograph cabinets that were not selling. In comparison with Models 30, 50 and 75 they are found infrequently but are known to British and Australian collectors. The Diamond D reproducer was developed especially for greater volume, although it has been said at the expense of quality.

AMBEROLA 75 phonograph. Each of the three drawers could hold 28 cylinders

AMBEROLA 60

Introduced:	Known to be in existence in October 1926
Dimensions:	Height 19 in; base 18 in. x 20 ½ in.
Motor:	Double spring, as fitted to AMBEROLA 50 and 75
Reproducer:	Diamond Model D
Horn:	13 in. x 9 ¼ in.
Cabinet:	The London No. 1 Disc Phonograph table model in mahogany finish. Oak finish has not been reported. A grille cloth was fitted.

AMBEROLA 60
phonograph

Close-up of the AMBEROLA 60 showing the balance wheel at the inner end of the mandrel and the Diamond D Reproducer supplied with this machine

AMBEROLA 80

Introduced:	Probably December 1928
Dimensions:	Height 44 ¾ in; width 19 ½ in., depth 20 ¼ in.
Motor:	Double spring, as fitted to AMBEROLAS 50 and 75
Reproducer:	Diamond Model D
Horn:	13 in. x 10 in.
Cabinet and Finishes:	Adapted from the Sheraton-sans-Inlay Diamond Disc Phonograph (upright) cabinet. Cupboard door opens on to two sliding trays, approx. 14 ¼ in. wide and 16 ¼ in. deep inside and each holding up to 42 cylinders in boxes. These models are finished in mahogany or oak. Model No. 1071 in oak has the remains of a dark grille cloth.

Production of all cylinder phonographs for amusement purposes ceased at West Orange in October 1929.

AMBEROLA 80 phonograph courtesy of Sotheby's, London

A corner of the Edison factory showing AMBEROLA 30 motors and a single AMBEROLA 50 motor awaiting installation. The horns hanging overhead are for Edisonic Disc Phonographs, and these would date the scene from late in 1927

1) The Phonograph Committee's original concept was a $25.00, $50.00 and $75.00 range.
2) U. S. Patent No. 1,265,179 for Phonograph or Talking Machine filed June 21st 1915 by John P. Constable, was granted May 7th 1918.
3) U.S. Design Patents 52,493 and 52,494 of September 24th 1918 by Walter C. Pitts and assigned to New Jersey Patent Company. Filed July 3rd 1917.
4) AMBEROLA business during the 12 months ended February 28th-
    1916 $641,000   1920 $1,430,000
    1917 $769,000   1921 $1,134,000
    1918 $1,081,000   1922 $112,000
    1919 $1,223,000
5) U.S. Patent No. 1,010,355 for Phonograph filed by Frank L. Dyer and Frank D. Lewis on June 19th 1909, gazetted November 28th 1911. Before this patent was granted there was an application (No. 550,037) by George L. Stone of March 10th 1911 for the swinging horn, and Dyer and Lewis offered him $200.00 for it.
6) Information from the New Zealand *Phonographic Record*, date not known.

Letters and production figures from the Edison Archives

TONE COMPARISONS

The Diamond Disc Phonographs may be said to have started their Tone Tests from early 1915 but it was really when the Edison company promoted the Disc instruments separately from the AMBEROLAS from 1916 that plans were made for setting the latter against a 'talking machine'. The make or type of talking machine was not specified but it was to cost at least twice as much as the AMBEROLA used in the test.

The Blue Amberol and shellac disc version of the same piece of music were recommended to be used in the comparison because artists of the day often recorded the same piece for several companies, but a few of the titles proposed were different but put over by the same artist. In most cases the Blue Amberols used were the brighter, more forward direct recordings made before 1915, although a small number of cylinders dubbed from the Diamond Discs are noticed.

The AMBEROLA 50 took part in an early Tone Comparison involving an Edison cylinder machine. This was in the ballroom of the Hotel McAlpin, New York on June 23rd 1916 before a trade audience of 650 so-called phonograph experts, when the 50 dollar AMBEROLA was pitted against a $115.00 'talking machine', both instruments being behind a curtain. The audience was given voting papers and two selections by the same artists were played in each instance on both phonographs and the AMBEROLA easily won. The items used were not reported.

The AMBEROLA, now described by the company as Jack-the-Giant-Killer was then sent round the country for further Comparison Tests and put against rival disc machines (described as 'the best-known needle type') costing from $110.00 to over $200.00, and was reported as 'slaying' them all. Among the cities visited were Indianapolis in October 1916, then Syracuse and Atlanta, In 1917 there were further victories in Minneapolis, at Kansas City in September, and at Detroit and Milwaukee in November.

There are indications that these Tone Comparisons went on into late 1918 and possibly beyond, a much scaled-down version of the Tone Tests, then in full flower with the Edison Disc Phonographs, but these often involved live performers.

AMBEROLA PRICE CHANGES FROM 1915.

	Model 30	Model 50	Model 75
Originally	$30.00	$50.00	$75.00
Oct. 25th 1917 (inc. new War Tax)	$30.90	$51.30	$76.75
January 1st 1918	$35.00	$58.00	$82.50
September 1st 1918	$41.00	$68.00	$100.00
April 1923	$30.00	$50.00	$75.00

Model numbers were adjusted to the new prices during this period

Edison Phonograph Works was selling AMBEROLAS to T.A. Edison Inc. at
February 1921 for:

	Model 30	Model 50	Model 75
	$19.52	$30.02	$48.84
	(oak)	(mahog.)	(mahog.)
		$27.32	$44.25
		(oak)	(oak)

UNITED KINGDOM PRICES

	Model 30	Model 50	Model 60	Model 75	Model 80
1915, June onwards	£6 6s. 0d.	£10 10s. 0d.		£15 15s. 0d.	
1922	£12 0s. 0d.	£21 0s. 0d.		£32 0s. 0d.	
August 1923	£10 10s. 0d.	£18 18s. 0d.		£28 7s. 0d.	
*post 1929	£6 0s. 0d	£8 0s. 0d.	£10 10s. 0d.	£12 12s. 0d.	£15 0s. 0d.
	(oak)	(oak)	(mahog)	(mahog)	(oak)

*these last prices were offered by the London & Provincial Phonograph Company

AMBEROLA OUTFITS

Undetermined dates in the late 1920s

Outfit No. 48   AMBEROLA 30 (oak)
12 customer selected records
12 free records of Edison selection $48.20

Outfit No. 68   AMBEROLA 50 (mahogany, golden or fumed oak)
12 customer selected records
12 free records of Edison selection $68.30

Outfit No. 93   AMBEROLA 75 (mahogany, golden or fumed oak)

12 customer selected records
12 free records of Edison selection $93.40

Advertising was founded on the slogan "Every Member of the Family needs the Phonograph"

Pre- October 1917	AMBEROLA 30 + 12 x 50 cent Blue Amberols $36.00
	AMBEROLA 50 + 12 x 50 cent Blue Amberols $56.00
	AMBEROLA 75 + 12 x 50 cent Blue Amberols $81.00
From Nov. 15th 1918	AMBEROLA 30 + 12 x 60 cent Blue Amberols $48.20
	AMBEROLA 50 + 12 x 60 cent Blue Amberols $75.20
	AMBEROLA 75 + 12 x 60 cent Blue Amberols $107.20

THE FIRST SIX MONTHS OF SALES OF THE NEW AMBEROLAS

1915	June	July	Sept	Oct	Nov-Dec.
Amberola 30	750	600	1187	1500	2770
Amberola 50	350	300	328	600	840
Amberola 75	-	400	298	400	630
Surviving earlier models					
Amberola V	75	50	19	-	-
Amberola VI	100	-	6	-	-

THE NEW DIAMOND AMBEROLA 'STORE'

Although intended solely for the trade and particularly the dealer, the New Diamond Amberola Store merits inclusion in this section as it is not unlikely that an example could be seen and passed over by an Edison collector who might think it 'just another cupboard'.

The Edison Company had established a New Amberola Sales Department to try and stimulate AMBEROLA business, and the Store could accommodate an example of each of the new table models 30 and 50, together with about 185 cylinders in six pull-out trays. The dealer, having paid $15.00 for the Store could lay out Edison literature on the top and stack leaflets in a built-in rack along the back, while the front doors and side panels were made especially for displaying monthly record hangers and other advertising matter.

The Store was finished in Blue Amberol shade of enamel and had gilded beadwork and the words THE NEW EDISON DIAMOND AMBEROLA appeared in gilt on the backboard of the rack. Dimensions: Height 3 ft. (approx.), width 3 ft., depth 23 in.

It was announced in the *Edison Phonograph Monthly* of October 1916. No examples have been reported in the United Kingdom but there was a wartime restriction on such imports then.

Chapter 15
PREMIUM
Phonograph

Although there are occasional rumours of a PREMIUM Phonograph somewhere in private hands, it does not seem likely that more than a prototype was built with perhaps one or two back-up examples for experiment and for showing selected traders.

The suggestion of a 'premium phonograph' of the small internal horn type came from F. K. Dolbeer, sales manager, to Frank Dyer, president of T.A. Edison Inc. in a letter of February 22nd 1911, saying he considered the time ripe for such an instrument.

These photographs were taken on May 19th, three months after Dolbeer's suggestion, but the machine was not put into production and no details are available of its mechanism, size or projected price, but from appearance might have found its niche in the catalogue at the GEM pages.

A late mention came in a letter of October 12th from Paul Cromelin, managing director in Edison's London works and a ready critic of expensive Edison models requesting "one of those which were made for premium purposes in the United States but not put out", to compare with cheap models imported from Germany by Murdoch. There is no evidence of one being sent.

PREMIUM Phonograph, exterior front view

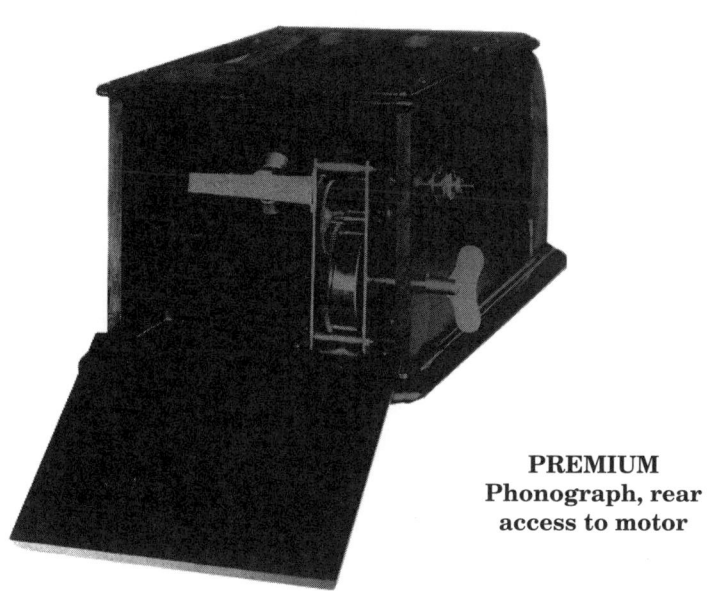

PREMIUM Phonograph, rear access to motor

PREMIUM Phonograph, front access to mandrel

Chapter 16
OPERA Phonograph

A bygone enthusiast has described the OPERA as "the peak of Edison's phonographic achievements, and in its day undoubtedly the finest producer of recorded sounds anywhere", and a look at its competitors leaves that statement to stand without fear of contradiction. With its silent all-geared motor, traversing mandrel and free-standing horn it played directly-recorded Blue Amberols made before 1915 with a fidelity unapproached by any disc or cylinder phonograph of its time. Nowadays it is a desirable instrument.

In describing the OPERA, later named the CONCERT, the reader should not become confused with the earlier and less sophisticated Edison machines that carried these names. Despite the name change and a cabinet option the mechanism remained the same and there was no model series designation.

The OPERA owed its origin to the falling popularity of the IDELIA - really a TRIUMPH in luxury clothes - reported in January 1911 as not selling in any quantity; this may be attributed to the trade's anticipation of the promised Disc Phonographs. In a memo of August 17th 1911 there is the first mention of a new type of phonograph designed by Peter Weber, to have the same mechanism as the projected AMBEROLA (B)-I and to be given a mahogany cabinet and self standing Music Master horn. It would sell for $90.00.[1] As soon as Weber had built the prototype it would be named, but in a further letter dated August 29th it was still un-named.

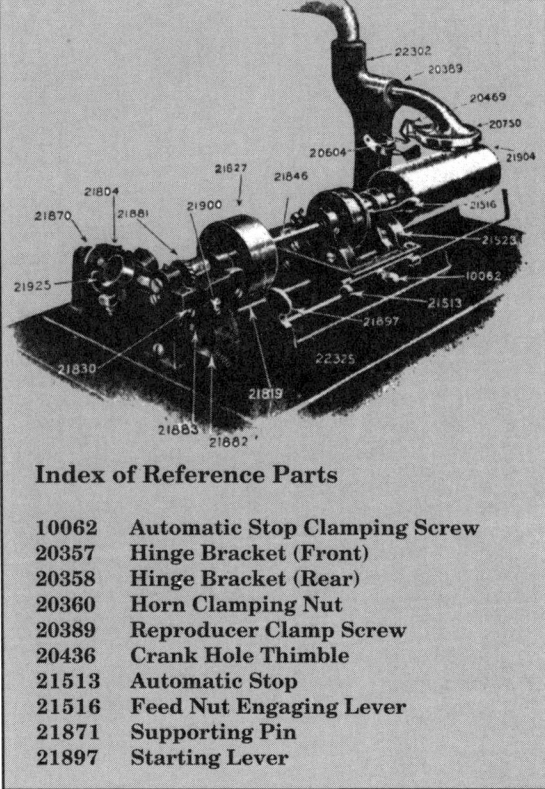

Index of Reference Parts

10062	Automatic Stop Clamping Screw
20357	Hinge Bracket (Front)
20358	Hinge Bracket (Rear)
20360	Horn Clamping Nut
20389	Reproducer Clamp Screw
20436	Crank Hole Thimble
21513	Automatic Stop
21516	Feed Nut Engaging Lever
21871	Supporting Pin
21897	Starting Lever

Introduced:	November 1911 (U.S.) and January 1912 (U.K.)
Type:	4-minute
Dimensions:	Height 14 ¾ in., base 18 in. x 12 ¾ in.
Motor:	Of the traversing mandrel type and derived from that in the AMBEROLA (A)-I,[2] the belt drive being replaced by gearing and the motor became that of the AMBEROLA (B)-I.[3] Simplicity was the rule both in its mounting, which was part of the top plate casting and in the sparing use of gearing, the first shaft driving the feed screw, the feed screw the mandrel. The double springs were the same as on the TRIUMPH Models F and G. The governor was placed above the top plate and driven from the mandrel shaft through a fibre worm gear; a flywheel was concealed under the governor cover. At first glance the controls of the OPERA suggest a similar operation to the first AMBEROLA but the brake action is through a separate lever and the control lever lowers the stylus (and cleaning brush)[4] on to the record while engaging the feed nut. An automatic brake was fitted.
Reproducer:	Model L playing wax Amberols. A special adapter was needed for home recording, described in the later chapter on Edison Recorders.
Cabinet:	Mahogany, piano finish, with pillars in each corner made this a unique Edison design. The cover rested on the case but could not be fastened for carrying by the top handle, and a hole in it allowed the horn to be mounted with the cover in position. It was not intended for the machine to be played with the cover closed, and it would not. The 'Edison' decal was on the front of the case.

OPERA Phonograph in mahogany finish

Horn:	Self supporting Music Master capable of being swivelled to play towards any direction. The horn stem supplied with these machines and the SCHOOL Phonograph was angled to make the horn sit squatly and is not readily adaptable to any other Edison phonographs fitted for Cygnet type horns.
Finish and Accessories:	The top plate and fittings were finished in brown enamel with gold lining, with the crank, reproducer, automatic stop setting, mandrel and lifting handles in oxidized bronze. Early machines have been noted with a gunmetal finish and one model (No. 12) has a horn stem in original bronze finish with lighter bronze on the upper and centre ring and with no evidence of wood graining. Oilcan and cleaning brush provided.
Price:	$90.00; £18 18s. 0d.

In February 1912 (U.S.) and April 1912 (U.K.) the OPERA could be bought in an oak cabinet with oak Music Master horn, price $85.00; £17 17s. 0d. This model had certain cabinet differences to the mahogany OPERA. The case had no carrying handles at the ends, but the cover had the securing clasps of the TRIUMPH, HOME and STANDARD of the time. It still had a hole in the cover for the horn stem. Some TRIUMPHS of the later style are reported in OPERA cabinets, and this is not thought to be anything but a local adjustment.

The OPERA was reported in April 1912 as moving quickly, as many as 1,234 had been sold by the end of February with many orders in hand. Threats of legal action from The United States Phonograph Company in the summer led to the Edison company deciding on August 20th to discontinue the name OPERA and substitute CONCERT. Name plates and changes in printed matter were ordered and the alteration was made public in October 1912 (U.S.) and January 1913 (U.K.) when the CONCERT was given a Diamond Model

Oak CONCERT Phonograph in closed position

A Reproducer for playing the new Blue Amberols. There were no price changes. The following were prepared for expected sales:

CONCERT, in oak 100, in mahogany 400.

Orders in hand for these types were reported on October 5th to number 176, and by the end of 1912 the assembly schedule for CONCERTS was 40 per week 15 in oak and 25 mahogany.

From a report by a British CONCERT owner who has a very late machine of 1914 (No. 4604) it seems the last models had a lid sufficiently deep to cover the horn support without a hole being needed in it. Most of the fittings have an oxidized bronze finish.

From October 1st 1913 it was announced from West Orange that no further horn machines would be made at the Edison plant except the SCHOOL Phonograph; by this date sales of the CONCERT had dropped off to a handful or so every week in the face of the AMBEROLAS, but were still being sent out in ones or twos for several months after.

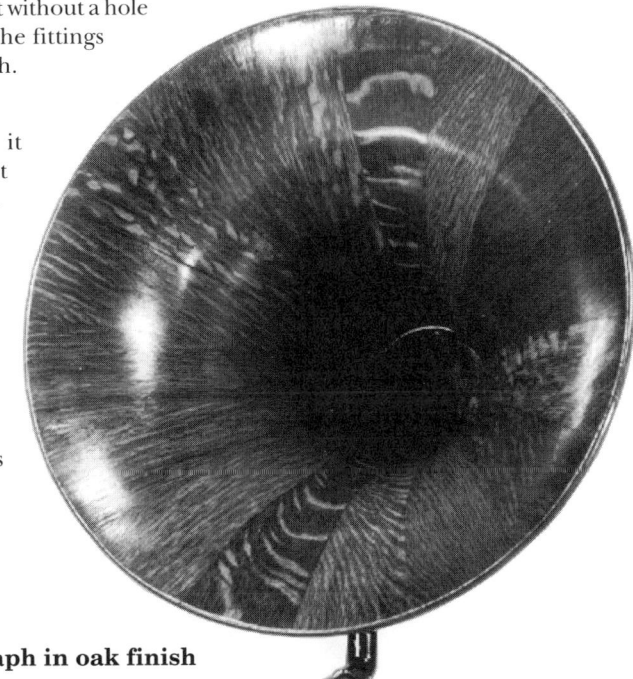

CONCERT Phonograph in oak finish

1) Letter from C.H. Wilson to Edison Amusement Phonograph Committee - Edison Archive
2) The first AMBEROLA motor was the feature of U.S. Patent No. 1,220,480 for Phonograph, filed on August 6th 1910 by Peter Weber and not granted until March 27th 1917
3) This AMBEROLA motor was depicted in a U.S. Patent No. 1,187,115 for a Stop Device (automatic brake) filed on December 7th 1911 by Peter Weber and granted June 13th 1916. The extended gestation periods of these two patents will be noted
4) The use by Edison of a Record Cleaning Brush was based on three U.S. Patent Nos. 831,987; 832,249 and 865,674, awarded to J. N. Blackman and the Company paid an annual royalty to Blackman.

Packing the
OPERA Phonograph

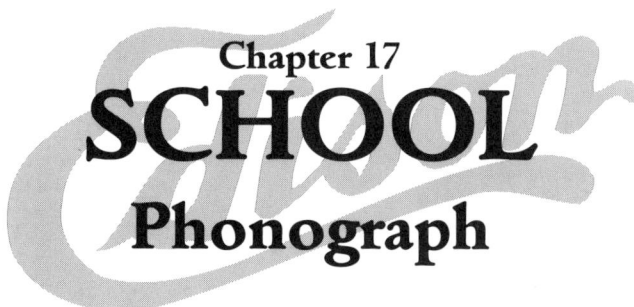

Chapter 17
SCHOOL Phonograph

From the earliest days of his invention Edison had visualized the phonograph as a means of instruction, particularly of languages, and the innovations of the durable Blue Amberol cylinder and diamond stylus combining to give clearer reproduction, were more suitable for classwork than the more restricted I.C.S. types of STANDARD, GEM and AMBEROLA. The SCHOOL Phonograph was not limited to language and business instruction however, because 54 Blue Amberol cylinders in the regular United States listing offered several subjects, mainly dictation, spelling and mathematics.[1]

The SCHOOL was the first and only specially designed Edison phonograph to reach the classroom, the later Disc Phonograph never getting beyond the prototype. It was announced with some solemnity and length in December 1912, and in a factory memo of December 30th production of 25 per week was directed.

Nevertheless the SCHOOL model seems to have been available some months earlier because it features in a Minute of the Executive Committee of Thomas A. Edison Inc. of August 28th 1912, and at that date the OPERA may have been used in or intended for the SCHOOL outfit before the metal-bodied phonograph was introduced.[2]

Introduced:	(officially) December 1912 (U.S.) and January 1913 (U.K.)
Type:	4-minute
Dimensions:	Height (without horn) 11 ¾ in., base 17 ⅝ in. x 12 ⅞ Height of machine and stand 45 ¼ in.
Motor and Movement:	Mechanically similar to the OPERA, later CONCERT phonograph, but there was a broader speed range from about 60 to 160 r.p.m. To reach the motor a steel access plate under the case had to be removed. An automatic record cleaning brush was fitted.
Reproducer:	Diamond Model A; recording equipment was available and is described in a special section on Edison Recorders.

Horn: No. 11 Cygnet, black with gold lining, fitted on the self-supporting stem supplied with the OPERA and CONCERT horn; this was painted black. The No. 10 Cygnet Horn was also used on this model; indications are that this was sent out with the later SCHOOL machines when perhaps the 11's stock was run down after horn phonographs were discontinued in October 1913. Some of the No. 10 horns in known SCHOOLS carry signs of having been drilled for suspension, and made good.

Cabinet: The elegant wooden cabinet of the OPERA and CONCERT gave way to a robust sheet steel case, mounted on a metal stand that could be moved around on casters. There were four shelves for cylinder boxes each holding 24 records, and a pull-out U-shaped metal bracket where a box could be rested for easy selection of records.

Finish and Accessories: The whole of the cabinet, stand and most of the top works were finished in hard wearing black enamel, but parts like the reproducer and winding crank were oxidized bronze as found on the OPERA and CONCERT machines. An oilcan and cleaning brush were provided.

Price: $75.00; £15 15s. 0d.
$60.00 from November 1st 1913

The SCHOOL phonograph was the only Edison horn model to be spared the axe in the Company's advertised clearance of open-horn machines in October 1913, but from figures available the weekly requisitions for SCHOOL machines were very low for much of its existence, sometimes falling to nil, and it was allowed to fade from the scene in early 1914.

SCHOOL Phonograph on stand with original cylinder containers

1) These comprised the Blue Amberol block 1657 to 1710
2) The Minute reads:

"The phonograph used with the SCHOOL outfit is an OPERA, the name of which machine has recently been changed to CONCERT. The matter of leaving off the name-plate when the machine is used with this outfit was discussed and it was decided that a name-plate bearing the new name CONCERT should be substituted for the old one".

Chapter 18
Electric Coin-Slot Phonographs

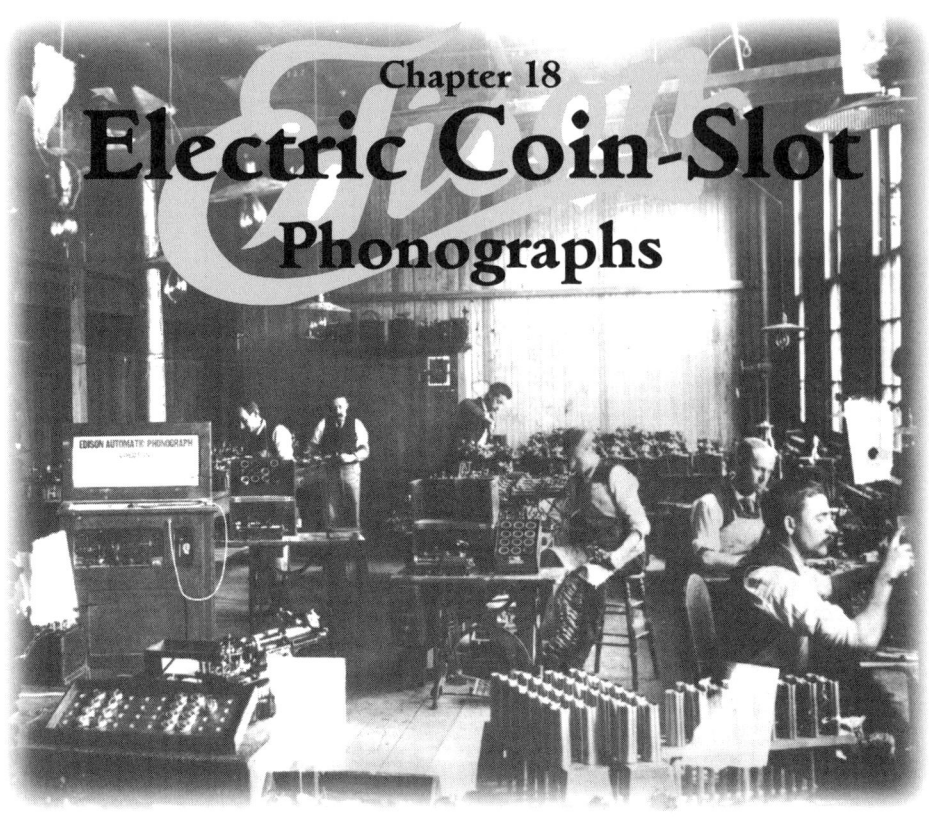

This view of the cylinder phonograph assembly department at West Orange is dated 1890

Electric motor phonographs are still necessary for use in slot machines, as no spring attachment has been devised which is sensitive enough to start the mechanism by the dropping of a nickel.
   James L. Andem of Ohio Phonograph Co., writing in 1896.

Although credit for the first successful coin automatic phonograph is usually given to Louis Glass and William Arnold of San Francisco in their December 1889 American application, there had been earlier stirrings elsewhere as shown in British patents 10,970 dated August 10th 1887 and 9762 of July 5th 1888, but it is not known if either of these was constructed and put into use.

The first by W. S. Simpson and W. S. Oliver of London was a 'speak-your-weight' weighing machine using a phonograph with foil 'electroed or hardened' and brought into action either by the weight of the client on the platform, or by moving a lever, the 'electric' part of the instrument being in the coin-chute where the dropping of the coin caused battery-operated solenoids to release the mechanism. Advanced for its time, this machine visualized compressed air amplification of the sound.[1]

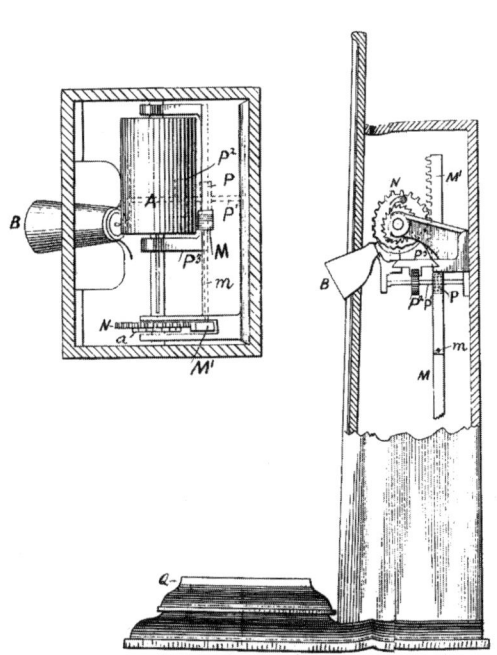 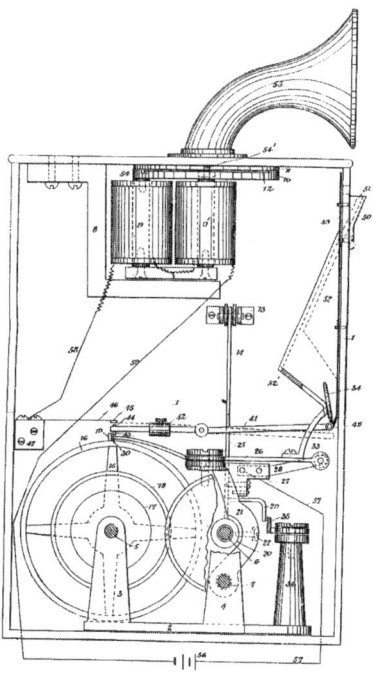

Details from Simpson and Oliver's British Patent No. 10,970 of August 10th 1887 for a coin-operated speak-your-weight machine

Randall's Pariophone as shown in his British Patent No. 9762 of July 5th 1888

    The second was nearly a year later and was the so-called Pariophone of C. Adams Randall of London. This was a coin-actuated sound reproducing apparatus for use in public places and again with a durable record, to be driven by an electric motor, as well as other suggested forms of propulsion. It would have interchangeable records. Better sound reproduction was one of the objects of the Pariophone including the proposal of a wooden diaphragm.[2]

    While these inventors showed ingenuity in their efforts to elevate the tinfoil style of phonograph to a coin-slot machine that could earn its keep, it was not until the coming of the electric phonograph, perfected in June 1888, with its more precise mechanism and wax cylinders that an automatic phonograph seemed really feasible. These very early experimental models were made to incorporate a repeating attachment in the form of a coarse screw carriage return, and not long after the machines became generally available for renting out to office businesses by the Local Phonograph Companies, coin-triggering devices began to be invented for the phonographs to be set up in public to play a musical item or comic snatch for a small coin. They were firmly in the hands of the companies from their foundation and the devices' patentees were usually employees of the companies, or closely associated.

    These local phonograph companies were established in 1889 by Lippincott's North

American Phonograph Company to handle Edison phonographs and North American Graphophone Company's instruments, but in fact very many more Edisons would be handled than the less effective Graphophones, and by 1893 surviving Graphophones had been converted to play Edison-type cylinders. At their peak at the beginning the local phonograph companies numbered 33 and remained in business in reducing numbers until 1896, some even later, and were formed with the intention of hiring out phonographs, maintaining them and supplying spares and records. In 1893 North American could claim to be represented in 'all states' and by Holland Brothers in Canada. Primarily this business was intended to handle machines for office use and the first rental charged was $40.00 per annum but the talent of the times for invention soon showed through and led to several variations of coin-slot apparatus and cabinet designs.

The Edison electric phonographs of the CLASS M and E types with their carriage return mechanism were eminently adaptable to coin working and the first of these devices was covered in the two patents of Louis Glass and William S. Arnold. Glass was prominent on the West Coast and an official of three phonograph companies in the North American group. He also constructed a spring motor for non-automatic phonographs. (Cf. chapter on EDISON SPRING MOTOR PHONOGRAPH) So comprehensive were his coin-slot patents and embracing such elementary necessities as multiple hearing tubes that he was later accused by other companies of extracting 'blood money' when they had to use them.[3]

Charles Cheever, prominent in the (New York) Metropolitan Phonograph Company and other local companies and an original Edison Speaking Phonograph Company director, financed Gilliland to producing cabinets with automatic apparatus[4] and placed 744 with 12 local phonograph companies before they were overtaken by Albert Keller's popular and reliable machines that he assigned to The Automatic Phonograph Exhibition Company of New York, this firm having acquired the rights to Glass's patents. Keller's were the square upright models with the prominent push-in knob at the right-hand end.[5]

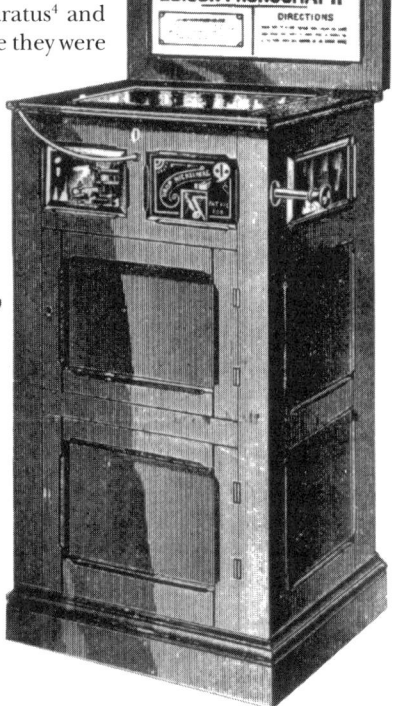

The New York Exhibition Company's Automatic model of pre-1892

Another conspicuous inventor of the day was Jacob H. Ling of Detroit, who was using a phonograph at his business as an advertisement, but it needed an attendant to return the arm when the record was over. Ling succeeded in assembling his own automatic coin operated phonographs, drawing large crowds and receiving a big contract for the Ling Attachment with The Michigan Phonograph Company, another of the local companies.[6] With others working in or alongside the local companies and producing and patenting automatic mechanisms, it is no wonder that although surviving numbers are small, they have a bewildering variety of coin-operating devices and designs of cabinets.

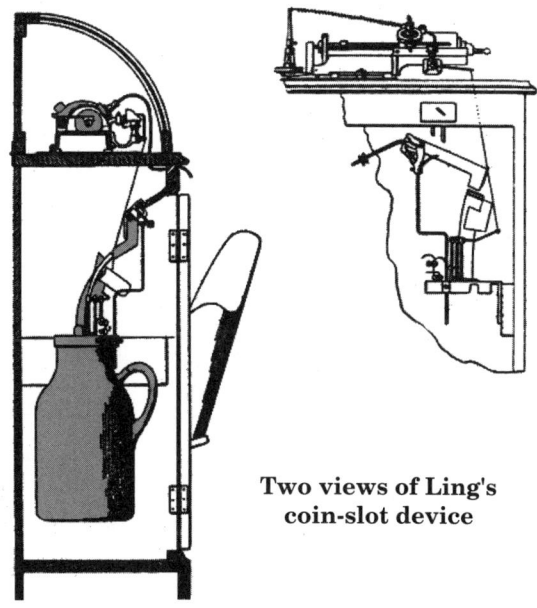

Two views of Ling's coin-slot device

Despite an oft-stated aversion to this coin-slot trade whose entrepreneurs more than anyone were commercializing the phonograph,[7] Edison signed a contract with The Automatic Phonograph Exhibition Company (of New York) on April 19th 1890 to make them a complete model of a slot machine and a duplicate; this style was to be the Standard Slot machine - the CLASS S. Delivery would not exceed 15 machines a day, to be regulated from time to time upon 30 days' notice, and in late November 1890 the first machine was ready for delivery. The CLASS M type machines were sold to the local companies to use in automatic phonographs, but in a letter of August 30th 1890 North American notified them that CLASS S phonographs were now being sent out; these were a CLASS M mechanism designed for use with the nickel-in-the-slot device. These machines were made to take the Standard Speaker.

Edison, reported in *The Phonogram* of January 1891 was denouncing the coin-slot operators for gaining an advantage over the businessman's aid and in his view the more worthy use of his invention, but the trade had its teeth into something that would make good money for many years to come and establish the phonograph as an entertainer. Some of them would later be accused of greed and of stifling its evolution after its pioneering 'booming' by Gouraud, Young and others.

The first Edison Phonograph Parlor was opened in the Arcade Building, Cleveland on September 15th 1890, an address said to have led to the generic use of 'arcade' in the coin-slot amusement machine sense. The next was the Exhibition Parlor in Cincinnati on November 8th 1890, and further parlors soon followed in Boston, New York, Philadelphia, Baltimore, Washington, Chicago, St. Louis, New Orleans and San Francisco. It was hoped to have one in each town of 10,000 inhabitants. There were 16 phonographs in Cleveland, 18 in Cincinnati and the best returns were claimed from coin machines in groups of from 8 to 10 in a central

Opened on September 15th 1890 the Cleveland Arcade Parlor was the first for Edison automatic phonographs. It opened day and evening with programmes changed daily

This Phonograph Parlor was opened at 5 Emery Arcade, Cincinnati, on November 8th 1890

The Vine Street Parlor, Cincinnati, in 1894

Edison Automatic Phonographs entertain a mixed crowd, possibly in Philadelphia

locality with an attendant in charge and a ready supply of small change.[8] It was 5 CENTS TO HEAR THE EDISON PHONOGRAPH and some machines were paired back-to-back. Running lights were added to some of these parlors as an extra attraction.[9]

Early experience showed that the first Automatic Phonograph Exhibition Company's machines were unreliable and people were treating them roughly; a lack of confidence and experiences with heavy-handed and large-booted customers caused The Georgia Phonograph Company to withdraw for a time, saying the instruments were 'unadaptable and defective'. The New Jersey Phonograph Company followed a policy of trying to place them at strategic seaside resorts where the habitués changed daily and the cylinders needed changing less often. The Old Dominion Phonograph Company preferred towns of up to 1,000 population where there was little other entertainment and expenses were low; in cities maintenance costs were higher and operators demanded more profit. Both The New England and Kentucky Phonograph Companies reported higher expenses clearing the coin chutes of bad coins, chewing gum and stuffed paper, the Kentucky company describing a shortfall of $4,000 in slugs and gun-wads, etc. Magnetic devices and 'bounce gaps' became part of the coin mechanisms to detect ferrous and lightweight slugs, and cutting away the sides of the coin chutes was intended to let stuffed paper drop out. The New York Phonograph Company introduced tokens in 1890.

After the early patents the coin-slot mechanisms leaned towards standardization with the incoming coin closing the electrical circuit through its diameter and causing the machine to play; on the reproducer's return to the starting position the money was tripped out -"the penny drops" - breaking the circuit and clearing the system for the next coin. Another feature of these amusement arcade phonographs was the use of a cork and rubber mandrel to reduce record breakages. Not everyone welcomed automatic machines, they had the reputation in some arcades of attracting rowdy elements and when in France in 1895 they became silent when copyrights became due to authors and publishers, it was said that "the phonograph has become a horror which we are better rid of".

Competition between nearby parlors brought an intake of fresh machines as new models were introduced, as well as some grumbling from the companies at the instability and constant re-designing. Frequent turnover and the rental system contributed largely to so few of these early automatic machines surviving today. In June 1891 it was estimated that there were 2,000-3,000 of these in operation, and in the same month James Andem of the Ohio company was speaking of 50 handsome and expensive coin-slot instruments being made by Standard Locomotive Works of Cincinnati. Were these the first de-luxe juke boxes?

The Ohio Company's model in 1892

In 1893 the Chicago company announced its intention of placing no fewer than 300 automatic phonographs at the World's Fair of that year.

The cylinder records for these public amusement phonographs could be obtained by the trade from the Edison laboratory from May 1889.[10] Edison had a duplicating process of dubbing from master cylinders, and the exhibitors found difficulty in getting sufficient records; some even sent in their own masters, to no avail. Columbia did not come in on the scene with musical cylinders for the automatic phonographs until mid-1890 when Edison wax blanks were used, and by 1894 were reported as sending out from 3,000 to 5,000 cylinders every day. Accounts of the time show that the clientèle, however heavy-handed, was short on sophistication;

exhibitors found that full announcements on cylinders were a necessity, that vulgar songs were not invariably popular and that "Nearer my God to Thee" was a favourite in a tough part of St. Louis. Several companies, nevertheless, got into trouble with risqué cylinders that today's listener might find hard to fault.

Since the time of the first satisfactory phonograph in mid-1888 there had been a tight Edison policy of leasing out rather than a cash sale; this caused friction among the local companies, some wanting to sell machines outright to raise capital, while others situated between large cities feared that any sold would gravitate quickly to those cities. Original buying companies were anxious to keep a rein on coin-slot machines out on hire.

The Chicago Company's model in 1892

Several of the local companies started to offer these for sale in the spring of 1891[11], leading to a limited relaxation by August when North American offered the local companies 1,000 mixed CLASS M, T and W types for sale only, but they were not permitted for coin-slot use.[12]

The electric coin-slot phonographs continued virtually unchallenged through most of the 1890s with the automatic disc trade not offering competition until the next decade. The prevalence of phonograph parlors encouraged some communities to tax them, and state levies of $2.50 for a nickel type machine and $1.00 for a penny (cent) type were reported. In December 1899 2,827 automatic phonographs were reported in Brooklyn when the authorities were proposing to tax them. By April 1906 when coin-slot arcades had become known as 'penny vaudevilles', one on Union Square, New York was operated by a corporation whose capital stock was $500,000, and it had 13 other arcades and about 100 Edison coin-slot phonographs in constant operation.

The Empire State Edison Phonograph of 1897

243

As the old century ran out the Edison company uplifted the appearance of all its models. From April 1900 to facilitate ordering, code words for all machines and accessories came into use, replacing many of the earlier more casual designations. In 1900 most of the Edison range were put into New Style cabinets with banner transfers, and for a time the automatic phonographs were given curved glass tops with side windows. By August 1904 the coin-slot CONCERT phonographs with the large cylinders had been phased out as the Gold Moulded process now made them obsolete, and by 1906 all the floor standing automatics had reverted to a flat glazed top with side windows; perhaps the curved tops were not able to stand up to the treatment they had to meet. By 1906 too, lighter and more compact electric motors were starting to replace the old CLASS M types, and these were usually bought in from outside makers. The automatic electric phonographs were joined by some spring powered styles from 1898 to 1906, but these had only limited success.

Edison coin-operated phonographs seemed to fade away rather than being officially curtailed, and they are reported in use in arcades in the mid-1920s and even into the early '30s, indicating that spares were still to be had. A number fitted with combination gearing are known.

Mention should be made of platform driven phonographs for use with coin-slot mechanism. In these the weight of the client stepping on to a platform caused winding of the phonograph. One invented by George V. Gress who also patented multiple phonograph apparatus (Cf. chapter on MULTIPLEX COIN-OPERATED PHONOGRAPHS) needed from 60 to 500 lb. to prime the phonograph motor to play one cylinder. Another one was invented by Walter Miller of the Edison staff.[13] George A. Moore of Moore Talking Scale Company of Maine established 6 patents for 'speak-your-weight' machines, but favoured discs.[14] It is not clear how far such adaptations of the Edison phonographs were developed, or if any have survived.

CLASS M, E and S ELECTRIC COIN-SLOT PHONOGRAPHS

The CLASS M was the workhorse for Edison coin-operated phonographs from 1889 until the following August when The North American Phonograph Company offered a form modified for coin-slot operation called the CLASS S that the local phonograph companies could build into their own cabinets. This practice continued until after 1896 when the term CLASS S went out of use and CLASS M was favoured when conjoined with automatic equipment. The mains CLASS E in its several forms had no similar change of style and was adapted for coin-slot phonographs as required, being employed less frequently than battery models.

In the 1890s the Edison electric phonographs - handled for half of the decade by North American Phonograph - were known as the Standard Slot Machine, the Nickel-in-the-Slot Phonograph, the Edison Automatic Coin-Slot Phonograph, and the 'M Electric' and 'E Electric' Coin-Slot Phonographs. The 'M Electric' became the IMPERIAL from April 1900 and WINDSOR in August 1904 (U.S.). The WINDSOR was re-cased in 1906. The 'E Electric' was known as the REGAL from April 1900 and MAJESTIC in August 1904 (U.S.). Both IMPERIAL and REGAL were the machines' telegraphic code-words before April 1900.

In general these 1890s Edison automatic phonographs were as follows:

Type:	2-minute
Dimensions:	Height: 55 in.; base 28 in. x 17 in.
Weight:	198 lb. with batteries and 130-165 lb. without.
Cabinet:	Antique oak, floor standing with cupboard below for coin mechanism and cash tray and giving space for batteries in CLASS M and S models. A flat top prevailed until about 1900 when the machines were standardized with a curved glass front and this persisted for four or five years, reverting to the glazed box cover probably in January 1905. The WINDSOR had square cabinet corner pillars from about the same time. A music advertising frame (sometimes at extra charge) and locking keys were provided.
Mechanism:	Regular electric upper-works with provision for coin mechanism causing the return of the reproducer carrier arm to the starting position after every playing. In the early models the coin itself completed the electrical circuit, but this changed so that in falling it triggered an electrical contact outside the chute. Edison machines were normally made to accept a nickel (5 cents), but could be made for other coins to order. The trade was apprised of new styling to these machines on May 3rd 1904 to take effect in the August and the automatic mechanism was changed to embody the latest return attachment and mercury contact device.
Reproducer:	Edison Standard Speaker (with reproducing sapphire only), then Automatic Speaker/Reproducer followed by Model B. A flexible (later telescopic) tube led from the reproducer collar to the horn or hearing tube fitting.
Horns etc:	Way rails for as many as 17 listening tubes were more popular than horns at first, but horns up to 24 in. with rear support became general after about 1900, especially where the single machine was set up in a hotel lobby or a store. The records of the day though tended to sound better through listening tubes than a horn.
Accessories:	Camel-hair chip-brush, oilcan and connecting wires. 1890s machines were often quoted with batteries and perhaps a dozen cylinders.
Prices:	The policy of leasing automatic phonographs persisted for several years, but some typical cash prices were as follows:

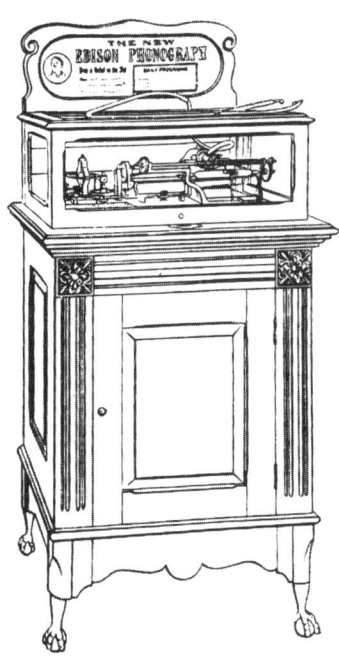

This CLASS M nickel-in-the-slot was described in detail by George Tewksbury in his 1897 book

This North American nickel-in-the-slot Phonograph cost $165.00 in 1896. Later it became the Edison Automatic Coin-slot Phonograph for $125.00. (Sam Sheena photograph)

North American CLASS M type, c. 1892. The carrier-arm has been replaced during its career

Unidentified CLASS M automatic of about 1905

Battery models:

	$185.00 (1895)		$125.00 (1899)
IMPERIAL	$125.00 (1900)	**WINDSOR**	$80.00 (1904)

Mains models;

REGAL	$125.00 (1900)	**MAJESTIC**	$90.00 (1904)

The CLASS S model was sold for adding to the automatic cabinet and equipment. Its April 1894 price:

> with battery, motor, hearing tube, chip-brush and oilcan; body box, speaking tube or shaving apparatus not included $95.00

or the complete instrument in the United States Phonograph catalogue for 1896:

> CLASS S equipment with automatic nickel-in-the-slot Kansas pattern, with new chute, patent slug ejector, electric motor, Automatic speaker, all in cabinet with records. Plate glass top. $165.00
>
> or without battery or records $140.00

In August 1896 the exporting Edison United Phonograph Company was paying the Phonograph Works $29.00 for CLASS S mechanisms (without slot equipment). At about the same time (Tewksbury's) United States Phonograph Company offered:

> Standard Slot Cabinet with automatic device only..... $50.00
>
> with automatic nickel slot mechanism...... $35.00

•••••••••••••••••••••••••

From November 1903 (U. S.) the coin-slot phonographs were separated from the domestic catalogues and listed on their own. New prices for accessories, such as way-rails and connectors were announced.

•••••••••••••••••••••••••

There is evidence that many of the smaller companies were finding coin-slot phonographs difficult to keep working and in a general shake-up in August 1904 the Edison Company announced the setting-up of a special department for installing these machines and keeping them maintained. Company appointed men could be called on in the event of serious trouble, although larger dealers were still entrusted with repairs. In the same month several machines had a change of name and the Concert cylinder automatic machines were discarded.

In 1906 further re-organization brought a lowering of prices. With the bulky CONCERT types gone and improved technology, the 20 year old vertically mounted Edison motor began to yield to a new compact style transversely mounted under the mandrel end of the top plate. This was seen in two newcomers, the ECLIPSE, wired for 125 v. DC and ACME, wired for 104-

110 v. 60 cycle AC. These replaced the MAJESTIC, built around the old 110-120 v. DC CLASS E motor and mechanism. The WINDSOR, still the old AUTOMATIC/CLASS M/IMPERIAL by another name was continued for a further year or two.

The automatic phonographs are listed as closely as possible to catalogue presentation because closer examination of survivors of this period shows departures from normal Edison construction and not conforming to a particular style that might be expected at a specific date. A policy of using up redundant stocks of parts is often accountable, but more likely is the replacement of faulty pieces or whole portions of the mechanism by repairmen. For example, the expected TRIUMPH Model B top works are reported but lacking an end-gate, combination attachments locked in the 2-minute mode are found on later models, and both Model J and K reproducers adapted to 2-minute playing have been notified. Gateless machines were recognized as giving problems in conjunction with the Model D Repeating Attachment, but such a combination is widely reported as functioning properly.

With these new mechanisms came a new cabinet of uniform design. It was floor standing with ball-and-claw legs. The greater floor clearance made it easier for sweeping underneath, finding dropped coins and doubtless less of an invitation to be kicked by the customer if it failed to play. Earlier cabinets had mostly been legless or with short and stumpy feet. The new cabinets had a cupboard that was more than enough for the batteries if needed, coin-mechanism and box, and there was a lyre on the front and pillar decoration at both front corners. The new design had a rectangular glazed cover - the curved glass fronts had gone - and this tilted back for access to the upper mechanism while the whole machine tilted back on a wooden base. Locking keys were provided.

Most conspicuous was the large frame with the title of the piece offered, and rows of these machines, each advertising a popular song or catchy tune of the day looked impressive in a Phonograph Parlor.

WINDSOR Coin-Slot Phonograph

Introduced:	In this style in 1906 but first named in August 1904
Type:	2-minute
Dimensions:	Height 72 in; (46 in. without back frame), base 27 in. x 17 in.
Weight:	150 lb. net, gross 217 lb.
Motor and Mechanism:	As the CLASS M. The new Edison Contact Coin Equipment was fitted, claimed to be simple, positive and reliable and made at the Edison works.
Cabinet:	Quartered oak, antique finish, square top fitted with bevel glass, and bevelled French plate glass mirror as interior backing. The cabinet corner pillars were rounded from 1906.

Reproducer:	Model B
Listening tubes etc:	Rubber hearing tubes with ear cups supplied with a 24 in. horn and crane as alternative.

Price: $65.00 - if 10 or more ordered $60.00

£13 13s. 0d. or £12 12s. 0d. for ten or more from May 1908 (U.K.).

The MAJESTIC, ousted by the ECLIPSE and ACME in the United States in 1906 was listed in the United Kingdom at these prices until discontinued in 1908.

WINDSOR phonograph with the large electric motor

ECLIPSE and ACME Coin-Slot Phonographs

These are dealt with separately, as follows:

ECLIPSE

Introduced: June 1906 (U.S.);
              May 1908 (U. K.)

Type: 2-minute

Cabinet, Dimensions and Weight:
Described in the introduction and under the Windsor heading above, the only difference being in the motor mounting board and having an electric mains lead fed through the back.

Motor: Model A with CLASS E motor

Model B with Emerson make for 125 v. DC circuit with speed control through governor contacts across a shunt resistance. Belt drive to top works. Other motor makes are known to have been used.

Reproducer: Model B

Listening tubes etc: Rubber hearing tubes with ear cups were supplied, with a 24 in. horn and crane as the alternative.

Price: $65.00
         if 10 or more ordered $60.00
         £13 13s. 0d
         £12 12s. 0d. for ten or more (U. K.)

The ECLIPSE was overtaken in 1907 (U.S.) by the ALVA Coin-slot Phonograph, but was still quoted in September 1908.

ECLIPSE Coin-slot Phonograph; the ACME and ALVA automatic machines were housed in similar cabinets

250

ACME

Introduced:	April 1906 (U.S.); May 1908 (U. K.)
Type:	2-minute
Cabinet, Dimensions and Weight:	Similar to the ECLIPSE above.
Motor and Mechanism:	Emerson-made induction motor to run on 104-110v. 60 cycle AC circuit. Speed regulation through the normal type of friction brake governor, similarly to the spring driven phonographs. The motor drove the TRIUMPH Model B type of top mechanism. Return effected by Model D Repeating Attachment. This was the first AC phonograph put out by the Edison Company. Until December 1907 it was possible to order the ACME to special frequencies, but there was trouble generally with the standard motor during 1907 and the offer was withdrawn.
Reproducer:	Model B
Listening tubes etc.:	Rubber hearing tubes with ear cups were supplied, with a 24 in. horn and crane as alternative.
Price:	$65.00, if 10 or more ordered $60.00
	£13 13s. 0d. or £12 12s. 0d. for ten or more (U. K.)

The ACME was phased out after 1907 and its place taken by the ALVA, although still quoted in September 1908.

ALVA Coin-slot Phonograph

Introduced:	Mid to late 1907 (U.S.)
Type:	2-minute
Dimensions:	Height 72 in. (46 in. without back frame); base 27 in. x 17 in.
Motor:	104-110 v. 60 cycle AC - DC universal motor of the domestic ALVA and identical to those found on the concurrent Edison BUSINESS Phonographs. These were frequently made by Emerson or Burke Electrical Company. The motor shell was aluminium with the normal friction governor on the extended motor shaft. Electrical ballast was supplied for the DC operation. Special motors were offered for

251

other currents.

Cabinet:	As supplied for the ECLIPSE and ACME
Mechanism:	TRIUMPH type upper works with Model B repeating attachment.
Reproducer:	Model B
Listening tubes:	One pair of hearing tubes with ear cups supplied, the horn being no longer offered.
Accessories:	Camel-hair chip-brush, oilcan and connecting wires.
Price:	$65.00 -if 10 or more ordered $60.00. It is not known if this model reached the United Kingdom.

Examples have come to notice of these Edison automatic machines with 4-minute playing only, and after 2-minute records were discontinued there would be no alternatives, and in the 1920s they would have played Blue Amberols, although the 3 ½ minute duration must have told against them in a public place.

As a statistic for a Book of Achievement of the Phonograph the following are offered: in 1903 two long-lasting Edison Gold Moulded records were given publicity after use in coin-slot phonographs, one in Pennsylvania had played an accountable 1525 times, and another in Memphis, Tenn. was reported as playing 3,000 times.

NOTES
1) British Patent No. 10,970 dated August 10th 1887 for The Combination of a Phonograph with Coin-freed apparatus for Indicating the Results of Operation and for other purposes
2) British Patent No. 9762 dated July 5th 1888 for Improvements in Apparatus for the Automatic Reproduction of Sounds from Records. Charles Adams-Randall is a neglected pioneer of the early phonograph. In his British patent 9996 of July 10th 1888 for instance, he proposed recording on a disc or cylinder of soft metal or a wax-like material a groove of uniform depth, but with the sound waves cut in the sides and using a diaphragm boosted by electromagnets, an elementary microphone. The patent also included electroplating and duplicating of the original recording.
The origin of the word Pariophone is derived from the Latin word parere = to produce, or give forth, and the Greek phone = voice
3) U.S. Patent No. 428,750 dated May 27th 1890, filed December 18th 1889 for Coin Actuated Attachment for Phonographs, the phonograph having up to four listening tubes, each with its own coin chute. U. S. Patent No. 428,751 dated May 27th 1890, filed February 3rd 1890 for Coin Actuating Attachment for Phonographs; in this operation the coin itself closed the electrical circuit. Glass was general manager of Pacific Phonograph Company, 323 Pine Street, San Francisco, a director of Spokane Phonograph Company, Washington, and of West Coast Phonograph Company, Portland, Oregon. The first two Glass/Arnold machines were set up in the Palais Royal Saloon, California on November 23rd 1889, and from then to the following May 14th took $1,035.25 and from December 4th to May 14th $938.57, while a third elsewhere took $580.50 from December 10th to May 14th. A fourth in a San Francisco ferry waiting room took $551.50 from February 14th to May 14th 1890, another took $248.00

4) Gilliland (and F. W. Toppan) patented an attachment for automatic phonographs on April 10th 1894 (U.S. No. 518,209), but this had been filed on March 6th 1890.
5) Keller's three U.S. patents 518,190/1/2 of April 10th 1894 embodied features in these machines. They were filed January 31st, February 14th and March 10th 1891.
6) Ling took out two U.S. Patents Nos. 440,046 for Automatic Repeating Mechanism for Phonographs, filed May 16th 1890, granted November 4th 1890, and 495,557 filed June 4th 1891 and granted April 18th 1893 for Coin-operated Mechanism
7) An early use of the coin-slot phonograph to promote sales of goods was reported from a Bloomington, Illinois newspaper of July 31st 1890. Two stores in the town were giving a free hearing of the phonograph to buyers of more than 50 cents worth of merchandise. Eighteen months later on December 9th 1891 phonograph business in the town was described as being good, with the five automatic machines having their cylinders changed every other day. The 65 lb. batteries had to be carried to the electric light works to be recharged.
8) James L. Andem, president and general manager of Ohio Phonograph Company, Cincinnati, writing in *A Practical Guide to the Use of the Edison Phonograph*, Cincinnati 1892.
9) *Edison Phonographic News*, November-December 1895
10) Listed in *Edison Cylinder Records* 1889-1912
11) Examples: S. S. Ott of Kansas Phonograph Company offered the Ott/Tewksbury Topeka machine with oak or sycamore cabinet and automatic mechanism for $35.00, not to exceed $40.00. These machines would average $1.25 a day for 50 cents expenses; Cary's Nebraska Automatic Slot Machine sold for $50.00 and would bring in $1.10 a day. For an outlay of $42.00 Missouri Phonograph Company could produce one St. Louis Automatic Slot Machine with cabinet, safe, money drawers, safety fuse attachment and free crating and delivery. The State Phonograph Company of Illinois offered not only a machine for $25.00 plus 10% of profits but a little experience as well
- "we try to place three to seven machines in areas where men can inspect them twice a day and change the music. We now have 65 coin-in-the-slot out and they are paying the expenses of our company entirely from these receipts......"
12) Letter of August 7th 1891 from Thomas R. Lombard, vice-president of North American Phonograph Company to New Jersey Phonograph Company. Lombard was a promoter of coin-slot phonographs and was later the first to see commercial and entertainment possibilities in Edison's motion picture machines - Edison Archive.
13) U. S. Patent No. 680,060 for Platform Motor for Phonographs filed April 26th 1898, granted August 6th 1901.
14) U.S. Patent No. 702,985 filed September 13th 1901, granted June 24th 1902. There was one earlier and 4 later allied patents.

LOCAL PHONOGRAPH COMPANIES

The following comprised the Local Phonograph Companies, set up in 1889 by Lippincott's North American Phonograph Company to handle Edison's Phonographs, and Graphophones. All those shown were represented at the first Convention in Chicago in 1890 and the figures show the total of business and automatic phonographs claimed to be under rental at the second Convention in the next year.

Alabama Phonograph Company	
Central Nebraska	
Chicago Central	200
Columbia (of Washington, DC)	400
Colorado and Utah	

253

Eastern Pennsylvania	over 100
Florida	
Georgia	over 50
Iowa	over 200
Kansas	56
Kentucky	78
Louisiana	45
Metropolitan Phonograph (of New York)	
- merged with New York Phonograph	
Michigan	
Minnesota	
Missouri	134
Montana	about 45
Nebraska	80
New England (Boston)	300
New Jersey	about 80
New York (merged with Metropolitan)	750
Ohio	161
Old Dominion (Virginia)	225
Pacific (San Francisco)	
South Dakota	
Spokane	
State (Illinois)	about 125
Tennessee	
Texas	110
West Coast (Oregon)	
Wisconsin	
Western Pennsylvania	
Wyoming	

Holland Brothers of Ottawa

Chapter 19
Multiplex
Coin-Operated Phonographs

Multiplex is an old word meaning "multiple" or "manifold"[1] and came into use as a phonograph term in the 1890s briefly for a $1,000 3-cylinder 3-horn Graphophone Grand, and earlier and more significantly as a unit of several cylinder mandrels that could be attached to an electric CLASS M or CLASS E Edison, either for an automatic amusement machine or for office use. Edison had also applied the term to a telegraph invention, but the idea of a multi-cylinder phonograph had either not appealed to him or had not arisen.

The Multiplex Automatic Phonographs are elusive as a research subject, though not lacking patentees, and much that is known depends on surviving letters between G. N. Morison, secretary of Edison United Phonograph Company and Stephen F. Moriarty of Edison Bell in London, and presupposes more activity in the British market than in the United States.

The 1890s were fruitful years for inventors of multiple mandrel phonographs. The pioneer patentee was James L. Skillin who proposed two or more mandrels held within a wheel-like frame at either end, the whole rotative to bring each mandrel successively in line with a drive shaft.[2] Nearly all the other multi-cylinder phonographs used a similar layout, culminating in the 24-cylinder ferris wheel magazine in the Multiphone of John C. Dunton.[3] This was a very large machine and possibly this fact alone cowed many a patron before he had to start winding the Edison spring motor.

Skillin's invention and his successors' depended on their being adapted to the drive

The Multiphone at Fort Myers Edison museum. It used the Edison Triton motor.

255

shaft of the electric phonographs of the CLASS M style, where they took the place of the normal mandrel; at first cylinders could be brought into playing in sequence while, as time went on, the customer could make a selective choice by moving a lever. The early Multiplexes had their drawbacks and broken records were an ever present complaint.

Another name prominent in this corner of phonograph history was George W. Moore, a mechanic of Atlanta, Georgia - "Moore's Multiplex Attachment" - of July 1896.[4] Again it was adaptable to a standard electric phonograph but needing the mandrel removing, the back rod supports raising and new carrier-arm fitted, and was recommended for:

1) Brief and letter dictation by lawyers
2) As an entertainer
3) For course of instruction in any study

Moore's achievement with 5 mandrels was soon overtaken by another from Atlanta, G. V. Gress, the most progressive and successful of the several promoters currently working on multi-mandrel cylinder players. Gress's Multiplex machine was advertised in *The Phonoscope* in 1896 and was made with mandrels for 5, 10, 15, or 20 cylinders for attaching to the Standard Edison Automatic Phonograph. The machine was explained fully in the December 1896 *Phonoscope*.

A Multiplex machine was bought by Edison United Phonograph Co. for $190.00 in August 1897, opening the way to a co-operation between Gress at his New York office and Edison, who seemed to get on agreeably with him to the extent of offering him his collaboration. Edison was uneasy at first lest Gress sold his invention to Columbia but in a letter[5] he promised Edison United all foreign business in his inventions on the Multiplex and the platform motor, and it soon became obvious that Gress could make money independently of Edison and could be difficult if he felt so disposed. The platform motor was part of a coin-operated phonograph. Powered by the weight of the operator standing on a platform it would enjoy some success.[6]

Following meetings between Edison and Gress they agreed that the latter would make and supply Multiplex units to the Edison works for attaching to the Edison-made bodies at the rate of about 300 a month. On the body of each was marked:

MULTIPLEX PHONOGRAPH CO., ATLANTA, GEORGIA

Pat: April 12 1892, April 19 1893, Sept. 22 1896

others applied for

while the Edison plate on the top casting would be omitted. Although Edison said he could make them cheaper, the attachments were bought in for $100.00 each[7] and Gress would be paid $5.00 each or $5,000.00 royalty for each year.

In the United Kingdom The Edison Bell Consolidated Phonograph Company Ltd. had

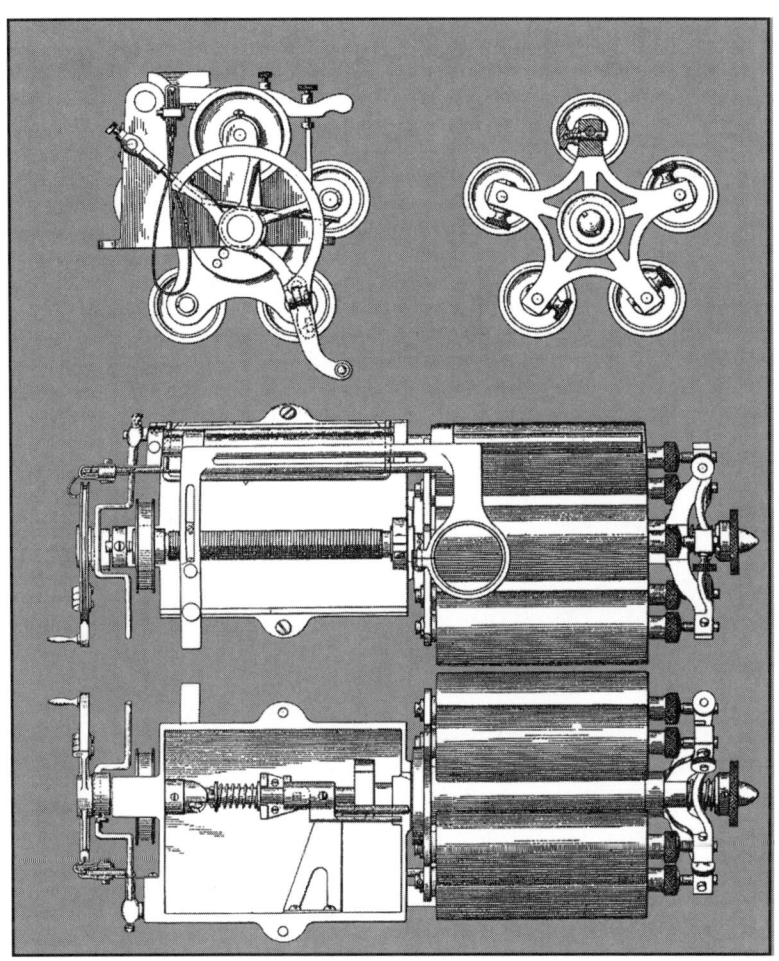

Details from Gress's British Patent No. 6923 of March 22nd 1898

been formed in December 1897 to take over the patents of the Multiplex (and Bettini's Microphonograph). The principal shareholder was Edison United Phonograph Company, and after Gress's initial qualms had been overcome, export of the machines was started and by May 1,000 had been ordered by London where complete in cabinet they would be known as the Type 5 (Gress Automatic).

In March 1898 Gress applied for and was granted British (No. 6923) and German (42714) patents.

The first Multiplex was said to be in London by December 1897 and the only other British sighting mentioned was also in London at Earls Court Exhibition Centre in August 1898 where six models were reported to be taking ten shillings a day each.[8]

In the same month in London Edison Bell secured an Agreement with Multiplex for patent rights in France and Germany and two months later a further 750 Multiplexes arrived in the capital.

In September 1898 the indefatigable Gress announced an improved Multiplex. Up to now the cylinders on the mandrels had to be exchanged in situ, but the mandrel clusters were now made readily removable for replacing the cylinders outside the machine; thus the programmes could be changed more frequently.

In the meantime Gress had also improved the platform motor, though still worked by the customer standing on a step in front of the phonograph, and by October 1898 200 were reported building at the Multiplex works. There were hopes of being able to put one in every United States railroad station. Their instructions survive:

1) Step on platform
2) Pull down lever and release - number you wish to hear appears on dial below
3) Drop coin in slot

Production details and further career of the platform motor automatic phonograph are not clear but it drew praise from Edison sources "the weight motor machine seems to run perfectly and I have never seen it fail to reproduce properly.... "[9] This unique phonograph style, despite a promising start, seems to have gone without leaving so much as a shadow.

The Gress Multiplex had largely run its course by the end of the decade, remaindered stock was stored in Brooklyn and Edison Bell was holding up payments. There were other makers of multi-mandrel phonographs in the market and more sophisticated machines were on the way, but the Edison works would still be assembling and casing small numbers of Multiplex for several years, in spite of misgivings about their prospects.[10]

By April 1899 Gress had other uses in mind for the Multiplex, and like George Moore was publicizing a commercial version 'to fit on a desk' in two versions - (1) spring motor driven for around $65.00, and (2) electric motor at $100.00 or more.[11]

Edison Bell in London had overstocked with Multiplex phonographs, and in 1905 offered these at prices much below their worth - the purchase price of $80.00 or around £17 0s. 0d. had been quoted in February 1899.

Type:	2-minute
Dimensions:	Height 54 in., width 27 in., depth 17 in.
Motor:	Standard electric CLASS M type, 2 ½ volts 2 amps.
Cabinet:	Oak floor standing with cupboard below, curved glass cover to mechanism and music advertising frame
Reproducer:	Edison Automatic
Horn:	Aluminium herald trumpet
Price:	£10 10s. 0d.

In the United States other makers of multi-cylinder coin-slot machines offered models with more sophisticated mechanisms and better cabinets. The Regina Company of Rahway NJ, makers of perforated disc musical boxes not only marketed a six-cylinder Automatic Reginaphone in 1905 but promised to campaign against laws repressive to playing musical instruments in public places. The improved Regina Hexaphone followed three years later, but by now Edison companies were out of the multi-cylinder instruments and on to the final series of their own single-cylinder automatic phonographs. The multi-record coin-slot disc phonograph trade was moving in quickly and in several years had largely ousted the cylinder machines.

NOTES
1) 1676 or earlier (O. E. D.)
2) U.S. Patent No. 472,684
3) U.S. Patent No. 797,102
4) U.S. Patent No. 568,116
5) December 7th 1897
6) Walter Miller of the Edison phonograph works also patented a Platform Motor for Phonographs, U.S. No. 680,060 of August 6th 1901, filed April 26th 1898, but no record of the machine's production has been seen
7) Quoted March 29th 1898
8) Letter of August 19th 1898 from G. Brossa to Moriarty. From this distance of time this does not seem a very large amount, being 120 playings at one penny in a presumably busy spot in an exhibition.
9) G.N. Morison to S.F. Moriarty, June 30th 1889
10) In a letter of February 17th 1899 G.N. Morison prophesied that the public would turn to small Edison-built coin-slot phonographs for the years ahead
11) G.N. Morison to S.F. Moriarty April 14th 1899.
Letters quoted are from the Edison Archive.

The principal Multiplex patentees were as follows:

		filed	granted
U.S.	472,684 James L. Skillin, New York	Sept. 12 1890	April 12 1892
	495,869 Joseph L. Atkins, Washington, DC	Aug. 27 1892	April 18 1893
	568,116 George W, Moore, Atlanta, GA	May 11 1895	Sept. 22 1896
British	6923 George V. Gress, Atlanta, GA	March 22 1898	April 30 1898
U.S.	634,025 Arthur B. Robinson, Dickinson, ND	Feb. 21 1899	Oct. 3 1899
	655,225 George V. Gress, Atlanta, GA	April 21 1898	Aug. 7 1900
	797,102 John C. Dunton, Grand Rapids, MI	Nov. 28 1904	Aug. 15 1905
	816,608 Cyrus C. Shigley, Hart, MI	Oct. 26 1904	April 3 1906
	864,686 Allison A. Pratt, New York	Jan. 17 1906	Aug. 27 1907
	883,971 Julius Roever, New York	May 29 1907	April 7 1908
	909,455 Cornelius Reinhardt, San Fran., CA	Dec. 6 1907	Jan. 12 1909
	925,430 James I. Gemmill, Cleveland, OH	Sept. 22 1905	June 15 1909
	948,675 Peter M. Ravenskilde, Carberry, IL	Oct. 20 1908	Feb. 8 1910
	978,014 James I. Gemmill, Cleveland, OH	July 11 1908	Dec. 6 1910

Chapter 20

Electric Coin-Slot CONCERT Phonographs

CLASS M CONCERT and
CLASS E CONCERT AUTOMATIC PHONOGRAPHS

CLASS M CONCERT became known as the AJAX in April 1900

CLASS E CONCERT became known as the VULCAN in April 1900

(originally these were their telegraphic names)

Introduced: Late 1899

Type: 2-minute Concert cylinders

Dimensions: Height: 55 in., base 28 in. x 17 in.

Weight: CLASS M CONCERT/AJAX 203 lb. with batteries, gross 420 lb., packed in 4 cases; this was the heaviest Edison phonograph

CLASS E CONCERT/VULCAN 170 lb. gross 325 lb. and packed in 3 cases

Motor: Standard CLASS M battery type at 2 ½ volts 2 amps., and CLASS E mains type at 110-120 volts DC. Both had the exposed vertical ball governor

AJAX Coin-slot phonograph. The VULCAN was identical except for use of 110v. mains current

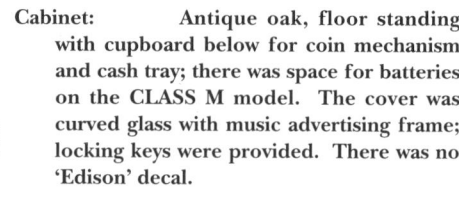

Cabinet:	Antique oak, floor standing with cupboard below for coin mechanism and cash tray; there was space for batteries on the CLASS M model. The cover was curved glass with music advertising frame; locking keys were provided. There was no 'Edison' decal.
Mechanism:	CONCERT upper works with provision for coin mechanism and repeating attachment to return to the starting place after each playing. This was effected by a lever and drawstring apparatus
Reproducer:	Edison Automatic followed by Model D in 1902. A telescopic tube led from the reproducer to the horn or listening tube outlet
Horn etc.:	A 24 in. brass horn with rear-mounted support was supplied at first; later a brass-belled black-bodied horn took its place. To increase revenue it is likely many of these models were fitted promptly with multiple listening tubes
Accessories:	Camel-hair chip brush, oilcan and connecting wires
Price:	$150.00 for both models

The rare CLASS M CONCERT Automatic Phonograph converted to playing Standard cylinders

These machines were officially deleted from the catalogues in 1904 but could still be ordered as the CONCERT WINDSOR and CONCERT MAJESTIC to the end of 1905.

No examples have come to notice in the United Kingdom. As with the domestic CONCERT Phonographs the large mandrel and carrier-arm could be replaced for using Standard cylinders.

A use for redundant AJAX cabinets was reported from San Francisco, where in January 1904 Peter Bacigalupi opened up a 'swell' Penny Parlor. On March 30th AJAX cabinets were being supplied to him for using with multiple mandrel automatic phonographs and may well have been used similarly elsewhere.

Chapter 21

Spring-Driven Coin-Slot Phonographs

Thomas Edison was essentially an electrician and with some of his inventions involving early forms of electric power, it followed that the first phonographs would be driven by electricity from early on and as a next step adaptation to automatic operation. In the 1890s there was still not much electric power outside the cities and an aversion in many quarters to using batteries, and for about ten years a range of Edison spring-driven coin-slot phonographs was made available.

Single 'S' style coin-slot phonograph

From today's vantage of the punching and rough treatment meted out to coin operated machines it seems incredible that these delicately adjusted wind-yourself phonographs lasted even long enough for any to have survived, but perhaps people were more restrained in the times when those machines flourished.

It is likely that the first spring-driven coin-slot phonograph was that introduced by Columbia in 1897 (Type AS) preceding the first advertisement for an Edison version in *The Phonoscope* for August 1898 (U.S.). This is believed to have been for the 'H' COIN-SLOT Phonograph, based on the HOME and code-named 'Domestic', a term that was hardly apposite.

In the same year The Manhattan Phonograph Company adapted the 'square-top' STANDARD and set it in an oak cabinet, a much cheaper proposition than any modification of the electric models. The customer had to wind the spring before every playing and a friction clutch forestalled overwinding. Some models were paired back-to-back. The Manhattan company

263

paid $1,000 a year for placing these machines in the various ferry houses of The Union Ferry Company of New York. The machine is generally referred to as the 'S' COIN-SLOT phonograph.

Production of the 'H' COIN-SLOT ceased in 1901 and two models took its place, the BIJOU built around the GEM, and the EXCELSIOR. This used a STANDARD mechanism. Both were table models.

They were joined at the same time by the CLIMAX, a bulky floor-standing model that played Concert cylinders.

Unlike the domestic phonographs each type ran to only one advertised model but each underwent mechanical changes.

'H' COIN-SLOT Phonograph

Introduced: August 1898 (U.S.)

Type: 2-minute

Dimensions: Height 21 in; base 18 ½ in. x 12 in.

Weight: 45 lb.

Motor: HOME motor of contemporary 'suitcase' period and adapted to coin operation[1]

Equipment: Horns varied, but it is known to have been offered either with a black japanned flared North American or 14 in. brass types. The Automatic reproducer was held in the carrier-arm by two wide-headed screws, and an oilcan and chip-brush were provided.

Cabinet: Antique oak table type with curved glass front cover to the mechanism and front door for access to the motor and money drawer. The side panels were not glazed on the early types. Both the glass front and drawer were fitted with locks.

Back-to-back 'S' style coin-slot phonograph

General:	There were two styles, the first with normal on-side reproducer and the later models had an on-top reproducer connected by a telescopic tube instead of the unsatisfactory flexible tubing. The coin-slot chute and mechanism at the back of the mandrel in earlier models was re-sited more forward in the later. The standard version of the machine was made to be operated by a nickel (5 cents) but adjustment to other coins could be specified.
Price:	$50.00

'H' style coin-slot phonograph, two views

BIJOU COIN-SLOT Phonograph

There were two distinct styles of this machine, the differences lying in the forms of their coin-slot mechanisms. The second style is found more frequently, signifying that all was not well with the machine in its original form.

In the early model the coin-triggering device is placed towards the right front with the coin-chute brought forward to feed it, but the reproducer carrier is actuated behind the mandrel and returned to its starting position by a drawstring; the rear of the body casting is cut out to give room to this mechanism.

Also on the earlier models the instruction card holder was fixed on the left and there was no decal on the cabinet front.

The siting of the mechanism was largely reversed in the second model with the coin-

chute placed at the back centre of the cabinet and the lifting straight edge being in front of the mandrel and the carrier-arm returned after each playing by a light tension spring.

The instruction card clip was now moved to the right of the glass cover and an EDISON BIJOU PHONOGRAPH banner decal[2] appeared on the cabinet body.

Introduced: 1901 (U.S.), also imported to the U.K. by Edison Bell, London

Type: 2-minute

Dimensions: Height 16 ¼ in., base 13 ¼ in. x 10 ½ in.

Weight: 17 lb.

Motor: Essentially the Model A GEM with the flat key. On standard models the BIJOU would accept a 1 cent piece with 5 ½ winds on the crank. The crank revolved as the mainspring unwound

Equipment: Initially a 14 in. North American funnel horn. An Automatic reproducer with shortened lever was supplied at first, but this soon gave way to the Model B

Cabinet: Antique oak table type, curved glass front cover and rear cash drawer both with lock.

Price: $30.00; £7 10s. 0d.

The early BIJOU coin-slot phonograph, three views showing the early style of mechanism

266

Two views of the later BIJOU

EXCELSIOR COIN-SLOT Phonograph

Introduced:	1901 (U.S.), also imported to the U.K. by Edison Bell, London
Type:	2-minute
Dimensions:	Height 18 ½ in., base 17 ½ in. x 11 ¼ in.
Weight:	28 lb.
Motor etc:	The first models were influenced by the 'square' STANDARD, then changing to the less severe lines of the 1901-1905 Model A. These early models had the automatic return mechanism placed behind the mandrel with the coin-chute in the right-hand rear corner. The later and more easily found models had a tilting straight edge with tension spring return at the front, with the coin operating equipment directly behind the mandrel.
Equipment:	14 in. brass horn, later black and brass type. Automatic reproducer held in place by two wide-headed screws, later the Model B was held by a knurled screw.

The later EXCELSIOR coin-slot phonograph

Cabinet:	Antique oak table type, the first models having no decal but soon to carry the EDISON EXCELSIOR PHONOGRAPH banner[3]. These first machines are reported with wooden side panels to the cover, but were soon glazed. Both front cover and side cash drawer could be locked
Price:	$50.00; £9 0s. 0d. (sold by Edison Bell as the Standard Automatic)

The BIJOU and EXCELSIOR were withdrawn after September 1908. This was the year the Amberol records were introduced, and falling sales and the need to concentrate factory resources led to the machines' demise.

CLIMAX COIN-SLOT Phonograph

Introduced: 1901

Type: 2-minute Concert cylinders

Dimensions: Height 54 in., base 22 ½ in. x 14 ½ in.

Weight: 95 lb. - when crated it grossed 335 lb.

Motor: The CONCERT with added coin mechanism, the standard model accepting one nickel (5 cents). The crank was then turned seven times and the reproducer automatically returned to the start after each playing.

Equipment: 24 in. horn suspended from a crane support fitted to the rear of the casing. Automatic reproducer, later superseded by Model B or D.

Cabinet: Antique oak, floor standing, with locking cover, cash drawer and door to lower cupboard.

Price: $125.00

CLIMAX coin-slot phonograph

The CLIMAX was withdrawn in August 1904; by this date Standard Gold Moulded cylinders were well established. It seems unlikely that this machine was offered in the United Kingdom.

NOTES

1) U.S. Patent No. 541,924 for Phonograph filed by Edison on December 3rd 1890 and granted July 2nd 1895 was for a powered carrier-arm return for the HOME (and TRIUMPH) style of phonograph.
2) The word BIJOU in the form depicted on this decal was the subject of U.S. Trade Mark No. 6,675 of August 22nd 1905, filed May 24th 1905.
3) The word EXCELSIOR in the form depicted on this decal was the subject of U. S. Trade Mark No. 6,673 of August 29th 1905, filed May 24th 1905.

Views of a Perfection coin-slot phonograph with the Edison top movement adapted to an Amet double-spring motor

Chapter 22
PHONO-KINETOSCOPE
1894-5

The coin-slot Phono-Kinetoscope combined 35mm moving film with a cylinder providing musical background

One of Edison's less successful phonograph ventures was the coin-operated Phono-Kinetoscope or Kinetophonograph. Not to be confused with his big-screen projected Kinetophone of 15 years later this was the crude 1894 Kinetoscope with a phonograph mandrel movement installed in its body and driven by the motor of the film equipment.[1] The intention was to give the viewer sight and sound, adding music thought to be appropriate to the film with no pretension to synchronization, and it was available only for a matter of months.

The composition of this phonograph mechanism is at first baffling because it was not the CLASS M as might be expected for that date, but the improved (spectacle) machine of 1888-9. The spectacle frame was cut down to one eye and secured at its pivot while the reproducer on the one Phono-Kinetoscope that is the 'most complete' has a recorder body from the perfected phonograph with a floating weight from an Automatic speaker fitted but turned 180° in the eye and causing the stylus bar to be reversed so the sapphire meets the grooves rather than trailing them in the normal way. In front of the mandrel a short return screw with 1 ½ in. of coarse thread - unique to this model - lifted the carrier-arm back to the start. These special phonographs had FOR USE WITH THE EDISON KINETOSCOPE ONLY marked in gilt on the body casting and the serial number was prefaced by a punched 'K'.[2] Additionally the original repeating attachment shaft was removed and its left-hand pivot ground out. The half-nut arm was shortened, and from what remains one can imagine the working of the feed and return mechanism.

The reason for using an obsolete movement and reproducer is given as enabling Edison interests to retain control of the Phono-Kinetoscope, especially outside the United States.[3] As a test case a Phono-Kinetoscope was shipped to Great Britain in 1895, and a further two sent to France at about the same time.

From the small amount of information on the Phono-Kinetoscopes, there is an inclination to write them off as soon as they appeared in the arcades, but some attempts were made to excite interest in them. Edison quoted The Continental Commerce Company of 44 Pine Street, New York, phonographs for Kinetoscopes at $50.00 each including connecting devices; with this came worldwide sales permission so long as the reproducer was not sold separately.[4] Through this agency it is known that seven Phono-Kinetoscopes were sold to a Launcelot Lee-Warner for £60 0s. 0d. each, and that within a few months Lee-Warner contracted to take 15 more. All went to a sterling area such as the United Kingdom, where the works of one are reported to have survived.[5]

The other side of the cabinet and the location of the phonograph

In spite of their being a 'good idea' these early Phono-Kinetoscopes failed to catch the public ear and soon disappeared. A reason for their disappointing performance could be their expense to buy, more trouble to maintain and the fact that they yielded no extra cash for it. Kinetoscopes (without the phonograph) could be bought until about 1900. These cost $200.00 against $350.00 for the Phono-Kinetoscope[6] and it has been estimated that about 1,000 Kinetoscopes were made between 1894 and 1899 and a figure of around 45 Phono-Kinetoscopes in 1895 is perhaps as close as will ever be known.[7]

1895 Phono-Kinetoscope phonograph shown in position in the cabinet. The carrier-arm peculiar to this machine is shown. The phonograph is driven by the motion picture motor. There is no repeating attachment embodied in this motor and it is not clear what form this took or how it functioned.

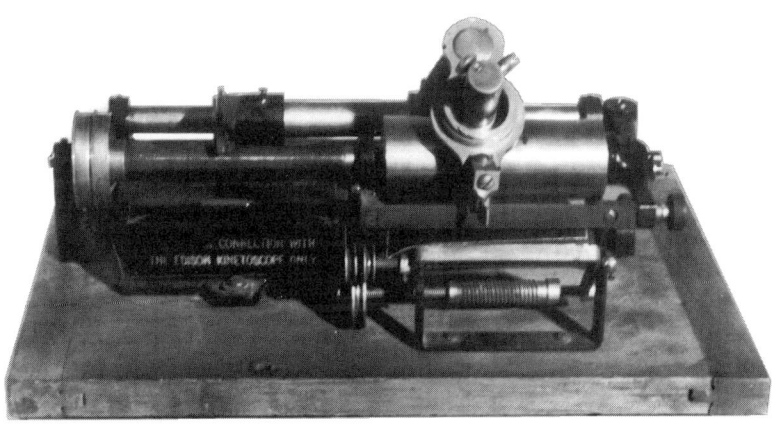

The same motor outside the cabinet. Although this example has a coarse return screw it is not clear what other parts are missing to cause the phonograph to repeat the cylinder.

1) The Perrett motor was said to give the best results. (Memo of January 16th 1895 - Edison Archive)
2) Correspondence with Ray Phillips
3) Opinion of Raymond Wile
4) Letter of May 9th 1895 - Edison Archive
5) Letter of August 28th 1895 - Edison Archive
6) Ramsaye - *Million and One Nights* pp 167-8. Ramsaye erroneously describes these machines as Kinetophones.
7) Gordon Hendricks - *The Kinetoscope*, quoted by Ray Phillips

It was reported on September 10th 1897 that the Graphophone had been used with a Kinetoscope instead of the Edison: "Result satisfactory in scene with a train, sound of bell and whistle perfect".

Chapter 23
KINETOPHONE
1909-1916

Preface

Although the later Edison Kinetophone was intended as an entertainment phonograph for an audience in providing voice and music in a motion picture theatre it had short-lived success and its history remained little-known until the publication of several informative papers by Art Shifrin, at the time Northeast Region Manager for Abekas Video Systems Inc.[1]

The Kinetophone was the inventor's final cylinder phonograph system and a study of its history has cleared up the justification for several Edison patents that have been difficult to understand. It was certainly one of Edison's failures, though like much of his work ahead of its time in some aspects, but in most books on the development of Talking Pictures it merits little or no mention, nor is credit given to the years of experiment and persistence of Edison's staff when everything seemed to be going wrong.

The account that follows has tried to avoid tramping through Art Shifrin's findings as much as possible and to look at further phases of this device, so that any reader fortunate to stumble across any of this equipment may perhaps recognize it and understand how it fitted in the system. Even now there are some features that are unclear. What was billed as "The Eighth Wonder of the World" - and much was in those days - was an untidy union of sight and sound, and failed for that reason, and a fully unified system made by others would not become general until the last years of Edison's life.

Development and Realization

> .... (Mr. Edison) wants to double the amount of sound and use it in combination with the Vitascope, for an audience to see an opera or play, to see the movement of the actors and to hear their voices as plainly as though they were witnessing the original production itself.
>
> Report in *Edison Phonographic News* July-August 1896

The above was credited to Edison about a year after the launching and subsequent rejection of the short-lived coin-operated Phono-Kinetoscope.[2] One assistant employed in the laboratory to help W.K.L. Dickson in the development of this apparatus in 1893 had been Eugene Lauste, who years later would photograph the sound on the film alongside the pictures and was still experimenting at Bloomfield, New Jersey, and close to West Orange, in the early 1930s.

The 1900s brought a rash of talking machine sound systems for the cinema; Little Tich in his big boots was seen and heard dancing to the cylinder phonograph in Paris, and among a number of others in the decade were the Cinephone, Hepworth's Vivaphone and Gaumont's Chronophone, all using films, discs and usually a synchronizer acting as a regulator between picture and sound.

There were several obvious difficulties that occurred in the coupling of a moving film and a phonograph disc or cylinder; after getting sound and picture synchronized the sound had to be made loud enough to fill a theatre. At the time the phonographs were being demonstrated in the 'nineties and were still a novelty, the people would have remained quiet during the lecture, the moving picture hall attracted a wider, noisier audience, there would be shuffling in and out and any sound would have to be bright and distinct.

Several inventors were starting to work on mechanical sound amplifiers, often using air under pressure. Had not Edison himself in 1878 demonstrated a speaking machine or Aerophone as an extension to his original Phonograph patent of February 19th 1878?[3] Robert Hope-Jones the improver of organ systems was working on air actuated comb devices,[4] as was Horace Short also in England a few years later, and his compressed air sound intensifier was bought by Sir Charles Parsons, improved and marketed by The Gramophone and Typewriter Co. Ltd. from 1905 as the Auxeto-Gramophone (or Aux-e-to-phone as sometimes advertised) and sold under Victor and Gramophone Company marques.

Research was continuing with sound intensifiers at West Orange too, led by Alexander N. Pierman and resulting in about a dozen patents. In his early endeavours he concentrated on a frictional method of amplifying cylinder records,[5] but after 1905 veered towards the comb valve and compressed air, but none of his reproducers was ever offered for sale. The abandonment of his work on the frictional sound amplifier may have been through pressure from W. E. Gilmore.[6]

Nearly a decade had passed from the Phono-Kinetoscope of 1895 before there was evidence of new thinking about sound films from Edison, this time spurred by the incursion of moving pictures into the coin-slot business. It took the form of a letter confirming a conversation between sales manager, president and factory manager:

> As I have already talked over with you, I believe it very important that we design a combination talking and picture machine. There are several concerns throughout the country now making this type and I find Slot Machine Parlors generally are putting them in. It is my opinion that sooner or later they will have preference over the regular slot talking machine which we are now turning out.
>
> Mr. Kohn of the Automatic Vaudeville Co. advised me yesterday that he had three machines of this kind in their 14th Street store, each of a different manufacture, and that he would be pleased to have Mr. Weber look over them at his convenience.[7]

Although the operating intention behind this letter still lay in the amusement arcades, the many failed attempts generally to lock moving pictures to a disc or cylinder phonograph were heeded at West Orange and some experiments there brought the following note of September 17th 1907 to Al Wurth from the Inventor:

> *Make experiment, connect Kinetograph to Phonograph by a shaft of focal length of Kineto beam. Run the Kineto by a governor that is accurately governed by the Phono being positively connected by the shaft. Will be in unison. The shaft should have no tension, hence use 2 in. tube and good bearings. A flywheel quite heavy should be used on the Kinetograph[8] - Edison.*

Drawings survive dated December 30th 1907 of 'Reproducing Pictures', combining a phonograph fixed to the back of a projector and driven by it. This was the machine that Wurth appeared to be working on. The phonograph reproducer carried a telephone type coil assembly with electric wires trailing to a compressed air amplifier and horn placed near the screen:

> *Object of this invention is to reproduce at a distance electrically the sounds from phonograph records. The invention consists in (sic) the combination of a magneto telephone, the diaphragm of which is moved by the record sound waves of the phono, and the reproduction of the sound amplified at a distant point by means of an instrument which gives motion by the electrolytic variation of friction to work a compressed air comb valve to reproduce the ....(incomplete)*

Experiments continued although disclaimed by the company to outsiders. The work must have become known within the trade because Daniel Higham, inventor of the friction sound magnifier already incorporated in some Columbia cylinder graphophones wrote to Gilmore on January 20th 1908:[9]

> *I have discovered some new methods in speech governing which will make Talking Pictures a success. Could you tell me if the Edison company would be interested in this direction?*

Gilmore wrote the following to Edison on February 4th:

> *We want somebody to work on such a thing as he suggests here, but I don't know what kind of an arrangement we can make with him.*

Higham outlined his proposals in greater detail in a letter of February 10th; he was prepared to make Talking Picture apparatus and achieve absolute synchronism under the control of an operator and increase the sound of the domestic phonograph 2 to 3 times with new features. He asked for $50.00 a week and demanded sole right to operate Edison Talking Pictures in Boston; he had free title to only one patent and would consider an offer.[10] Higham's purpose in approaching Edison, rather than Victor or Columbia, was that he thought cylinders would give a better sound response. It seems certain that he had already seen talking pictures with badly synchronized sound, using discs.

A meeting with Edison took place at West Orange a few days later and Higham was taken on. He seems to have got his $50.00 per week, but in May 1909 a projected salary of $3,000 and not more than $5,000 appears for discussion in a memo, so he may have achieved more.

There was still doubt in the autumn of 1908 as to whether an air or friction device would be used to magnify the sound. It was not to be as loud as the Auxetophone which was ideal for the open air, but of an improved quality for interior use.[11]

Higham's New Friction Phonograph was reported built on December 29th 1908 and at the same time he announced he was ready to start Talking Pictures, this being the stage of synchronizing the phonograph with the projector. To what extent Higham and Pierman worked together, or if at all is not known; both had worked independently and achieved analogous patents over the same period.

Even before this synchronization was realized there was a flurry of concern as to what the new Talking Pictures were going to be called, and the following names were suggested:

NONPAREIL - CLARION - HERCULES - IROQUOIS - AMBASSADOR PICTUREPHONE - KINETOPHONE - SONIDO - VOX MAGNA

Further lists of up to 100 titles were produced, but KINETOPHONE won handsomely and was adopted in March 1909.

As so often happened the Edison publicity jumped the gun, Edison giving interviews about Talking Pictures to the Press from July 1910. The title Kinetophone was first used openly on August 23rd just before a demonstration to the Press three days later at West Orange, a sorry failure that did nobody any good, but it brought Edison's comment that:

> *the present Kinetophone has been in experimental work in this laboratory for eleven years ...... not quite perfect enough to bring out grand opera yet.*[12]

The friction sound magnifying device was incorporated into the phonograph between the stylus bar and the diaphragm and comprised a vulcanite shoe located in the linkage and in light contact with a constantly revolving amber wheel, called a friction roll. A projection on the shoe ran in a central groove on the friction roll to steady it. Sound impulses from the cylinder on to the stylus bar increased the friction of the shoe on the roll, intensifying the sound from the diaphragm. This could be regulated.

Further amplification took place at the recording end of the process, the sound being cut on oversize cylinders called 'jumbos'. These were transferred pantographically to the larger master cylinders.[13] The advantages of such a step allowed the recording horn to be kept out of camera range and the performers a little more room to move about. This amplification and Higham's friction roll were said to build up volume to a magnitude of four times and to be able to fill any hall. It is not clear if Higham's sound magnifier was ever part of the recording process.

In the absence of the later 'clapper board' slate to synchronize film and sound, each take was marked by the striking together of two coconut shells and these were briefly and simultaneously recorded on film and cylinder for later assimilation. It is certain that in early experiments sound and speech were recorded after the filming had been made and printed, but synchronous filming and recording became the rule in 1911 and perhaps went some way towards Frank L. Dyer's note to McGeachy of the Kinetophone section:

> ..... glad to hear the demonstration of the Kinetophone was so entirely satisfactory.... reason to believe we will be ready to do something definite with the device round the first of the year or in early spring.

An experimental studio was set up in November 1911 at 645 W. 43rd Street, New York for Kinetophone trials.

Works assembly of the apparatus went ahead cautiously during 1912 and by November 200 Kinetophonographs were nearly ready. Higham reported that with the exception of the motors all parts were now decided, and four weeks later the Emerson factory was contracted to produce the first AC and DC types. Daniel Higham was replaced as engineer by Miller Reese Hutchison in the January of 1913.

A great boon at this time was Edison's acquisition of the celluloid moulding patents from November 24th 1912, allowing durable cylinders to be made in Blue Amberol material. Had this not been available the company might have turned to one of Aylsworth's plastic compounds he was developing for the Diamond Discs.

Experimental Kinetophone player or recorder of 1912

The final months of 1912 saw distributing companies set up across the United States. The Kinetophone equipment on offer included the Edison 'Underwriter's Type B' projector, the special loud-speaking phonograph and the synchronizing device. The agreements with the companies proposed 50 Kinetophones per week at $200.00 each, lease of films at 6 cents per foot and $1.00 for each record. 50 exhibitors signed at first. Delivery was advanced to December 15th in expectation of some Christmas trade. It was hoped all the earliest films would be vaudeville turns, but in Frank Dyer's words the first subject list was too elaborate. Hutchison, too, found that five releases a week of silent films were already working the studio space to capacity and that Kinetophone work was pushed to Saturday afternoon and Sunday, and he asked for greater priority to be given to the sound films.[14]

The first public showings of the Kinetophone were when the Keith-Orpheum circuit of vaudeville theaters took up the option, starting with Keith's Colonial Theater in New York. Two days after Christmas 1912 work began on equipping it, in this case a 500 ft. length of driving cord was needed between the phonograph and synchronizer and was supported on pulleys over the length of the auditorium. The first performance was given on February 18th 1913 and respectfully received, although on subsequent occasions when synchronization failed, the audience was less than enthusiastic and reports exist of 'hooting, jeering, hissing and rowdyism'. Similar equipment was installed in other New York theaters.[15] *Variety* treated the Kinetophone coldly, describing it as a "novelty for a vaudeville programme for a week or two".

The Colonial Theater booking was cancelled after 16 weeks, Keith-Orpheum paying Edison to terminate the contract. After this The (Edison) American Talking Picture Inc. was formed, offering 'Perfect Synchronism, Startling Illusion'.

Two talking films were presented at these early demonstrations, the second being a six-minute minstrel show, but in time the programmes were extended to two hours. Of interest particularly is the first film and record of the Kinetophone being introduced to the public. The film has not been found but the script and cylinder record have survived, being made a few days before the first opening date of February 18th; the speaker is thought to be Allen Ramsey, director of the Bronx studio. The typescript is much amended and includes a 'cast', who presumably stood behind Ramsey, and a number of props:[16]

> *People on stage:*
> *Bugler in bugler's uniform*
> *Quartette*
> *Only one horn - no whistle (sic)*
> *Xylophone (omit chimes)*
> *Saxophone, drum, cello instead of violin and small 22 cal. pistol*
> *Break lamp globe*
>
> *Ladies and Gentlemen:*
>
> *A few brief years ago Mr. Thomas A. Edison presented to the World the Kinetoscope, and today countless millions of people in every section of the civilized world are patronizing the thousands of motion picture theaters.*
>
> *The phenomenal success of motion pictures can perhaps be more directly attributed to realism than to any other single cause. They portray the real farmyard, the real city street, the real locomotive, not merely painted canvas as used on the dramatic stage.*
>
> *This realism, unfortunately, has been limited to sight only. The motion picture actor's lips moved, but he said nothing; the pianist played inaudibly; the giant locomotive rushed by in ludicrous silence. It remained for Mr.*

> Edison who has so aptly been called 'The Wizard of Sound and Light', to combine his two great inventions, the Kinetoscope and the Phonograph into the machine we call the Kinetophone, which produces simultaneously both sound and action with all the realism of nature. Many attempts have been made, heretofore, to produce so-called talking pictures by first making a phonograph record by talking directly into the recording horn, and then having the artist, or in most cases, an entirely different artist attempt to follow the record so made while the picture was being photographed. Of course the results thus attained have been crude indeed, and absolute synchronism impossible. The Edison Kinetophone pictures are positively the only genuine talking pictures ever produced. The artist performs exactly as he does upon the stage, moving freely about, and his every word and every action are precisely recorded. In only this way can perfect synchronism and illusion be obtained. I will now give you a few examples of reproducing familiar sounds:
>
> An automobile horn, breaking a plate, firing a revolver, a piano, a song, a cello, a bugle, dogs
>
> Ladies and Gentlemen:
>
> I believe we have shown enough to prove conclusively that talking moving pictures are a reality. Time alone will show to what vast purposes they may extend. Consider for instance the historic value of a Kinetophone reproduction of Christopher Columbus,* if it were possible to show it now, and you will realize the splendid opportunities which this great invention will afford future generations to study the great men and women of today. The political orator may appeal to countless thousands while remaining at his own fireside. In short there seems to be no end to the possibilities of this newest invention of that greatest of inventors, Mr. Thomas A. Edison.

*Before Christopher Columbus was pencilled on the script, earlier contenders had been Julius Caesar and George Washington.

Performance

An explanation of the Kinetophone system will show it to have a number of weaknesses, all open to giving trouble; there are also features that only close examination of original equipment would make clear.

The cycle of making the films started at the Kinetograph, the camera powered by an electric motor.[17] Nearby a recording phonograph was set up, having a spring motor drive and a synchronizer linked to the camera by a cord and pulleys. This was the first weak spot of the system, frequently breaking down and getting out of phase. The sound was recorded on 'jumbo' brown wax cylinders through a horn. Surviving plans favour this at a height of 6 feet above the floor, sometimes set above the camera and with side sound baffles out of range of the lens.

Kinetophone cylinder shown with standard Blue Amberol

The incoming sound would be at a fairly low level but when the jumbo cylinder was transferred to a master for making a metal mould, a pantographic system and greater mandrel speed helped to amplify the sound, giving the Edison system an advantage over rivals and allowing the performers more freedom to move about. When the sound and picture were 'locked' at the beginning of filming by the sound and visual recording of the coconut shells, the 'crack' of the shells on the cylinder was marked by a dab of white paint on the following groove; the frames with the picture of the shells being struck together were cut from the finished film and replaced by several of opaque film immediately following the opening titles.

The phonograph's motor would be running with the mandrel and record isolated by a clutch, and the stylus placed on the white mark; immediately the opaque film was seen by the phonograph operator he would release the clutch when the frames following appeared and sound and film would be in phase.

The phonograph was usually set alongside, behind or below the screen and incorporated the Higham sound magnifier, and was powered by a 220 volt D.C. motor. Horns were straight and usually larger than those used on the domestic phonographs, and were hung from a crane.

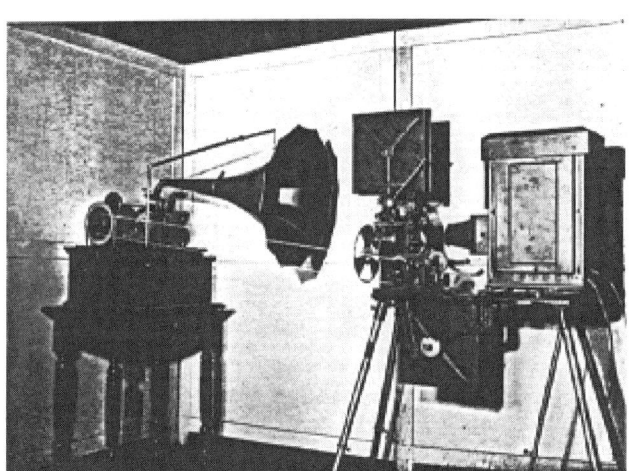

Kinetophone set-up of projector, and horn phonograph. The synchronising box on the projector was driven by a cord from the phonograph

There was a synchronizing box on the projector driven by the cord belt from the phonograph at the phonograph's speed of 120 r.p.m. By means of a brake shoe this governed the speed of cranking by the projectionist to 60 r.p.m. Should the sound run ahead of the picture the projectionist could move a lever on the synchronizer to by-pass the brake and allow faster cranking until the film caught up. There was a small revolving marker dial for the projectionist to watch as he cranked.

In the early experiments with the Kinetophone speed correction had to be made on the phonograph, but it was soon obvious that altering the projector speed would be less apparent to an audience.

The cord connection from phonograph to synchronizer was often long and complicated, stretching and slipping; loss of film through breakage had to be made good with blank stock.[18] The cylinder was normally locked against slipping. Projection and operation of the phonograph called for extra skills and Edison let it be known in October 1912 that all operators would have to attend training and be approved before being allowed to take charge of a Kinetophone. The first two to pass the course, Thompson and Corbett were promoted to act as instructors.

It is interesting to note that at one time sound points were proposed for the backs of the seats but not pursued, although in the 'thirties such facilities were sometimes available to the deaf.

March 1913 held out promises of 'entirely new outfits' for all theatres equipped with Kinetophones and referred to buzzers, telephones and head telephone sets between the two vital operators. At the same time an electric synchronizer Hutchison was working on was found to be too noisy to use.

The Edison fire of December 1914 did not affect the Kinetophone project directly although the outbreak started in the Film Inspection building, but the Kinetophone work had been carried on outside the affected area.

1915 saw the start of the wind-down of Kinetophone activities and the withdrawal from foreign markets brought about by war conditions and the system's unreliability, in spite of Edison's frequent urging of its perfection. It lingered to the end of 1916 when there was only one set of equipment on tour. Edison instructed John Constable, his chief engineer, to keep remaining apparatus ready for instant use, but in an inventory dated December 12th 1916 all that was left in storage trunks were:

> *1 Kinetophone, without motor*
> *1 Model D Kinetoscope, complete with transformer*
> *1 Kinetophone telephone outfit*
> *1 110 volt A. C. motor*
> *1 synchronizer*
> *1 film re-winder*
> *1 screen*
> *2 spools of synchronizer cord*
> *lenses and lens tubes*

It was reported on September 17th 1917 that the studio was closed down and Kinetophone material removed.

Some equipment specifications:

Kinetophone cylinders were moulded in Blue Amberol celluloid with an internal plaster lining and titling on the flat end -

>   *Diameter of record 4 $^{13}/_{32}$ in.*
>   *Length of record 7 $^{1}/_{2}$ in.*
>   *Revolutions per minute 120*
>   *Threads per inch 105*
>   *Width of Thread 0.0095 in.*

Diameter of sapphire 0.038 in.
Width of cut 0.0083 in.
Ratio of width cut to thread 6:7
Speed of recording 1662 in. per minute
Maximum duration 6 $^{1}/_{2}$ min.
Mandrel length 7 $^{29}/_{32}$ in.
Mandrel diameters 3 $^{5}/_{8}$ in. - 4 $^{1}/_{16}$ in.

Phonographs and horns for the Kinetophone

The 35 mm film normally ran at 16 frames per second or 60 ft. per minute and with opening and closing titles was about 400 ft. in length. Some Edison titles were multi-reel.

The phonograph used with the Kinetophone equipment had a wooden case, all those seen being of oak:

> Length 24 in.
> Width 13 ½ in.
> Height 10 in.
> Total height 22 in. (about)

The ciné horns remaining at the Edison Laboratory are straight panelled horns of the TRIUMPH/HOME/STANDARD design and finished in black enamel:

> Length 7 ft.
> Diameter across mouth 42 in. maximum.

A set of directions for the two operators of the Kinetophone have survived, together with adjustment, repair and assembly instructions for working on the synchronizer. The inclusion of the former in toto will help to clarify the operation of this part of the Kinetophone.

To open Phonograph:
> Open latches 1 & 2 on ends
> Open door in front: inside find
>   lamp cord with plug
>   attached
> Draw out cord
> Screw plug into lamp socket
> Insert horn holding rod into hole
>   provided, attach horn to
>   reproducer with short rubber
>   tube
> Attach chain to ring provided
>   on the horn
> Oil all bearings, putting one or
>   two drops in each oil hole,
>   including the two on the end
>   of the mandrel
> Oil the mandrel guide rods freely
> Slide mandrel back and
>   forward several times to see
>   if it moves freely over the
>   guides

Kinetophone Cinema advert
from Liverpool 1913

Turn the mandrel round on its shaft to see if it revolves freely
Draw out mandrel as far as it will go
Remove record from box, holding it on inside, do not handle the outside of record.
Place record on mandrel with name end towards you. See that it goes all the way on.
Draw out the spring hook in the end of mandrel.
Turn hook until it engages record and release

To adjust Phonograph:

Start motor by pulling up key switch in top plate
With motor running... slide record in a little and drop the reproducer upon it by pushing down the reproducer lever.
Press starting key and note the speed of record, it should be 120 r.p.m.
If speed is not correct it may be adjusted by means of the governor regulating screw. If speed is low turn screw to left, if speed is high turn screw to right.
Check speed until it is 120 r.p.m.
Note the position of the reproducer friction weight. The position of this weight indicates whether you have proper friction on the amber wheel, i.e. whether the loudness of the Phonograph is correct. If the friction is correct the pointer attached to the weight will point directly at the index pin attached to the frame.
If the friction is low, the speaking is not loud enough - to correct turn the friction adjusting thumb screw a little to the left until weight takes correct position.
If the friction is high turn same screw to the right until weight takes proper position.
When speed and friction are correct the Phonograph is ready for use

To set Phonograph:

Raise reproducer (keep motor going)
Slide mandrel forward or backward by means of the handle until the white spot on inner end of the record is just inside of the reproducer point
Drop reproducer by pushing down controlling lever
Turn mandrel slowly until a loud click is heard in the horn. After click is heard turn one more complete turn and enough more (sic) to bring the white index spot opposite the end of the reproducer balance weight
The Phonograph is now ready to start.
Start picture in Kinetoscope
First appears title. Frame properly
After title appears a short space of dark places, followed by the picture
The Phonograph operator should watch the screen from behind and the instant the first picture appears he presses the starting button
The Phonograph man has nothing more to do until the end of the picture

In order to become proficient at starting right it will be necessary to practice starts

Instructions for Synchronizing:

The man at machine turns crank continuously keeping a free easy swing one per second. If the speed is correct the small synchronizing disc will be stationary; if the small disc turns to right the speed is low.

The speed cannot be too fast as any tendency to run fast is stopped by the braking effect within the synchronizer. If the operator is slow, that is the Phonograph is ahead of the picture he may speed up as follows: turning synchronizing disc to left and turn faster until synchronism is again established. If the picture is ahead of the Phonograph the operator may slow down a little until the Phonograph catches up.

When picture and Phonograph are in synchronism the operator should keep up a steady easy swing keeping the small synchronizing disc standing still. Once in synchronism it is very easily maintained.

1) Published in *American Cinematographer*, September 1983, *db* December 1982, *Journal of Audio Engineering Society* November 1983, etc. Art Shifrin has become an authority on surviving Edison films and cylinders for the Kinetophone and has demonstrated synchronized examples, using equipment of his design. He also specializes in restoring sound from commercial cylinders of all types.
2) This first system is sometimes seen mistakenly referred to as the Kinetophone, but Edison sources used Phono-Kinetoscope or Kinetophonograph.
3) U.S. Patent No. 201,760 for *Speaking Machine* filed by Edison on March 4th 1878 and granted March 26th 1878.
4) British Patent No. 15,245 of 1890 expiring September 26th 1904.
5) Vide U.S. Patents 829,123 and 867,597 of March and April 1905.
6) On May 25th 1905 F. L. Dyer reported Gilmore wanting this work abandoned.
7) C.H. Wilson to W. E. Gilmore and Peter Weber November 1st 1905.
8) The word Kinetograph was usually applied to the camera, though not always, and the combined projector and phonograph system become the Kinetophone. The 1890s peepshow box was the Kinetoscope, but mixed usage of these terms was not uncommon and here Edison referred to a projector.
9) Higham was then living at Bridgeport, Conn., also the location of Columbia's factory.
10) U. S. Patent No. 772,938 of October 25th 1904 for *Phonograph Reproducer Apparatus*, the sound magnifier used on some cylinder graphophones. This was filed February 18th 1904
11) Letter from F. L. Dyer to T. Graf, managing director in London, dated October 30th 1908.
12) A note from Edison of August 1st 1911 still showed he was keeping his options open: "Pierman, continue to work on our reproducer with disc machine. Get some of the latest commercial discs where no crackles (are heard). Want it for moving picture theaters".
13) Jumbo cylinders were in production by February 19th 1910. Note from G. Schiffl to Edison: "... designed a cooling table necessary to manufacture the Phono-Kinetoscope record". 200 Kinetophone records are noted as made by November 28th 1910.
14) Letter to Edison December 19th 1912
15) Union Square, 5th Avenue and the Alhambra and in Chicago and St. Louis.
16) Art Shifrin finds that two versions of this demonstration film were made and suggests August 1910 for the earlier
17) At first battery DC, but following the first 10 models a few were powered by 110v. 60 cycles AC.
18) "This entire apparatus is the most unsatisfactory product we have ever turned out and I can see all sorts of troubles ahead" - Hutchison to Edison, January 16th 1913.

Correspondence and instruction sheets from Edison Archive

Chapter 24
Reproducers and Recorders until 1912

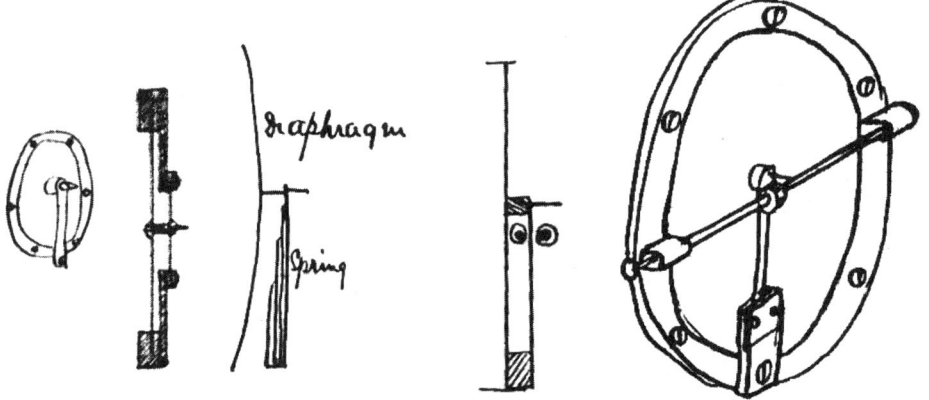

Sketches from Charles Batchelor's Diary of June 1887 showing progress with a 'talking diaphragm'.

Unlike the Gramophone and its first 50 years of using steel needles, its precursor the Edison cylinder phonograph strove from early days at a more scientific method of cutting and playing back recordings. Beginning with bent steel and crude hard wire points, gauged ball-shaped steel styli were tried for a short time, then sapphires and finally diamonds. There was a brief dalliance with a Carborundum stylus but how many were produced and sold is not evident.

The early steel pointed recorders and reproducers are included in detail under their headings, while the sapphire reproducer types fall readily into three well defined groups. The earliest were lightly loaded for playing the soft wax cylinders and took on more weight when the metallic soap cylinders were introduced. The next began with the new moulded 2-minute cylinders of 1901-2 that were harder and gave a more acute response with a heavier weight. These sapphires were seen firstly in ball shape and then in 'door knob' outline. The arrival in 1908 of the wax Amberol 4-minute cylinder brought a third sapphire type with a button shaped stylus running on edge in the groove.

Nineteenth century recorders and reproducers were inefficient in their rigidity and not very effective by later standards, but the Gold Moulded cylinders caused the range of reproducers to be widened, and with diaphragms of larger area and better designed horns coming along played very much better. Nevertheless, Edison owners being very conservative were often reluctant to part with their old tried and tested reproducers and buy one of the new range, and the company had to resort to tempting part-exchange offers and an outright confiscation policy to call in the old types and get the new models accepted.

All sapphire reproducers from B to S carried a letter on the movable weight - it is omitted on a very few - and this should not be confused with the Model letter of the Phonographs; there is no connection.

As a result of a 1906 Court Injunction Edison was obliged to give up using mica diaphragms from the July, adopting copper instead until the laminated Japanese rice paper with cork disc began to be used with the diamond reproducers of 1912. The trade was reluctant to accept copper diaphragms, complaining that these were prone to rattling, and mica was continued for some months in the domestic realm. Mica continued to be put in export consignments and in December 1907 London was warned to expect copper diaphragms, now of a superior quality. Several patterns of corrugated rings and spoked ridges were tried with the copper diaphragms to impart better audio response.

Study of Edison's 1908 patent for Amberol 4-minute cylinders and their recorders and reproducers shows the original recorder to be a button-shaped stylus with a shank, resembling a pin-head and with a cutting notch made in it;[1] the reproducer would be a straight cylindrical sapphire with a rounded tip. What came to be marketed was to the contrary, the reproducing stylus for the Amberols is button-like with a shank, the recorder a straight rod-shape but with a concave tip. In time several reproducers would have a 2 and 4-minute stylus mounting that swivelled or turned over in a similar way to the record player pick-up of the 'fifties. Edison phonograph owners will find the 4-minute reproducing sapphire may be used for the later Blue Amberol cylinders, but the correct diamond reproducer will play far better.

The choice of models among recorders was more limited, but these pursued their furrow alongside the reproducers, eventually being designed to cut 200 threads per inch in Amberol-like blanks for recording at home and could still be bought with these blanks after the Blue Amberols took over entirely.

THE EARLIEST REPRODUCERS 1887-1889

The first reproducers for wax cylinders were only a short step ahead of those used with the tinfoil machines, but from the first wax record phonograph designed by Edison and built by Gilliland in 1887[2] they were improved a step at a time over the next two years until established in the Standard Speaker and found fully acceptable as the Automatic in 1892.

The reproducer on the Gilliland machine was paired with the recorder in the spectacle frame carrier-arm and was of simpler construction. The diaphragm was gold-beater's skin, the 'stylus' was a phosphor-bronze wire anchored to the reproducer body and cemented to a rubber block on the diaphragm, drawing it down to be under tension. The rounded and burnished wire point bent towards the cylinder at a 45° angle and was finer than the chisel cut of the recorder's stylus that formed a square-bottomed groove on the cylinder. The top of the reproducer was slightly recessed, having a squat collar made a little wider than the recorder's, for differentiation. These reproducers were made of brass, polished and lacquered.[3]

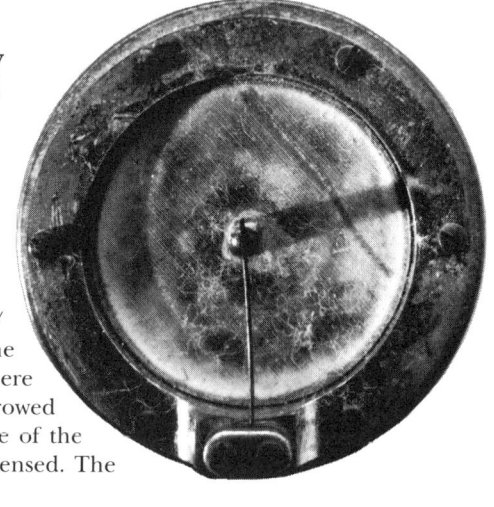

Early speaker from Gilliland's New Phonograph, to Patent No. 386,974 (from Smithsonian Institution Collection)

On the reproducer of the next Edison/Gilliland phonograph built in early 1888 the wire stylus gave place to thin metal, hinged where it fastened to the reproducer body and narrowed at the stylus end; it was fixed to the centre of the shellacked silk diaphragm by rubber and tensed. The tube plate was flat.[4]

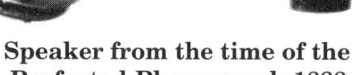

Speaker from the time of the Perfected Phonograph 1888

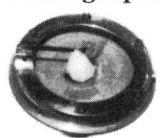

Speaker and recorder from Edison's Perfected Phonograph, July 1888

Edison's work on his electric phonograph reached its climax in the middle of June 1888 and inspired a number of reproducer styles. A good step forward was the substitution of the various diaphragm materials by thin glass held in place by a threaded tube plate from the top and insulated by thin metal and soft washers on both edges[5]. The result was a reproducer with a steel ball stylus and vertically movable weight playing a U-shaped groove and its achievement is recorded in Charles Batchelor's diary for March 19th 1889.[6] This shallow U-shaped groove cut by the companion recorder would eventually make possible the practical moulding of cylinders, and the recording stylus at 0.040 in. and reproducer at 0.035 in. gave a new clarity and greater sound output.

After a short while there were complaints about the steel styli being corroded by chemicals in the cylinder composition and were replaced by sapphires,[7] and at the same time the tube diameters were brought into line. These were the reproducers used on the phonographs made for the North American Phonograph Company and leased to the public in the second half of 1889. They were made of brass and nickel finished.

Three views of the earliest type of weighted reproducer, second half of 1889

Although these reproducers had the hinged weight, the recorders did not until both were combined into one device, the Standard speaker in November 1889. It was the only combination recorder/reproducer in Edison's entertainment range and did away with the need of a spectacle frame carrier-arm.

THE STANDARD SPEAKER 1889-1902

In spite of limitations the Standard was ingeniously thought out and well suited to the early carrier-arm eye fitted with the twin curved speaker clamps. These allowed the reproducer to be turned by up-or-down movements of the speaker arm, to record in the upper position and to play back in the lower. This lever first appeared on the Standard Speaker and limited the semi-rotative movement within the clamps, but the stylus assembly was rigid and prone to mis-tracking despite fine adjustment with the speaker adjusting screw on the carrier-arm. This was a fault freely and peculiarly admitted in Edison literature for several years until 1902 when the Standard was featured no more. As a safety precaution against accidental erasure some Standard Speakers had a pin in the cup recess which, used in conjunction with a pin in the carrier-arm eye fitted notches in the recording and listening tube plates, ensuring the speaker was set in the right position of engagement with the tube placed on it.[8]

The cutting end of the recording stylus on the Standard Speaker was slightly concave.

Apart from a serial number there was no lettering stamped on this speaker, and it was normal equipment with the CLASS M types until 1899:

Price: $9.00; reducing to $5.00 in mid-1890s

The Standard Speaker

In British Patent No. 20,330 of 1896 J. H. Greenhill patented a recorder/reproducer for Edison Bell. This turned bodily 180° in the carrier-arm for whichever function was needed. No example has been seen.

DIRECTIONS FOR USING THE

NEW TYPE EDISON PHONOGRAPH

TO RECORD.

Place the cylinder on the taper mandril, bring the swing arm into place, lock the same by springing the lock-bolt into place, and start the instrument.

Lower the diaphragm arm and pull down the T shaped lever on right of diaphragm.

Place the speaking tube in position and put diaphragm at point where record is to begin.

Then lower the lever in front of diaphragm frame and commence dictation.

TO REPRODUCE.

Follow above instructions, except that the right hand lever on diaphragm frame should be raised instead of lowered, place hearing tubes in position and listen. To throw reproducer point into "track" use screw at right of diaphragm.

CAUTION.

On this machine use only cylinders that have one end beveled.

NOTICE.

In the new type of Phonograph it is intended **to do away entirely with adjustments of any kind** in making and reproducing the record, making the machine absolutely **Automatic.** Our customers are therefore advised that to this end **all the Phonograph cylinders should be carefully shaved off by the type-writer or other clerk, when the machine is not in use for other purposes.** In this way the user is enabled to dictate much more rapidly, and is saved much trouble, and by having a number of clean cylinders at hand when commencing the morning's dictations, the user will be astonished to see how rapidly a large accumulation of letters can be answered.

The suggestions above made, if followed, will ensure perfect results; if any difficulty should arise, it will be caused by a non-observance of directions. The instrument must necessarily be of a somewhat delicate character to accomplish its wonderful work, and therefore is not intended to be used roughly, or by incompetent and unskilful persons. It should be handled with intelligent care and not allowed to be trifled with or abused.

The instrument is the property of the North American Phonograph Company, 160 Broadway, New York City.

1889 instructions for the Standard Speaker, not yet named when this leaflet was drafted. It appears that 'Automatic' might have been considered.

Standard Speaker for Model C Phonograph

THE AUTOMATIC REPRODUCER 1892-1902

Its name was derived from being able to track grooves automatically through having a little lateral play between the body and the floating weight. The ball sapphire was held vertically in a straight stylus bar. As time passed and formulations for wax and soap cylinders were changed, the weights on the Automatic were increased and had some lead weights added.[9] Its heavier weight made it more suitable for coin-slot work than the Standard, and two Automatic reproducers were also used in Leon Douglas's Polyphone. (q.v.)

When first advertised in September 1892 the Automatic Speaker (sic) cost $10.00 soon reducing to $9.00 and was also termed a 'repeater' and 'for transcribing', and was recommended as bettering the Standard Speaker for musical items. From early 1896 it was reduced to $5.00 when substituted for the Standard Speaker and ceased to be issued with domestic machines from February 1st

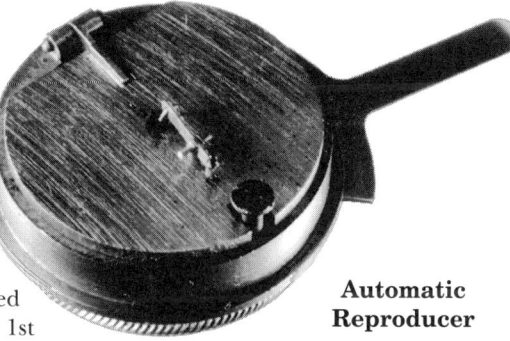

Automatic Reproducer

1902 when the Model C reproducer was issued generally and stocks of the Automatic run down. The Company declined to repair the Automatic after September 1910. There were said to be no more glass diaphragms nor weights and the Model C was recommended.

A special Automatic reproducer for use with CONCERT phonographs was produced in 1900, price $5.00, but had a short career.

MODEL B REPRODUCER 1902-1907

With the Model C reproducer coming into prominence from February 1902, it is not at first clear why the Automatic was continued in modified form as the Model B. The reason was that through Edison's large export business the Model B was supplied with phonographs sent to Edison Bell in Great Britain. The newly-styled GEM in particular was popular there, Edison Bell was taking up to 70-80 per cent of Edison's output of these machines and the Model B with its lighter weight was suited to playing the brown wax cylinders that still dominated the British trade. The Model B, having no tail weight could also be used on CONCERT-type machines.[10]

The British trade soon found the Model C superior to Model B and to ensure the success of the GEMS there Model C was supplied with them to Edison Bell orders from June 1902, but the Model B continued to be supplied with GEMS in the United States until 1905,[11] there being no similar reaction apparent in American trade circles.

Model B always had a ball sapphire and glass diaphragm, but the latter could be of mica if specified. When Gold Moulded cylinders came out the Model B was given an extra weight fixed underneath by two screws, but in time this was incorporated into making the existing weight heavier. There was never an adjusting arm and the letter 'B' was

Model B Reproducer

normally punched on the weight. As the Model Bs lost way to the Model Cs their owners were invited to exchange them for Model C on payment of $3.00.

Price $3.00; 12s. 6d.

A transitional reproducer that may be between the Automatic and Model B is reported from Ohio.

The top resembles a Model C with its sloping tube plate, but differs in profile and size of limit loop. It also lacks the notch for securing in the carrier-arm eye, but has an adjusting arm as used with speaker clamps. Underneath there is a Model B weight, but not marked as such, nor are there any holes for the extra weight.

National Phonograph license details are pressed round the perimeter of the tube plate, an early instance this practice. It is numbered 16259.

From March 1909 Company policy hardened towards obsolete Automatic and Model B reproducers and by September 1910 there were said to be no more glass diaphragms or weights. These reproducers were to be held and changed for more up-to-date models if returned on a machine for repair to the factory, and charged at list prices. With more advanced Edison reproducers on the market it is remarkable that these models lasted for so long.

EDISON DUPLEX SPEAKER 1896-1899

The first style was simply an adapter that screwed into the top of the Automatic Speaker with the glass diaphragm being placed in a sound chamber in the adapter, a long connecting link between it and the stylus bar, and the knurled compression ring screwed down on top of the adapter to hold down the tube plate.

Duplex Speaker

When the body was made in one piece this became the New Duplex Speaker.

295

By re-siting the diaphragm, output from either side of it could be led into two horns or listening tubes, and sound from two opposed horns could be thrown into adjoining rooms or different parts of the hall.

Price: 1896 $10.50, later $9.00

EDISON GEM SPEAKER 1899-1902

The earliest reproducers for the GEM were built into the carrier-arm and did not exist as separate entities. The weight and stylus bar were the same as the Automatic Speaker and there were two known variants in the upper portion or tube plate; these reproducers are not transferable.

During 1901 these were superseded by a special GEM reproducer (nearly always termed a 'speaker'), slightly smaller in diameter than the contemporary Automatic and needing a smaller carrier-arm. The reproducer dropped into this, was turned to the right and secured by two knurled screws. The speaker casing was cheap and simple, pressed in two pieces and held together by two small screws and enclosed a glass diaphragm. The first models had a light circular weight, but this was thickened slightly and had a chord cut away at the hinge. This style is found also with an extra weight held by two screws, and with a modified stylus bar and sapphire mounting.

The GEM speaker was supplied with the phonograph for about a year, then gave way to the Model B in the normal size carrier-arm. The GEM speaker looked what it was, a cheaply made product afloat in a competitive market. It would not fit any other Edison phonograph.

Price: $3.00

Gem Speaker

MODEL C REPRODUCER, 1902 onwards

Introduced in February 1902 the Model C was the most widely used of the 2-minute Edison reproducers. To a lesser degree it was a victim of its own success and was copied, but itself owed features to others. The Standard Speaker had established the size of the hole in the carrier-arm and its geometry, the Automatic took this a stage further with less rigidity for the stylus, and the Model C played 2-minute cylinders well and would last little altered for over ten years. Its most novel feature was the extension of the weight to a fish-tail.[12] This had already happened on Edwin Mobley's reproducer of 1901, (q.v.) and Mobley had based his invention on Edison's Automatic reproducer, introducing an overhanging tail and in the first consideration was sued successfully by Edison. The Model C was marketed at the beginning of 1902 with Edison's heavier fish-tail for playing Gold Moulded cylinders. Two holes in the tail of early models were for an extra weight to be screwed on, but this was not evolved to lessen the risk of record damage. It would have been the equivalent of an American 10 cent piece.

Model C Reproducer

The Model C was a non-rotating reproducer, held in tracking position by a notch in its perimeter and hip at '12 o'clock' on the carrier-arm. It was retained by a knurled screw through the carrier-arm side, superseding the several forms of speaker clamp. The first models still retained the side lever, now serving no useful purpose except to carry the word REPRODUCER and was soon discontinued. The earliest models had no identifying MODEL-C stamped on the tail-weight.

Until September 1906 Model C reproducers had built-up mica diaphragms, or else glass, and the stylus was button shaped, but copper diaphragms were later used.[13] Owing to opposition to these some Model Cs were still being sent abroad fitted with mica for a further year, but legal objections from Edison Bell made it impossible to continue using glass diaphragms in British exports.

Model C became regular equipment with most machines from its inception, but did not oust the Model B from the American GEM until 1905. It remained regular issue with the first Combination phonographs and was still offered in American catalogues almost until

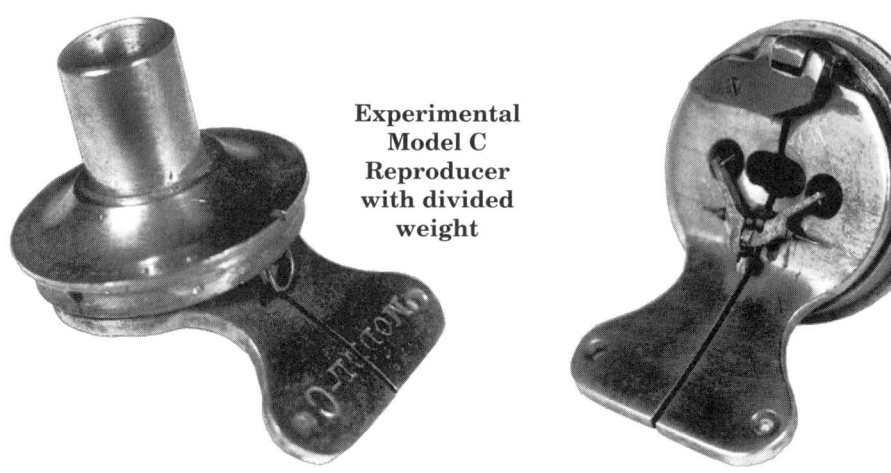

Experimental Model C Reproducer with divided weight

horn phonographs had faded out in 1913, but could be bought from the Edison works for many years after.

Many experiments were made in the Edison Laboratory using the Model C as a starting point and occasionally these curiosities are found by Edison collectors.

Original price:	$5.00;	£1 1s. 0d.
June 1909	$3.50;	14s. 0d.
1911	$3.50;	9s. 0d.

Each Model C reproducer cost the Edison company 85 cents to make.

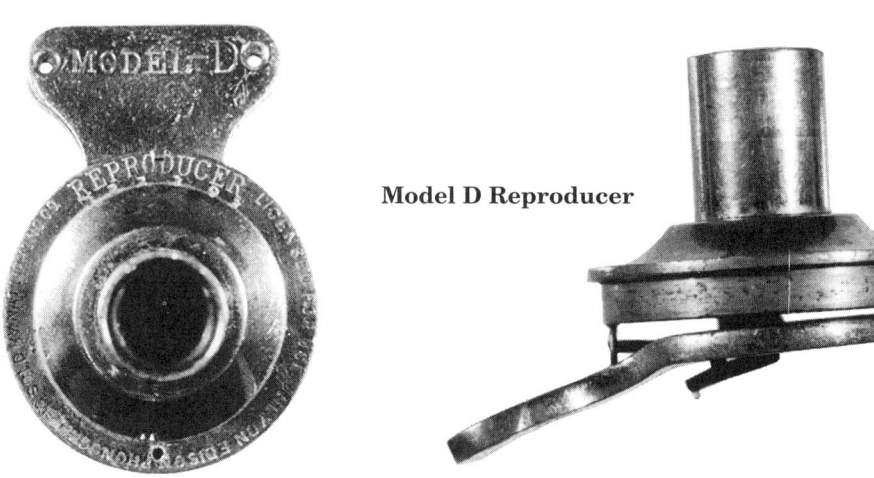

Model D Reproducer

MODEL D REPRODUCER 1902-1911

This was announced for introduction for February 1902, and although not unlike Model C there was a wider angle to the tail weight for playing Concert cylinders. Because of this a hole was made through the weight to allow it to clear the limit loop. Model D became standard issue with the CONCERT types of phonographs after 1902 and continued to be listed until declared obsolete in February 1911, nearly four years after these machines were dropped from the catalogue. It was fitted with a ball sapphire.

Price: $5.00; £1 1s. 0d.

MODEL E REPRODUCER

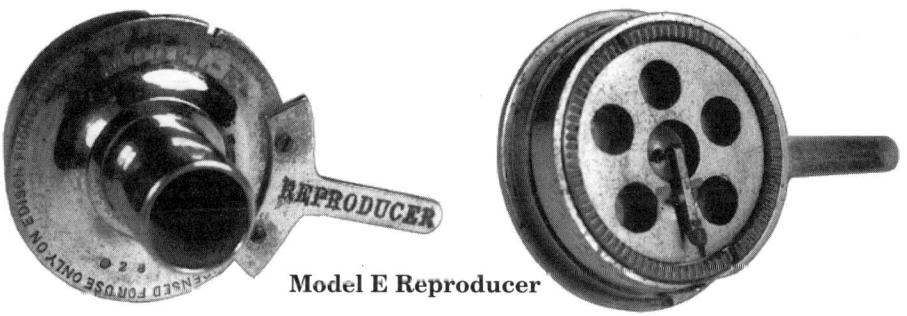

Model E Reproducer

One example is known to survive in private hands. It has the low serial number of 28 and uses the body of Model C.

MODEL G REPRODUCER

This classification was reserved for business phonograph reproducers.

MODEL H REPRODUCER 1908 onwards

This was the first 4-minute reproducer from Edison, outwardly similar to Model C but having a sapphire with a flattish button head that ran edge-on in the fine Amberol cylinder groove.[14] The early versions are found with a stylus bar in two thicknesses on a mounting that allowed swivelling and with an extended tail that would centre within a V-piece.[15] There was a likelihood of this type fouling the cylinder and the mounting was then fixed, although the

299

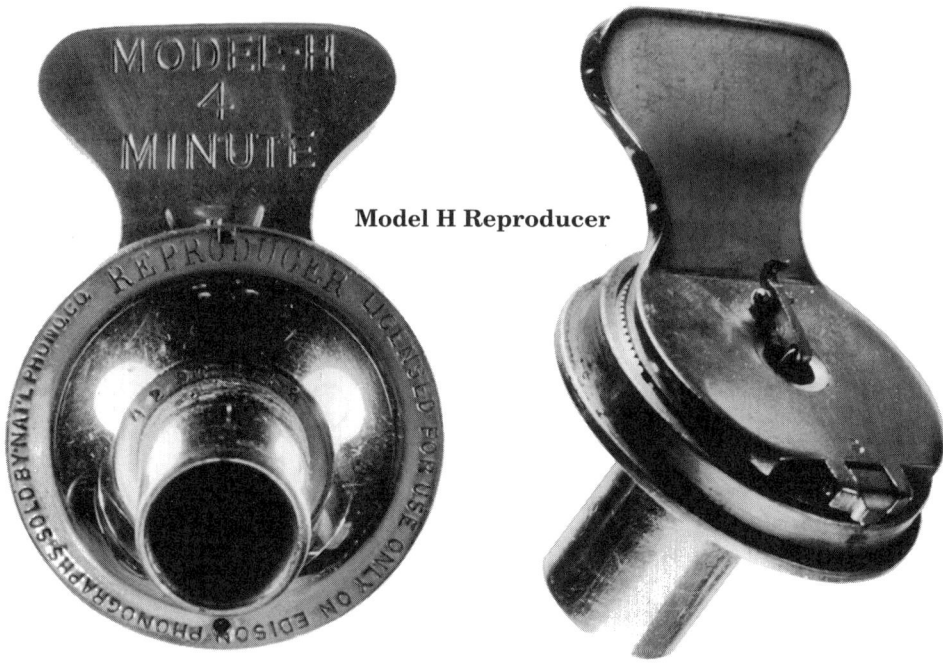

Model H Reproducer

pinning now allowed a little side play. The uniform stylus bar was shortened and the V-piece discarded. The reproducer was fitted with a corrugated copper alloy diaphragm and the tube plate stained green for easier recognition.

This reproducer was unveiled in the autumn of 1908 to coincide with the introduction of the Amberol cylinders, and it was supplied initially together with the Model C on most Combination Attachment outfits. The Model H was pushed aside from 1910 by more advanced reproducers such as the Models N, O and R, but could be bought afterwards.

Price:	$5.00;	£1 1s. 0d.
July 1909	$3.50;	14s. 0d.
December 1911	$3.50;	9s. 0d.

Each Model H reproducer cost the Edison company 85 cents to make.

A modified Model H reproducer with adapter ring was supplied with the I.C.S. AMBEROLA 30 equipment; this had the tail weight cut short and a half-moon section ground out from the front top edge of the tube. A right-angled elbow could then be mounted over the tube and led back to the neck of the horn. It was mainly intended for playing back recordings of language exercises made into the horn on the Edison 4-minute cylinder blanks.

Modified Model H Reproducer for the AMBEROLA 30 Phonograph for International Correspondence School's use. The docked tail weight and cut tube will be seen. This reproducer is also shown in the special adapter ring. When the lift lever is applied, it presses the round stud, and the two lugs push the weight up clear of the cylinder.

MODEL J REPRODUCER 1908-1911

This reproducer enabled owners of the obsolete CONCERT machines, now fitted with a mandrel for standard cylinders to convert to playing Amberol records.

In laboratory testing with the new Amberol cylinders the Model H reproducer was found too heavy in the 'on top' position of the carrier-arm and apt to cut the records, so the Model J was given a lighter weight. The first weights were hand-made, but from December 4th 1908 500 of the Model J were ordered.

The earliest were marked MODEL H with an added letter J. There is no record apparent of this model being sold separately from the CONCERT Amberol attachment.

A Model J with a 2-minute sapphire and marked Model J 2-minute on the weight is known to have been supplied with a coin-slot phonograph, but the reason for this is not known.

Like the Model D the weight was pierced to allow the limit pin to pass through, but the reason for the wide-angled tail weight remains unclear because the Model J was incompatible with the large Concert records. It was declared obsolete in 1911 and is infrequently found today.

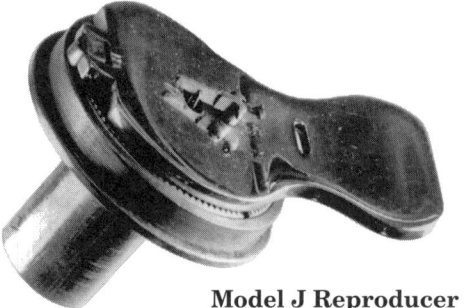
Model J Reproducer

A Model J Reproducer converted to 2-minute cylinders. The '4' appears to have over-punched

MODEL K REPRODUCER 1909-1912

This was Edison's first combination reproducer, designed to play both 2 and 4-minute records. It retained the body of the Models C and H as well as the fish-tail, but incorporated a turntable swivel on the floating weight which by a half turn could bring a 2 or 4-minute stylus into playing position.[16] It was announced in July 1909 (U.S. and U.K.) and was for use with the new FIRESIDE phonograph and Combination GEM.

The Model K was the last reproducer style with the 32 mm diameter diaphragm. It has also been found adapted to coin-slot machine use.

Price $5.00; £1 1s. 0d.

Model K Reproducer

MODEL L REPRODUCER, 1909 onwards

First introduced on the AMBEROLA I in December 1909 (U.S. and U.K.) and also later with the AMBEROLA III and OPERA phonographs. All three had a travelling mandrel, the reproducer remaining stationary and being suspended by its own output tube over the record; a knurled screw bayonet lock held it in the horn support neck, and the action of engaging the motor automatically lowered the stylus on to the record.

The 4-minute stylus was mounted as in the Model H. The larger diameter (42 mm) copper diaphragm was stamped with raised rings and spoked ridges for a more even sound response. Like the Model H early examples had a swivelling stylus-bar mounting with the V cradle, but this made for record wear, the swivel was removed and the stylus bar shortened, and with a spiral spring fitted round the link between the crosshead and stylus bar, was found more satisfactory.

Model L Reproducer showing spring modification to stylus bar

Price:	initially	$7.50	
	1911	$4.75;	£1 0s. 0d.

MODEL M REPRODUCER, 1910 onwards

Officially this reproducer was to be ready in May 1910 but small numbers are known to have been circulating from January of that year. The Model M was a combination version (2 & 4-minute) of Model L and rather similar in appearance. The M had a protruding horizontal rod when mounted for playing, and a knob on its end indicated choice of sapphire. By not having to remove the reproducer from its mounting, the selection of the correct stylus was much simpler than the swivel types of combination reproducers, Models K and S.

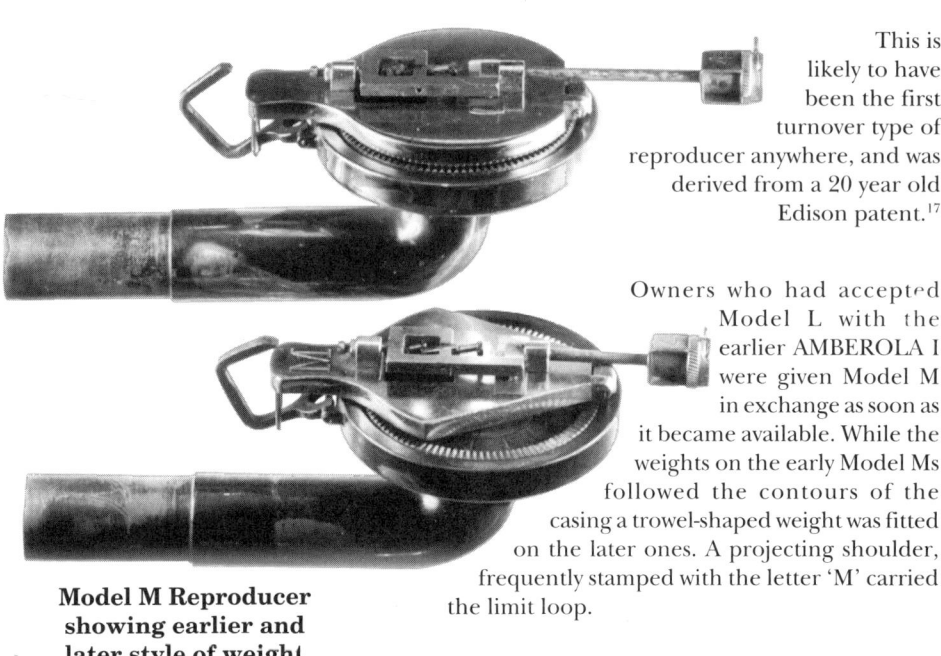

This is likely to have been the first turnover type of reproducer anywhere, and was derived from a 20 year old Edison patent.[17]

Owners who had accepted Model L with the earlier AMBEROLA I were given Model M in exchange as soon as it became available. While the weights on the early Model Ms followed the contours of the casing a trowel-shaped weight was fitted on the later ones. A projecting shoulder, frequently stamped with the letter 'M' carried the limit loop.

Model M Reproducer showing earlier and later style of weight

Price: $10.00; £2 2s. 0d.

In March 1913 it was estimated that prior to the arrival of the Diamond Model A Reproducer in October 1912 (U.S.) a total of 5647 phonographs had been sent out equipped with Models L and M reproducers, and of that number 1710 owners had ordered a Diamond A since its issue.[18] The memo recommended that a campaign should start to 'push' the balance of 3937 Diamond A.

MODEL N REPRODUCER, 1911 onwards

Announced in November 1911 (U.S.) and January 1912 (U.K.) the Model N conformed to the general shape and tail weight of the earlier series that included such as the Model C, but had the large (42 mm) copper alloy diaphragm and would fit only the large carrier-arm. It played the 4-minute Amberols with the sapphire mounted as on Model H. The Model N was part of the equipments of several machines, or as an optional extra after Blue Amberols had come into production. It then became the only sapphire reproducer of its type offered in the catalogues.

The Model N started by being sold fitted with a Model H tail weight, and being smaller than the Model N casing the pin-ears of the Model H weight were extended towards the hinge block; at the opposite end there was a longer limit pin to bridge the extra gap. Further modifications followed, the weight being made specifically to cover the diaphragm area with an extension shoulder to take the limit loop. This weight caused the stylus to jump grooves so a compression spring was inserted between the stylus bar and crosshead. A small 'N' was stamped on the weight extension.

The first fish-tail weight had the letter 'N' stamped over the 'MODEL—H 4-MINUTE' followed by 'MODEL—N 4-MINUTE and then 'MODEL—N' in slightly larger lettering and then an oversize 'N'. Similarly most of these reproducers had a domed top, but some are found with the flat stepped tube plate of the Model O.

Price: 1911 $5.00;   £1 1s. 0d.
               1913 $2.00;   8s. 4d.

In March 1913 following a Phonograph Committee report, the Model N-56 was announced for June 1913 (U.S. and U.K.). This as its number implies, was made for the two AMBEROLAS, V and (A)-VI and does not readily fit any other AMBEROLA carrier-arms.

Model N Reproducer

The N-56 had a trowel-shaped weight not unlike the second Model M, and a raised pillar or stud with a V-socket filed in it. When the feed was disengaged on the AMBEROLA V and (A)-VI a small metal arm raised the reproducer weight. Unlike the Model N the N-56 limit pin was located on the body of the reproducer, while the weight had the cage loop, but as on Model N this reproducer had the spiral spring fitted between the stylus bar and diaphragm to restrain a tendency to rattling in the early versions.

Price: $2.00; 8s. 4d.

The GEM Phonograph Model E had a special carrier-arm to take the Model N Reproducer in the side position

305

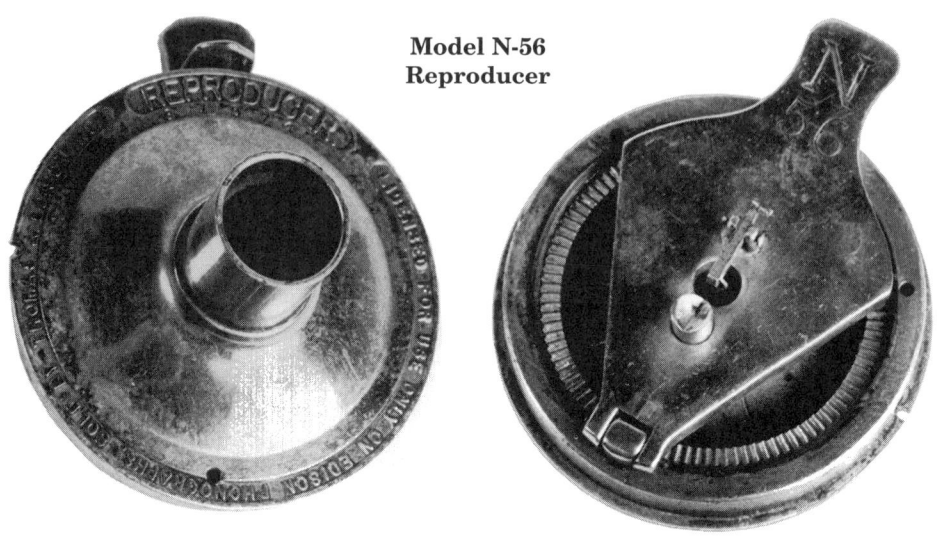

Model N-56 Reproducer

MODEL O REPRODUCER, 1910 onwards

This combination reproducer used a similar style of body to the Model N. The earlier examples had a round weight of similar diameter to the diaphragm and a truncated shoulder tailpiece, but in later versions this weight became trowel-shaped. Earlier ones had a flat stepped tube plate and this was changed to the more familiar dome. Like the Model M the Model O had a protruding horizontal rod that brought either the 2 or 4-minute stylus into play by a half turn. It would fit only the large carrier-arm set along the top of the cylinder and was available initially with TRIUMPH Model E and IDELIA, ALVA and BALMORAL phonographs in September 1910 (U.S.) and November 1910 (U.K.). Its arrival called for a longer crane upright rod to support the Cygnet Horns, known as the Model O (or Type E) crane.

Sold separately the Model O was offered complete with large carrier-arm and adapter ring. From known examples the earliest bodies were

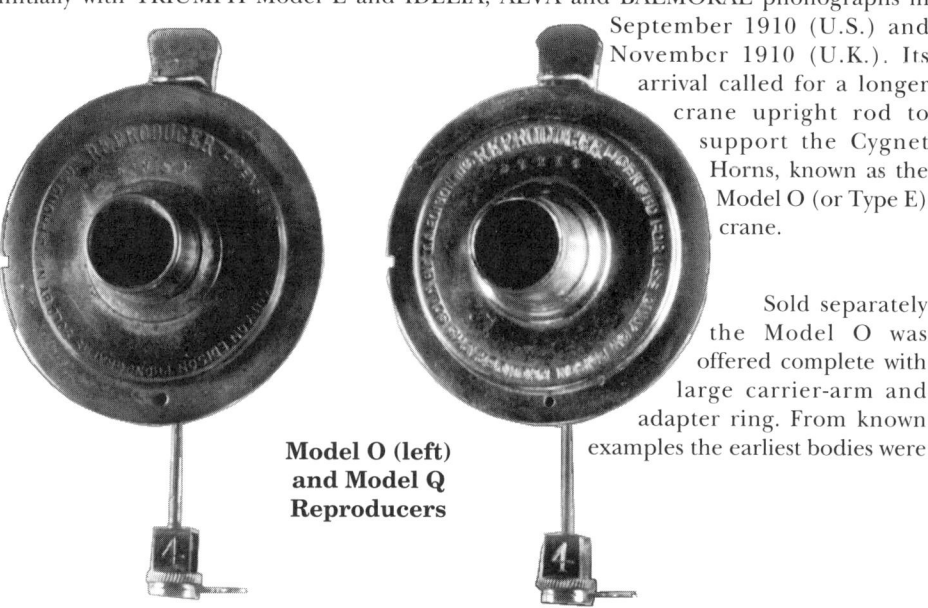

Model O (left) and Model Q Reproducers

made of brass, then iron with a brass label surface, followed by a pot-metal alloy.

Price $10.00; £2 2s. 0d.

Model O (left) and Model Q Reproducers

MODEL P REPRODUCER

No example of such a reproducer has been reported, but 'P' is likely to have been allocated to a model not put into production.

MODEL Q REPRODUCER

The early full-weight Model O reproducers sometimes damaged wax records and could be returned to the Edison factory through local dealers. There they had their weights trimmed to trowel shape and were re-stamped with a Q to denote the modification. Some of the very last Model Os sent out are believed to have been labelled 'Q'.

MODEL R REPRODUCER, 1911 onwards

These last two sapphire reproducers were directed at the Edison owner who was 'Amberolized' but whose machine still had the small carrier-arm and where the superior output of the larger diaphragm was desired. While the reproducer body fitted the carrier-arm eye in the usual way the oversize diaphragm casing sat atop and neither this model nor Model S could be coaxed into the large size carrier-arm. The Model R was announced for March 1911 (U.S.) and July 1911 (U.K.).

Edison machine enthusiasts were unhappy with the first form of this model and complained of the excess of lateral movement found in this design, leading to groove jumping. By making firm the pivoted stylus bar mounting, removing the V-cradle and extension to the stylus bar and putting a spiral spring along the link, the trouble was largely cleared up.

Model R Reproducer

A slot was cut in the reproducer shell for access to adjusting the diaphragm clamp.

Price $5.00; £1 1s. 0d.

MODEL S REPRODUCER, 1911 onwards

Outwardly similar to Model R, the Model S was a combination reproducer with a swivel plate on the floating weight to bring the 2 or 4-minute stylus into use. This arrangement was the same as on the earlier Model K and there were again separate stylus bars. Later versions were modified with the spiral spring between the stylus bar and diaphragm crosshead.

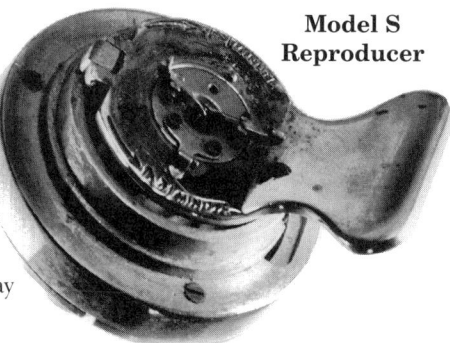

Model S Reproducer

This model was announced in November 1911 and supplied as part of the Model F STANDARD Phonograph equipment. It was not generally available in the United Kingdom but may have been imported unadvertised. Price: $6.50

An index entry is made for a Model T reproducer in a dealers' catalogue of Edison machines and accessories dated October 16th 1911, but this is an error for Model S. Nothing is known of any development past Model S in the sapphire range.

Several of the sapphire reproducers could be bought in oxidized bronze finish at extra cost for use on IDELIA phonographs.

Whereas the introduction of Edison reproducers is normally clearly dated, few were ever denoted as withdrawn or obsolete and most just faded away. Several of the more popular types were certainly still on supply until 1929 and could be bought after that.

The period up to 1911 saw many Edison patent applications for various improvements in Reproducers, including a series by Alexander N. Pierman feeding compressed air to enlarged Model Cs to boost volume in connection with the Kinetophone experiments. Another of March 1912 and filed by Edison in June 1908 (U.S. 1,019,440) had dual styli following each other closely in the groove with the aim of achieving more dimension to the sound. Another (No. 855,562) of June 1907 and filed by Edison in the previous March used a double diaphragm sealed round the periphery and each having radial slots but staggered in relation to one another.

REPRODUCERS INSPIRED BY OR USING PARTS OF EDISON MODELS

The simplicity and success of the Model C in particular produced a number of imitations, but with the Edison organization having markets through most of the world, the total of copied or modified models will never be known. In general there seemed to be three types of usage of the Edison range. The first copied the complete Edison original, the second used the body, with or without tube plate but had a modified weight and stylus assembly, the third placed a new diaphragm and housing on to a regular Edison weight and reproducer.

1) ARGOSY REPRODUCER

A reproducer for the German-made Argosy combination phonograph and a close copy of the Edison Model B tube plate with the spring-loaded stylus bar of the Columbia Lyric Reproducer fixed underneath. This so-called 'Extra Tension Reproducer' had a diamond stylus that would play 2 or 4-minute Indestructible Records, but not wax cylinders. Probable availability May 1910 onwards (U.K.). It cost 15s. 0d.

The Argosy Reproducer (from a sketch in *Hillandale News* for April 1991)

Blackman's Reproducer

2) BLACKMAN'S REPRODUCER

M. M. Blackman was an Edison salesman and manager of The Phonograph Company, exclusive Edison distributors in Kansas City, Missouri. Three of his patents were for the record brush fitted to the carrier-arm of some cylinder machines, and he may be remembered as the author of the statement that "Edison's Re-Creation of Music is his most sublime gift to Mankind".

3) COLUMBIA

The first semi-floating reproducers from Columbia - described as "a direct infringement of Model C" - were reported on September 29th 1904 in a letter from George Nisbett, Edison Western Manager, to W. E.. Gilmore. This was the Lyre, sold with the AZ Graphophone, and two successors with the Edison type tube plate.

4) EDISON BELL 'NEW MODEL' and CRYSTOL REPRODUCER

First reported on March 22nd 1904 the New Model was made available in Great Britain by Edison Bell with their Standard Phonograph, a close copy of Edison's STANDARD, and followed on other models. The New Model was based closely on Edison's Model C but the

Edison Bell New Model; the tail-weight came in two shapes

Edison Bell Crystol Reproducer

overhanging part of the weight is differently shaped and readily recognizable on that count, and the words NEW MODEL are cut into its weight. Frank Dyer, Edison's legal adviser in a letter of April 16th 1904 says: "unable to pursue (the reproducer) except perhaps unfair competition". As well as the New Model, Edison Bell offered the similar Crystol (or Chrystol) reproducer for playing the current 4-minute cylinders. Edison Bell produced its own 4-minute Crystol cylinders at the beginning of 1910 but they are rarely seen today.

5) FLETCHER REPRODUCER

Fletcher used the body and compression ring of the Edison Automatic Reproducer but substituted a domed tone chamber for the Edison tube plate with its flat interior. He also changed the stylus mounting. In a Court case in June 1902 Fletcher claimed these reproducers were old and were changed when he repaired them. The judge found for Edison's, but Fletcher was still adapting Edison reproducers according to a further report of October 8th 1902.

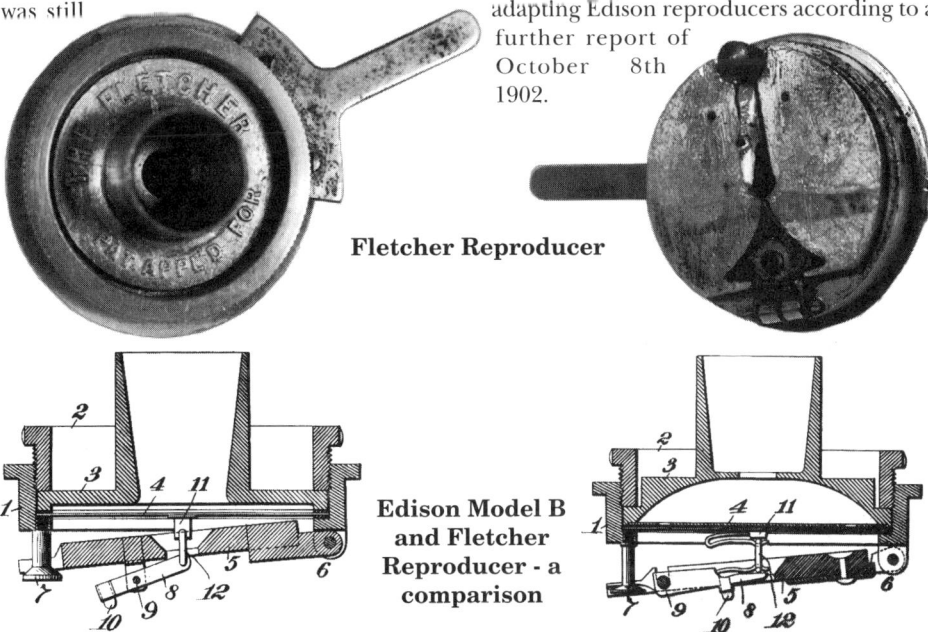

Fletcher Reproducer

Edison Model B and Fletcher Reproducer - a comparison

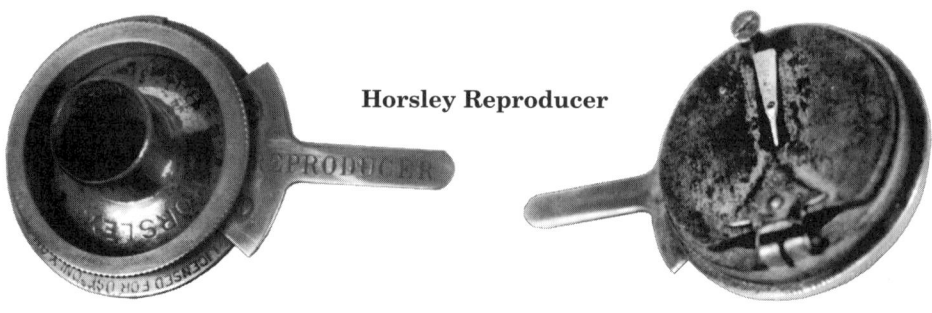

Horsley Reproducer

6) HORSLEY REPRODUCER

Another adaptation of the Automatic reproducer and described as a 'bayonet model'.

7) INDESTRUCTIBLE REPRODUCER

Marketed from September 28th 1908 by Indestructible Record Company this was a new reproducer with a stylus identical to the re-issued Model C patent. It had a large stylus 0.040 in. diameter and curve to engage the record surface 0.015 in. longitudinally. In time Indestructible Records in the U.K. were marketed by John D. Murdoch & Co., Ltd. who advertised 2-minute tension reproducers to fit Edison and Columbia machines, 10s. 0d. or 15s. 0d. with diamond stylus. The tube plate was similar to the Model C.

Indestructible Record Company's reproducer

8) MOBLEY REPRODUCER (ATTACHMENT)

This was a special form of lever extension to the floating weight of an Edison Automatic Reproducer and was claimed by Edwin H. Mobley in his U.S. Patent No. 690,069 of December 31st 1901. Mobley was accused of infringing three Edison reproducer patents: 397,280 of 1889, 430,278 of 1890, 484,584 of 1892.

Mobley Reproducer

The extension was added to the weight to improve tracking and to yield more volume. There was a dome plate and metal diaphragm fitted. Edison sued Mobley as he had Fletcher for altering his reproducer, and won. In his defence Mobley claimed his patent had been infringed by Edison and is thought to have been warned.

He was again reported by Louis Buehn of Wells Phonograph Co. of Philadelphia on October 10th 1902 as still selling his attachment to an Edison reproducer, but his activity was believed to be 'local and limited'.

9) SUTTON'S REPRODUCER

No drawing or photograph of this Australian instrument has been seen, but on January 1st 1908 it was described as a variation of Edison's chalk wheel (as used on telephones) and Higham's amber wheel amplifier.

10) MAX WURCKER REPRODUCER

Max Wurcker's Reproducer

This used the weight and stylus assembly of the Model C, but the diaphragm was larger, with a larger output collar. Wurcker was an Edison jobber from Sydney and his reproducer was reported to West Orange by W. W. Wyper, managing director of National Phonograph's establishment in Australia. In a report of July 29th 1908 the Laboratory found that Max Wurcker's instrument was "not as good as the Model C", but that no action would be taken on account of the three Australian Edison patents being weak. The reproducer was made by J. G. Coombs. These reproducers came in 5 types (0-4), three with 2-minute stylus, one with 4-

minute, and a combination model with change-over, said to be simpler than Edison's. Prices in 1908 Australia and New Zealand £1 10s. 0d.

SAPPHIRE SIZES

The following sapphire sizes should suit Edison reproducers:
> 2-minute ball (Model B types) 0.75 to 1.00 mm
> 2-minute ball, extra small (for indestructible records) 0.5 mm
> 2-minute 'door knob' (Model C types) radius 0.008 in; major diam. c 0.030 in., minor diam. c 0.016 in., tip radius 0.008 in.
> 4-minute disc end (Model H types) diameter of disc 0.050 in., radius of disc edge 0.005 in.*
> This was the first elliptical stylus in the industry

*measurements by D. M. Field

Early glass diaphragms were 0.005 in. thick

Max Wurcker's Reproducer

THE LAMBERT COMBINATION

Dating from the early 1900s the Lambert Combination consisted of the non Edison floating Matthews Reproducer and a special carrier-arm made to fit the GEM (17s. 6d.), STANDARD (£1 1s. 0d.) and HOME (£1 2s. 0d.). The Lambert Company Ltd. had an address at Water Lane, London, E. C.

**Lambert Combination, comprising the Matthews floating reproducer and Rawlinson sound-tight joint fitted to carrier-arm, and suited for:
GEM 17s. 6d.
STANDARD £1 1s. 0d.
HOME £1 2s. 0d.**

2-minute reproducer — make not known

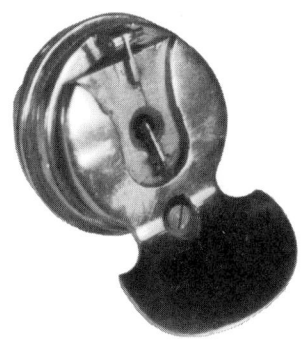

THE RECORDERS 1887-1912

Much of the credit for work on the recorders must be given to Charles Batchelor who was designing them from June 1887. Whereas the recorder-reproducer device of the tinfoil phonographs had been of no great consideration, immediately Edison began to give the wax cylinder phonograph his attention the recorder became of vital importance and with the reproducer was fitted into the spectacle frame carrier-arm from the earliest machine. This was the one constructed by Ezra Gilliland to Edison's pattern at the end of 1887, and the recorder was made of brass, polished and lacquered, had a slightly recessed tube plate and used a celluloid diaphragm.[19] The neck on the recorder was short but of smaller diameter than that on the reproducer to avoid confusion. The stylus was cut out of thin steel plate forming its own mounting and rested on a limit stop at its back end; it was fixed to the diaphragm centre and to a cross pin pivoted on mountings set on the body of the recorder. A spring raised the stylus bar to keep the diaphragm under tension, and was described by Edison as a 'closed' or 'constrained' system, likening it to the tympanum of the ear. The chisel end to the stylus produced a square-bottomed groove.

Square-bottomed grooves of the earliest wax cylinders

Gilliland constructed the second and improved style of phonograph to Edison's design in early 1888. It still had the recorder with the steel stylus ground to a chisel and set to a rubber block on a varnished silk diaphragm.[20] The brass tube plate was flat and the collar raised to near standard height.

Recorder (left) and speaker, December 1887

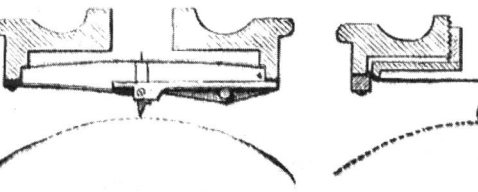

Edison's work culminating in the 'perfection' of the phonograph on June 16th 1888 led to a number of experimental recorders, but the inventor still adhered to the fixing of one end of the stylus bar to the recorder body, with tension being exerted to the centre of the diaphragm.[21]

So as to impart a clearer, more abrupt sound to the recording, experiments were tried with cutting styli with sharply hooked ends in advance of their stock,[22] thus prolonging the principle of the square-bottomed groove for a little longer. The first instance of the stylus bar assembly being fixed to the centre of the diaphragm and not attached in any way to the recorder body was in mid-1888[23] but this appears unwieldy, though in simplified form was successful 13 years later. The first recorders with glass diaphragms set in insulating washers on each edge were developed in time for Edison's work on the phonograph in June 1888. The tube plate was threaded round its rim and screwed into the reproducer shell for tightening or relaxing the diaphragm and the recording stylus cemented directly to the diaphragm centre, although still pivoting from the body of the reproducer.[24] In all these experimental models the stylus was still thick and cut a square section groove, and this was traced by a very much thinner phosphor-bronze wire stylus on the reproducer.[25]

By early 1889 the recorder had reached the following style; it was still made of brass:

Earlier 1889 recorder

The earliest spectacle phonographs first leased to the public in the latter half of 1889 had recorders similar to the above illustrations except that they were nickel plated and with a steel stylus, shanked and with a curved and recessed cutting edge[26] that was tracked by a steel ball. Batchelor's diary of March 19th 1889 chronicles this recorder and a reproducer as 'new models sent to me today'.[27] They combined later that year to become the Standard Speaker. Although the reproducers now had a hinged weight, the recorders were still rigid and had to be lowered into the wax to the depth desired. After a short time these steel styli were replaced by similarly cut and polished jewels, usually sapphires, as these were not affected by chemicals in the cylinders.[28] On these models the diameters of the tubes became standardized for the next 40 years.

Early sapphire recorder

By November 1889 the Standard speaker had arrived, combining both options into one unit. The dual spectacle frame was needed no longer although it lingered for several decades on office phonographs, and the Standard became regular issue with domestic phonographs until the arrival of the Automatic reproducer when a separate recorder was issued as well. This last was like the Standard, but without the reproducing sapphire. The day of the 'closed' spring-loaded diaphragm was over.

As the phonograph moved further towards a role as

Early 2-minute recorder

an entertainer the status of the home recorder declined and the emphasis moved towards better sound reproduction. It changed little over the years, being made in one model only. The dissipation of energy by the stylus bar with its contact with the recorder shell must have been recognized early, but was not remedied until 1901 when the stylus was cemented directly to the hinged diaphragm and had no other physical contact with the recorder. A sliding sleeve fitting inside the neck of the tube plate concentrated the sound on the centre of the diaphragm. This was the New Edison Recorder,[29] and these had their tops dyed orange from this period.

After alteration in 1905-6 the recorder became the Improved Edison Recorder, but after a year reverted to being just the Edison Recorder, the price remaining the same:

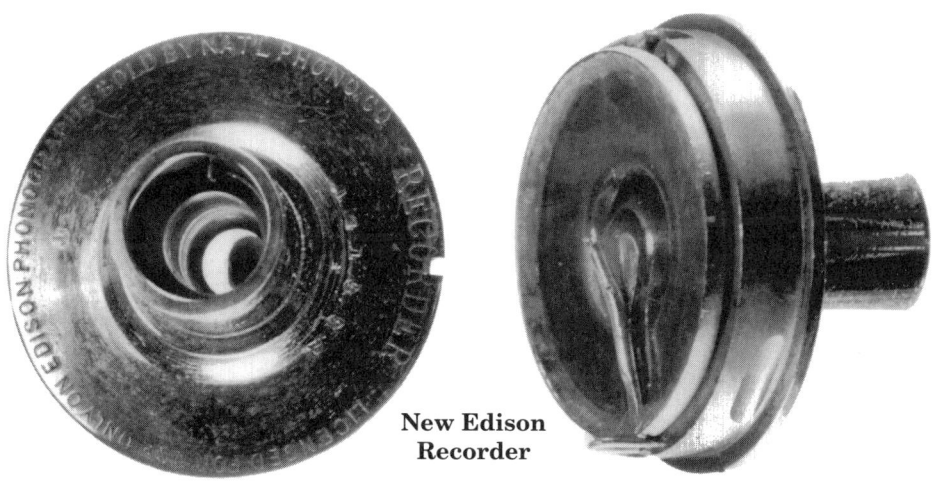

New Edison Recorder

Edison Recorder to 1901 $5.00;   £1 1s. 0d.
New Edison Recorder to 1906 $3.00;   12s. 6d.
Improved Edison Recorder to 1912 $3.00;   12s. 6d.

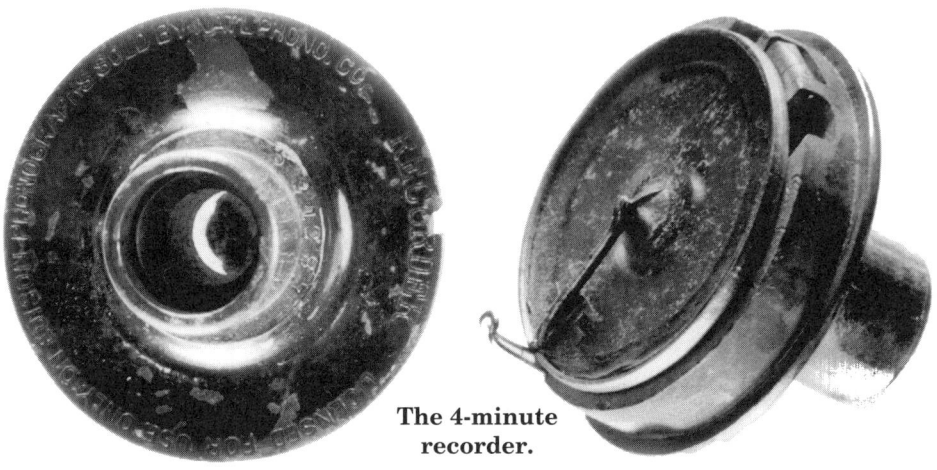

The 4-minute recorder.

Recorders remained strictly 2-minute until 1912 (U.S. and U.K.) but as 2-minute phonographs and cylinders were no longer being made, a 4-minute recorder[30] was included with the Edison Home Recording Outfit together with blanks of black material and a special shaver. This recorder was distinguished by green dye on the tube plate and could be bought separately for $3.00 or 12s. 6d.

The GEM recorder flourished briefly from mid-1900 until 1902, having the same smaller diameter of the GEM reproducer and looking very much like it at a casual glance. This recorder came as part of the GEM equipment, and its system of weight and linkage was the same as the regular Edison recorder of that time.

The GEM Recorder

Recorders were never offered with the large diaphragm that became general on reproducers after 1909, and needed a reduction ring in machines with a large carrier-arm. This so-called adapter ring cost 50 cents or 2s. 1d.[31] On the more sophisticated travelling mandrel phonographs, the early AMBEROLAS, the OPERA, CONCERT and SCHOOL a specific recorder arm was available for $1.25 or 5s. 3d. A special 14 in. recording horn was also recommended costing 55 cents or 2s. 6d. The arm fitted into the horn support on these machines in the normal place of the reproducer, and a regular diameter carrier-arm was pivoted to it.

Recorders continued to carry an adjusting arm for several years after the speaker clamps on carrier-arms had been displaced. The reason was for recognition as the word RECORDER was usually stamped on it.

Recorder and small recording horn shown fitted to an Edison SCHOOL Phonograph.

1) British Patent No. 28,759 for Improvements in Sound Records of July 23rd 1908 and filed January 3rd 1907. There was no comparable American patent.
2) U.S. Patent No. 386,974 for Phonograph filed November 26th 1887 by Edison and granted July 31st 1888
3) U.S. Patent No. 394,106 for Phonograph Reproducer filed November 26th 1887 by Edison and granted December 4th 1888
4) U.S. Patent No, 488,190 for Phonograph Reproducer filed June 7th 1888 by Edison and granted December 20th 1892
5) U.S. Patent No. 400,646 for Phonograph Recorder and Reproducer filed June 7th 1888 by Edison and granted April 2nd 1889
6) U.S. Patent No. 430,278 for Phonograph filed April 10th 1889 by Edison and granted June 17th 1890. This was the fundamental Standard speaker patent
7) U.S. Patent No. 484,584 for Phonograph filed by Edison on May 27th 1890 and granted October 18th 1892
8) This device featured in two of Edison's U.S. Patents, 453,741 of June 9th 1891 and 465,972 of December 29th 1891
9) U.S. Patent No. 484,585 for Phonograph filed on July 30th 1890 by Edison and granted October 18th 1892 described an early weighted reproducer
10) The Model B featured in Peter Weber's U.S. Patent No. 744,266 for Phonographic Recorder and Reproducer filed February 6th 1901 and granted November 17th 1903
11) Letter of June 12th 1902 from Judge Hayes to W. E. Gilmore - Edison Archive
12) The overhanging weight of the Model C was anticipated by E. H. Mobley's Phonograph Reproducer, U.S. Patent No. 690,069, filed July 3rd 1901 and granted December 31st 1901. This was an improved version of the Automatic and Mobley was sued by Edison who then put out the Model C with a similar weight of fishtail shape
13) The diaphragm built up of several discs of graduated size was first specified in Peter Weber's Patent No. 454,941 of June 30th 1891, filed May 24th 1890, but was not implemented until Model C was marketed. U.S. Patent No. 975,377 of November 8th 1910, filed March 22nd 1907 is for the copper diaphragm. The change resulted from James Andem's suit against Edison in New York state that precluded his use of mica diaphragms, and is explained in more detail in Appendix V
14) An early method of setting the sapphire is shown in Edison's U. S. Patent No. 996,625 for Phonograph-Reproducer, filed March 18th 1908 and granted July 4th 1911, but the Model H is effectively embodied in U.S. Patent No. 951,496, filed October 8th 1908, granted March 8th 1910
15) A feature of U.S. Patent No. 1,049,216 for Phonograph-Reproducer filed by Frank L. Dyer and Peter Weber on March 20th 1909 and granted December 31st 1912
16) U.S. Patent No. 905,033 for Phonograph-Reproducer filed by Peter Weber on March 26th 1908 and granted November 24th 1908
17) U.S. Patent No. 605,667 for Phonograph filed by Edison on December 3rd 1890, renewed February 4th 1897 and granted June 14th 1898. In the original patent application one side was a recording stylus, the other a reproducer, and Model M had two kinds of playback styli. With the arrival of the LP in the early '50s this mode of turnover styli came into use again, really the development of a 19th century phonographic device
18) Minutes of the Amusement Phonograph Committee, March 14th 1913 - Edison Archive
19) Celluloid was invented by the Hyatt brothers and patented July 1870 (U.S. No 105,338)
20) U.S. Patent No. 488,190 (see Note 4)
21) A typical recorder of this time features in U.S. Patent No. 393,466 for Phonograph Recorder filed July 17th 1888 by Edison and granted November 27th 1888. The stylus bar was pivoted and spring loaded
22) Three such experiments are detailed in U.S. Patent Nos. 393,966/7/8, all filed by Edison on July 17th 1888 and granted December 4th 1888
23) U.S. Patent No. 397,280 filed by Edison September 27th 1888 and granted February 5th 1889. In this case the recording stylus was spring loaded with a retarding device working in the air like a fan
24) U.S. Patent 400,646 (see Note 5)
25) U.S. Patent No. 400,647 for Phonograph filed by Edison on July 7th 1888 and granted April 2nd 1889

26) U.S. Patent No. 430,278 (see Note 6)
27) Edison Archive
28) U.S. Patent No. 484,583 for Phonograph Cutting Tool filed by Edison on May 27th 1890 and granted October 18th 1892. Besides the sapphire recorder this patent included a turning-off and polishing jewel
29) Designed by Peter Weber and filed on February 6th 1901 as U.S. Patent No. 800,890, granted October 3rd 1905 in this form. In U.S. Patent 802,212 of two weeks later Charles L. Hibbard (for Edison) proposed the stylus holder be fastened through the diaphragm by metal tongues, but the Weber method of fixing by adhesive is met more often
30) U.S. Patent No. 1,024,839 of April 30th 1912, filed on January 3rd 1907 envisaged a 4-minute button type of stylus with a notch, but the production model used a cylindrical stylus with a concave end. (see Note 1)
31) With the adapter ring the Edison recorder could be used on AMBEROLAS VIII and IV, but the lift lever is found to strike the mica on the AMBEROLAS V and VI

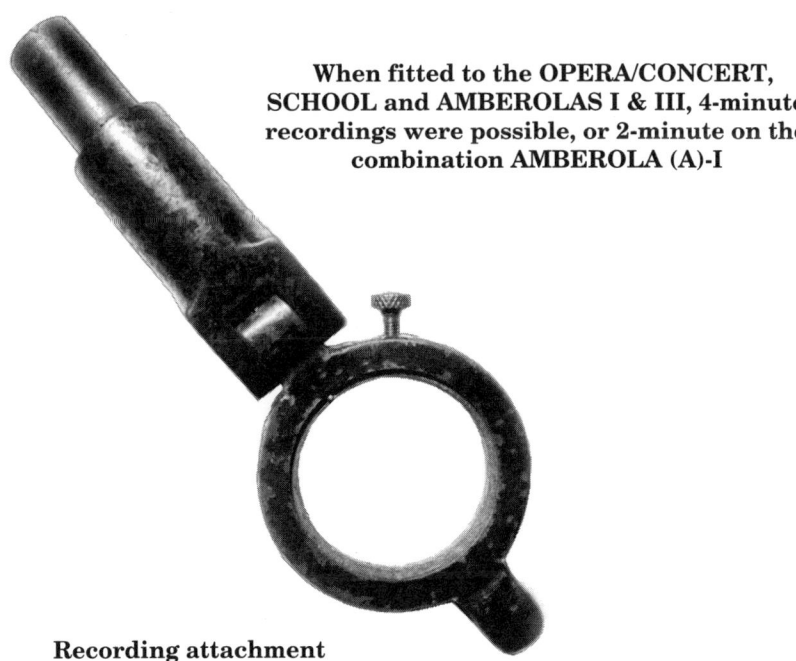

When fitted to the OPERA/CONCERT, SCHOOL and AMBEROLAS I & III, 4-minute recordings were possible, or 2-minute on the combination AMBEROLA (A)-I

Recording attachment

Chapter 25
Diamond Reproducers

This was a series of four designed to play the celluloid Blue Amberols, but would also function satisfactorily on most makes of indestructible cylinders.[1]

The Model B is seen the most often. A very great number of these were sold to convert horn phonographs to playing Blue Amberol cylinders and they were also supplied with several of the AMBEROLA models.

Unlike sapphire reproducers the diamond stylus models bore *no letter marking* but may be identified readily as follows:

Diamond A was the only one to be finished in highlighted oxidized bronze

Diamond B was the only one to have the sound outlet coming out vertically, and generally had a nickel finish.

Diamond C had a horizontal outlet tube, was usually painted black (although a few nickel plated examples are known) and will fit only the AMBEROLAS 30, 50 and 75 range.

Diamond D was closely based on the Diamond C, but with an added weight partly circling the cylinder and a spiral spring round the connecting link. It is not seen very often.

All four reproducers had the larger 42 mm diameter diaphragm, normally made of Japanese rice paper.

DIAMOND MODEL A REPRODUCER 1912 onwards

This was intended for the traversing mandrel machines and had features in common with the earlier models L and M reproducers, being suspended by its output tube from the horn bracket. It was normally finished in highlighted oxidized bronze.

The reproducer was introduced in October 1912 (U.S.) and December 1912 (U.K.) and supplied from those dates with the AMBEROLA (B) - I and III and CONCERT and from December 1912 (U.S.) with the SCHOOL. Like Models L and M the stylus was automatically lowered on to the record on engaging the motor.

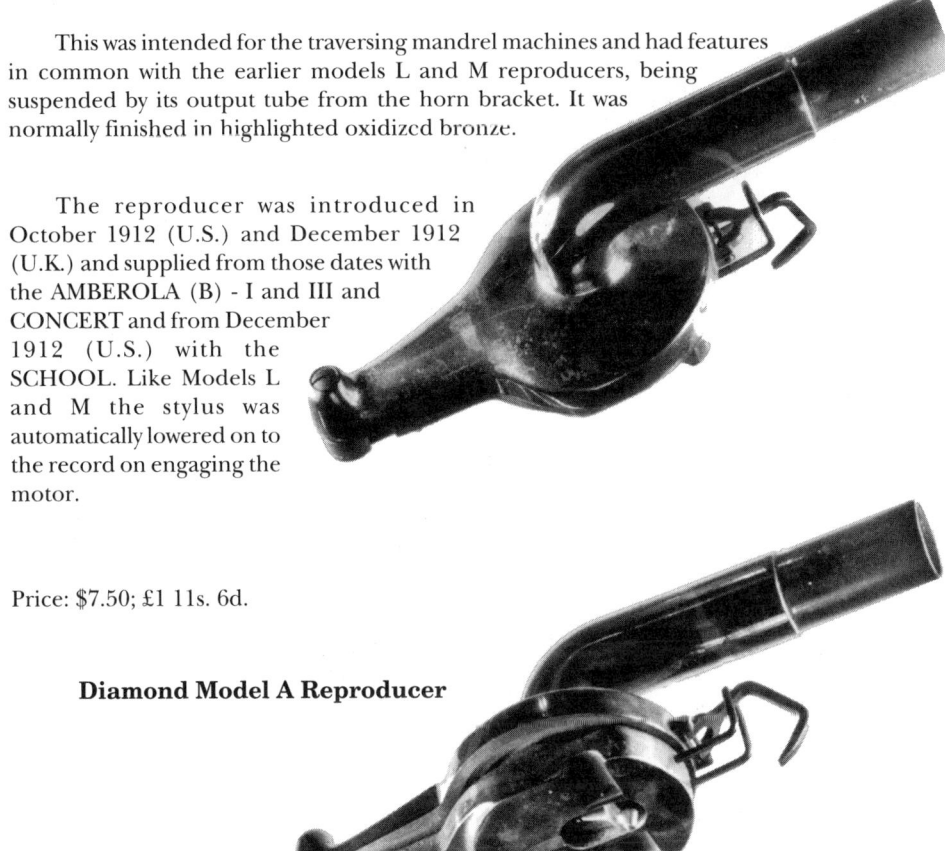

Price: $7.50; £1 11s. 6d.

Diamond Model A Reproducer

DIAMOND MODEL B REPRODUCER

This was introduced in October 1912 (U.S.) and January 1913 (U.K.) and was sold with horn machines, except the GEM, from those dates. This versatile reproducer was also found with combination attachment outfits for adapting older machines to the new records, and also as standard issue with AMBEROLAS IV, V, VI, VIII and X. Except for a rare oxidized bronze finish to match the IDELIA, the reproducer was always nickel finished.

Price: $7.50; £1 11s. 6d.

Diamond Model B Reproducer

After the Great War world trade was slow to pick up, and the Edison Company, eager as ever to launch advertising campaigns to keep the cylinder in front of the public, estimated that of all the people who had ever bought two million TRIUMPH, HOME and STANDARD phonographs, ninety per cent had still not gone over to using the Diamond B Reproducer and that these may have discarded their machines now that 2-minute cylinders were no longer made. Therefore in August 1919 Diamond B Reproducer Outfits were made available in eight types and prices for the FIRESIDE, STANDARD, HOME and TRIUMPH machines, and included carrier-arm, horn connector and other parts.

Diamond Model B Reproducer

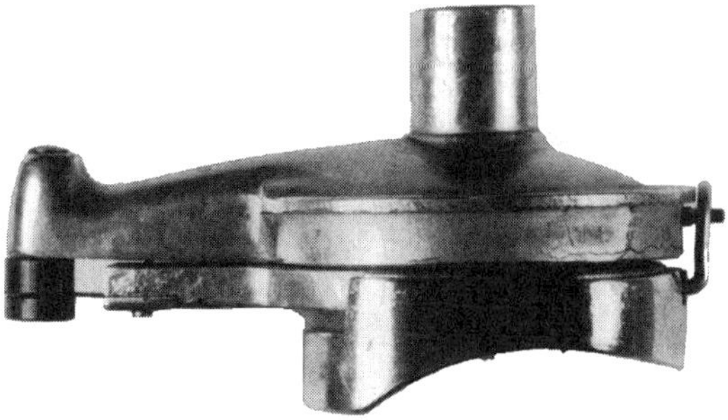

Diamond Model B Reproducer fitted with additional weight

DIAMOND MODEL C REPRODUCER

This was an entirely fresh design for the new range of AMBEROLAS 30, 50 and 75 and was the only issued reproducer on these machines from the first half of 1915 until all cylinder phonograph production ceased in 1929. The carrier-arms on this range were the same diameter as the large ones on the horn phonographs, but were modified expressly to accommodate this new reproducer. The tube plate and weight on this model were not unlike the Diamond Model B, but the sound outlet was now turned through a horizontal tube where the neck of the internal cabinet horn was suspended and pivoted. For about their first two years these models had a nickel finish and the sound tube was an inserted brass ferrule, but from October 1916 they were diecast with a machined ferrule and the visible parts black lacquered. These are often found to have swollen in storage.

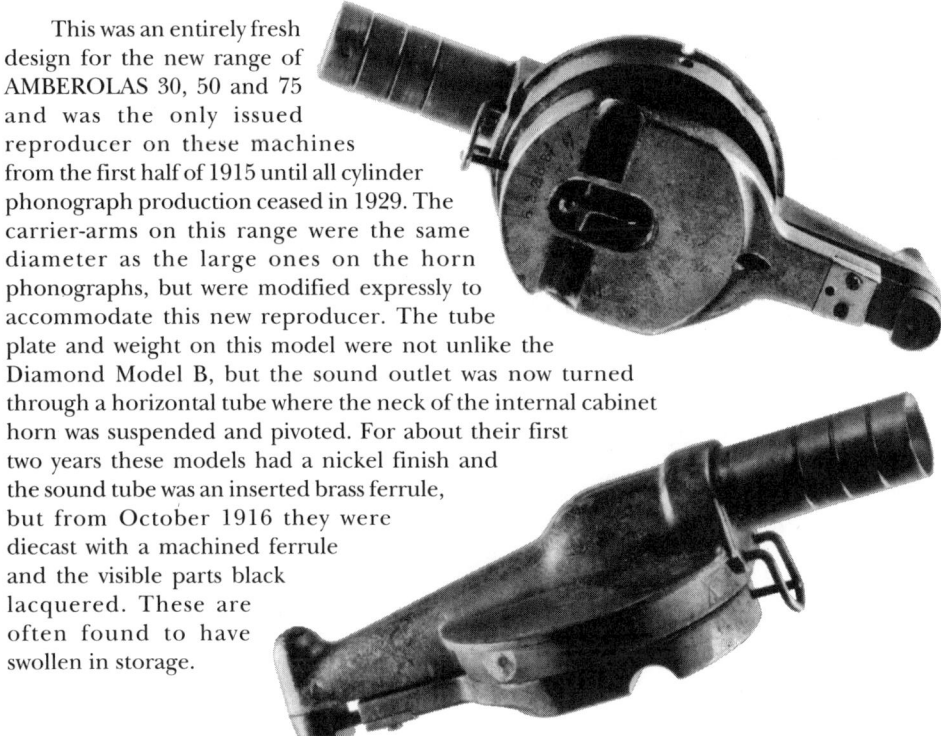

Diamond Model C Reproducer in its earlier nickel form. The later die-cast models had a dull black finish

In November 1916, anxious about the rise in the cost of diamonds due to the war, the Edison factory management was contemplating a rise in the prices of Diamond Model B and C reproducers. At that time they cost $3.03 and $3.15 each to produce, and it was decided to double the number of points derived from each carat of diamond. The price was not increased however, as it was felt desirable to continue trying to induce owners to convert their 2-minute phonographs to playing Blue Amberols through the Diamond Model B Reproducer.

DIAMOND MODEL D REPRODUCER

This was introduced in 1928 for use with the AMBEROLAS 60 and 80. It was very similar in appearance to its predecessor, the Diamond Model C, but there was a hook and tension spring at the extremity of the stylus bar, and an additional weight screwed on to the standard weight produced more volume. It is believed that all these reproducers were nickel plated.

Neither this reproducer nor the AMBEROLA 60 and 80 for which it was intended are much known in the United States although these machines were sold in the United Kingdom and New Zealand. Both this reproducer and the Diamond C were sold only with their respective AMBEROLAS and no record of their individual selling price has been noted; it is thought that there must have been provision for lost or damaged models.

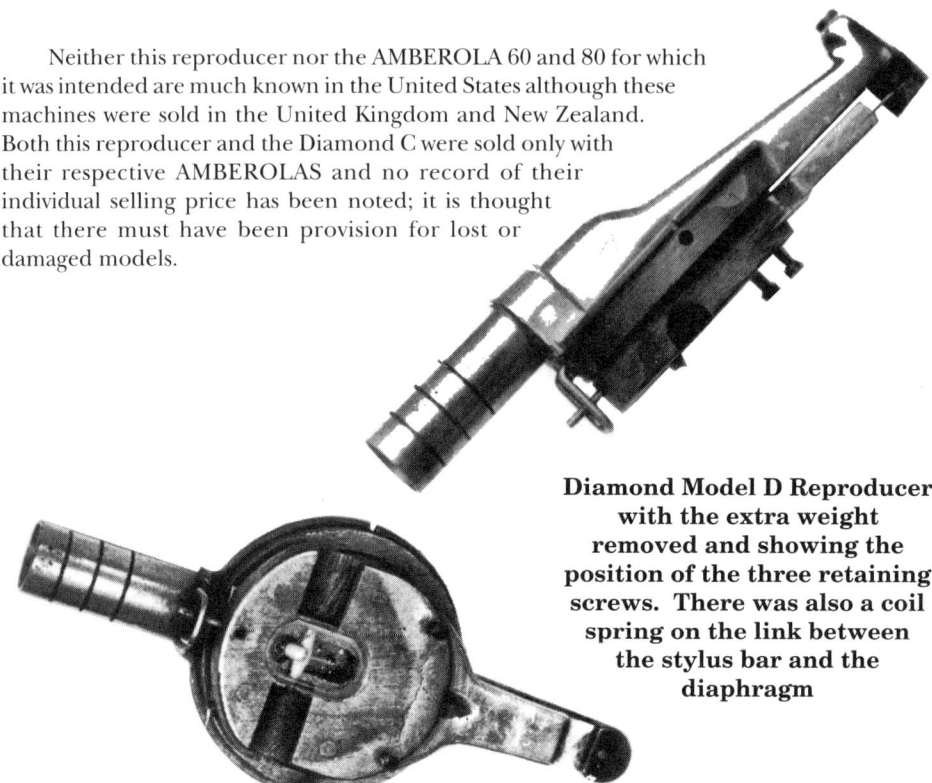

Diamond Model D Reproducer with the extra weight removed and showing the position of the three retaining screws. There was also a coil spring on the link between the stylus bar and the diaphragm

THE SYKES ELECTROGRAPH

Some British collectors will be familiar with the 'Electrograph' pick-up attachment for phonographs, depicted nearby. This was introduced in 1935 to followers of British Edison and presumably made available for export as needed. It was the creation of Adrian F. Sykes, BSc., a noted British physicist of his generation, acoustics expert and inventor and lifelong champion in Great Britain of the Edison Phonograph. The Electrograph was the culmination of a number of experiments, some of these

The British Adrian Sykes introduced his Electrograph in the mid-1930s, a time when pick-ups for playing gramophone records through the family radio were becoming popular

being granted provisional patent numbers. The stylus assembly, floating weight and linkage from a Diamond Model B reproducer acted on a moving iron pick-up housed in a bakelite moulding and could be amplified through a radio set.

Price: £1 1s. 0d. (21/-)

This sort of electric pickup would be called a variable reluctance type today. The output could be controlled up to a point by adjustment of the screw in the top but should not touch the iron paddle or it will vibrate with the stylus through the connecting link. If the gap is too small, distortion will result. By feeding the signal into an equalized (tone controlled) amplifier the high and lows will be flattened out and more detail derived from a Blue Amberol than ever a Diamond Model B reproducer will portray.

NOTES:
1) The layout of these reproducers and the multi-layered Japanese rice paper diaphragms were embodied in Edison's U.S. Patent No. 1,055,621 for Reproducer, filed May 18th 1911 and granted March 11th 1913. The British equivalent of this patent is 3,814 of 1912. The rice paper used was 0.001 in. thick, shellacked, dried and compressed to 0.005 in. thick in 2 in. squares. Cork was then shellacked to its centre and a cap of hard material secured to the top as anchor for the link from the stylus bar. The diaphragm was then stamped to size.

The Diamond Model D Reproducer with weight shown mounted on an AMBEROLA 60

Chapter 26
Language Courses

The earliest pronouncements by Edison on his newly invented phonograph and its uses included the storing of dying languages and changing dialects, and he particularly envisaged it as a means to learning a foreign language without a teacher and in the quiet of the home, and certainly one of its earliest applications was to this end.

It was only on the realization of the Edison electric phonographs from June 1888 that the experience of hearing from these instruments the uttered word in its full syllables individually impressed itself on two of the established linguistic experts of the day in the United States that this might be a means of offering spoken foreign language courses to the public.

The first of these was the Count Rafael Diez de la Cortina, who had established The Cortina Academy of Languages in New York City in 1882. He was reported as experimenting with phonographs as early as 1885, three years before Edison's perfected wax cylinder machine, but may have had access to the Bell and Tainter wax-coated experiments of that time. Professor Cortina was an early convert to the 1889 Edison electric instruments with their more durable solid wax cylinders, and offered these in advertising his courses until 1893. His first language course on cylinders was *Spanish in Twenty Lessons* in 1889. From 1893 a Columbia Graphophone was shown, and then, as they came on the market the CLASS M, SPRING MOTOR and STANDARD, all these being recommended in the catalogue of Cortina's Language Academy in 1899. On whatever phonograph, his system of instruction was called *The Cortinaphone Method*.

By 1897 it was stated that he had sold more than a thousand Edison phonograph and foreign language sets, and although the early recordings were made individually by Cortina himself at his Academy of Languages, it is likely the Edison company took over production at the factory from 1896 to 1901.[1] There was no obvious involvement by The International Correspondence School in Edison products at this time, indeed at the end of 1900 a Special Announcement in Edison catalogues read:

> *In response to a popular demand for Language Study Records, there are now being manufactured at the Edison Laboratory complete sets of such records in French, Spanish, German and Italian exclusively for Professor R. D. Cortina, 44 West 34th Street, New York from whom all particulars can be obtained. Prof. Cortina is the originator of the adoption of the phonograph for the teaching of*

languages and with an experience of 15 years making language records. These records are for sale in sets only (10 records to a set) by all dealers in Phonographs, Records and Supplies.

It is apparent that this announcement made no reference to the use of Edison phonographs, because Cortina was edging away from Edison and beginning to buy the machines from outside, and although he now moves out of the compass of this book it is worth recording that *The Cortinaphone Method* still flourishes from its Academy of Languages in New York.

The second pioneer who was quick to follow Cortina was Dr. Richard S. Rosenthal, a Potsdam-born emigrant to the United States, and reputed to have brought over with him the mastery of 28 languages! The earliest reference to his involvement with the phonograph appeared in *The Phonogram* of 1891, where his *Meisterschaft System* was offered on 24 cylinders for each of four conversational languages. Although these cylinders were made through the Columbia Company of Washington, D.C. the phonograph first offered with them was the Edison electric machine, and its successors continued probably until some time between 1894 and 1896 when North American Phonograph was in bankruptcy and Rosenthal had to turn to American Graphophone for a more certain source of supply. Again it is possible he may have waited a year or two before crossing the road to this company, for in 1898 it was marketing the 'Eagle' and 'Five Dollar Graphophone', and these Rosenthal adopted.

In retrospect both Cortina and Rosenthal must have found the price of the phonograph something of an obstacle when pushing their language courses, unless the student had access to one already, when it is remembered that the Edison electric phonographs of the early 'nineties were listed in the region of $200.00, and both were not slow to transfer allegiance to the very much cheaper Graphophone range.

As public taste began to turn from the cylinder and espouse the disc, so did Rosenthal in 1914 with his *Language Phone Method*, and although his systems of language tuition, advanced for their day, no longer flourish, his book *Spanish (French, Italian, German) Self-Taught* survived him to a very last printing in 1947, and even that edition still faithful to the original text-book of 1893, made reference to 'turning the lever of the machine', meaning a phonograph.

If by 1900 Rosenthal had already deserted the Edison phonograph for playing his language systems, and Cortina procured his machines both from Edison and Columbia, a third correspondence school turned to the Edison company to supply phonographs and language tuition records, and this is the system that is known better to students of Edisoniana than either of the earlier two, because examples of the phonographs are not infrequently found. Most have either the distinctive repeating key or an ivory plaque engraved with the International Correspondence Schools, or sometimes both. Single specimens or sets of I.C.S. language cylinders are not uncommon either.[2]

Whereas Cortina and Rosenthal offered the regular Edison (and other) phonographs to reproduce their language courses, I.C.S. machines were the first to be equipped with the repeating device.[3]

STANDARD Phonograph Model A with repeat lever for use with I.C.S. Language records. This example has had a Combination Attachment added

The background of the International Correspondence Schools is unusual in that they started in a very small way in 1891 at Scranton, Penn., then a flourishing anthracite mining area, to provide the miners with correspondence courses to help them pass examinations and improve themselves in the industry. The Schools expanded rapidly and by 1901 instruction in modern languages was offered. Early in the following year a catalogue was devoted to *Instruction in Foreign Languages* with the help of the Edison phonograph and moulded cylinders. These I.C.S. cylinders became a minor landmark in phonograph history, being the first to be made by the Edison moulded process, and they were offered in September 1901, preceding the first moulded entertainment records by four months.[4] The term Gold Moulded for these latter cylinders was first used in October 1902.

This use of a cylinder of harder composition for language tuition made for a more incisive reproduction and allowed a repeating device to be fitted to the phonograph. By pressing a button the reproducer was taken back a few grooves to reiterate a word or phrase that would have been destructive to the softer brown wax records. The phonograph chosen for the repeating device was the Edison STANDARD Model A, then just being marketed in its New Style cabinet, and the device was continued with Models B and C, and a Combination STANDARD not earlier than Model D has been reported with it. Much was made in advertisements of this phonograph's dual abilities, to teach at 90 r.p.m. and entertain at 160 r.p.m.

The I.C.S. system was certainly available outside American shores and I.C.S. were persuaded to agree to offer Edison cylinders exclusively with outfits sold in foreign countries, although the terms of the agreement are not known.[5]

International Correspondence Schools designed a cabinet that they were shrewd enough to offer both for language study and amusement. It contained an Edison STANDARD Phonograph with repeating lever, lowering into a compartment at the top when not in use. By

The International Correspondence School's cabinet of 1904 was equipped with an Edison STANDARD Phonograph, two pull-out peg trays for cylinders, two storage compartments, and a rest for the instruction book

raising the lid this positioned the phonograph where it latched, at the same time creating a book rest. Behind, a flap covered a space for speaking and hearing tubes and other accessories, and in a cupboard below there were two sliding shelves with pegs for 25 cylinders each; underneath there was space for text books, horn and other cylinders in boxes. The cabinet measured 34 in. high, 18 in. depth and 13 in. width, and was finished in weathered oak. It was announced in March 1904. The price for this rather splendid cabinet is not known, and it was followed in the next month by a simple bent rod book rack for fitting to existing STANDARDS; this attachment slotted in the lid catch holes, but its price has not been seen.

In February 1910 a specially built I.C.S. GEM, resembling the 2-minute Model C, replaced the STANDARD. Low gearing and a governor restraint kept its speed within the tolerance of the 90 r.p.m. I.C.S. cylinders and it could not be speeded up to play entertainment records.[6] This Language Outfit complete with 11 in. horn, hearing tubes with headband and oilcan was offered for $35.00.

By July 1915 I.C.S. were pressing the Edison company for a 2-minute version of the AMBEROLA 30 for its students' use, but the assistant chief engineer John P. Constable resisted

Special GEM phonograph introduced for I.C.S. use in 1910

this as being different to the regular AMBEROLA 30 and the factory was too busy to make special orders. In the September it was decided to offer this model to the I.C.S. with a 4-minute recorder in an adapter ring, sapphire reproducer and special connector to the horn.[7] It was felt that the way was now open to the user to buy a diamond reproducer if he or she wanted the machine for entertainment use.

By the beginning of December 1915 the factory was ready to send out these phonographs. The staff was instructed to check that the carrier-arm raised the reproducer and recorder weight correctly. These AMBEROLA 30s seem to have been offered by I.C.S. for many years, the last-noticed mention in Edison company records being April 1927.

In 1903 (U.S.) typical I.C.S. Language Outfits with the option of French, German and Spanish were as follows:

25 I.C.S. Records and Text Books initially $25.00,	$30.00
Complete Outfit, Records & Text Books, without correspondence instruction	$50.00
I.C.S. Phonograph (STANDARD Model A with groove repeating attachment)	$30.00
25 I.C.S. Records	$18.00

This I.C.S. phonograph included Model C reproducer, listening tubes and headphones, recording tube, oilcan, camel-hair chip-brush and 14 in. horn

From a 1907 British source I.C.S. Language Study Outfits were offered in the following forms:

Complete Outfit, STANDARD Phonograph with repeating attachment and equipment, 25 Edison Gold Moulded Records and four bound volume Text Books   £12 12s. 0d.
As above but with pamphlet Text Books   £11 11s. 0d.
Records and Text Books consisting of 25 Edison Gold Moulded Records and four bound volume Text Books   £ 6 6s. 0d.
As above but with pamphlet Text Books   £ 5 5s. 0d.

Languages for the above included French, German, Spanish, English-French, English-Spanish, Polish, English-Slovak, English-Lithuanian, English-Ruthenian

Only recently have another pair of American companies come to light during research. These were the associated Technical Supply Company and International Textbook Company, who bought STANDARD and HOME phonographs from Edison. Both machines were fitted with the back-spacing attachment, 14 in. horn, recorder, speaking tube, special head-band hearing tube, oilcan and chip-brush. Details are thin but these concerns were billed as follows on October 19th 1907:

STANDARD Home Language Study Outfit $12.42 net.
HOME   " $17.31 net.

Retail prices have not been seen but this use of the HOME in language study is unique.

While the above article has been constructed from material of original research, it readily acknowledges several Papers published in the 1970s in American Phonograph journals by Dr. Phillip Petersen on the Cortina, Rosenthal and I.C.S. language courses.

Top movement of the AMBEROLA 30 I.C.S. Phonograph of 1915, showing details of the special Model H reproducer adapter

1) During this period Edison cylinders and other principal makes were 'dubbed' or duplicated by the pantographic method.
2) The I.C.S. Trade Mark No. 87,895 of March 25th 1902 showed two fingers of a cuffed hand holding up a cylinder. Filed January 30th 1902 and use claimed since December 28th 1901
3) The repeating device on these machines was the subject of Peter Weber's U.S. Patent No. 744,267 of November 17th 1903 and filed April 14th 1903
4) Earlier moulded cylinders like Lioret and Lambert had been made of celluloid; these new I.C.S. cylinders were so-called 'black wax'. The Gold Moulded label was registered August 9th 1904, filed January 23rd 1904.
5) Letter of October 21st 1904 from W. Schermerhorn to James White of National Phonograph in London -Edison Archive
6) The cylinders offered with this machine were the 100 t.p.i. black wax types, later moulded in the Blue Amberol celluloid.
7) The courses offered with this phonograph were on Blue Amberol type of cylinders, 200 t.p.i. and playing at 90 r.p.m.

A Full Edison Hand

Double Service
FOR EVERY PHONOGRAPH

Chapter 27
The Polyphone Attachment

The names of both Leon F. Douglass and Henry Babson were closely associated with the development and sale of the Polyphone Attachment. Their connection dated at least from 1892 when they and Charles Dickinson founded the Talking Machine Company of Chicago.

At the age of 21 in 1890 Douglass was a precocious patentee and in 1898 filed a patent for the Polyphone attachment for Phonographs and Graphophones.[1] It was really quite a simple idea, two reproducers set in tandem with their styli ⅜ in. to ½ in. apart and running in the same groove. There were two horns.

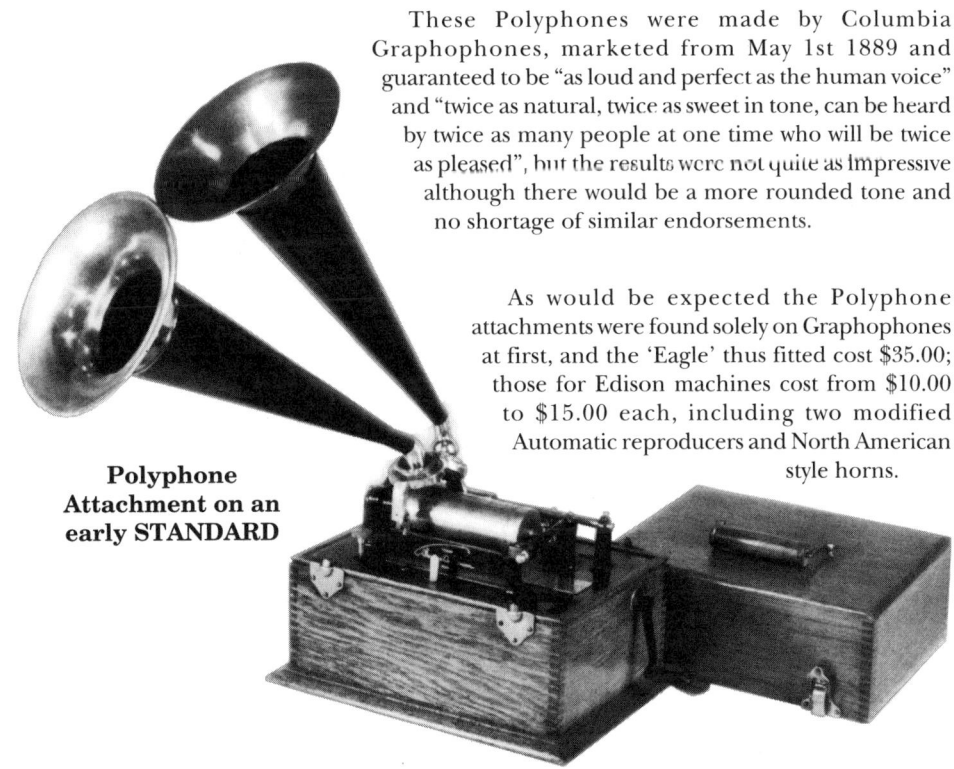

Polyphone Attachment on an early STANDARD

These Polyphones were made by Columbia Graphophones, marketed from May 1st 1889 and guaranteed to be "as loud and perfect as the human voice" and "twice as natural, twice as sweet in tone, can be heard by twice as many people at one time who will be twice as pleased", but the results were not quite as impressive although there would be a more rounded tone and no shortage of similar endorsements.

As would be expected the Polyphone attachments were found solely on Graphophones at first, and the 'Eagle' thus fitted cost $35.00; those for Edison machines cost from $10.00 to $15.00 each, including two modified Automatic reproducers and North American style horns.

The 'suitcase' HOME with Polyphone Attachment

The Polyphone Company operated from 107 Madison Street, Chicago, the address of Babson Brothers the mail-order firm, who were big distributors and friends of Edison and National Phonograph began making Polyphones for Babson. Edison unusually agreed to allow him to sell the device attached to Edison phonographs. An account for these survives from November 30th 1900:

21 Polyphones for CONCERT	@ $15.00 each	
277 " STANDARD	@ $12.00	"
248 " HOME	@ $12.00	"

These attachments only existed for a short time and became obsolete when the brighter-sounding Gold Moulded records came on sale in 1902. Babson himself said later that Edison stepped in and forbade the use of double reproducers and double horns on his phonographs very soon after.

Until this time four Polyphone-fitted Edison phonographs were offered by Babson Brothers:

GEM Polyphone   complete $15.00

STANDARD with Polyphone
1 oak carrying case
2 extra loud Automatic reproducers
Double bell concert horn
1 oilcan
1 chip-brush   complete $25.00

HOME with Polyphone
1 oak carrying case
2 extra loud Automatic reproducers
Double bell concert horn
1 oilcan
1 chip-brush   complete $35.00

CONCERT GRAND (sic)
with Polyphone Grand attachment, 2 - 24 in. brass horns
and stand   complete $105.00

1) U.S. Patent No. 613,670 for Talking Machine filed February 14th 1898 and granted November 8th 1898. Douglass later patented a number of other phonograph inventions.

CONCERT phonograph with Polyphone attachment

Underside of Polyphone HOME Attachment

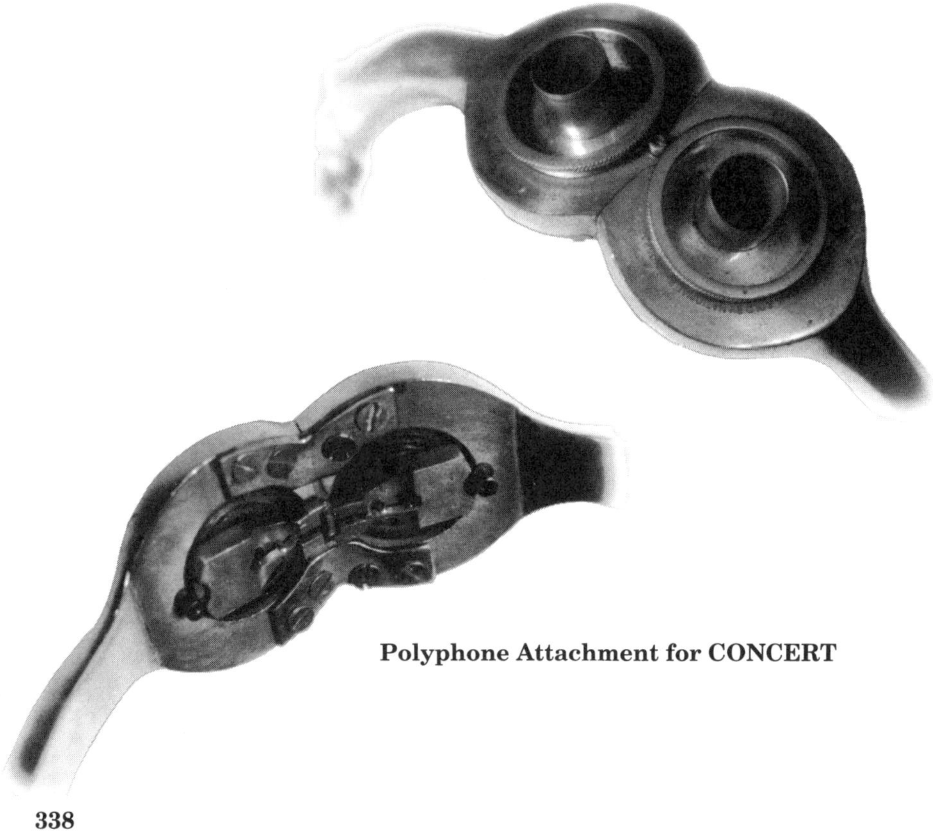

Polyphone Attachment for CONCERT

Chapter 28
Repeating Attachments

A glance at any of the earliest models of the wax cylinder phonographs frequently shows a built-in mechanism that returns the reproducer carriage to the starting position by means of a coarse reversed screw thread. This was soon considered an essential principle of the phonograph in an office where repetition of dictated matter was desirable, and from such machines to the amusement parlour phonographs with an added coin-slot mechanism was an obvious step and one that opportunists of the day were quick to take.

It is not clear quite why the early Phonographs had this integrated repeating attachment; the hearing over-and-over again of the same piece was hardly desirable and the machines' designers could not then have foreseen the day when the trade would have a phonograph playing the same record time and again inside or prominently outside their stores. Repeating attachments had little to offer the domestic owner.

Strangely, the first United States patent for a Feed and Return Mechanism for Phonographs was granted to Edison in May 1888[1] two months before his 'New' Phonograph patent was published,[2] although the patent application for the phonograph had been made two months before the mechanism. This feed and return mechanism used a coarse retracting (or return) screw set in parallel with the mandrel shaft and an electrical solenoid was introduced to lift the carrier-arm at the end of its travel; this novel device does not seem ever to have been put into use but in November of the same year Ezra T. Gilliland was granted a patent on the spectacle frame for recorder-reproducer in combination with its carriage and return mechanism.[3] This last took the form of a coarse retracting screw driven by a cord from the mandrel shaft, the arm for the half-nut carrying a cylindrical weight, and this engaged the retracting screw on being tripped forward. This weight is prominent in pictures of early electric Edison phonographs.

Before the end of 1889 coin-slot versions of Edison machines were built, fitted with a return screw shaft. A triggered cam arrangement lifted the reproducer carriage thus disengaging the half-nut from the feed screw. In the lifted position the carriage contacted the retracting screw shaft with a tracing edge. This acted as would a feed screw half-nut but was shaped somewhat like a knife and rode in the coarse groove of the retracting screw.

In their elementary way the Edison Dolls of 1889-90 used a return and repeating device in the hand-cranked mechanism. Also the Phono-Kinetoscope of two or three years later had a short retracting screw that swung up and under the return tracing edge, thus lifting the carriage and disengaging the feed screw and half-nut.

The construction of the first coin-operated phonographs in late 1889 by Louis Glass and William Arnold, using an electric Edison phonograph with their patents on the coin apparatus and other features showed that a reasonably unfailing return mechanism had been achieved.[4] Several further mechanisms by Edison and others were patented over the years, usually built into the machines and for office and arcade phonographs. George Tewksbury's company, United States Phonograph of Newark, New Jersey patented a repeating device of July 1894 that could be fitted to domestic or coin-slot phonographs.[5]

With the unfolding of the spring motored models in the late '90s an unusual Edison repeater made its appearance. It came in two sizes, one for the SPRING MOTOR and HOME machines, and one for the large CONCERT phonograph, and was worked through a windlass and cord drawing the carrier-arm back after playing.[6] Smaller spring driven phonographs like the STANDARD were not strong enough to carry a repeating device, but the coin-operated models built around the STANDARD, HOME and GEM generally had their carriages tripped and drawn back by a coil extension spring after each playing, but earlier styles sometimes used a drawstring.

The successor to the windlass repeater was one of Peter Weber's, released in September 1903 and produced for only one year.[7] It had a chain drive from the mandrel shaft to the retracting screw, and was reported as being complicated to install. The model for the HOME was gear driven. The Model D that followed was Edward L. Aiken's repeating attachment of August 1904[8], and was the most successful, remaining in the catalogues until 1910 (U.S.) and 1912 (U.K.) and could in all likelihood be ordered after those dates. The Model D was also used on the WINDSOR, ECLIPSE and ACME coin-slot phonographs.

Although this final version of the Edison repeating attachment was designated Model D, one seeks in vain for written indications of Models A, B and C. The Edison system of numbering or lettering its products was normally so logical that the draw cord and chain-driven models were surely Models B and C, but what constituted Model A is not clear.

These attachments were as follows:[9]

Draw-cord Model B (?) 1898-1903

for	CONCERT, OPERA, ORATORIO	$15.00
	SPRING MOTOR and Standard electric phonographs	$15.00

Peter Weber's Model C (?) 1903-4

for   TRIUMPH and electric phonographs of similar layout $15.00
        HOME phonographs $15.00

Edward L. Aiken's Model D 1904-1912

for   HOME phonograph $7.50; £1 11s. 6d.
        TRIUMPH, VICTOR, CONQUEROR, ALVA $7.50; £1 11s. 6d.
        CONCERT, electric OPERA, ORATORIO $7.50; £1 11s. 6d.
        IDELIA (special finish) $12.50; £2 12s. 6d.

A repeater for a different purpose was built into the STANDARD phonographs supplied to International Correspondence Schools by Edison. By depressing a lever on a saw-tooth rack the carrier-arm was moved back several grooves each time to allow a phrase to be re-heard.[10]

Several inventors not in Edison's employ patented repeating or carriage returning devices for Edison phonographs. These included T.F. Morrisey and Elam Gilbert[11] while The Douglas Phonograph Company of New York offered repeating attachments for the HOME for $6.50 and for the TRIUMPH for $7.50.

The introduction of combination attachments in November 1908 (U.S.) and February 1909 (U.K.) was made without thoroughly checking their working on machines already fitted with the repeating attachment, and mechanical malfunctions led to a number of complaints particularly from TRIUMPH owners. The fault was overcome by supplying a special mainshaft pulley with the combination attachment if requested, and with this unwieldy explanation of January 7th 1909:

> *In filling orders for pulleys and gears for combination attachments to drive repeating attachments, please note that the Model C combination main shaft pulley will answer for the TRIUMPH A combination attachment, TRIUMPH B (which has no shift lever), TRIUMPH C, HOME A and B (which have no shift lever) and Model C.*
>
> *The Model B main shaft driving pulley will answer for the TRIUMPH B machine (with shift lever) and the Models A and B HOME attachments (with shift lever).*
>
> *When repeating attachment pulleys are ordered for combination machines, we should know whether the machine is a regular type D phonograph, and, if an old machine, whether the combination attachment is equipped with a shift lever or without it.*

For the Model D type of machines we furnish the D pulley.

For machines that are equipped with combination attachments and have no shift lever, the Model C pulley is furnished. For all machines that are equipped with combination attachments having a shift lever, the Model B pulley is furnished.

1) United States Patent No. 382,416 for Feed and Return Mechanism for Phonographs filed by Edison January 5th 1888 and granted May 8th 1888.
2) United States Patent No. 386,974 for Phonograph, filed by Edison on November 26th 1887 and granted July 31st 1888.
3) United States Patent No. 393,640 for Phonograph, filed by E.T. Gilliland on June 7th 1888 and granted November 27th 1888.
4) United States Patent No. 428,750 for Coin-actuated Attachment for Phonographs filed December 18th 1889 and granted May 27th 1890
5) United States Patent No. 523,556 for Coin-operated Mechanism for Phonographs filed November 30th 1892 and granted July 24th 1894.
6) United States Patent No. 541,924 for Phonograph filed by Edison on December 3rd 1890 and granted July 2nd 1895 showed a phonograph carrier-arm drawn along by a wire and windlass.
7) United States Patent No. 771,851 for Repeating Attachment for Phonographs filed October 1st 1903 and granted October 11th 1904.
8) United States Patent No. 798,087 for Repeating Attachment for Phonographs filed June 10th 1904 and granted August 29th 1905
9) These attachments were coded for much of their lives as 'Iris' (CONCERT type), 'Diana' (TRIUMPH type) and 'Sirius' (HOME type),
10) United States Patent No. 744,267 for Phonographic Repeating Mechanism filed by Peter Weber on April 13th 1903 and granted November 17th 1903.
11) United States Patent Nos. 831,455 filed June 16th 1903 and 911,491 filed November 8th 1904 respectively. 911,491 was the last of Gilbert's 6 phonograph patents and had he not died insane might well have contributed much more to the industry.

Chapter 29
The Coming of the Amberols & Combination Phonographs

You better order and send to John Ott three or four standard types of Graphophones - want to devise and patent every practicable way of changing from 100 to 200 thread - then when they steal our thunder we will have a fight on the patent.

Edison to W. E. Gilmore, 1908

Until the Amberol cylinders of September-October 1908 Edison records had been established on a playing time of 2 minutes, except for some finely grooved export cylinders of the 1890s. This was far too short for the average song or piece of music, while the 4-minute 12 inch Gramophone disc had long overtaken the cylinder in popularity since its appearance in 1903. The answer lay in four-plus minute cylinders with a finer thread, but now Edison had no patent access to the use of celluloid, considered ideal for their more critical manufacture. Instead, the new cylinders would continue to be made of metallic stearic salts but with added Montan and Ozokerite waxes to make the record more durable, though as it turned out, more brittle.

The naming of any new Edison product usually led to lengthy discussions by a committee, and the new cylinders were no exception. At a meeting of the Phonograph Committee on April 30th 1908 the following names were put forward for their consideration:

AMBER, AMBERITE, AMBEROL, BESINOL, CEROL, EBONITE, EBONOL, FOUR-MINIT, 4-MINIT, PALMOL

At first EDISON FOUR-MINIT RECORD held the running, but Frank Dyer, Edison's legal adviser felt that such a name might invite imitation and that Amber or Amberol would make an acceptable and patentable trade mark.

A further committee meeting was fixed for May 15th and the list narrowed down to four contenders:

EDISON AMBER RECORD
EDISON AMBEROL RECORD
EDISON RECORD
EDISON FOURMINIT RECORD

EDISON AMBEROL RECORD attracted the most votes and the name was made official from this date.[1] Mrs. Edison was sometimes credited with the choice of Amberol, 'pure tone' (sic).

The thinking behind this name has puzzled generations of owners of Edison phonographs ever since. Why amber? The records bear no resemblance to the usually translucent fossilized resin, much in use at that time for items of personal adornment, umbrella handles, cigarette holders and mouthpieces for pipes; all the committee members being Victorians would be familiar with such articles, especially their smooth feel when polished - and when rubbed the ability to generate negative electricity as well as give off a pleasant odour. Such traits, especially the smoothness, associated with a product of Edison's might just carry a hint of magic as well as the qualities the Edison customers looked for. The name Amberol would be used for these wax-type records for four years, and then followed by Blue Amberol for the celluloid cylinders until 1929.

The agenda of this committee meeting of May 15th is important as it set the stage for turning away eventually from the Standard records and for an Edison four-minute future and deserves inclusion in its entirety:

1) *Determine definitely the name for a 4-minute record*
2) *How many 4-minute selections are we to have before announcement of the new record is made, that is by September 1st?*
3) *How many 4-minute master records are to be made monthly after September 1st, that is how many selections will the monthly list consist of?*
4) *What will be the list and net prices of the 4-minute record?*
5) *How many records of each selection should be made up and in stock on September 1st to take care of the first orders?*
6) *Should anything be engraved on the record to designate it as 4-minute?*
7) *Should the name of present 2-minute record and labels for same be changed to contain the new name that will be adopted for the 4-minute record?*
8) *Determine on the carton label for the 4-minute record*
9) *Determine definitely the kind of attachment that is to be adopted on new machines of each type*
10) *Determine on the different kind of attachments to be supplied for machines already out, and which will from time to time be changed over*
11) *Determine definitely if new machines are to go out equipped for both 2 and 4-minute records, and if they are should list prices be increased?*

12) Determine definitely list prices and discounts on extra attachments to be supplied for machines already out, both on a straight selling basis and exchange basis.
13) How many extra attachments of each style should be made up and in stock by September 1st, to take care of orders received for the extra attachments, so that machines then out may be changed over to the combination?
14) How many combination machines of each type should be made up and in stock September 1st. to take care of orders received at that time?
15) Determine the type of reproducer that is to be adopted for the combination machine
16) Determine the kind of reproducing point to be adopted for the combination reproducer
17) Committee to give an opinion as to whether we should go into high class music to get some of the Victor or higher class trade; for instance, band and orchestra selections by such leaders as Damrosch, Herbert, Sousa, also songs, recitations etc. by high class artists. It is, of course, understood that in all cases where the combination attachment is referred to in any of the above, it includes both the attachment and reproducer necessary to change a machine over so it will operate both the 2 and 4-minute records.

A factory letter to all foremen was sent round on July 14th, giving notice of intention to market the new combination phonographs and attachments on October 1st 1908. These would be the Model D types and would be offered at a price higher than existing Model B machines; the new types would be given new names, particularly the STANDARD, HOME and TRIUMPH. The cabinets of the STANDARD and HOME would be made to the same width at the bottom so the STANDARD horn crane would fit on both.

It was further decreed that production would be stepped up with the factory on full time from July 20th, and as well as the Model D phonographs, combination attachment outfits and reproducers would be started. The Model D of the STANDARD, HOME and TRIUMPH would be given the top plate of the Model C with combination gearing fitted, and all Model B machines would be discontinued as soon as the stock of castings was exhausted.

The decision to retain the existing model names had been taken by August 11th and in a further exhortation to all foremen reminding them that they had "four or five weeks in which to get ready for the new Fall orders", the following schedule was specified by Peter Weber, the general superintendent:

Machines
TRIUMPH Model D   Combination   300 per week
TRIUMPH Model C   50   "
TRIUMPH Model B   50   "
HOME Model D   Combination   2,500   "

HOME Model C		100	"
HOME Model B		1,000	"
STANDARD Model D	Combination	4,000	"
STANDARD Model C		100	"
STANDARD Model B		2,000	"
GEM Model C		1,500	"

(Model D GEMS were not ready until October 1909)

Total machines   11,600 per week

Attachments

TRIUMPH Model DA	Attachments	150 per week	
TRIUMPH Model DB	"	150	"
TRIUMPH Model DC	"	25	"
HOME DA and DB	"	5,000	"
HOME DC	"	250	"
STANDARD DA and DB	"	7,000	"
STANDARD Model DC	"	300	"
Total attachments		12,875	"

Reproducers

For machines	Model H	6,800
	Model C	11,600
For attachments	Model H	12,875

By September 19th the order books were starting to fill up.

Orders received for Model D machines to date

		Immediate	Future
STANDARD	21,879	12,004	9,875
HOME	13,361	6,798	6,563
TRIUMPH	1,784	1,027	757

Orders received for attachments to date

STANDARD B and C	35,446	24,874	10,572
HOME B and C	25,555	15,920	9,635
TRIUMPH B and C	3,695	2,483	1,212

Orders received for Amberol records to date

First orders	737,799
Second orders	51,006
Total	788,805

Model D machines and attachments were delayed because of the slow assembly of the Model H reproducers, but production improved and by November 6th the machine schedule had been reduced to the following:

STANDARD Model D	2,000 per week
HOME Model D	1,500 "
TRIUMPH Model D	300 "

and overtime and night work on them was stopped.

Size variations in the top castings of the different models of the TRIUMPH and HOME led to Peter Weber's entangled instruction of January 7th 1909 that was intended to clear up confusion at the works and in the trade:

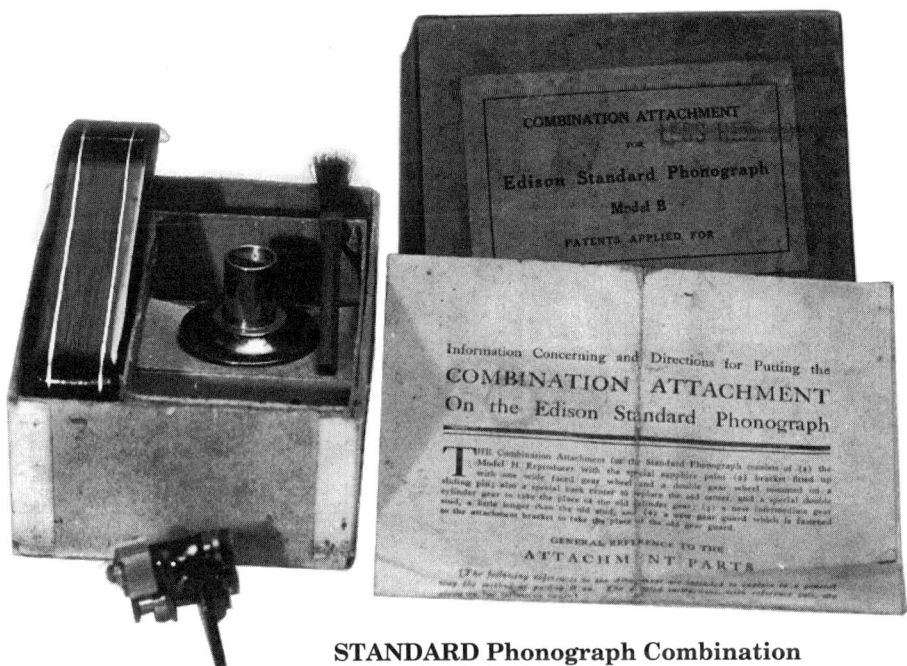

STANDARD Phonograph Combination Attachment Outfit

347

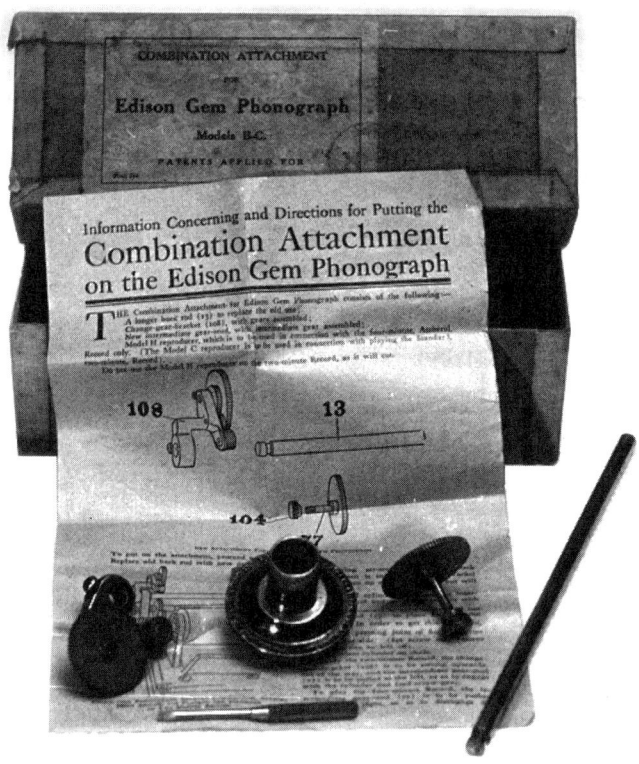

Please note that the Model C main shaft pulley will answer for the TRIUMPH A combination attachment, TRIUMPH B (which has no shift lever), TRIUMPH C, HOME A and B (which have no shift lever) and Model C. The Model B main shaft driving pulley will answer for the TRIUMPH B machine (with shift lever) and the Models A and B HOME attachments (with shift lever).

When repeating attachment pulleys are ordered for combination machines, we should know whether the machine is a regular type D phonograph, and if an old machine, whether the combination attachment is equipped with a shift lever or without it.

For the Model D type of machines we furnish the D pulley

For machines that are equipped with combination attachments and have no shift lever, the Model C pulley is furnished. For all machines that are supplied with combination attachments having a shift lever, the Model B pulley is furnished.

Combination attachments continued to be made and supplied after the horn phonographs were declared obsolete; on September 18th 1916 the price was lowered and the 10 'free' Blue Amberols offer abandoned, the price for the attachment only being $5.50 for the STANDARD and $6.75 for the TRIUMPH and HOME.

The early distribution of combination attachments abroad was held up because of difficulties in getting sufficient sapphires set in the reproducers, and priority was naturally given to the home trade. The slow production of machines too meant that none would be available for exploitation in the European market until after the beginning of 1909. Although Thomas Graf, managing director of National Phonograph in London was sent 3 each of the Combination STANDARD, HOME and TRIUMPH for showing the trade, the United Kingdom business was not considered ready for combination models as these would cause the large number of 2-minute machines on the shelves to be left unsalable. Therefore, to convert these and other phonographs in the hands of Edison enthusiasts 8,300 Combination Attachments and 165,000 Amberols were shipped to London on October 20th 1908, and it was hoped that by the end of the year the new Amberol cylinders would head an Edison revival in the United Kingdom and that Amberol operatic cylinders would be issued to compete with HMV discs. Combination phonographs were eventually marketed in the United Kingdom in August 1909, but the operatic Amberols failed to reach expectations.

This material has been derived from the Edison Archive

NOTES:
1) U.S. Trade Mark No. 72,560 filed October 29th 1908 and registered February 2nd 1909. U.S. Patent No. 964,221 for Sound Record filed by Edison January 3rd 1907 and granted July 12th 1910

Attachments for Playing Amberol Records
With 10 Special Amberol Records

For Gem Phonograph	$5.00
For Standard Phonograph	6.00
For Home and Triumph Phonographs	8.50
For Concert Phonographs	10.75

A Model H Reproducer is also included in each of these Attachments.

(For Concert Phonographs, see page 32.)

Amberol Attachment for
Gem
Phonograph

Amberol Attachment for
Standard
Phonograph

Amberol Attachment for
Home and Triumph
Phonographs

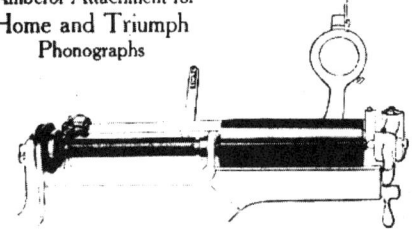

Ten Special Amberol Records

Simple and easily applied attachments have been designed by which all types of Edison Phonographs may be equipped to play the new Amberol Records. These attachments embody the principles of the differential gear, and include an additional Reproducer, known as the Model H. This model has a smaller reproducing point, but possesses all the advantages of the Model C Reproducer.

As an inducement to Phonograph owners to equip their machines with Amberol attachments, ten special Amberol Records are being included with each attachment, the cost of the complete outfit being but little more than the cost of the attachment alone. These special Records are equal in every respect to any in the regular catalogue. They can only be had with an attachment. Ask a dealer for detailed information about this proposition. These attachments are sold without the ten special Records as follows:

For Gem Phonograph	$4.00
For Standard Phonograph	5.00
For Home and Triumph Phonographs	7.50

Chapter 30
Edison Horns

Recording and reproducing horn No. 3 in the North American catalogue of 1891, fitted to an electric CLASS M model

In the first years of the Edison Phonograph - or for that matter the first Berliner Gramophones - emphasis was on listening tubes rather than horns, and no doubt the listener of the day felt in more intimate contact with the recorded voice through ear tubes in the same way as headphones of today. Early Edison literature on the subject spoke of the horn as still being in the experimental state, but the original Edison wax cylinder phonographs were commercial and meant for office use where privacy was desirable.

Some of the very first tinfoil phonographs were depicted with cone-shaped mouthpieces, or later, simple attendant horns that could be used for recording or listening, and as they tapered to an elbow could well have been influenced by the ear-trumpet of the day; one or two such examples will be noticed in contemporary Edison literature.

Earlier, the little 1886 Graphophone of Bell and Tainter was photographed with a lean funnel horn and Gilliland's New Phonograph of 1887 was shown with a small cone horn. The first picture noticed of the 14 in. japanned tinplate flared horn is in *Harper's Young People* for February 5th 1889, and another self-supporting horn of spun brass or copper was shown at the Paris Exhibition of later that year.

The earliest comprehensive listing of horns appeared in the 1891 (North American) Edison Phonograph Catalogue:

Large Recording Horn No. 1, length 6 ½ ft., diameter 30 in.
    in block tin, japanned and with wooden tripod $20.00
Recording and Reproducing Horn No. 2,
    length 26 in., diameter 10 in. $2.50
    in block tin, japanned;   folding stand extra $3.00
Recording and Reproducing Horn No. 3,
    length 20 in., diameter 10 in. $4.00
    in heavy brass, flared,   support crane $1.00
Typewriter's Horn No. 4, length about 12 in.   complete $2.50
    in nickelled brass, supported by crane from back of the machine
Reproducing Horn No. 5, length 14 in. $1.00
    japanned tin, flared
Reproducing Horn No. 6, length 12 in.
    in nickelled brass with bell $2.00

These styles continued for several years and the No. 5 14 in. black japanned tinplate horn survived into the new century because its shape made it handy for recording and reproducing. It is sometimes called the North American horn.

By 1896 when the phonograph business had passed back into Edison's hands, his National Phonograph Company established what were called standard sizes. These horns were made of sheet metal, black japanned with gilt trim and in the following lengths and styles:

    14 in. flared   36 in. conical
    26 in. conical   56 in. flared

The 36 in. was said to be best for concert work, and a 30 in. papier-maché style was available. Brass was not recommended and said to be "seldom used nowadays".[1]

The brass horn however, was always in the background if sometimes out of favour, having arrived in the late 1880s when commended for its 'ringing tone' and a decade later became part of the equipment for several Edison phonographs. At the turn of the century the brass body gave way to japanned sheet metal, a likely economy measure, and the 14 in. black and brass horn had arrived to become standard equipment with nearly all domestic Edison phonographs until 1907. Only the CONCERT phonograph had anything larger at 24 in. and in the other direction the GEM had to make do with a 10 in. conical horn in black with a gold band, in company language known as the 'B and G'. These conical horns were not very efficient and many years passed before horns were made on an exponential or logarithmic curve. A sample sent to Edison on April 16th 1900 from an outsider Edmund D. Spear of Boston, Mass. was claimed to be made to a mathematical curve - 'a conchoid curve' - but was not followed up. Perhaps the soft wax cylinders of the day did not justify improvement.

For much of this time Edison offered alternative reproducing horns up to 4 ½ ft. long, and some of these were collapsible and could be nested.² They were not offered in machine catalogues after 1901 but separately in accessory lists and the company gave the impression of losing interest. Any Edison owner wanting a horn larger than the standard equipment could now find himself being offered cut-price non-Edison types outside, and this was interfering considerably with company trade.

C.H. Wilson, sales manager of National Phonograph asked for an opinion in 1904 as to what should be done to stimulate sales of machines by supplying better horns. Following experience on the sales staff, J. W. Scott a senior salesman in the United States and Canada put forward several views:

The collapsible horn he described as a Jonah, especially with the New England trade, but improvements of the black and brass style would be favourably received, and the consensus of opinion (in the trade) would approve the following:

GEM with 18 in. black and brass horn		All with extra special bell -
STANDARD 24 in.	"	not specified - and horn crane,
HOME 30 in.	"	the TRIUMPH with full nickelled
TRIUMPH 36 in.	"	horn stand

Regrettably none of these suggestions was adopted, and a further 2 or 3 years went by before anything was done.

A long black horn with Japanese decoration, called the Kyoto horn, was sold for Edison and other phonographs around 1906 in the San Francisco area. An example has been noted as bearing the logo ALLEN 1/9/1906 No. 1022 (Wm. J. Schroth), but it was likely put out by a trader who was finding small-horned machines difficult to sell; perhaps the earthquake curtailed its run. Large concerns like Babson Brothers and Hawthorne & Sheble bought mainly from such makers as The Tea Tray Manufacturing Company of Newark, N.J. or Standard Metal Manufacturing Company, and had been substituting straight panelled horns, some with floral decoration. These were becoming more favourably accepted by the public to the detriment of Edison interests. Towards the end of 1906 the holders of patent rights in straight panelled horns, The Searchlight Horn Company (formerly U.S. Horn Co.) started to issue

353

warnings to the trade and public not to buy horns of a morning glory (flower) type, claiming infringement of these rights.[3]

Meanwhile National Phonograph, claiming to have tested scores of horns over several years approved the adoption by the Phonograph Committee on July 8th 1907 of the flower (polygonal) horn in three sizes at an increased price. The Committee had also considered adopting a collapsible 11-panel (Cygnet type) horn in 1907, but getting the straight horns into production and on to the machines was urgent.[4] On July 23rd an order was placed for 100,000 of 10, 11 and 12-panel horns with Tea Tray Manufacturing, this representing two-thirds of Edison requirements at that time.

The Edison company was licensed to use these horns by Charles Eichhorn, the patentee and assignor to The Tea Tray Manufacturing Company and in August made known the new range to be ready from September 16th, and for a dash of self-protection in the announcement threw in the phrase "the solid metal polygonal horn (is) somewhat different to any now on the market".[5] It was still to run foul of the Searchlight company and a Court hearing resulted eventually in January 1916, after Edison had finished with horns.

The bell of the so-called Kyoto horn

With the new horns came the regular Edison habit of arriving late for the market, this time attributable to a shortage of rod stock for the cranes in spite of shop orders for brackets and cranes being issued on July 10th; the promised September date was extended to the next month. In the meantime frustrated traders were cabling the makers direct, to the annoyance

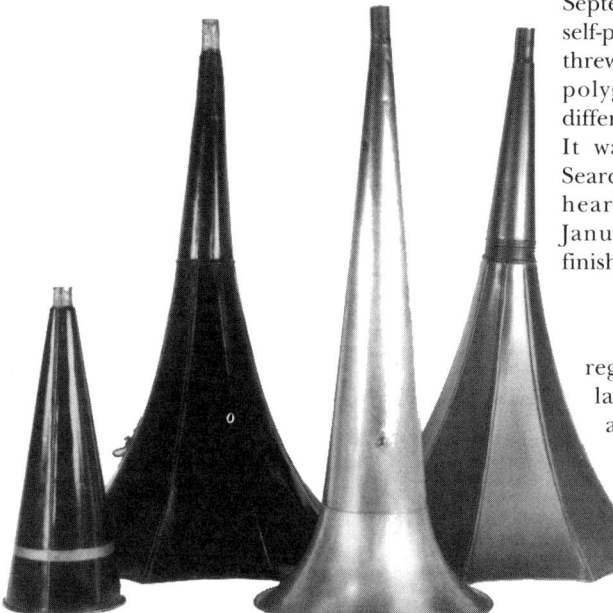

Four typical straight Edison horns, the 10 in. GEM, the 19 in. panelled horn, the all-brass GEM horn of 1901, and the two-part FIRESIDE

of all concerned and leading to a reproving Edison circular of October 10th.

When the horns appeared eventually two weeks later it was seen that they were designed to be of a size proportional to the **GEM, STANDARD, HOME** and **TRIUMPH** and carried the names of those instruments on a blue and gold decal, while the **BALMORAL, CONQUEROR, ALVA,** and **IDELIA** would have one style of horn in mahogany finish marked IDEAL - soon IDELIA. That for the GEM was smaller and had 8 panels. The crane support at first was made to fit only the horn intended for it, and jobbers and dealers were instructed by the Edison company to see that all phonographs already on the shelves were re-equipped and sent out priced to take in the new horn and crane fittings.[6] This equipment on the GEM added $2.50, on all other machines $5.00.

The neck of the horn fixed to the reproducer by a short flexible connector and was suspended from the crane by a ring near the horn mouth; the crane fixed to the front of the Phonograph cabinet in a special clamp, this being braced to the machine's front and carrying a shoe to prevent tipping forward. All GEMS were now sent out with a crane socket as part of the top casting.

The sizes of these straight horns were as follows:

GEM	length 19 in.	diameter at bell 11 in.,	8 panels
STANDARD	30 in.	19 in.,	10 panels
HOME	32 in.	21 ½ in.,	11 panels
TRIUMPH, BALMORAL, ALVA, CONQUEROR, IDELIA			
	33 in.	24 in.	12 panels

The United Kingdom had to wait until January 1908 for the new horns with the curving flare. This followed a letter from London:

> ... *the introduction of new machine equipment is becoming more and more necessary over here ..... present small aluminium and 14 in. horns not doing justice to our machines ..... .*[7]

The first GEM horns were shipped on December 31st, in fact these were the largest straight panelled horns that London would see except for the luxury IDELIA, sent over with its own 12-panel horn from December 1909. With the light 19 in. horn one type of crane and support was sufficient for all (except the GEM with its own socket) and differed to the American style by being screwed to the front panel of the phonograph. In the United Kingdom horn and crane could be bought separately for 11s. 0d. to convert existing machines.

In the United States the new horns could be bought separately from November 1907 as follows:

	horn	crane
*GEM	$1.50	25 cents
STANDARD	$2.10	90 cents
HOME	$2.40	90 cents
TRIUMPH	$2.70	$1.15

*The GEM horn was made in one piece and finished in black and gold, although original blue and green finishes are known.

These cranes were recommended as easy to fit to the cabinets, being screwed to the wooden baseboard and a brace piece was pushed to clip over the front top lip under the motor board. The recommended distances from the inside of the cabinet end to the centre of the holder were:

STANDARD	3 ¼ in.
HOME	7 ¼ in.
TRIUMPH, ALVA, CONCERT	7 ¾ in.
BALMORAL and CONQUEROR	12 ½ in.

The horn crane socket on the GEM was enlarged from $\frac{3}{16}$ in. to ¼ in. on all new machines from about August 1907 and cranes could be bought to fit either type.

Prices of horns and cranes were advanced slightly from February 1908 (U.S.) and mahogany finished horns were also offered to match owners' existing cabinets, as follows:

Black and gold finish

	horn	crane
GEM	$2.25	$1.25
HOME	$2.50	$1.25
TRIUMPH, BALMORAL, CONQUEROR, ALVA	$2.75	$1.25

Mahogany Finish

GEM	$2.60
STANDARD	$6.00
HOME	$6.25
TRIUMPH/IDELIA	$6.50
IDELIA horn crane in oxidized finish	$2.50

From April 1908 (U.S.) the options were simplified and one horn crane sufficed for the STANDARD, HOME and TRIUMPH instead of three, and again the prices moved upwards by a few cents, as did the existing GEM crane. Through the supply of these straight-horned phonographs the Edison company largely stopped the cut-price sources of horns and crane stands that had been eroding this side of its business for years. The use of a swinging arm attachment for a tone-arm phonograph was seriously contemplated by the Edison company in May 1909 but never put into production. Hawthorne and Sheble had one in their catalogue[8] and the handful of Columbia Graphophones with tone-arms were derived from patents awarded to Lewis P. Halladay; his Patent No. 857,169 of June 1907 was for a tone-arm suitable for an Edison machine.

The entirely new FIRESIDE Phonograph appeared on the scene in July 1909 (U.S.) and August 1909 (U.K.) and with it the FIRESIDE horn made in two threaded sections to facilitate packing. Similar in shape to the existing 19 in. horn it was finished in maroon and marked FIRESIDE. It was also supplied with the GEM Model D from October 1909 (U.S. and U.K.) and the later Model E, and a blue finish is known. The metallic quality of the maroon finish is ascribed to the horn being plated before the paint application.

In spite of the success with this new horn range a pronounced drawback was the space they occupied in front of the phonographs, and if the larger ones could be contained as much as possible within the area of the machines' base and could be turned and made directional, this would be a popular selling factor. To this end in September 1908 the Edison company entered into correspondence with Charles A. Beppler of Brooklyn over his sectional 'new S-shaped Phonograph Horn'. This was constructed in three sections, bell, curved tapering body and curved tapering elbow, and from illustrations was rather ungainly.[9] The company bought Beppler's creation and Peter Weber designed what became the Cygnet Horn, covered by two patents and one trade mark registration.[10] It would be very much a curved version of the existing straight panel horns and in its first conception was in one piece, but in the version marketed the mouth part was detachable from the supporting elbow. Its crane too was made in two parts, the lower support rod and upper suspension rod.

Cygnet Horns were available from September 1909 (U.S.) and October 1910 (U.K.) as standard equipment with the TRIUMPH, HOME, STANDARD, FIRESIDE and ALVA models. They came in two sizes with 10 panels for HOME, STANDARD and FIRESIDE (the No. 10) and with 11 panels for larger machines such as the TRIUMPH, IDELIA and ALVA (the No. 11), and like some of the straight horns some were made by The Standard Metal Company. The first Cygnet Horns had a rather rigid bolt suspension and the connection to the semi-forward facing reproducers was by a curving hose or ball joint. With the arrival of the Model O reproducer and the 'on-top' carrier-arm the horn had a spring suspension that gave it 180° movement about a vertical axis and a lighter pressure on the carriage, and the lower crane support rod was heightened by 1 ½ in. and known as the Type E crane. When the Cygnet Horn was part of the Model D phonograph kit the machine was then known as the Model D2, a rare occasion when a horn addition influenced a model designation.

Two sizes of fixing plate for the horn support socket will be found, having over-all measurements as follows:

Width across top 4 ⅛ in. x depth of side 3 ⅛ in.
     "   4 ⅛ in. x   "   2 ½ in.

The Cygnet Horns bought separately with crane, socket and metal flexible connection were priced as follows:

No. 10 black and gold finish*	$7.50;	£1 15s. 0d.
11 "	$8.00;	£2 0s. 0d.
No. 10 oak or mahogany finish	$12.50;	£3 0s. 0d.
11 "	$13.00;	£3 5s. 0d.
Cygnet Horn cranes	$2.15;	10s. 0d.
" oxidized for IDELIAS	$4.25	

IDELIA mahogany finished horn with oxidized crane and fitting £3 15s. 0d.

*original green is also known

Thus the Cygnet Horn could now be fitted to all domestic Edison horn phonographs to date except the GEM, and this would always be sent out with the 19 in. straight horn. Polygonal straight horns continued to be sold with other remaining earlier models to help clear stocks, until early in 1911 when the range of options was simplified to help the trade.

A favourable memo on adopting the Music Master wooden Cygnet Horn was circulated to the Phonograph Committee by Peter Weber on May 11th 1910, specifying that it would be of one size only and had the same bell dimensions as the No. 11 metal Cygnet Horn (21 ½ in.) and fitted existing cranes and elbow pieces. The Music Master brand of horns were made by Sheip and Vandegrift Inc. of Philadelphia and are also found on some Columbia disc machines from 1908. The use of bent wooden staves glued edge to edge to form the circular bell was after the style of wooden barrel construction, and they were considered very effective.[11]

As with the earlier metal Cygnet Horns the Music Masters were offered as part of the equipment of the current phonograph range at an increased price, but were soon available separately at the following:

Oak or Mahogany	$15.00;	£3 2s. 6d.
Spruce (to order)	$20.00	
Inlaid Mother-of-pearl (to order)	$50.00	
Crane connections, etc. extra		

The oak and mahogany Music Master horns were ordered from the manufacturer in batches of 500.

Metal Cygnet Horns supplied with the SCHOOL phonographs and Music Master horns on the OPERA/CONCERT phonographs were self-supporting by the stem of the specially shaped metal elbow. A few straight Music Master horns are known in the United States, fitted to a nickel plated cone with a short taper, but dates and prices of such 'specials' have not been seen. Spruce horns are also seen in the United States, but the Mother-of-pearl types must be very rare. Spruce as a wood for these horns was certainly derived from its traditional use in making the belly of violins.

The success of the Cygnet Horns in both metal and wood meant the Edison company found itself with quantities of straight horns on the shelves and some of these were cleared by making up the Model E STANDARD in November 1911 as a 4-minute only phonograph for the mail-order trade. Numbers of black and gold 10-panel straight horns were returned to Standard Metal to be stripped and refinished in blue with floral decoration. This unusual step was inspired by Babson Brothers of Chicago who had been buying black straight horns from Edison and had added a decorated horn of their own for the mail order trade. Edison's recognized the value of Babsons' business and the wisdom of adapting this machine specially for them, and was prepared to offer it to the trade and public generally.

This was nearly the last development in reproducing horns for the open-horn phonographs, and as the AMBEROLAS came on sale interest in the earlier styles declined. An official announcement of their discontinuance was made in October 1913 (U.S.). By then very few indeed were being sold, but works records show a small activity in clearing orders until early in 1914. In the United Kingdom the Cygnet horned FIRESIDES and straight horned GEMS were still being sold during 1914 alongside the AMBEROLAS. From West Orange came an adaptation of the AMBEROLA 50 and 75 internal horn and put out as the West Point Horn and largely intended as a replacement for phonograph owners who had lost or damaged the horn on their machines, as the old Cygnet range was no longer being made.

Until the Cygnet and Music Master horns crossed the Atlantic, the average British owner - and Edison was well supported in that country - had never been offered a large Edison panelled horn, and naturally quite a trade existed in locally made products. One of the best of these was a Music Master look-alike sold by F. W. Saitch of Stoke

The West Point horn in position

Newington, London, but made of hard cardboard or whaleskin, and these are sometimes found, fit the Edison crane and reproduce the cylinders well.

All the Edison horns mentioned were made of sheet brass or steel plate or wood, and only once was aluminium known to be used. This was in the United Kingdom where the 10 in. conical GEM horn failed to please and a 10 ½ in. x 8 in. aluminium 'herald' horn was supplied instead from October 1904 to late 1907.[12] This was a defensive policy of Edison's as the chief rival in the London trade was Edison Bell, a company that carried a range of spun horns in their catalogues.

Mention should be made of a 26 in. x 5 in. recording horn that could be bought from about 1907 to 1912 (U.S. and U.K.) for $2.00 or 8s. 6d. The last Edison horn was a 14 in. conical japanned tinplate recording horn for use with the OPERA and AMBEROLAS I and III in conjunction with the August 1912 (U.S. and U.K.) 4-minute Home Recording Outfit. It cost 50 cents or 2s. 1d.

Two features of the straight panelled horns that were repeated on the metal Cygnets were the concave ends to the panels and the slightly projecting ribs of the seams which were meant to carry the weight of the horn when stood mouth downwards on a surface. This was an important claim of the Eichhorn patent. All Edison panelled horns had the concave-ended panels, other makes often had convex 'petal' ends and a regular undulation is found on those of Victor/HMV. Tapered tone-arm attachments for mounting horns like those on disc phonographs were offered for Edison machines by The Chicago Stand Company from October 1907 for $7.50.

As a postscript it might be of interest to remark on the carrying power of a phonograph under ideal conditions but with an unspecified horn and reproducer. It was reported at some length in the 1910 *New Phonogram* that on a still evening in Jeffersonville N.Y. a party on the piazza of the Jeffersonia Hotel could hear an Edison phonograph enunciating clearly across a deep valley from a known distance of 3,000 ft., and it seems every word could be heard distinctly.

Form 33.

Instructions for Adjusting Cygnet Horn on Horn-Crane with the New Spring-Suspension.

The Edison Cygnet Horn is suspended from the horn-crane by means of a spiral spring attached to an adjusting bolt on top, and at its lower end to a half round ball, which is part of the bell of the horn.

A rubber tube connects the horn to the reproducer. The rubber tubing is to be slipped over the small stem of the horn, and when the horn is adjusted to hang in the proper vertical position, the lower end of the rubber connection will meet the top of the reproducer, and can be readily slipped over. When the lower end of the spring is connected to the half round ball, and the upper end is affixed to the suspension-bolt, the complete horn can be attached to the crane without the necessity of taking the thumb-nut off the bolt. The bolt has a flat space right above the hole that holds the spring, and this flat space slides into a slot at the extreme end of the crane.

The important point to be observed in adjusting the vertical position of the horn, is that a slight portion of the weight of the horn rests on the reproducer when the latter is in playing position. This slight pressure on the reproducer and arm will guard against the feed-nut slipping or skipping in the threads of the feed-screw. When the lift lever raises the reproducer-arm, the bulk of the weight of the arm is supported by the spring.

By means of the adjusting bolt and nut on top, the horn can be set in proper vertical position. The Cygnet Horn can be turned to point in different directions, by holding the rubber tubing stationary and turning the horn so that its stem will turn in the tubing.

Thomas A. Edison, Inc.
Orange, N. J., U. S. A.

The West Point horn was issued at the end of the career of the open horn phonographs. It was adapted from the AMBEROLA horn.

1) *Edison Phonographic News* July/August 1896
2) Subjects of United States Patent Nos. 820,158 and 878,029 of May 1906 and February 1908 and awarded to Peter Weber. Filed February 1905 and June 1904 respectively.
3) These rights were invested in U.S. Patent No. 771,441 for a horn made up of panels, filed April 14th 1904 by Peter C. Nielson and granted October 4th 1904
4) Internal memo from W. E. Gilmore to C. H. Wilson July 8th 1907 - Edison Archive
5) U.S. Patent No. 797,725 for Amplifying Horn filed June 14th 1905 by Charles Eichhorn and granted August 22nd 1905.
6) U.S. Patent No. 998,218 for Phonograph Horn Crane filed by Peter Weber on September 11th 1907 and granted July 18th 1911.
7) Letter of November 27th 1907 from Thomas Graf, London managing director to C.H. Wilson, now assistant general manager National Phonograph - Edison Archive
8) Thomas Kraemer's U.S. Patent No. 960,560 filed March 10th 1909 and granted June 7th 1910
9) U.S. Patent No. 881,843 filed May 13th 1907, granted March 10th 1908
10) U.S. Patent No. 1,010,333 for Phonograph Horn of November 28th 1911 by Peter Weber and filed March 31st 1908. This was the two-piece Cygnet Horn with flexible connection to the reproducer. U.S. Patent No. 1,058,284 for Phonograph of April 8th 1913 by Peter Weber, filed October 14th 1907. This patent, filed earlier than the one above was for the one piece Cygnet Horn with crane. U.S. Trade Mark No. 77,478 of April 12th 1910, the name Cygnet being used continuously since July 22nd 1909.
11) U.S. Patent No. 889,480 filed April 6th 1908 by Stanislaus Moss and granted June 2nd 1908 and assigned to Sheip and Vandegrift.
12) Although aluminium in mineral form is widespread, it was not until about 100 years ago that establishment of hydro-electric systems and the availability of cheap electricity made economic separation from the ore possible. Both in spun and sheet form it was used by phonograph firms but had the reputation of imparting a nasal quality to the playing back of records.

Chapter 31
Some Notes On Shavers

The earliest design of an Edison shaving device appears on British patent 17,175 of December 14th 1887 for Edison's first wax cylinder phonograph, the so-called 'New' Phonograph, assembled by Ezra Gilliland. This example was threaded through the supporting leg of the spectacle frame carrier-arm, a form of mounting that would appear on HOME and STANDARD machines ten years ahead. Alongside it and attached to the carrier-arm was a burnishing tool for following the cutter and polishing the record surface; this was heated either by an electric current or a spirit lamp. In the United States patents that followed, the phonograph[1] and burnisher[2] were separated, but a heated tool of this type was evidently not followed up. For blanks that still needed polishing Edison designed a smoothing tool, a rolling or ironing cylinder for dressing the surface and for use with a solvent if needed,[3] but if it had any public distribution is not known.

The manner of removing the recorded layer from a cylinder surface became known by several names in these first years, and words like paring, turning off, erasing and reducing were used constantly.

The shaver had started in a position behind the cylinder, but the next style had the blade acting on the top surface of the record, but still pivoting from the carrier-arm; it had an oblique cutting edge.[4] In a further move a coarse shaving blade was fixed to an eye of the spectacle frame or carrier-arm for the purpose of preparing blanks that had become hard or brittle, especially in offices.[5] The last form of the shaving blade to be set forward of the record's axis was fixed under the shell of a recorder or reproducer that had had its diaphragm taken out, the blade facing the revolving cylinder with a small chute to deflect the swarf.[6]

When a photograph of the CLASS M was first seen in December 1889 the shaving knife was now back behind the cylinder and mounted on the side of the carrier-arm above the guide rod. On this model the knife was pushed down against the cylinder, set and finely adjusted and then locked by a lever. This was a type in use for several years and sapphire was now substituted for the hard steel shaving knife.[7] The similar lever type of shaver, later familiar to owners of the SPRING MOTOR, TRIUMPH and domestic electric phonographs came into use during the 1890s[8] and was dispensed with when the Model C range of phonographs was introduced.

The first patented record shaver separate from a phonograph was in 1890 and called the Phonograph-dressing Machine. Constructed like a book-press the cylinder spun on the end of a descending screw and came into contact with a shaving knife at the side. Invented by an outsider from Iowa,[9] it could not have been what the trade was looking for, because an individual shaving machine instead of a knife on the phonograph was called for at the 1890 Convention of Local Phonograph Companies, and made an appearance shortly afterwards in treadle-powered form for both domestic and office use, using a CLASS M phonograph body mounted on a sewing machine table. It cost $50.00 complete, or $35.00 for the manually turned CLASS M body, and lasted into the 1900s at reduced prices of $40.00 and $25.00 respectively. Since 1890 many of the business phonographs had adopted a 6 in. long cylinder and the shavers were given a longer mandrel when in commercial form. The CLASS M body, now called the VICTOR, continued on these machines.

Shaving machines with an electric drive had been commended in 1897 by George Tewksbury for working up a good cylinder speed.[10] 1500 r.p.m. were said to give fine results and commercial high speed shaving could be done at up to 2800 r.p.m, without damaging the sapphire or the cylinder disintegrating. Indeed the owner of the domestic CLASS M and CLASS E models was advised to throw off the governor belt and give the motor its head! None the less electricity in those days was still something of a luxury, a novelty even outside the larger towns, and electrical equipment expensive and not widely understood. At this distance it seems inconsistent for shaving knives to be fitted to such spring driven phonographs that had no possibility of attaining high revolutions, though there is no sign of dissatisfaction on this account. However, fitted they were, and the SPRING MOTOR/TRIUMPH, IDELIA, HOME, STANDARD and early CONCERT range all carried a shaving device for much of their existence, their owners having to pare their cylinders several times for an acceptable new recording surface.

With the arrival of the Model C phonographs in 1908, all the Edison machines lost their shaving mechanisms but the Model A HOME and STANDARD had been without them from 1904. New designs of shaving machines were marketed in the United States from March of that year and in the United Kingdom shortly afterwards. This was the Edison Universal Shaving Machine in manual or electric choice and with its long mandrel able to shave both the regular and business cylinders.[11]

Simple hand turned Edison shaving machine on an oak base

It embodied several innovations, and followed closely phonograph designs of its day. There was for instance the novelty of a fan exhauster to draw the shavings down a chute into a drawer below it. This drawer was set in the right end of the cabinet below the crank position and had holes to help air circulation. The mechanism was gearless but used belts and pulleys to achieve a high shaving rate when turned by hand at 50 to 75 r.p.m.

Edison Universal Shaving Machine

Two styles of wooden cabinet are known, and later on metal casings were used for office machines. These cabinets had the usual rounded cover, and might be mistaken at first for phonographs, although it was several years before a decal was applied. In or after 1908 the cabinet was enlarged and the end drawer became an outward opening flap in the front. This admitted to a chute bag removable for emptying, but the motion remained the same.[12] Improvements were a double-cut shaving knife, oil grooves cut in the back rod and chute re-arrangement.

In 1904 the model originally cost $35.00 or £7 7s. 0d., or with electric drive $55.00 or £11 11s. 0d., rising to $60.00 or £12 12s. 0d. from March 1911 after re-styling. The motor and bracket to convert the hand machine to electric drive cost $20.00 or £4 4s. 0d. and were generally made by Emerson or Burke Electrical.

Mention should be made of a simpler shaving machine on offer after 1906 for home use. Consisting of the top casting, mandrel and feed mechanism of the TRIUMPH Model B, it was rotated by a geared shaft and crank handle parallel to the feed screw, the whole being fixed to a wooden base with heavily bevelled edges. There was a removable lead plug in the carrier-arm eye to weigh it down.

In January 1911[13] it was realized that some time in the future the whole range of Edison cylinder phonographs would become 4-minute only. While terminating the 2-minute home recording feature, this was reported as now being little used. On the following August 3rd it was decided to go for 4-minute only and that October 1st 1911 would be the launching day of the new models. At the same time 4-minute recorders and a new black wax blank would be available, as well as a new shaver, but there was delay and by January 15th 1912 a working model was demonstrated and approved at a meeting of the Entertainments Committee, with a further dozen ordered to be made up and tested. A price list followed on April 24th when the new machine was shown at $4.50 or with a 4-minute recorder and three new-type blanks $8.00 or £1 13s. 4d.

Instead of the high-speed paring of the record with a small sapphire knife, the new shaver was made to be rotated slowly by hand while a steel knife as wide as the record cleaned its surface in only a few turns. There were many complaints that the trial model could not be made to work properly, even the London office returned theirs, and an internal letter reveals it was decided to hold back manufacture until the instrument was foolproof,[14] and it was released for August 1912 (U.S. and U.K.).

From the number of examples met with, this last version of the Edison shaver must have enjoyed fair sales, but was reputed to be difficult to operate properly.

●●●●●●●●●●●●

What is claimed to be the earliest practical shaving device is reported by Aaron Cramer and Allen Koenigsberg in *A.P.M.* Vol. X No. 3 in a report on a cylinder machine constructed by Frank Lambert about 1879-1880. This used a solid lead sleeve and from a recital of the hours that survives on it appeared to be for use with a speaking clock, and is the earliest recognizable recording. It has a shaver to erase a previous recording. Lambert was better known as the inventor of a typewriter sold by the early Gramophone Company in the U.K.

Later Edison Universal Shaving Machine

1) This Phonograph patent was U.S. No. 386,974 filed by Edison November 26th 1887 and granted July 31st 1888.
2) Edison's Burnishing Attachment for Phonographs was U.S. No. 382,414 filed November 26th 1887 and granted May 8th 1888. The transposed dates of appearance of these two patents will be noticed.
3) U.S. Patent No. 457,344 for Smoothing Tool for Phonograph Blanks filed by Edison November 21st 1890 and granted August 11th 1891
4) U.S. Patent No. 393,465 for Method of Preparing Phonograph Recording Surfaces filed by Edison July 7th 1888 and granted November 27th 1888
5) U.S. Patent Nos. 406,570/1 for Phonograph and Process of Treating Phonogram Blanks filed by Edison February 11th 1889 and granted July 9th 1889
6) U.S. Patent No. 414,760 for Phonograph filed by Edison March 30th 1889 and granted November 12th 1889
7) U. S. Patent No. 484,583 for Phonograph Cutting Tool filed by Edison on May 27th 1890 and granted October 18th 1892
8) U.S. Patent No. 465,972 for Phonograph filed by Edison on November 18th 1889 and granted December 29th 1891
9) U.S. Patent No. 441,609 for Machine for Paring and Polishing Phonograph-Cylinders filed by George A. Beach, Sioux City, Iowa on June 16th 1890 and granted November 25th 1890
10) *Complete Manual of the Edison Phonograph* pp 76-77
11) U.S. Patent No. 796,857 for Machine for Shaving Sound Records filed by John F. Ott June 24th 1903, granted August 8th 1905
12) Dimensions: Base 17 in. x 12 in., height 17 ¼ in. with cover, cabinet 10 ¼ in. without cover
13) Report of Entertainments Committee January 17th (?) 1911 - Edison Archive
14) F.K. Dolbeer to C.H. Wilson August 16th 1912 - Edison Archive

Edison shaving machine for 4-minute wax blanks of 1912

Chapter 32
Batteries

The first electric phonographs from the time of the Gilliland models hired out by Edison were supplied with the Grenet primary battery. This was the glass flask using potassium dichromate and a vertical slide rod to control the reaction, and was claimed to run the phonograph from 12 to 15 hours. It was fairly easily recharged by adding more solution and it cost $6.00 complete. This simple accumulator had much to be said against it, its short life, component expense, trouble in containing the chemical, but it was a useful cell for the early phonograph users, operating out of reach of any electrical generating plant.

One of the many things Edison did on a visit to Europe in 1889 was to buy the rights to the Lalande Battery, and these in several sizes were a great improvement, providing a more reliable and long-service primary source than the Grenet. Normally four cells (cylindrical jars) were linked and supplied in an oblong or square metal-lined wooden box, but could be used without this for stationary installations such as coin-slot phonographs. At first there were two types on offer, one for domestic use, and one for office and coin-slot machines.

<u>1891</u>

Type K (100 hours), 4 glass cells in wooden box	$13.60
without box	$10.00
Type T (300 hours), 4 porcelain cells in wooden box	$25.00

Dimensions and weights of each cell were as follows:

Type K, diam: 5 ⅝ in., height 13 ¼ in., weight filled 13 ¼ lb. empty 5 ¾ lb.
Type T, diam: 8 ½ in., height 16 ¼ in., weight filled 44 lb., empty 20 lb.

The Edison-Lalande was an alkaline battery system, using zinc elements with a caustic potash exciting solution. Later other Edison-Lalande primary batteries became available as follows:

Type S (100 hours), 4 porcelain cells in wooden box	$15.00
box dimensions 25 ½ in. x 8 in. x 15 in.	

Type V (50 hours), 4 steel cells in wooden box $12.00
box dimensions 13 in. x 13 in. x 9 ½ in.
Type V was recommended for portable work

The small glass bottles that are sometimes found lettered with the words 'Edison Battery Oil' were for use with these batteries. A film of floating oil sealed the surface of the electrolyte.

The earliest days of the electric phonographs coincided with experiments to build practical secondary or storage batteries, batteries that lead plates and dilute sulfuric acid electrolyte would not make unattractively heavy, perhaps with the combination of two or more separate cells. These would need a regular charge from a direct current source.

The first storage battery recommended for Edison electric phonographs was made by The Consolidated Electric Storage Company and was the Julien Type S-17, sold in an oak case for $17.50, or in a painted case for $16.00. It had a 30 hour performance. The weight and dimensions of this battery are not available and it may have been imported from Europe.

The electrolyte comprised one part of pure sulfuric acid to five parts of water (23° Beaumé or s. g. 1.189). After cooling for four hours this was added to the battery cells and charged at a rate of 10 to 20 ampères per hour.

The Julien Battery soon gave way to the similar Chloride Accumulator Storage Battery, also using lead-sulfuric acid despite its name. This weighed 35 lb., its casing measured 4 in. x 10 in. x 14 in. and it cost $14.50 and ran a phonograph for 30 continuous hours.

Into the 20th Century accumulators for driving Edison phonographs were soon subordinate to spring-driven and mains-current machines, but were still available at the same price after the battery-driven machines had been dropped. The last noticed Chloride Accumulator was in a list dated October 16th 1911.

Chapter 33
Some Notes on Business Machines

There are still many people who remember coming first to the phonograph by way of cylinder office machines, the generical Dictaphones,[1] or less often the Ediphones.[2]

In their careers the Dictaphones would become more widely recognized and accepted than the Ediphones and in their early days despite both constituting Lippincott's North American Phonograph Company a strong rivalry existed, but Edison phonograph business was led by events to be directed towards the domestic and amusement trade, and American Graphophone towards domestic and office phonographs.

Edison cylinder office phonographs were made until 1947, but some old models still being used were reported in the 1970s although production of cylinders for them ceased in the mid-sixties in Great Britain and perhaps earlier in the United States.[3]

The use of recording machines in offices was the first of Edison's ten intended functions for his new invention reported in 1878,[4] and it is noticeable in that year and the next that a number of tinfoil phonographs found their way to companies, firms and public bodies as well as to individuals (see Appendix I). Short messages and letters could be left on the tin-foil, and enquiries about these machines to use in place of stenographers exist in Edison files.

An electrically driven Dictating Cylinder Phonograph with tinfoil wrapped round a vertically mounted mandrel and the phonet driven up it was shown in laboratory sketches of October 6th 1878,[5] but tinfoil as a recording surface was limited and once removed from one machine could not be played back on another, and little further work was done by Edison on phonographs for the next 9 years.

In the 1880s in the meantime the Bell and Tainter experiments led to the wax-coated cardboard cylinder that was readily transferable, and on May 8th 1887 Charles Batchelor reported seeing one of these phonographs with an ozokerite cylinder set up on display as an office machine with a typewriter alongside.[6]

Several testimonials in the booklet *The Description of the Phonograph and Phonograph-Graphophone*[7] show the Bell-Tainter Phonograph-Graphophone was in use from about May 1st

1888, being endorsed largely by government offices and committees.[8] Despite this approval the Bell-Tainter machines gave a deal of trouble and Edison let it be known he would be perfecting his Phonograph shortly. This much-publicized but valuable achievement of June 1888 soon opened the door to its employment in business offices with a reusable wax cylinder that would hold up to five minutes of speech at slow speed. The Bell-Tainter cylinders attracted many complaints that the ozokerite peeled from the cardboard base; this was built up of spirally wound paper. Although normally 6 in. long, shorter cylinders were obtainable. It was also reported that the stylus wore out after about a month's use, and the feed nut had to be replaced regularly.

The phonographs of Edison's make were much more robust and as well as having a recorder and speaker came equipped with a shaving knife; with a record shaveable for up to a hundred times these were an attractive choice for the businessman who could come to a rental agreement with North American. The machines offered were the CLASS M from 1889 and CLASS E soon after, and special desks and cabinets could be bought to accommodate the instruments with room for typewriter and accessories. In the North American company's machine catalogues of the day office and residential (or social) phonographs were offered together, although the emphasis was still on business use, but from 1893 were differentiated into Catalogue A (Commercial) and Catalogue B (Home Entertainment, Education). These early models were supplemented in offices by CLASS T treadle types, especially in country districts, and to a lesser extent by the CLASS W water models.

At the beginning the going rental for the electric office phonographs was quoted at $40.00 though rising in 1890 to $60.00 per year, $50.00 for treadle and $40.00 for hand-turned graphophones, but the trade was soon pressing for outright sales to avoid heavy losses on bookkeeping, repairs, improvements and exchanging.[9] The earliest prices seen for the sale of Commercial Phonograph Outfits date from the early 1890s and are as follows:

No. 1 CLASS T Phonograph on treadle stand, with speaking and hearing tubes
and 1 dozen cylinder blanks $140.00
No. 2 CLASS M electric type with battery, speaking and hearing tubes
and 1 dozen cylinder blanks $170.00
No. 3 Ditto, plus typewriter table $180.00
No. 4 Two CLASS M electric types with batteries, speaking and hearing tubes,
typewriter table, stand for dictation machine
and 2 dozen cylinder blanks ... $350.00
Outfits 2, 3 and 4 could also be furnished with CLASS E machines
for mains operation up to 120 volts.
CLASS W water motor with blanks but no cabinet $150.00

The Edison Commercial Phonographs were described as the "ideal amanuensis for business purposes", and it is not surprising that stenographers did not take kindly to the new equipment invading their province. Not only were their services dispensed with but in testimonial letters sent to North American this was made a prominent reason for endorsing the office phonographs and in Kansas City in 1890 some resistance was reported and nine different opposing bodies organized, but the protest soon faded out.[10] They were early days for such demonstrations to be effectual.

The CLASS M and CLASS E with adaptations remained the chief Edison office machines in the United States until the BUSINESS series of 1905. The longer playing 6 in. Edison wax cylinders were introduced by North American in 1890, probably in June, and the lengthened mandrel appeared on office phonographs.[11] At the same time a one inch diameter miniature postal cylinder "not larger than your finger" was in circulation in the trade[12] though which phonograph could accommodate it is not clear because the forthcoming series of commercial machines was not ready for sending out until the likely date of April 7th 1891, and most of these went for export. It is probable that prototypes were being moved among selected American dealers for evaluation.

The safe mailing of recorded cylinders was always a problem and special boxes were provided, but the Bell and Tainter cylinders were lighter and cost only 2 cents to mail. Although work was carried out at the Edison laboratory on collapsible and folding cylinders and patents awarded, no evidence has been seen of their coming into general use.[13] A lot of money was lost on sales of the Edison office cylinders in their early days and Edison was restricted in endeavors to improve the cylinder structure by the Tainter patents.[14] Although the Bell and Tainter and Edison laboratories were supposed to be working together in Lippincott's North American Phonograph Company, they were described as "fighting like Kilkenny cats".[15]

The trade was confused by the two types running side by side and appealed to North American for one commercial system only and preference was shown for Edison's machines with their all-wax cylinders. The Bell-Tainter equipment had shown too many defects, not only with the lightly-made phonographs but often the cylinders were faulty when received; neither could they be re-used. At the same time there was a call for a shaving machine independent of the phonograph.[16]

The small Edison postal cylinders were the answer to the shortcomings of the Bell Tainter, and the North American CLASS C COMMERCIAL Phonograph that played them was an important innovation. It was the first purpose-designed Edison office machine, and although no photographs have been found it is featured in several line drawings in a British patent applied for by Col. G.E. Gouraud in September 1891 on Edison's behalf.[17] This was a battery driven machine, unusually with the motor placed right underneath the phonograph movement and with the governor alongside, thus shortening the top plate and saving space. These illustrations do not show any cabinet-work but could mean that the machine was intended to be dropped into a table or a desk-top. Three layouts are depicted; with the feedscrew on the mandrel shaft, with the feedscrew at the front and parallel, and with it at the back and parallel to a shorter mandrel shaft, rather in the style of the STANDARD model that came later. In the last two the feedscrew was driven from the mandrel shaft by a perforated leather belt and sprockets, a convenient way of reducing its speed to make a 200 t. p. i. cut on the cylinder. There was a 6 in. long standard diameter rubber covered mandrel that was slipped over a smaller one made for the postal cylinders. The larger cylinder was intended to revolve at 96 r.p.m., the postal size at 176 r.p.m. A spectacle frame carrier-arm easily adapted to both of these by having the lift lever raised for standard cylinders or lowered for the smaller ones.

These smaller cylinders were those described by W. K. L. Dickson, for years Edison's assistant and associate, in commending the COMMERCIAL phonograph as "simple to handle for any merchant or clerk" and that the recorded phonogram was "enclosed in a little box especially adapted for mail transportation". He also noted that cylinders of differing lengths could be bought "answering to our note, letter and foolscap paper and embracing any number of words from 500 and 800 to 4,000".[18]

Edison Postal cylinder (centre) shown with its box and compared with a standard wax cylinder. The label is addressed to Stephen Moriarty. (Sam Sheena photograph)

Several further innovations were included in Gouraud's patent. When making a recording the carrier-arm could be lifted clear by pressing an electric button on the recording tube without breaking the motor circuit. A safety feature was built into the recording tube and recorder/speaker tube plate to guard against existing material being gone over, and an electric bell signaled the approaching end of the cylinder. In this patent Gouraud also registered sapphires or similar jewels as cutting, reproducing and turning-off tools, and an unexpected addition established the lateral cutting of sound waves on cylinder records, claiming that:

vibrations are more truly recorded in this manner ..... the reproduced sounds being accordingly improved.

This inclusion was more for strategic rather than practical reasons in the United Kingdom.

This Edison COMMERCIAL Phonograph and its successor were pointed in the direction of export and a large number were taken up by Edisonia Ltd. in London. Was this machine the Edison COMMERCIAL Phonograph Model A, and could the one that followed be the Model B, and were these labels bestowed retroactively?

This second COMMERCIAL model is recorded as being first shipped on May 12th 1893 and it would remain the office phonograph for overseas for the next decade. The motor and governor were once more set under the phonograph mechanism for the sake of compactness. The feedscrew ran behind the mandrel, operated by a perforated belt, and the controls were improved. Again it recorded and played at 200 threads per inch and used the 6 in. long cylinder and the small postal cylinder;[19] this cost ninepence in the U.K. with the former at one shilling. These CLASS C machines continued to be available in Great Britain through Edison Bell until 1905. (Reference should be made to the chapter on the ELECTRIC PHONOGRAPH and also to Appendix IV)

Edison CLASS C COMMERCIAL Phonograph as it appeared in the United Kingdom when marketed by Edison Bell. This example has the single rubber-covered mandrel

This plate on the COMMERCIAL Phonograph determines its date as not later than 1898

In the United States following the abandonment of the Bell-Tainter ozokerite cylinder, Graphophones were adapted to the Edison-type wax cylinder and after the break-up of North American Phonograph in 1894 the commercial phonograph policies of the two companies clashed, with neither side agreeing on the groove pitch to adopt. The new Columbia graphophones used 160 t.p.i., Edison's regular machine 100, so a cylinder recorded on one make could not be played back on the other. Edison's 100 t.p.i. was achieved with a 50 t.p.i. feedscrew with a 2:1 rating gearing; later the feedscrew was cut at 75 t.p.i. and the gearing 2:1, making the cylinder cut 150 t.p.i. The Edison company continued to justify the discrepancy by advising that the thicker wall between their grooves avoided possibilities of 'echo' especially in warm weather, but Columbia would not budge from 160 t.p.i., so the Edison feedscrew was cut at 80 t.p.i. and the 2:1 spur gears translated this to a cylinder cut of 160 t.p.i. Such feed screws and nuts were stamped '80'. Later, Edison standardized at 150 t.p.i. using a 50 t.p.i. feed screw with helical gears of 3:1 ratio, but to achieve 160 t.p.i. special gears were available. Where both Edison and Dictaphone machines were to be used together customers were advised to attach tags to their machines and mark the cylinders accordingly. The years when these modifications were made have not been determined.

A major reorganization took place when the Edison Commercial System was advertised on July 1st 1905. For two years the now-named Edison BUSINESS Phonograph had been placed on trial with a number of suitable firms in New York City and

373

its environs, and round these brand-new models the Commercial System was fashioned. Promotion was co-ordinated from head offices at 31 Union Square, New York, a floor below the existing offices of National Phonograph, and branch offices were opened in Boston, Buffalo, Chicago, Philadelphia and Pittsburgh. Distinction between the domestic and commercial businesses was stressed and the office machines continued to be catalogued separately. The first manager of the system was Nelson C. Durand who held several patents on Edison's behalf for improvements in commercial machines and equipment. These headquarters were soon moved back to West Orange.

The BUSINESS phonograph had been planned in 1903 and publicly shown in the April, having shed its earlier Commercial or Office Outfit conception. Designed by Peter Weber the works manager, and Charles L. Hibberd who would carry these machines and equipment through various improvements, the new instrument was more compact and easier to use than its predecessors.[20] Both spring driven and electric versions came in the same oak case, and had a typical rounded hood and conventional lifting handle and latches and were a size between the STANDARD and HOME models of the day. The feedscrew was now set at a standard pitch of 150 t.p.i. These machines established the dimensions of those that followed, having an approximate base of 11 ½ in. x 8 in. and an overall height of 11 ½ in. The spring motor had two springs and electric versions of the 'open frame' motor were furnished for either mains or batteries. The characteristic banner transfer EDISON BUSINESS PHONOGRAPH was on the front of the case and on lifting the hood the machine's commercial layout was obvious. The recorder and reproducer were set in a spectacle frame carrier-arm and the 6 in. long mandrel had a bullet end; it was supported on a central bearing. The dog-clutch on the mandrel shaft was controlled from two press buttons and later by remote means. The equipment consisted of a recording tube and hearing tubes and would allow the dictator to hear repetitions and make paper scale corrections.

The BUSINESS Phonograph Model C of 1905 owed much to the domestic machines of the time. The cases could take either form of drive and the hole for an electric lead is visible next to the crank handle.

A special monthly journal for users called *The Edison Business Record* appeared from March 1904.

In the absence of a guide to prices it appears that the customer's outlay on the BUSINESS phonographs was determined by how much of the Edison Commercial System was bought, but was around $400.00 for three or four machines. The sales agent who was required to buy the system from the Edison company received a 20 per cent commission on completion. He was responsible for seeing it installed, and there was a back-up of repairmen and spare parts.[21]

The second layout for the so-called New BUSINESS Phonograph of March 1907 and listed as Model D, was designed by Edward L. Aiken and incorporated several new features[22] although the oak case and hood still remained. The lowering of the spectacle frame carrier-arm was now simplified to a lever on top of the carrier-arm that was arranged also to secure the floating weight of whichever recorder or reproducer was inactive.

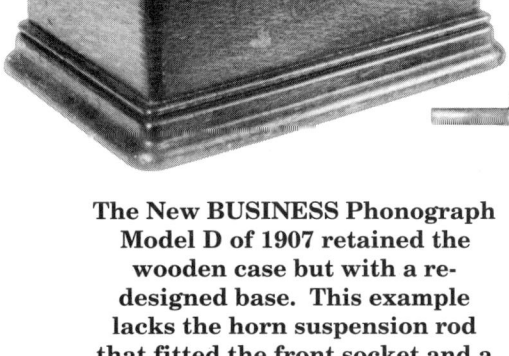

The New BUSINESS Phonograph Model D of 1907 retained the wooden case but with a re-designed base. This example lacks the horn suspension rod that fitted the front socket and a swivelling connector between horn and recorder

The mandrel was again bullet-ended and the equipment included the new long straight recording horn fixed to a support from the front of the case. This horn was elliptical in section and joined the neck of the recorder by a ball and socket coupling.[23] Recorder and reproducer were also bridged at their necks by a curved adapter tube with a ball controlled sound valve inside, an ingenious isolating device.[24] The hood was hinged to lie over the back when the machine was in use. These early wooden cabinets still carried the banner decals but were soon changed to the word 'Edison' in signature style.

The electrically driven versions of this machine incorporated for the first time a Universal Burke type of motor for use from all lighting circuits.

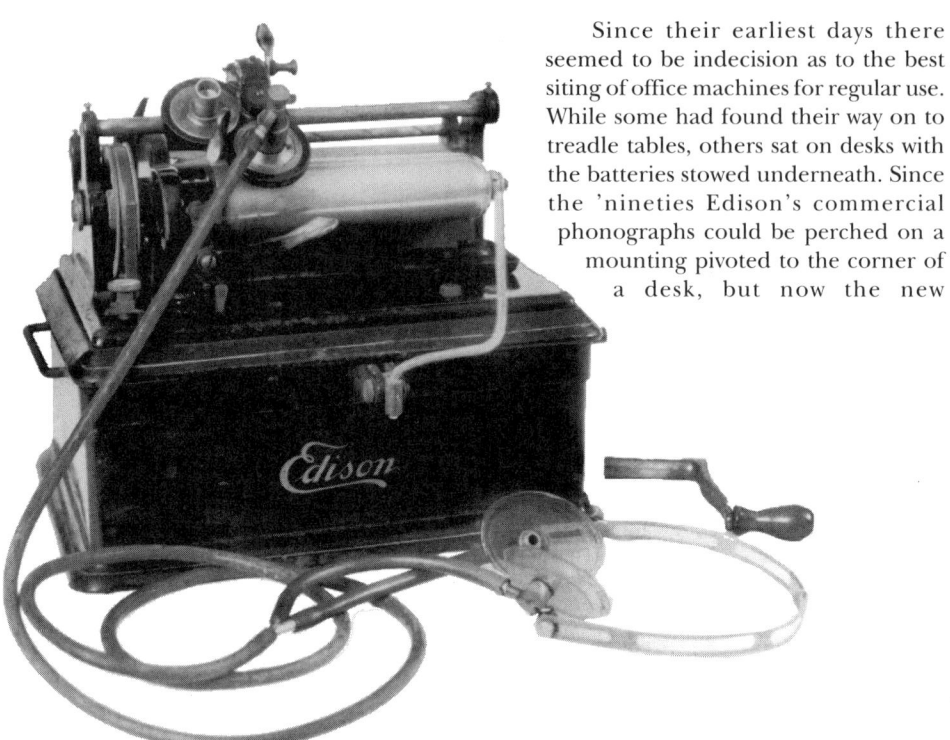

Since their earliest days there seemed to be indecision as to the best siting of office machines for regular use. While some had found their way on to treadle tables, others sat on desks with the batteries stowed underneath. Since the 'nineties Edison's commercial phonographs could be perched on a mounting pivoted to the corner of a desk, but now the new

The New BUSINESS Phonograph Model D in metal body made after the style of the wooden cased dictating machines, and found also on the SCHOOL models. The fixing of the lower end of the horn support will be noticed

BUSINESS machine was handy enough to be moved about the office on a pedestal table with tripod and casters. The next stage was a 4-post steel knock-down pedestal with casters and a single shelf, a scaled-down version of the mobile metal stand that came with the SCHOOL machine. Improved trolley stands with pigeon holes for cylinders and cupboards for equipment gradually came into use.[25]

The SCHOOL also had one noticeable influence on its contemporary BUSINESS phonograph, another type of the Model D. The case for this was of a black-finished metal but moulded and shaped like the preceding oak cabinets. It had two other unique features, the horn support rod being held by a metal strap and bolt projecting from the upper front of the case, and pull-out carrying handles of metal rod. The gilt decal 'Edison' in signature style was still applied to the case front. After this model the office phonographs became metal cased, and cast off the drawing-room look of the domestic range of machines. BUSINESS phonographs were interchangeable for dictating or transcribing and carried the following equipment in 1912:

Phonograph, spring or electric universal motor
4-post steel pedestal trolley
Rubber cover
12 cylinders in system cartons*
Carrying rack (for 6 cylinders)
Choice of speaking tube or dictating horn with support cranes when ordered for dictation
Choice of aluminium or headband hearing tube when ordered for transcribing
Pneumatic foot trip
Tool kit
One pad of correction system forms
Attachment cord for electric motor
Winding crank for spring motor

*From July 1911 all dictation cylinders had 'Edison Voicewriting Blank' stamped on the end, and in the next year a metal cap and spring to grip the cylinder was supplied on the base of the carton; this cap was transferable to other cartons.

The Ediphone - 'A Tool for Thinkers' (Edison pamphlet)

From 1918 the BUSINESS phonograph became The Ediphone, at first marked in an arching Edison-style signature, but changing after 1921 to 'The Ediphone' in gilt upper and lower case. As well as black, cabinets were also available in a grey finish. The stub feet of previous metal cabinets were eliminated.

Tapering mandrels were replaced from about 1912 by an ingenious skeletal frame of three longitudinal rods that could be eased for withdrawing the cylinder by pushing in a spring-loaded knob at the end of the mandrel shaft, a refinement that the domestic phonograph owner of earlier days would have relished.[26] The more traditional shaped mandrel returned in the 1930s but with expanding ribs to support the interior ends of the cylinder that could be contracted for its removal, again by pressing the end knob.[27] A significant improvement took place during 1915 with conjunction of recorder and reproducer into the same shell and fitting a single-eye carrier-arm. This made for a simplified control system and gave less purpose to the spectacle frame carrier-arm, although individual recorders and reproducers continued to be improved. The new so-called Combination Arm was regulated by a 3-position lever set above the guide rod that also brought in a safety guard. A flexible metal recording and listening tube - called a Sanitube - came with the executive Ediphones and there was a push-pull control cable running through it. The mouthpiece on the tube was either of ebonite or glass, and when out of use it was rested on the stop-start cradle on the machine.[28]

As a guide to dating at this time copper diaphragms on recorders and reproducers were nickel plated from June 1915, and chip brushes were attached to the carrier-arm from January 1912.

Production figures for office phonographs through the 'teens remained steady at 125 per week or so, or about 120 mixed DC and Universal, and 5 spring motor machines.

For an unspecified time from 1926 Ediphone cabinets bore a Grand Prize emblem to mark their success in the Sesqui-centennial Exposition of that year. Ediphones became Voicewriter Ediphones from the mid-1920s, merely a re-translation of the word Phonograph.

Without a doubt the most striking design of the range was the Pro-Technic Ediphones from 1933 onwards, housed in dark olive Art-Deco metal cabinets with flared corners and gliding on concealed casters.[29]

As well as the double spring motors on the earlier models the BUSINESS phonograph series had come with every combination of electric motors and resistances to suit the broad conditions of local electric supplies. The first such motors were the 'open frame' type for Direct Current, followed by the Edison Ekonowatt series that became the regular Universal motor from January 1918. The Burke Universal Motor was also supplied in the earlier days, and may be found in its first form with a 2-ball governor and flywheel, or later a 4-ball governor.

From the early times of the commercial phonographs accessories were introduced to advance the system and add efficiency, starting in 1890 with a primitive foot pedal for the operator that pressed on a rubber bulb and caused the carrier-arm to lift by pneumatic means.[30] Electrified and acting on the clutch this became the Ediphone Toe-Trip, the Electric Toe-Trip and the Electrip.[31] The principal who dictated his letters to the Executive Ediphone Voicewriter used the Typefase electric remote controller with 'Speak' and 'Repeat' digital buttons.

The Transophone of 1915 was claimed as 'the complete machine for transcribing' and had an electric back-spacer worked from the side of the typewriter keyboard.[32]

The Telescribe for recording phone messages on a cylinder and with a desk amplifier was introduced in 1914,[33] followed about 1920 by the improved Telediphone. As far back as 1878 Edison had foreseen the Telescribe principle as the first of his Ten Prominent Uses for the Phonograph. Electrical recording and reproduction 'by vibrating means' was tried in 1917, using a small earphone or microphone pushed on the neck of a reproducer or recorder,[34] and developed into an electric cutting recorder with its magnet close to the diaphragm; this was available by September 1917,[35] but no valve amplification was used at this date.

Just as many early automatic phonographs had multiple hearing tubes joined to a metal gallery of listening outlets, so did the Ediphones if needed. A 10-point bar tube and 'headphones' were available from 1920 so that one Ediphone could supply dictation to a class of pupil typists in a commercial school. Sometimes a pipeline was fixed from desk to desk, so the entire class could take the same dictation. For this a ⅜ in. diameter pipe was recommended, and not longer than 20 ft. Special Eldridge Dictation Records were available for such schools.

The magnitude to which the domestic phonographs were neglected after 1913 when the Edison Discs and their machines officially arrived on the scene is revealed by the progressive development of these office phonographs and their accessories. Whereas nothing was done to better the AMBEROLAS 30, 50 and 75 until they withered away in 1929, the office phonographs and Ediphones were constantly updated by a team whose names appeared with regularity on American patents. Electrical recording and playback of a limited nature was available for the office before Victor and Columbia came out with it in 1925, but the Edison chiefs were unwilling to resuscitate the domestic cylinder machine trade that had been losing money for years.

Work was started in 1935 on disc Dictating phonographs, but not until 1947 – the centenary of the inventor's birth – did the first Disc Electronic Voicewriter (D.E.V.) appear, and cylinder phonograph production cease. Marketing of all Edison dictating and audio equipment stopped in 1973, four years short of the Phonograph's 100th birthday.

Aside from its use in business offices of nearly two hundred different industries, several special or unique uses of Edison Dictating Phonographs were listed in publications of the early 1900s:

> *Clergymen in composing and memorizing sermons*
> *Actors in rehearsing and memorizing roles*
> *Playwrights and Authors*
> *Architects and Engineers dictating specifications while working over a draughting table*
> *Callers leaving messages while visiting when the principal is busy or absent*
> *Outside workers who need to file office reports can call in and leave them on a dictating machine*

Further information bearing on Edison Office Phonographs will be found in the chapters on:

THE EDISON ELECTRIC PHONOGRAPHS

THE EDISON PHONOGRAPHS AND EDISON BELL (Appendix IV)

NOTES
1) Term first used in mid-1907
2) Term first used in 1918
3) The writer visited this factory at Maidstone, Kent in 1966 and bought some cylinders. Unhappily the plant was never preserved
4) In *The North American Review* of June 1878 he wrote of "letter writing and all kinds of dictation without the aid of a stenographer"
5) A feature of Edison's patent No. 227,679 of May 18th 1880, filed March 29th 1879
6) Charles Batchelor Papers - Edison Archive
7) Published July 1888 by North American Phonograph Company and describing the Edison and Bell-Tainter machines, almost certainly the first published writing on them
8) The Columbia Graphophone Company was responsible for servicing machines in government offices
9) *Proceedings of the 1890 Convention of Local Phonograph Companies*, p44
10) Ibid., p. 52
11) Ibid, p. 136
12) Ibid., p. 139

13) Several U.S. patents for collapsible or flexible blanks were granted at this time:
    Edison's 400,650   filed October 17th 1888   granted April 2nd 1889
    Edison's 406,568   October 17th 1888   July 9th 1889
    Isaac Heysinger's 460,338 February 7th 1888   September 29th 1891
    Edison's 488,191   January 19th 1889   December 20th 1892
14) *Proceedings of the 1890 Convention of Local Phonograph Companies*, pp 147-9
15) Ibid., p. 111
16) Ibid., p. 155
17) British patent No. 15,206 for Improvements in Phonographs, applied for September 8th 1891 and accepted July 9th 1892
18) W.K.L. and Antonia Dickson: *Life and Inventions of Thomas A. Edison* (1894) p. 132
19) At an unknown date it reverted to a single standard mandrel but retained 200 t.p.i. facility certainly until 1905 for office use in the United Kingdom. Edison Bell who handled it there also offered it for home use with 100 t.p.i. and with a Capps spring motor installed in both types if required.
20) U. S. Patent No. 772,485, filed September 10th 1903 and granted October 18th 1904
21) *Edison Phonograph Monthly* August 1905 p. 3
22) U. S. Patent No. 847,631 filed February 20th 1906 and granted March 19th 1907
23) U.S. Design Patent No. 38,943 of Edward L. Aiken, filed October 11th 1907 and granted December 10th 1907
24) U. S. Patent No. 855,622 of Nelson C. Durand filed October 26th 1906 and granted June 4th 1907
25) U. S. Patent No. 1,821,621 of Nelson C. Durand, filed March 21st 1929 and granted September 1st 1931. The reason for this late patent may have been due to opposition from Dictaphone.
26) U. S. Patent No. 1,167,500 of Newman H. Holland, filed October 6th 1911 and granted January 11th 1916
27) U.S. Patent No. 2,010,717 of H.F. M. Gramann, applied for January 23rd 1932 and granted August 6th 1935
28) U.S. Patent No. 1,297,466 of Newman H. Holland, filed July 13th 1914 and granted March 18th 1919
29) U.S. Design Patent No. 89,521 of Smith, Langley and Braun, filed January 26th 1933 and granted March 21st 1933
30) U.S. Patent No. 443,507 of T. A. Edison, filed December 27th 1889 and granted December 30th 1890
31) U. S. Trade Mark No. 172,259, filed November 11th 1920 and registered August 23rd 1923. Used since March 1920
32) U. S. Trade Mark No. 98,495, filed March 6th 1914 and registered July 21st 1914. Used since February 1914
33) U. S. Patent No. 1,420,317 of Newman H. Holland, filed November 30th 1914, renewed December 16th 1920 and granted June 20th 1922
34) U. S. Patent No. 1,229,749 of Newman H. Holland, filed September 17th 1914 and granted June 12th 1917
35) U. S. Patent No. 1,465,764 of Newman H. Holland, filed November 6th 1920 and granted August 21st 1923

The Edison office phonographs were well endowed with patents and those shown above are selective.

Appendix I

First Edison Phonograph Sales, April 1878 to Jan. 1880

This list of the first 22 months of sales by The Edison Speaking Phonograph Company has been compiled from statements prepared for Edison to show his 20 per cent royalty on sales. There are unaccountable gaps, and several instances where the phonograph was returned and re-sold. A few of the customers bought more than one machine, and although the clients were described as Lessees there was a rule at this stage 'No phonographs loaned or rented'. Selling price differences can not be explained, but both iron and brass instruments were being sold, and some would have had extra decoration.

Date	Purchasers & Lessees	Address	Machine	Price
1878				$
May	Chas. H. Sewall	Albany, NY	1	95.50
Sept.	to A.M. Musser			
May	J. N. Pratt	Brooklyn, NY	2	95.50
	K. K. Eldred	St. Louis, MO	3	95.50
	J. S. Vale	New York, NY	4	95.50
	F. B. Smith	Albany, NY	5	95.50
	F.L.C. Lundy	Morristown, NJ	6	95.50
April	J. Gutheridge	New York, NY	7	95.50
	Thos. Mason	St. Louis, MO	8	95.50
Sept.	to Jacob Backus			
May	George H. Iott	Grand Rapids, MI	9	95.50
	J. S. Vogler	Concord, NH	10	95.50
April	Ball Bros.	Ironton, OH	11	95.50
May	G. S. Pike	New York, NY	12	95.50
April	Richard Hampton	Brewster, NY	13	95.50
June	George W. Marston	—	14	95.50
April	J.G. Turner	Mt Washington, MD	15	95.50
May	W.J. Chappell	Susquehanna, PA	16	95.50
	J.B. Cook	New York, NY	17	95.50

Date	Purchasers & Lessees	Address	Machine	Price
	B.V. Eaton	Clinton, PA	18	95.50
	R.P. Staats	New York, NY	19	95.50
Sept.	to H.A. Parr			
June	Elliott Mason	—	20	95.50
	to W. Chamberlain			
May	Macdonald &Simmons	New York, NY	21	95.50
	L.W. Camp	Clayton, IL	22	95.50
	A. L. Rauck	Lancaster, PA	24	95.50
August	George W. Sherwood	—	25	95.50
	C. C. Cogswell	—	26	95.50
May	A.D. White	Toledo, OH	27	95.50
	Wm. McMahon	Boston, MA	28	95.50
Jan 1879	T.C. Ballard	—	35	40.00
June 1878	W. F. Wheeler	—	46	95.50
	Samuel Hubbard	—	51	95.50
August	J. R. Smith	—	52	95.50
June	Fred W. Jones	—	55	95.50
	C.H. Fiske	—	57	95.50
	Fred W. Jones	—	58	95.50
	C. H. Fiske	—	59	95.50
August	to E.B. Hamlin	—		
June	J. M. Nixon	—	60	95.50
	C.H. Thayos	—	61	95.50
	J. J. Gleason	—	62	47.75
	H. C. Ford	—	63	95.50
	Samuel Hubbard	—	64	95.50
August	John T. Mason	—	65	95.50
	Young & Swilner	—	66	95.50
June	C. Barnes	—	67	95.50
August	W. J. Westwood	—	69	95.50
June	L.T. Weld	—	70	95.50
	G. H. Bliss	—	71	95.50
	J. R. Smith	—	72	95.50
August	to H. Clay Ford	—		
June	G. H. Bliss	—	73	95.50
	G. H. Bliss	—	74	95.50
	G. H. Bliss	—	75	95.50
	J. Ross	New York	76	95.50
	F. W. Smith	Newark, NJ	76	95.50

Date	Purchasers & Lessees	Address	Machine	Price
	Alf Burnett	Philadelphia, PA	76	95.50
	W. F. Wheeler	—	77	95.50
	C. B. Harris	—	79	95.50
Sept.	Silver & Laws	—	80	185.00
July	H. Clay Ford	—	81	95.50
August	Morris Simmonds	—	83	185.00
July	Victor Spaenhoven	—	84	185.00
Sept.	J. N. Furtenburg	—	86	185.00
July	U.B. Dinsmore	—	87	185.00
Nov.	J.D. Easterling	—	88	85.00
June	E. McCroskey	—	89	95.50
August	George H. Bliss	—	89	185.00
		Double numbering not explained		
June	E. T. & P. R. Gilliland	—	A	95.50
August	John Pritchard	—	90	185.00
Sept.	M.T. Higginbotham	—	91	185.00
August	D. A. de Leuna & Co	—	92	185.00
	Wexel & Degress	—	93	185.00
	George Washburn	—	94	185.00
	W. F. Jamieson	—	95	185.00
	C. A. Sullivan	—	96	185.00
	E. B. Hamlin	—	97	185.00
Sept.	E. B. Hamlin	—	98	185.00
	E. B. Hamlin	—	99	185.00
	W. L. McGee	—	100	185.00
Dec.	M. Echereivia	—	101	135.00
Sept.	E. H. Harvey	—	102	135.00
August	C. C. Cogswill	—	104	95.50
Sept.	A. C. Lovell	—	105	185.00
	E. B. Hamlin	—	106	185.00
	M. P. Lopez	—	107	185.00
	J. P. Calvert	—	108	185.00
	Orrin Bros.	—	109	185.00
	E. B. Hamlin	—	110	135.00
Oct.	J. B. Johnston	—	112	185.00
	John H. Hunter	—	113	135.00
Dec.	A. H. Crunu	—	114	110.00
Oct.	Dr. J. J. Villiers	—	115	135.00
	F.O. Field	—	116	110.00

Date	Purchasers & Lessees	Address	Machine	Price
Dec.	J.D. Erdman	—	117	85.00
	A. A. Walderman	—	118	135.00
	A.F. Annabel	—	119	85.00
Oct.	C. M. Page	—	120	135.00
	H.A. Clute	—	121	85.00
May 1879 to C. F. Maashommet(when re-sold)				90.00
Oct. 1878 Rev. Thomas Douglas—			122	135.00
Feb. 1879	Darling & Co.	—	123	85.00
1878				
Oct.	Wexel & Degress	—	124	110.00
Nov.	Irving Moses	—	125	85.00
	A. Shorter Caldwell	—	126	110.00
	Robert Murray	—	127	85.00
	Flint & Warner	—	128	135.00
	J.W. Rohler	—	129	135.00
	G. P. Humphrey	—	130	85.00
	Brown & West	—	131	85.00
	Dr. J.L. Castilla	(noted as brass)	132	175.00
Oct.	N. F. Dexter	—	133	85.00
	S. N. Gorsuch	—	134	85.00
	H. Murray	—	135	85.00
	Edward Jones	—	136	85.00
	James Lowe	—	137	85.00
	A.J. Howell	—	138	85.00
	W. W. Wheatley	—	139	85.00
	Dick Martin	—	140	85.00
	George H. Bliss	—	141	85.00
	Wm. E. Adams	—	142	85.00
	John L. Burton	—	143	85.00
	E.A. Kennedy	—	144	85.00
	Prof. Albert Johnson	—	145	85.00
Nov.	Roman Catholic Cathedral Fair	—	146	110.00
	L. Averill	—	147	85.00
	A.P. Westcott jr.	—	148	110.00
	L.A. Ludwig	—	149	85.00
Dec.	James A. Carey	—	151	85.00
	W. F. Ferlor	—	152	85.00
Jan. 1879	George W. Hutchings	—	153	90.00
Dec. 1878	W.C. Chamberlain	—	154	85.00

Date	Purchasers & Lessees	Address	Machine	Price
	D. Clark	—	155	85.00
	A. S. Mills	—	157	85.00
	Col. H. S. Scott	—	158	no charge
	A.S. Cameron	—	159	85.00
April 1879	F.W. Bogardus	—	160	90.00
Dec. 1878	Richard M. Hair	—	161	85.00
Jan. 1879	R.C. Bruckner	—	162	90.00
Dec. 1878	S.R. Wells & Co.	—	163	85.00
Jan. 1879	Percival Hawes	—	164	90.00
	Emil Costello	—	165	90.00
May	to Professor J. Halwick	(re-sale price)		90.00
Feb.	J.G. Tillotson & Co.	—	166	75.00
Jan.	L. Kline	—	167	90.00
	H.W. Applebaugh	—	168	80.00
Feb.	United States Military Academy	—	169	85.00
Jan.	Frederick Probst & Co.	—	170	85.00
March	Herr Budd - Berlin	—	171	225.00
June	Wells & Hope Company	—	174	160.00
Jan.	H. Marquardt	—	175	210.00
Feb.	T.C. Ballard	—	177	85.00
April	Lee H. Dowling	—	178	90.00
Feb.	W.H. Peck	—	179	85.00
	Oscar Carpenter	—	180	no charge
	J. M. Jones	—	181	85.00
	N. F. Canaday	—	182	85.00
	Paul Jench	—	183	85.00
March	Wm. Crane	—	184	90.00
Feb.	C. C. Delhommer	—	185	85.00
	A. E. Hall	—	186	85.00
March	Burr Robbins	—	187	90.00
April	D. Lee Jr.	—	188	90.00
March	B.N. E. Fletcher	—	189	90.00
April	Batchelor & Dorris	—	190	85.00
	Paul Healy	—	191	90.00
	T. A. Edison	—	192	no charge
June	A.H. Simms	—	193	90.00
May	Col. G.E. Gouraud	—	194	no charge
	to D. Ramage	—		90.00
	Charles Broussard	—	195	90.00

Date	Purchasers & Lessees	Address	Machine	Price
	J.W. Barber	—	196	90.00
	W.A. Clarke	—	197	90.00
	Dr. A. Shellack	—	199	90.00
June	Fred'k Probst & Co.	—	200	85.00
Oct.	E. Mathers	—	202	90.00
Sept.	R. U. Alaasi	—	203	90.00
July	T. A. Edison	—	205	90.00
Sept.	B. Avery	—	206	90.00
July	W.R. Palmer	—	207	90.00
	J. W. Barber	—	208	80.00
August	C. H. Shaw	—	209	90.00
July	J. W. Barber	—	210	80.00
June	A. W. Shewey	—	211	85.00
	J.E. Powers & Co.	—	212	90.00
Jan. 1880	George Smith	—	216	90.00
Nov. 1879	Dr. Charon	—	217	90.00
Dec.	Bryant & May	—	218	90.00
Oct.	M. Ferguson	—	219	90.00
	Echeusne Company	—	220	90.00
Nov.	Dr. Clelland	—	221	80.00
Jan. 1880	Cutler & Company	—	223	80.00
	Anthony & Company	—	224	80.00
	Cutler & Company	—	225	80.00
Dec 1879	Dr. Clelland	—	228	80.00

The following sales of small Phonographs are noted from 1879:

Date			
Feb. 1879	12 small phonographs		$96.00
	3 @ $15.00		45.00
March		2	28.00
		2	16.00
		1	12.00
		1	15.00
		1	15.00
April		1	10.00, # 1102
May		1	7.00
		1	12.00
June		1	10.00
		4	20.00

July	1	10.00
Sept.	3	nos. 1082, 1125, 1127
Nov.	6	nos. 1124, 1136, 1147, 1149, 1158, 1179
Dec.	26	nos. 1033, 1087, 1134, 1141, 1144, 1176, 1177, 1588, 1627, 1634, 1682, 1706, 170?, 1724, 1797, 1809, 1815, 1837, 1841, 1862, 1866, 1874 1889, 1897, 1903, 1907.
January 1880 45 small phonographs		nos. 1602, 1604, 1614, 1619, 1622, 1642, 1643, 1678, 1697, 1704, 1709, 1755, 1756, 1758, 1759, 1760, 1768, 1783, 1785, 1795, 1800, 1818, 1819, 1821, 1825, 1827, 1828, 1838, 1840, 1846, 1848, 1852, 1853, 1864, 1868, 1869, 1879, 1881, 1894, 1899, 1900, 1901, 1904, 1945, 1969

No selling price is indicated on these small machines from September 1879, but Edison received royalty of 50 cents for each machine.

Appendix II

THE TINFOIL PHONOGRAPH ABROAD

Just as there was somebody to carry the wax cylinder 'Perfected' Phonograph across the Atlantic to London eleven years later, there was a representative from England who had met Edison some months earlier but who happened to be at Menlo Park Laboratory probably on Thursday December 6th 1877 at the time when Edison and Kruesi were trying out the first recordings on the newly constructed tinfoil phonograph. This was Henry Edmunds, a prominent engineer and inventor who leaves his peculiar mark on history as the man who introduced the Hon. C. S. Rolls to the engineer Henry Royce in 1904 thus leading to the beginning of their motor and aircraft engine company.

Edmunds later described seeing Edison

> *in a dimly-lit interior... his assistant working on a small brass cylinder covered with tinfoil. Edison held up his hand dramatically. We halted. He slowly turned the cylinder with a handle and an unearthly, metallic voice with a strong American accent spoke the words 'Mary had a little Lamb'. We had arrived in time to hear the reproduction of a mechanically recorded speech.*[1]

The British Professor Tyndall and William Preece with locally made phonographs early in 1878

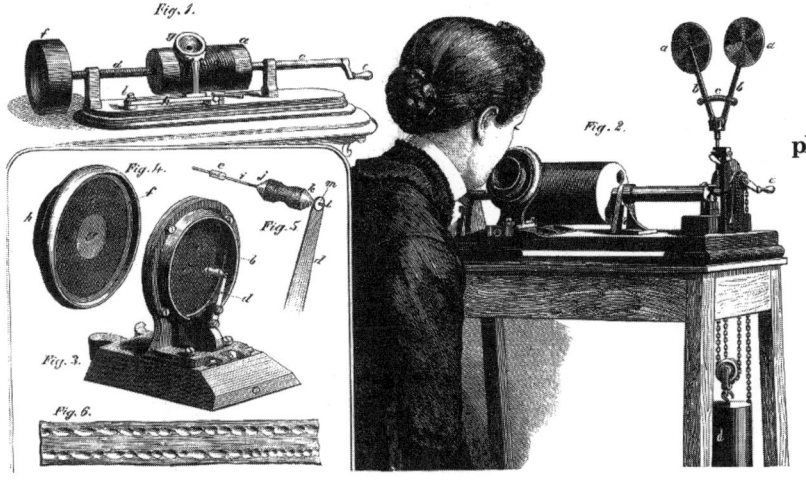

August Stroh's tinfoil phonographs of 1878

Impressed by what he had seen and heard Edmunds wrote a letter on his return describing the phonograph to *The Times* for January 17th 1878, but had been beaten by several weeks with a description of the machine from Charles Batchelor sent over on December 9th to *English Mechanic*, however it was Edmunds's *Times* letter that struck the public's fancy. A few days later Edmunds met William Preece, chief engineer of the General Post Office who agreed to demonstrate a tinfoil phonograph at the Royal Institution on February 1st, as well as the new telephone, and Augustus Stroh built him a machine. From line drawings of the time, the body of this phonograph was made of wood, but Stroh constructed a more robust weight-driven tinfoil phonograph for a further Preece demonstration on February 27th at The Society of Telegraph Engineers. There were two other phonographs demonstrated, a copy of Edison's original built by a W. Pidgeon and his son of Putney, London, and a more recent Edison model sent over. Preece was so impressed that he arranged to have the following message cabled to Edison:

> *The Society of Telegraph Engineers at their meeting tonight send congratulations and thanks to Mr. Edison for the services he has rendered to applied science by the invention of the Phonograph which interested and delighted a crowded audience.*
> Norvin Green, secretary

It was a pity that by June relations between Edison and Preece would become soured to the point of public recriminations in the press.

On February 8th Theodore Puskas, Edison's foreign patent lawyer and promoter in London reported to the inventor that he was in touch with a 'first-class house' ready to advance £2,000 and offer half profits for the phonograph agency in Great Britain.

The source of that offer is unclear, but certainly by March 7th, George S. Nottage, managing partner of London Stereoscopic and Photographic Company of 54 Cheapside was writing to Menlo Park to ask if his company could handle Edison phonographs in the United Kingdom under licence, and an agreement was reached through Puskas in the sum of £1,500. London Stereoscopic and Photographic was a small firm specializing in scientific novelties and had done official photography for one or two members of the Royal Family.

Prospects must have looked bright in London to Puskas, because on February 14th 1878 he was cabling Edison for a 'promised phonograph' and asking the rate for an order for a thousand.

The first small phonograph to arrive was reported on March 18th to have broken adrift in its box and was damaged, but a clockwork phonograph - presumably the one demonstrated by Preece on February 27th - was obtained from Augustus Stroh and sent to the Crystal Palace in south east London where it was demonstrated by Stroh and J. P. Edwards on April 19th in the Board Room. There was a Good Friday Concert on that day and several musicians taking part had entrusted their talents to the Stroh machine. These included the singers Signor Foli and Madame Lemmens-Sherrington and the conductor Augustus Manns, and Sergeant Hardy of the band of the Scots Guards played "The Last Rose of Summer" on his cornet. All the recordings were clearly audible to those in the room. This is the earliest reported instance of musicians of professional standing making a recording, but there is no mention of the other principals in the concert, Sims Reeves, Madame Patey and Edward Lloyd singing for the phonograph.[2]

In due course a small phonograph was put on show at the Langham Hotel in London and Professor W. P. Barrett was engaged by London Stereoscopic to take another phonograph out on exhibition and lectures at five guineas per lecture, plus expenses.

The term 'plate phonograph' appears on several occasions in London Stereoscopic's correspondence during 1878 although there is no evidence of their being sent any, yet a number must have been in existence in British scientific circles for them to become known about.

Puskas, who was Hungarian and whose brother represented Edison in Budapest looked to the Continent and began organizing a phonograph gathering in Paris. He succeeded in having it presented by the Compte du Moncel, author of the new book *Le Téléphone, le Microphone et le Phonographe*,[3] and he was able to get the phonograph to utter some publicity for itself - and himself - "Le Phonographe présente ses compliments à L' Académie des Sciences".[4]

These academic demonstrations were followed by an Exhibition of Phonographs at the Boulevard des Capucines from April 23rd to September 23rd 1878, where there were three demonstrations daily in the afternoon and three in the evening - "where will its colossal success stop?" - and advertised in German, Dutch, French, Italian, Spanish and English. A profit of more than 36,000 francs was made and to turn the glow of Parisian enthusiasm to good purpose Puskas sought out E. Hardy in Paris to quote for making small inexpensive phonographs for sale in France and also for the London Stereoscopic Company.[5] Some of Hardy's machines that were imported were cheap versions, largely made of wood and with a plaster mandrel-flywheel. Other Edison phonographs made in France were by A. Du Michel of Paris.

After the demonstrations at the Crystal Palace and Langham Hotel the attitude to the phonograph of The London Stereoscopic and Photographic Company seemed to lack direction and zeal, but the reason for this is not apparent although bad feeling developed between Puskas and George S. Nottage who described Puskas as "fierce and litigious".

It was said in letters by Professor Barrett that the company was enthusiastic about his lectures because they made money with little effort, and in December while imploring Edison for small machines Barrett reported the company was dragging its feet "as not having supplied a phonograph to the public yet". This was stretching the truth but the company blamed its slowness on being unable to find the right sort of engineering workshop to make them. By October it was quoting phonographs for private use for £31 10s. 0d. with a 3-week waiting list, and for £10 10s. 0d. in December when "immense demand" was reported. Although Augustus Stroh was generally considered to be the builder of the larger London Stereoscopic phonographs, it is likely some of those from France were imported for a time. No early London Stereoscopic catalogues have been seen but in 1886 the following were offered:

1) Hand cranked and without flywheel	£5 0s. 0d.
2) Hand cranked with flywheel	£10 10s. 0d.
3) Weight driven	£25 0s. 0d.[6]

The reproducer on at least one large Stroh phonograph had a floating weight, the earliest noticed of this construction.

By the spring of 1878 tinfoil phonographs were being sold or presented in other parts of the world. In May, one was sent to the Emperor of Brazil "to open up the Brazilian Empire and Argentine Republic", a toy phonograph (?) was sent to Germany for exploitation and almost by return the Germans produced a 'clockwork' phonograph.[7]

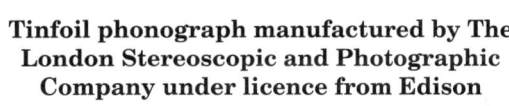

Tinfoil phonograph manufactured by The London Stereoscopic and Photographic Company under licence from Edison

Not all the instruments exported were successful or extended the Edison empire. Dobbie Brothers of Adelaide who applied for the Australian franchise in March were sent a phonograph, but the agency was abandoned in the September for unstated reasons. In October, after correspondence, a phonograph was sent out to George Street, Dunedin, where A. Solomon became the first reported owner there with a prospect of handling it in New Zealand, but he was not able to make it work despite close instruction, exchanges of letters and expenditure of £25, and Edison was glad to let him go.

**Stroh Phonograph converted to playing wax cylinders
(A Mark Ulano photograph)**

Other countries where there were requests to buy or have them for demonstration were Russia, West Indies, Turkey, Panama and Japan and colleges, schools and laboratories made appeals to buy or to be given them, and to some Edison showed generosity. In September he gave a machine to the French National Lottery, and on the phonograph's first birthday, December 6th 1878, an example was already being sought for the Royal Industrial Museum in Stuttgart, Germany.

NOTES

1) Paul Tritton - article in Rolls-Royce house journal Vol. II No. 1
2) *The Times, Daily Telegraph* and *Daily News* April 20th 1878
3) Published Libraire Hachette, Paris 1878
4) *Manchester City News* March 30th 1878
5) Hardy was already making Edison electric pens
6) Chew - *Talking Machines* p. 6
7) The term clockwork is frequently ambiguous in phonograph descriptions of this nature and at this time, some were weight driven, others spring

Also Edison Archive correspondence sources

Appendix III

THE 1888 GIFT FOR COLONEL GOURAUD

The account of the carrying of the first Perfected Phonograph from Edison's Menlo Park laboratory to Colonel George Gouraud, his agent in London by his emissary H. de Courcy Hamilton will be known to many. With this phonograph Gouraud was able to demonstrate Edison's inventive skill, and holding dinner parties and other social gatherings allowed him to corner the guests, purposely some of the most eminent people of the day, who were flattered to be asked to say some words into the Phonograph. Generally few of them had anything ready that was very profound to judge the surviving recordings, but they are of singular historic importance. In this way the Phonograph drew a brief spotlight to itself, something the Graphophone never managed. Edison had earlier been irked that the improved Graphophone had overtaken his tinfoil instrument while his attention was concentrated on the electric light.

Architects' drawing for "Little Menlo", Beulah Hill, Upper Norwood, London, Colonel Gouraud's home. It was pulled down in April 1964.

The inventor's promise to send a phonograph over to Colonel Gouraud after its perfection was made more than six months before the vital date of June 16th 1888, and is borne out by a letter of November 30th 1877 from Gouraud to Hamilton stressing confidentiality when transporting the finished machine over to London.

Little Menlo,   *Nov. 30th 1887.*
Upper Norwood,
London

Dear Hamilton:

I am very glad to hear from Mr. Edison that he will send you over in charge of the first phonograph. As soon as you are reasonably sure of the date of your starting, will you please cable me day of sailing and name of steamer.

Of course you will not yield to the curiosity of passengers who may wish to see the instrument on ship, as this would diminish the interest and dissipate the mystery with which I have arranged to surround the first appearance of the Phonograph in this country.... better not mention to anybody that you have the Phonograph.

(signed) G.E. Gouraud

Secrecy was further reinforced by an undated note from Edison to Hamilton asking that he inform anyone on the voyage who became curious about his journey that he was "simply Botanizing for amusement - catch on?" (sic)

The long wait before the phonograph's realization was more than Gouraud could contain and his public admiration for his friend drew an irritated Edison to ask him to "talk phonography, not Edison - I don't propose to be Barnun-ized".[1]

The Colonel was already dropping hints to selected journalists that 'something big' was going to be revealed at Menlo Park laboratory during 1888, and paid a visit to Edison in the spring. This is confirmed in a letter of May 24th reporting his recent departure for home on ss 'Elbe'.[2] It is likely that a reason for this visit was to discuss squeezing the most publicity out of the forthcoming invention. Two days after perfecting the phonograph on June 16th, Edison sent Gouraud the first Phonogram - Edison's name for a message recorded on a cylinder. It no longer exists but a transcript was made:

Friend Gouraud: *June 18 1888*

This is my first mailing phonogram. It will go to you in the regular United States mail from New York, via Southampton, North German Lloyd steamer 'Aller'. I send you by Mr. Hamilton a new phonograph - the first one of the new model that has left my hands, It has been put together very hurriedly and is not finished, as you will see. I have sent you a quantity of experimental phonograph blanks so you can talk back to me. I will send you Phonograms of talk and music by every mail leaving here until we get on to the best thing for the purpose.

Mrs. Edison and the baby are doing well. The baby's articulation is quite loud enough, but a trifle indistinct. It can be improved, but is not bad for a first experiment.[3] With kind regards.

T.A.E.

Hamilton and the machine arrived at Gouraud's house in south-east London on June 26th and there was haste to get it working because Gouraud sent Edison a cable on the following day:

"First phonograph received today every word perfectly clear and distinctly understood by every member of family including child seven years old accept heartiest congratulations on this unparalleled triumph of mind over matter"

Gouraud

Colonel Gouraud with a perfected phonograph, arguably the one depicted with Edison on June 16th 1888

Before the end of June accounts of the new phenomenon appeared in the British national and local newspapers and journals bolstered by letters from Gouraud, all quoting the first phonogram wholly or in part. Reporters were entertained at Little Menlo where they were regaled with Edison's words from the phonogram. Gouraud responded, also by phonogram on June 30th.

> Little Menlo 30th June 1888
> Upper Norwood,
> London
>
> Dear Edison,
>
> Ahem. I cabled you the due receipt of your first phonogram. It was an indescribable sensation to us all to hear perfectly distinctly the familiar tones of your voice here in England 3,000 miles from where you had spoken, and ten days after...... The entire press chronicled this latest triumph of your genius in appropriate terms. I am literally bombarded with letters and besieged by visitors ......
>
> Very sincerely yours, George Edward Gouraud.

Gouraud started a practice of sending two phonograms a week but Edison had not sent any more by August 24th despite his promise in his phonogram. It was found that Gouraud's cylinders were arriving broken and cracked in New Jersey owing to careless handling by 'postal officers' - presumably customs examiners - and Edison gave written instructions to Gouraud to have secure transit boxes made at the London end.[4]

On August 15th Gouraud held the first of a number of gatherings "to meet Mr. Edison - eloquentem sed not presentem," speaking but not present, and a programme of cylinders included several recitations by the inventor and also simple musical items. Hamilton operated the phonograph and also coped with a breakdown. This social muster at Little Menlo was the first of many similar.

These episodes make a good story and superficially run easily together and have been accepted in this form in several articles and books by serious researchers and writers. Edison perfected the phonograph, it was carried over in secrecy to Gouraud who 'boomed' it, launching it at Society level, while its American promotion was noticeably less vigorous, relying almost entirely on press reports and some hall demonstrations.

The first to deviate from the accepted account lighted on the phonograph part of the story and called this into doubt,[5] that Edison would surely not have parted with a successful machine that had needed so much time and effort, but would have had reserve parts made up into the machine for Gouraud. This is of course hinted at in the first phonogram of June 18th:

> "........ the first one of the new model that has left my hands, It has been put together very hurriedly and is not finished......"

Early recording scene in the Music Room of "Little Menlo", with Colonel Gouraud on the left with family and friends. This room is the one on the left of the tower in the architect's drawing. The small boy is Powers Gouraud and J. Lewis Young is said to be operating the phonograph

Edison spoke this first phonogram more for the public's ear than for Gouraud's, all part of the promotion they both sought. As will be shown we do have Edison's word that there was only one completed model available.

Again, Gouraud was reported by an outsider as having left America on the 'Elbe' on the Monday prior to May 24th 1888 and presumably crossed to England. He must have returned within two weeks as he appears in W.K.L. Dickson's photograph bearing the date of June 16th 1888 and showing Edison and the Perfected Phonograph and several close staff at Menlo

Park. It is now certain that Gouraud accompanied Hamilton and the phonograph on June 18th on the 'Aller' on the voyage to London. As well as the first phonogram of that date they also brought over a further cylinder that Gouraud refers to in his phonogram of July 24th:

> "..... the two phonograms I have, one the first phonogram and the other one the dialogue between yourself and myself and not sufficiently distinct for the ordinary hearer ..... you spoke very loud and I spoke a little loud too"

Although never likely to be confirmed it is probable that Edison and Gouraud jointly composed the first phonogram. The piece of news about 'the baby' was merely a stratagem maintaining that Gouraud was in London over that period. Put together where do these inconsistencies lead? Why should Gouraud's American presence and return with the Phonograph and cylinders be clothed in such secrecy - presumably to meet Gouraud's intentions of his letter of November 30th 1887. Yet he allowed himself to be pictured at the laboratory, perhaps out of regard for his hero. Publicity is not a blanket answer for Edison's and Gouraud's joint duplicity, however mild and harmless, but it is difficult to offer another hypothesis. It was an elaborate staging for a simple play, but some of Edison's actions at times were puzzling.

Finally, a letter that Edison probably dictated unmindful of its future interest to researchers; it is dated June 18th 1888, two days after the Perfected Phonograph and the day of his first phonogram; it was a reply to Mrs. Joseph Swan, who had written to Edison asking for a

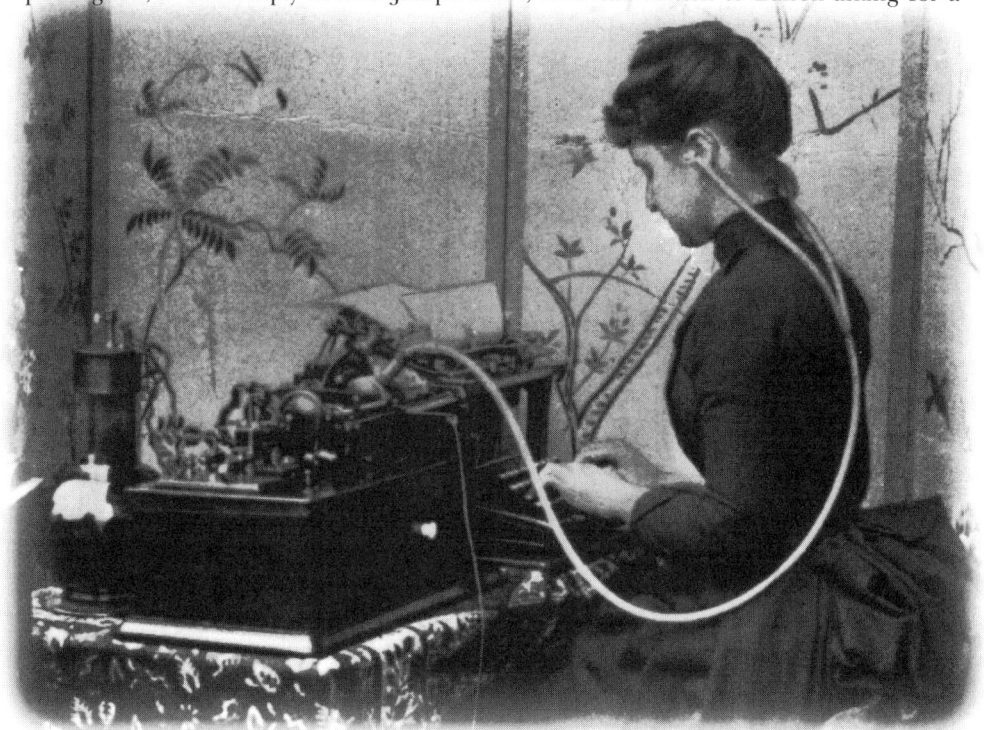

Mrs. Ferguson taking typing from an Edison phonograph at "Little Menlo", probably the first woman to do this in the United Kingdom

phonograph, She was the wife of the prominent British electrical engineer and inventor, then living in South-east London:

> Orange, N.J. June 18 1888
> Mrs. Joseph W. Swan,
> Lauriston,
> Bromley,
> Kent,
> England.
>
> Dear Mrs, Swan,
>
> It would give me much pleasure were I able to comply with your request contained in your letter under date 1st inst. Col. George E. Gouraud, who represents the Phonograph in Europe, came over here specially to obtain a Phonograph and returned to England this morning, taking with him the only perfect instrument which has yet been turned out of our factory. It will be at least six weeks before we have even a small supply of instruments........
>
> (signed) Thomas A. Edison

This again confirms Gouraud's visit to Edison just when he was supposed to be expecting the imminent arrival of the phonograph at his London home, but the courteous excuse to Mrs. Swan's unusual and eager request still leaves the door slightly ajar on the matter of which phonograph, and the reader may decide on the evidence shown.

It is a pity that none of the very first Perfected Phonographs has survived.

Notes

1) Memorandum of March 2nd 1888
2) Letter to Edison dated May 24th and sent at Gouraud's direction
3) Madeleine Edison, born May 31st, and the first child of Edison's second marriage
4) Arthur Payne to Hamilton, July 24th 1888
5) Peter Martland: article in *Hillandale News* June 1988

Material from the Edison Archive or from private sources

Appendix IV

EDISON PHONOGRAPHS and EDISON BELL

The full story of the setting-up of Edison phonograph sales outlets beyond the United States and especially in Great Britain is told in detail in Frank Andrews's book *The Edison Phonograph - The British Connection*. The following account is necessarily much abridged, but serving to introduce the reader to the several special models sold by Edison Bell.

Edison's National Phonograph Company Ltd. began operating a British branch in London in May 1903[1] for the purpose of making records and selling phonographic equipment. This was the culmination of more than a troublesome decade of the Edison United Phonograph Company selling the products of the Edison works in the United Kingdom and on the continent of Europe at first through a branch in London established in 1890 and then through the British organized Edison Bell Phonograph Corporation Ltd. Edison United had disposed of 20 Edison Letters Patent in Phonographs and Graphophones to this company for £40,000 between November 1892 and February 1893, passing Edison Bell control over all cylinder machine sales in Great Britain and some other countries, with the result that all other traders had to apply to them for a licence. This now meant that not only could Edison not sell his own Phonographs directly there, but Edison Bell had rights over any improvements his laboratory might make to the phonograph in the meantime.

The consequence of this situation should not be underrated, because following objections by Edison Bell, features on Edison Phonographs underwent changes that appeared on machines produced for world markets.

Relations between Edison in New Jersey and Edison Bell in London were bad and led to legal actions, but Edison Bell took large shipments of machines and Edison was only waiting for the day when his patents would start to expire in 1903 and a move to London would be worthwhile. The man who had brought the Perfected Phonograph to London, Colonel Gouraud, had set up Edison United Phonograph Company there in 1890, but his pronounced individuality caused him to be ousted; the London Stereoscopic and Phonographic Company, remembered for its poor promotional service to the tinfoil Phonographs was out of handling Edison goods by December 1891, but on the scene would come James E. Hough of The London Phonograph Company, later with Edisonia Ltd. and the Edison Bell companies, and he would be a thorn in Edison's side even after Edison's company had started trading in London as The National Phonograph Co. Ltd.

Machines sent over for distribution in Great Britain were the following:

pre—1891

The first models that would have arrived in London were electric models of the CLASS M type (battery); these were called:

Exhibition

with 14 hearing tubes and 6 free records cost £50 royalty + £50 a year quarterly in advance.

Drawing Room

with 8 hearing tubes cost £10 annual rental, records 5s, to 6s. 6d. (home use only)

from April 1891

The first MODEL C electric phonographs, having the motor situated centrally under the top plate to save space by shortening the machine.[2] The governor under the top plate controlled the motor speed by breaking the circuit.[3] There were two layouts available to this machine, the earlier with the feedscrew on the main shaft, probably cut to 100 threads per inch; the second design had the feedscrew cut more coarsely on a parallel shaft and driven by a perforated belt on pinned pulleys. The ratio of these determined the rotation of the feedscrew and 200 t.p.i. was used on the commercial (or office) machines. By slipping off the mandrel a smaller mandrel for mailing blanks was exposed.

A secondary cell battery was recharged from DC power sources.

From May 1893

A similar-looking version of the above was produced but the belt-pulleys driving the parallel feedscrew were changed to make the outside face of the belt drive the secondary pulley, a unique arrangement in the Edison Phonograph series. This successful machine continued into the first years of the 20th Century as either a 200 t.p.i. commercial machine with secondary cell battery or a clockwork form with Capps motor for £15 0s. 0d. each or as a 100 t.p.i. electric Drawing Room Phonograph for £15 0s. 0d. and supplied with a 14 in. flared horn. This was also available with spring motor at the same price. Pre-recorded 200 t.p.i. cylinders for some of these phonographs and called London records were available from 1893 to 1897 and perhaps later, but no listing has been seen.[4]

Measurements: height 13 in; base 17 in. x 10 in.

Weight: 54 to 58 lb. according to sources

(This machine is depicted in the chapter on Edison Business Phonographs)

December 1897

The first Multiplex (Gress Automatic) Phonograph arrives in London. 1,000 were ordered for London by May 1898 where they would be known as Type 5. The last of these 5-mandrel slot machines were still being cleared out in 1905 for £10 10s. 0d. each.

For some years from 1896-7 Edison Bell persisted in ordering and distributing Edison phonographs in the United Kingdom using their own Type numbers for identification. Sometimes, as they came into production, different machines were allocated to the numbers and leading to confusion in transatlantic correspondence with Edison United Phonograph. These phonographs generally bear a plate with a Licence declaration and Type Number. No plates were put on at the Edison works.

Most of the Types have been identified, as follows:

TYPE 1 GEM (originally to be Type 3)	early 1899
TYPE 2 STANDARD	April 29th 1898
TYPE 3 HOME (originally to be Type 1)	October 1897
TYPE 4 Large Clockwork Commercial - displaced by SPRING MOTOR with Automatic Reproducer	1898
TYPE 5 Multiplex, complete with cabinet and coin-slot phonograph (The Gress Automatic)	April 22nd 1898
TYPE 6 CLASS M with Bettini attachment (known as The Exhibition with Bettini's Diaphragm)	April 3rd 1898
SPRING MOTOR with Bettini horn and reproducer Also additional markings such as Type "CONCERT"	

By July 1900 Edison Bell's holdings of some of Edison's 16 current British patents had been sustained in the United Kingdom and an opinion was sought from an eminent American lawyer Judge Howard W. Hayes on what modifications would need to be made to Edison machines sent to Edison Bell territory, at the same time making allowance for the impending expiry dates of several of these patents. The most sensitive would be No. 19153 of 1889 (applied for Nov. 28th 1889, expiring Nov. 28th 1903) Claims 7 and 8 embodying cam lift lever, spring lock to swinging gate, twin nuts on the feed mechanism and sliding spring actuated knife for the shaving device. The first three of these were replaced by the pin lift, locking latch and single half-nut, but the sliding spring was left unchanged. National Phonograph was warned to expect litigation over the recorder diaphragm clamped with yielding material, and the glass diaphragm, tapering mandrel, straight edge, recorder and reproducer with retarding device, circular cutter, ball reproducer, jewel recorder and reproducer, the soap blank and the cylindrical blank with tapering bore. Several of these patents had a short time to run and it was thought unlikely that Edison Bell would sue on all of them.

To this end Edison procrastinated and received warnings from Edison Bell's legal advisers as well as from Judge Hayes, but Edison Bell started suing unlicensed British persons or firms found in possession of these illegally equipped phonographs, and moderate costs were usually awarded against them.[5] By April 1902 it was agreed to send replacement parts to the Edison depot at Antwerp for altering the offending machines to having a lift pin on the carrier-arm, locking latch on the swinging gate and a single half-nut welded or brazed to its arm.

In an attempt to clear the air W. E. Gilmore, president of National Phonograph Company at West Orange wrote to James Hough, then sales manager of Edison Bell, to stop further litigation; Hough agreed, subject to a commission of 5 per cent on Edison's United Kingdom sales, and Gilmore accepted.

Curiously the one patent (British No. 26219 of December 1898) over which Edison Bell had no control was owned by The American Graphophone Company of Washington. D.C. Under this, its licencees, including Edison Bell were restrained from offering a phonograph that could play Concert (or Grand) cylinders. Edison Bell meanwhile had been selling both Edison and Graphophone large cylinder phonographs, the Edisons of the old-style case period, the Graphophones (called 'Combination A-1 Grand') from September-October 1900 or even earlier, and was prepared to sit out the slow turning of legal machinery until the patent holders could get a restraining injunction through the courts.[6]

The outcome was that Graphophone threatened proceedings against anyone handling Edison CONCERT phonographs, whereupon Edison Bell counterclaimed for the infringement of the Edison Bell licence the company held, and the cases were held simultaneously in the summer of 1900 but in different courts. One of the results was that Edison Bell was restrained from supplying Graphophones and large cylinders of 12.5 c.m. in diameter (Grand or Concert-size) covered by Graphophone Company's aforementioned patent.

It is not known whether there was a resulting privately-made reciprocal agreement between Edison Bell and Graphophone, but the verdict seemed to make no difference to Edison Bell who continued to offer Concert-type phonographs of Edison and Graphophone origin, made only to play the large cylinder.

A new catalogue, floated on July 16th 1902 offered some fresh machines from Edison Bell, and of especial interest were two modified Edison CONCERT Phonographs. The first was the Edison CONCERT GRAND, being the regular Edison CONCERT but with a mandrel for Standard sized cylinders as well as a slip-on Concert mandrel. This came with a large nickel horn and stand and with accessories cost £25 0s. 0d.[7] The second was the Edison NEW DUPLEX with similar Standard and slip-on Concert mandrel, but with the single spring Edison HOME motor assembly in place of the Capps 3-spring motor, and this was said to run for four records. Complete with self-supportive aluminum horn the price was £15 0s. 0d.

The £25 0s. 0d. would soon prove a high figure because next year Edison's National Phonograph Company was offering the CONCERT in Great Britain for £15 15s. 0d. Could it have been that Graphophone was demanding a high licence fee following the settlement of the litigation? As a way out these two CONCERT-based phonographs from Edison Bell were

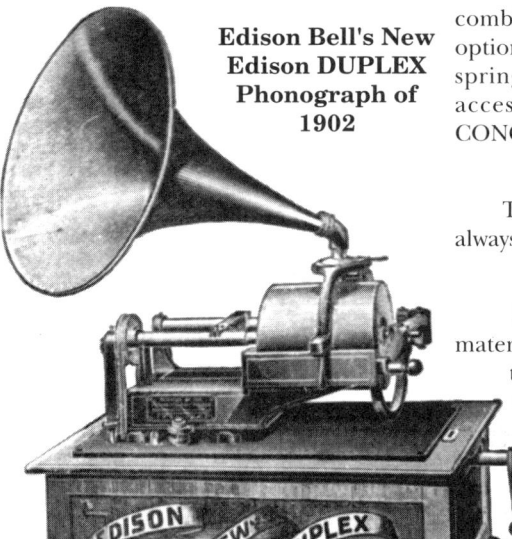

Edison Bell's New Edison DUPLEX Phonograph of 1902

combined into the CONCERT DUPLEX, with optional Concert and Standard mandrels and 3-spring motor and priced at £17 5s. 0d. with accessories. It was the same as the earlier CONCERT GRAND.

The large cylinders made by Edison Bell were always marketed as 'Concert Grand'.

Searches among Edison machine archive material have not yet revealed any reference to these 'specials'. Although the mechanisms are obviously Edison-made, the cabinets bear marks of local construction and finish; were the Standard-Concert conversions carried out in London? After 1903 Edison Bell's supplies were cut off from Edison, and the post-1903 CONCERT DUPLEX would probably have been offered from stock on the shelves, and for a time the company resorted to dubious expedients to import them.[8] Nevertheless Edison Bell made plans to manufacture its own, and the Edison Bell STANDARD, a close copy of Edison's STANDARD is first noticed in November 1903 when it sold for £2 12s. 6d. The Edison Bell GEM followed in 1905 when it sold for £2 5s. 0d. in a fumed oak case or £2 10s. 0d. in a 'highly polished' case.[9] The Edison Bell New Model Reproducer was sold with these machines; it closely resembled the Edison Model C Reproducer.

The HOME motor took the place of the 3-spring Triton motor in Edison Bell's DUPLEX machine

James Hough was told to cease using the words GEM, STANDARD and HOME, and when Edison Bell's version of Edison's HOME came out in 1906 it was named the Homestead, and the GEM and STANDARD were displaced by an entirely new range. Hough agreed to stop trading in Edison machines in May 1905 on condition that Edison bought back phonographs already supplied to Edison Bell, but the inventor refused and Edison Bell resorted to stratagems to clear stocks.[10]

This feuding between Edison and Edison Bell in London is now more fully researched, but the full story of the special phonographs and the conversions are not known. Were they sent over assembled, who made the cabinets, and why were the electric CLASS C not sold in the United States in any quantities, and why were the 200 t.p.i. cylinders not followed up until 15 years later? These are only some of the questions.

The Edison Company occupied the upper floors of 52 Grays Inn Road, London, for a few months in 1903, before moving a mile away to Clerkenwell Green.

NOTES
1) The first address was 52 Grays Inn Road, London
2) British Patent No. 15,206 of July 9th 1892, applied for September 8th 1891 by Col. G.E. Gouraud on Edison's behalf. This style was not given an American patent.
3) U.S. Patent No. 513,097 for Phonograph originally filed December 3rd 1890 by Edison and granted January 23rd 1894. Two brushes, one in permanent contact with the governor shaft comprised the circuit.
4) Said to have 136 yards of groove per cylinder and to play for 6 minutes. The only two survivors reported however are said to be short on recorded area.
5) For example in April 1902 Edison Bell sued Waterfield Clifford for having a SPRING MOTOR phonograph with twin half nuts and locking bolt actuated by a spring. Costs of £30 18s. 10d. were awarded, but settled for £28 0s. 0d. Another case against H. Heathcote was settled for £45 5s. 0d.
6) It is thought that Pathé Frères were licensed to make duplex Graphophones for European distribution, and in support a picture of the Edison Bell Combination A 1 Grand suggests one or two Pathé features. However a reversible motor-board Edison Bell Duplex Grand has been seen, numbered 311; although bearing no particular distinguishing marks it is of a European continental make other than Pathé, so Edison Bell had several sources of supply. To add further to the confusion, the Edison Bell Victor Concert Phonograph, a small duplex machine in the 1902-3 catalogue, is noted as being a 'Graphophone type'.
7) On July 1st 1902 James Hough wrote to W.E. Gilmore at West Orange that CONCERT machines becoming obsolete through the Gold Moulded process should have dual mandrels and adapter as Hough had earlier shown Edison. It might sell for $60.00. Hough further recommended to Edison that the CONCERT machine should have an improved cabinet and made mechanically more reliable, a roller on the carrier-arm and a shaving box would help.
8) Hough used business friends and employees to try and import Edison machines. One batch was traced to an address that was found to be his stable.
9) The Edison Bell GEM had a motor similar to Edison's, but with the governor contained within the motor frame and a different stop-start and speed control.
10) One Edison Bell advertisement of February 1904 placed in the *Ironmonger's Gazette* had 'Edison' and 'Bell' on different lines and in different type.

Use has been made of items of correspondence from the Edison Archive.

The Edison Works at Chandos Road, Willesden Junction, London, from 1907-1913. It was said that the sign was 456 ft. long and had an average height of 20 ft. The lettering was painted in two colours

Appendix V

THE CIRCUMSTANCES OF THE INTRODUCTION OF THE EDISON MODEL C PHONOGRAPHS

The Model C phonographs were the hurried outcome of the last major lawsuit involving Edison's companies and which incidentally brought to an end Graphophone molestation of them. It was a protracted legal process over 14 years, absorbing large sums of money that could have been better spent; leading it was a former friend of Edison.

Edison was frequently unfortunate in his friends, and James L. Andem formerly of The Ohio Phonograph Company and a one-time Edison manager, had with backing from Graphophone organized opposition to Edison interests ever since 1894 when North American went into bankruptcy. One of the main grudges was the strict Edison control of licensees, still requiring them to sell machines instead of leasing them, a policy that produced a faster financial return.

Andem, now secretary of The New York Phonograph Company, one of the survivors of the original 1890 group of Local Companies set up by Lippincott and others, started to retaliate and by 1905-6 was producing injunctions forbidding National Phonograph to sell phonograph products that involved a number of assigned patents granted Edison from 1888 to 1894.[1] A start was made on what now may seem to be minor items, the cylinder with plain or spiral ribs (414,761 of 1889) and the use of the mica diaphragm (454,941 of 1891). This brought about the substitution of mica by copper diaphragms and for a while cylinders were given a smooth interior, though soon reverting as the patent ran out. It also brought a letter from the Edison company to all New York traders offering them protection if proceeded against for allegedly infringing these patents.

In 1907-8 further pressure led the Edison staff to declare 29 or more patents on which the Edison phonographs, domestic and office, records, shaving machines, accessories and processes depended, and after lengthy Court actions Edison was found guilty of violation and fined $2,500 with $1,500 costs. Andem's company immediately threatened every trader in the State of New York for violations over the past two years and brought 228 actions against jobbers and dealers in New York City, but did not pursue them pending a test case against one of them.

This sorry business led in 1908 to hurried changes being made to the Model B range of machines and Gold Moulded cylinders supplied to the trade in New York State and in due course this would affect the style of the Edison company's entire machines, records and some accessories. From that time cylinders were no longer made by the vacuous gold deposit method but by the graphite process. This was apparently just as efficient and opened the way to its use in all cylinder making and the term 'Gold Moulded' disappeared from all Edison literature.

In a letter of February 7th 1908 from Edison's legal adviser Frank L. Dyer he recommended features to be eliminated from Edison phonographs to comply with legal restraints, and these modifications affected equipment thus:

1) (sapphire) Shaving apparatus to be dispensed with
2) Material other than a jewel as recording and reproducing styli[2]
3) A single feed nut instead of a twin
4) This to be riveted, brazed or soldered to the arm
5) A pin lift device to be substituted for the cam lift lever
6) The end gate to be dispensed with on all but the GEM
7) All electric machines to have horizontally mounted motors
8) All electric motor machines to have a friction governor
9) A belt tightener on electric machines not dependent on sliding the bedplate; this now had to be fixed
10) On these machines the cushions between frame and bedplate to be dispensed with

All business correspondence and transactions with the trade in New York State and offices there were closed. Repairs would be carried out on machines sent in from the area but no parts could be renewed, only repaired; even sapphire points could only be repolished and replacements would be glass or Carborundum.[3] Edison phonograph owners will understand how difficult could be the implementing of such restructuring, although one or two of the changes were minor. To the outside world the company gave its reasons for discarding the shaver as being the substitution of the centre bearing for that on the end gate, thus making a smooth shaving operation more difficult; it was also stated that removal of the end gate eliminated a source of damage to cylinders when being put on or removed.

The first substitute tried for a sapphire stylus was glass, and instructions were given by the factory superintendent Peter Weber to make styli from hard Jena glass. From April 4th 1908 he stipulated reproducers on phonographs to have the stylus point made from Carborundum. It is not known how many of these styli were actually sent out because patent rights of the New York company were running out, and so were its funds, and Andem was indicted for forgery in another phonograph company. National Phonograph won an appeal in Andem's prosecution of Sol B. Davega, the trader in the test case.

Having gone over to production of the gate-less, shaver-less Model C range of machines for New York and complied with several other of the earlier retrogressive requirements, the Edison company made the best of them and commended them in advertising material as technological improvements; hardly true, but that was the Edison way of putting a brave face on the situation. Though seen through this number of years it seems little more than a storm in a teacup, but the future of the Edison phonograph was put in jeopardy. The vindictive Andem and his supporters goaded the phonograph into technical retreat, but this spurred Edison and his mechanics to give fresh thought to 20 year old styles and soon led to the first AMBEROLAS in a matter of months and the OPERA in a couple of years, the highest forms the phonograph would achieve.

The Company maintained secrecy over this new Model C phonograph, as there was up to three months stock of Model B machines and spares, and concern was expressed lest Edison dealers outside the State of New York should start placing orders for the new models before the Model Bs had been cleared. Typical instructions to the Company's managing director in London were that "should you instruct us to forward you samples of the different Model C machines, they should be kept in a room at Willesden under lock and key, in order to prevent any possibility of their being seen by any of your trade or our own people other than yourself." Apart from the managing director, who would be left to see them?

Looking back, it is difficult to understand how The National Phonograph Company could have expected its New York traders to keep silence on the arrival of new Edison models while everyone outside was handling obsolescent stock. Could it have been that transgressors would find themselves on the Company's Suspended List?

Notes:
1) Edison had lost his patents to Lippincott's North American Phonograph Company, but acquired them again when this concern was made bankrupt in 1894, and he turned them over to National Phonograph on its formation in January 1896.
2) Frank L. Dyer wrote once that up to 1893 Edison had upwards of 65 patents in jewelled styli - Edison Archive
3) February 1908 memos between C. H. Wilson and Peter Weber - Edison Archive

Appendix VI

CHARLES BATCHELOR'S RECOLLECTIONS OF THE PHONOGRAPH INVENTION

In the chapters on the development of the early phonographs credit has been given to the work of Charles Batchelor (1845-1910). Batchelor liked writing articles on the Edison experiments either for such journals as *The English Mechanic*, or for his meticulous diary, knowing that he was in the presence of the making of history. The following appears in the entry following Friday October 12th 1906.

"My recollections of Mr. Edison" - No. 1, the invention of the Phonograph

"This occurred at Menlo Park N.J. in the Edison Laboratory about the middle of the month of November 1877. I was Mr. Edison's chief assistant at that time and had been so for some years - we had been at work off and on for years previous to this time and had developed a system of automatic telegraphy, one of the instruments for which consisted of a rapidly running small wheel carrying forward a strip of paper, with a stylus resting on it to record chemically the dots and dashes that came over the line. Some of these instruments we had in the laboratory and much of the paper. We had also for a long time been developing the Edison Carbon Telephone, an instrument in which a diaphragm produced the human voice. Many of these instruments were in the laboratory at the time and we used them daily. Some years previous to this date we had designed and made some machines for coating paper with paraffin (similar to the paper now used to wrap candy in) for making condensers for electrical work and a large lot of variable thicknesses of this paper coated and uncoated was stocked away in the cupboards.

When making different sized telephone diaphragms it was a very common usage to mount them in a frame with a mouthpiece, hold them up and talk to them in a loud or low voice; at the same time putting a finger close to the centre to feel how much vibration was communicated to them.

One night after supper (which was prepared for us a midnight) and at which all the principal workers sat down together, Mr. Edison who had been trying different diaphragms in this manner suddenly remarked 'Do you know Batch I believe if we put a point on the centre of that diaphragm and talked to it whilst we pulled some of that waxed paper under it so that it could indent it, it would give us back talking when we pulled the paper through the second time' - the brilliancy of the suggestion did not at first strike any of us - it was so obvious that it would do so that everyone said 'why of coarse it must!'

I said 'We'll try it mighty quick!' and we went to work. Mr. Kruesi the chief mechanican took the diaphragm to solder on to it at the middle a needle point about ¼ in. long; he also took one of the automatic telegraph wheels and stands to fasten the diaphragm to so that we could draw the paper through easily. I cut and got ready some strips of paper of different thicknesses of paraffin coating. It was a matter of an hour or so when we all got together again to make a trial - we fixed the instrumentation to a table and I put in a strip of paper and adjusted the needle point down until it just pressed lightly on the paper. Mr. Edison sat down and putting his mouth to the mouthpiece delivered one of our favorite stereotyped sentences used in experimenting on the telephone 'Mary had a Little Lamb' whilst I pulled the paper through.

We looked at the strip and noticed the irregular marks, then we put it in again and I pulled it through as nearly the same speed as I had pulled it in the first place and we got 'ary ad el llam' something that was not fine talking but the shape of it was there, and so like the talking that we all let out a yell of satisfaction and a 'Golly it's there!!' and shook hands all round. We tried it many times and in many different ways continually improving the apparatus during the early morning. During the time that some of these changes were being made Edison and I would talk about the possibilities of such an invention and it was then that we fully realized the brilliancy of suggestion and the magnitude of its possible applications. Before breakfast the next morning we had reproduced almost perfect articulation from a strip of the wax paper which I had embossed as it were with a ridge in the middle running the whole length, the middle point in this case was ground chisel shaped.

Before the next night we had reproduced speech from a strip of tinfoil using again a rounded point needle; this was so remarkable that we decided to design a machine to experiment with. In a few days about the beginning of Dec. 1877 we had this instrument finished. It consisted of a cylinder of brass turned by hand that was provided on its surface with a spiral groove running the whole length and being about ⅛ in. apart; the shaft was cut the same pitch so that when the handle was turned the cylinder moved forward uniformly.

A talking diaphragm was mounted on one side of the cylinder to record the speech, and a more delicate diaphragm was mounted on the other side to reproduce the same. Each diaphragm could be moved away from the cylinder at will so that only one was in operation at a time. The nut that the screw thread on the shaft engaged with could also be disengaged so that cylinder could be set back quick.

The cylinder was covered with a sheet of tinfoil and a suitable device was provided to hold it. This sheet could be put on and reproduced many times; the needle most generally used was a rounded point. Many thousands of experiments were made with this machine, and similar ones made immediately after, some of which were exhibited in different parts of the country and Europe whilst great crowds of people came almost every day to Menlo Park to hear with astonishment the reproduction of their own voices."

Appendix VII

SOME SELECTED POEMS IN PRAISE OF EDISON PHONOGRAPHS

The flush of 19th Century invention attracted many writers of poetry often to the most unlikely subjects, and with each new creation, poems good and bad appeared in the press, encouraged also in competitions arranged by journals and newspapers. Those published about the Cylinder Phonograph ran into scores, probably hundreds eventually, and these started to appear as soon as Edison's TINFOIL Phonograph began to be known about from the first days of 1878.

The earliest such verses to be found were in an unidentified journal dated February 27th 1878 by Perry F. Nursey and dedicated to Henry Edmunds. Edmunds had been present on the previous December 6th at Menlo Park laboratory when Edison and Kruesi had been experimenting with the new invention, and had had a letter published in the London *Times* of January 17th that drew public attention to what Edison had achieved. (See Appendix II)

> LINES ON HEARING THE PHONOGRAPH
> Now Adam, Noah, Melchisedic,
>   And all their friends would laugh,
> Could they but visit earth again
>   And hear the phonograph
>
> Sure Memnon, son of morning's voice
>   Could not be more melodious,
> Nor could old Stentor's roaring lungs
>   E'er utter sounds more odious
>
> The former's smooth as brooklet flows,
>   The latter's harsh as medicine,
> But smooth or rough, like honour goes
>   To Thomas Alva Edison.

The attention that the poets were giving his invention must have appealed to Edison because two months later he copied out the following lines in his own hand and the paper is still in the Edison Archive files.

AN UTTERANCE BY THE EDISON PHONOGRAPH
Behold! What marvels meet our sight,
Where science sheds her wond'rous light
I'm but a brass and iron thing
Yet I can talk and laugh and sing,
Can cough and sneeze and also kiss
If but quite near, a sweet young miss.
Give me a message to your friend,
Your very voice he'll hear, depend.
Ah! I'll re-hear what you have said
When years are passed and you are dead.
Perchance in time I may repeat
Niagara's roar-old oceans beat,
The thunder roll-the battle's stroke
The siren's song-the organ's note.
I'm made by one whose worthy name
His thoughts and deeds exalt to fame
And Edison shall ever stand
Among the famous of our land.
               M. Hudson, New York author, April 1878

After some further attention from the poets, interest faded for 10 years until the arrival of the 'perfected' phonographs in 1888 when the very first poem had the most frequently quoted verses of them all. It was recorded by its author, Rev. Horatio Nelson Powers D.D. of Piermont on the Hudson, NY at the West Orange laboratory on June 16th 1888, the very day of the perfection of the Edison phonograph. This cylinder in all probability crossed the Atlantic with Colonel Gouraud and the phonograph, although it does not get a mention on that account. At the same time a leaflet commemorating the event was issued. The poem was dedicated to Mr. Edison and addressed to Col. Gouraud - Powers was Gouraud's brother-in-law - but it was widely reported as being played at social gatherings organized by Gouraud at Little Menlo, London.

THE PHONOGRAPH'S SALUTATION
I seize the palpitating air. I hoard
Music and Speech. All lips that breathe are mine.
I speak, and the inviolable word
Authenticates its origin and sign.

I am a tomb, a Paradise, a throne;
An angel, prophet, slave, immortal friend:
My living records, in their native tone,
Convict the knave, and disputations end.

In me are souls embalmed. I am an ear
Flawless as truth, and truth's own tongue am I.
I am a resurrection; men may hear
The quick and dead converse, as I reply.

> *Hail English shores, and homes, and marts of peace!*
> *New trophies, Gouraud, yet are to be won.*
> *May "sweetness, light" and brotherhood increase!*
> *I am the latest-born of Edison.*

That poem was re-used over the years when it was thought perhaps that Edison readers had forgotten about it; it was shortened and condensed on occasion, and the final verse adapted to saluting someone other than Edison, H. M. Stanley for instance in January 1893:

> *Hail, broadening realms of knowledge and of peace,*
> *The trophies, Stanley, by steadfast faith were won,*
> *May light, and truth and brotherhood increase!*
> *I am the latest boon of Edison.*

Only one poem of this time has been found that favoured the Graphophone.

Often the most ingenious verses were those submitted by dealers who had perhaps used them in window displays or in local advertising. After its appearance in the *Edison Phonograph Monthly* of April 1903 the following ten lines were repeated on occasional Edison printed matter over the years, but the publishing of phonographic verses had practically ceased by the end of the first World War.

EDISON'S LATEST

P stands for Phonograph of Edison's make
H stands for Him who will no other take
O stands for Orders which exceed the supply
N stands for Natural Tone of records you buy.
O stands for Others of inferior kind
G stands for GEM not left behind
R stands for Records, the best in the land
A stands for Artists in Edison's Band
P stands for People who own a machine
H stands for Happiness there to be seen.

Newspaper advertisement submitted by a Mr. Bowen,
a dealer at Kawanee, IL.

WHAT DID IT COST? SOME PARALLELS WITH 1900

In 1900 an Edison GEM Phonograph cost $7.50, an Edison STANDARD $20.00 and an Edison CONCERT $100.00!

Today these seem like great bargains, and we all have a spare seven dollars and fifty cents which we would readily spend on a GEM. But in 1900....

We cannot properly judge the cost of merchandise from our vantage point so close to the end of the twentieth century. A pound of sugar for 4 cents, a dozen eggs for 14 cents and a pound of butter at 24 cents all sound like marvellous bargains.

Further bargains by today's standards include a 2 quart rice double boiler for 25 cents, a 4 quart gray enamelled coffee pot for 29 cents and the Sunday *New York Times* for 3 cents. Gentlemen's Madras pajamas were available $1.00 a suit, ladies' summer dresses on sale for $25.00; ladies' black kid skin boots at $1.00 a pair. Gentlemen's suits were to be had at a cost of $20.00 to $25.00, with selected styles and fabrics as low as $12.00. For entertainment the well-dressed lady or gentleman could attend a performance at Proctor's Vaudeville Theatre with a choice of tickets at 15 cents, 25 cents or 50 cents or take a nine-day cruise from New York to Bermuda, all expense paid for $37.50.

A special sale of building lots in Brooklyn, NY, in the fashionable Flatbush area, just one mile from Prospect Park, ranged between $190.00 and $590.00 each, and could be purchased for $2.00 down, and $1.50 to $2.00 weekly at 4% interest[1]; or a high-stoop house on 183 Street in New York, just off Broadway rented for $45.00 per month.

But all of these bargains had to be balanced against the amount of income that a family had. In very few cases did a wife work; once she was married, a young woman left the job market to care for her husband, children and home. The exception might be a husband and wife domestic team, but most did not have families to raise.

For the husband, the workday started at seven or eight o'clock am., and continued until six o'clock pm; Saturday was often only a half a day's work! An article in the June 23rd 1900 issue of *The New York Times* dealt with a gentleman who threw his father out of the house, contending that on his $60.00 a month salary as a painter, he could not afford to take care of his own family and his father too! New York City gardeners were protesting the fact that most earned only $65.00 a month while a few selected men in their ranks commanded $75.00 a month.[2]

Starting salaries for a young man in an office were not nearly so generous. A salary of $30.00 per month for the first six months was offered and the position probably was filled very quickly. The average salary for a worker at the turn of the century ranged between $40.00 and $50.00 a month.

Young ladies had few options open to them in the job market; a (home) nurse commanded $20.00 a month, a dressmaker $1.50 a day, and a cook $25.00 a month.

One ad read: "Wanted, a refined Protestant seamstress and maid for three young girls; one capable of giving some assistance in management of the household preferred. Wages $20.00......"[3]

Funds for entertainment had to come out of the small monthly earnings, and when the cost of an Edison STANDARD Phonograph equalled approximately three weeks' wages, it became a major purchase. Despite that, Edison GEMS and STANDARDS and HOMES did sell, and sell by the thousands! And so did the cylinder records. Each week when new records were received by the dealers, owners of Edison phonographs lined up to hear the latest songs or vaudeville routines and buy them for the family's enjoyment at 35 cents each.

1) *New York Times* June 9th 1900
2) *New York Times* October 1st 1900
3) *New York Times* June 6th 1900

Contributed by Neil Maken

Acknowledgments

The author would like to express thanks to those who have helped in the preparation of this second edition by furnishing new material and photographs or making suggestions for improvement, thus enabling the earlier book to be expanded.

Of these, first and foremost must be mentioned the Edison Site at West Orange where the Archivist George Tselos and his staff did everything possible to find the appropriate files. In particular I must record my gratitude to Leah Burt for locating photographs and machines in the laboratory and vault, and for help with photography and overall encouragement.

The senior collector, Ray Phillips has most generously opened his files and sustained a protracted exchange of letters with his customary patience and knack of spotting errors, as well as loaning a number of fine photographs. Another, equally supportive with information and photographs has been Charley Hummel, expert in rare machines. Without the help of these kind people much would have been overlooked.

Again, many of Allen Koenigsberg's publications have supplied the answers, as well as his occasional letter, and this ready help and permission to quote from them is much appreciated. Likewise an extended help from Neil and Tracey Maken has uncovered fresh facts about the Edison Dolls, and their assistance in a difficult area is appreciated, as well as Neil's chapter on cost parallels.

Due to commitments my colleague of last time, Al Sefl has not been able to join with the edition, and he is missed. There are not many to touch his familiarity with the evolution of these machines and accessories, or close-up skill with a camera, and a number of photographs are included from the earlier book.

In conclusion I am indebted to Mark Ulano for allowing use of several high-grade photographs of early machines, and to many friends for photographs or loan of research material, including:-

Frank Andrews	Karl Frick	Seiro Shinagawa
Mike Appleton	Robert Halgrim	P & J Slikker
Mike Ball	Peter Martland	Dennis Teuscher
Ron Dethlefson	Dennis Norton	Tom Valle
John Fesler	Sam Sheena	John Woodward

Recommended Reading

The reader may find some of the following helpful, embracing as they do the several aspects of the Edison Phonographs. Some of the earlier, obscure and lightweight books have been omitted from this edition; some may still be bought from publishers listed at the end, while others may be hunted through specialized book dealers. List compiled July 1994.

ANDEM, James L. - *A Practical Guide to the Use of the Edison Phonograph* (1892) - Cincinnati, OH, U.S.A.

ANDREWS, Frank - *The Edison Phonograph - The British Connection* (1986) C.L.P.& G.S. booklet

BELLE, Harry - *Spreekmachines* (1989), in Dutch with supplemental description of the machines in English - Zaanenlaan 52, 2024 ZB HAARLEM, Holland

CHARBON, Paul - *La Phonographe à la Belle Epoque* (1977), in the French language - 19 Rue de Kembs, 67100 STRASBOURG, France

CHEW, V. K. - *Talking Machines* (1981) - Science Museum, London, SW 7

CLARK, Ronald W. - *Edison, the Man who made the Future* (1977) - George Rainbird, Ltd., 36 Park Lane, London W1Y 4DE

CONOT, Robert - *Thomas A. Edison, A Streak of Luck* - Vestal Press Ltd.

DETHLEFSON, Ronald - *Edison Blue Amberol Recordings* 1912-1914 (second edition 1997) *Edison Blue Amberol Recordings* 1915-1929 (1981)

DICKSON, W. K. L. and A. - *Life and Inventions of Thomas Alva Edison* (1894) - Chatto & Windus, London

FROST, Lawrence A. - *The Thomas A. Edison Album* (1969) - Superior Publishing Co., SEATTLE, WA U.S.A.

FROW, George L. - *The Edison Disc Phonographs & the Diamond Discs* (1982)

GELATT, Ronald - *The Fabulous Phonograph* (second edition 1977) - Cassell & Co., London

GILLETT, William - *The Phonograph and How to Construct It* (1892) - Reprinted by George L. Frow

JEHL, Francis - *Edison, a Biography* (1959) - McGraw Hill Book Company Inc., New York, Toronto, London

JEHL, Francis - *Menlo Park Reminiscences* 3 vols. 1936, 1938, 1941 Edison Institute, Dearborn, MI, U. S. A.

JOSEPHSON, Francis - *Edison, A Biography* (1959) McGraw Hill Book Company, inc., New York, Toronto, London

KOENIGSBERG, Allen - *The Edison Cylinder Records 1889-1912* (1990) *The Patent History of the Phonograph 1877-1912* (1990) - APM Press, NY, U.S.A.

MAKEN, Neil - *Hand Cranked Phonographs, it all Started with Edison* (1994) - PO Box 6773, Huntington Beach, CA 92615

MILLARD, André - *Edison and the Business of Invention* (1990) - Edison National Historic Site

MOORE, Wendell - *Edison Phonograph Monthly* (1903-1916) - reprinted in 14 hardbound volumes and published by Wendell Moore, 6 E. Park St. Brazil, IN 47834

NATIONAL Phonograph Company - *The (Edison) Phonograph and How to Use It* (1900) - Facsimile Reprint by APM Press

PROUDFOOT, Christopher - *Collecting Phonographs & Gramophones* (1980) - Vista Division of Cassell, 35 Red Lion Square. LONDON WC1R 4SG

REISS, Eric L - *Compleat Talking Machine* (1986) - Vestal Press

SEYMOUR, Henry - *The Reproduction of Sound* (1918) - W. B. Tattersall Ltd, LONDON

TEWKSBURY, George E. - *Complete Manual of the Edison Phonograph* (1897) - National Phonograph Company

VANDERBILT, Byron M - *Thomas Edison, Chemist* (1971) - American Chemical Society

WILE, Raymond R - *Edison Disc Recordings* (1978) - a complete compilation; from The Edison National historic Site

WILE, Raymond and Ronald DETHLEFSON - *Edison Diamond Disc Re-Creations, Records and Artists 1910-1929* (1985)
Additional pages to above (1990)-Enquiries to R. Dethlefson

WELCH, Walter L. - *Charles Batchelor, Edison's Chief Partner* (1972) - Syracuse University, NY U.S.A.

WELCH, Walter L. & BURT, Leah S. - *From Tinfoil to Stereo* (1994 edition) - University Press of Florida ISBN 0-8130-1317-8

YOUNG, J. Lewis - *Edison and his Phonograph* (1890) - Edison United Phonograph Co. The Phonogram (London 1893), several issues bound into one booklet - C.L.P. & G.S. booklet

Addresses (1997)

A.P.M. Press, 502 East 17th Street, BROOKLYN, NY 11226 U.S.A.

C.L.P. & G.S. (City of London Phonograph & Gramophone Society) Booklist, c/o Don Moore, Woodbine Cottage, Brigg Road, CAISTOR, Lincs LN7 6RX Great Britain

DETHLEFSON, Ronald, 3605 Christmas Tree Lane, BAKERSFIELD, CA 93306 U.S.A.

EDISON National Historic Site, Main Street & Lakeside Avenue, WEST ORANGE, NJ 07052 U.S.A.

FROW, George L., 48 Woodfields, Chipstead, SEVENOAKS, Kent TN13 2RB Great Britain

VESTAL PRESS LTD., P.O. Box 97, VESTAL, NY 13850 U.S.A.

Springs for Phonographs

		Long ft.	Wide in.	Thick in.	Hole in.	Weight oz.
GEM Model A				-various-		
	B-C	11	5/8	0.020	3/8	-
	D-E	10	5/8	0.021	3/8	-
FIRESIDE A-B		10	7/8	0.030	7/16	14
STANDARD A*		10	7/8	0.030	7/16	14
	B-C-D-E-F-G	11	1	0.032	7/16	18
HOME A		11	1	0.032	7/16	18
	B-C-D-E-F	13 ½	1 5/16	0.030	7/16	24
SPRING MOTOR/TRIUMPH						
	A-B-C-D-E	14	2	0.022	7/8	34 ½
	F-G	13 ½	1 5/16	0.030	5/8	24
CONCERT (old style)		14	2	0.022	13/16	34 ½
	The earlier TRIUMPH spring will fit as replacement for CONCERT					
IDELIA	B-C-D-E	14	2	0.022	7/8	34 ½
AMBEROLA	(A)-I	16	2	0.024	7/8	-
	(B)-I III	13 ½	1 5/16	0.030	5/8	24
	IV	13 ½	1 5/16	0.030	7/16	24
	A-V	13 ½	1 5/16	0.030	7/16	24
	B-V	14	1	0.028	13/16	21
	A-VI	15	1	0.025	7/16	-
	B-VI C-VI	11	1	0.032	7/16	18
	D-VI	14	1	0.028	13/16	21
	A-VIII B-VIII	11	1	0.032	7/16	18
	(A)-X	10	13/16	0.021	3/8	-
	(B)-X	12	7/8	0.021	3/8	-
	(C)-X	11	1	0.032	7/16	8
	D-X	12	1	0.025	7/16	-
	30-50-6-75-80	14	1	0.028	13/16	21
OPERA/CONCERT/SCHOOL		13 ½	1 5/16	0.030	5/8	24

* Early versions had a lighter spring
Particular care is recommended when looking to replace AMBEROLA X springs because of the possibility of overlaps of the different motors.

Some Phonograph Sales 1899-1905

	1899-1900	1900-1901	1901-1902	1903-1904	1904-1905
GEM	15062	13363	9923	12540	21458
STANDARD	14053	13199	17946	10976	15197
HOME	15350	12561	10165	3565	4257
TRIUMPH	615	1009	881	267	510
CONCERT	2317	2710	2917	83	75

The chapter on AMBEROLAS contains some statistics for these models

The Edison Phonograph Companies

A number of Edison phonograph companies and their subsidiaries and dependents over the early phonograph years can be confusing and the presentation of this book in Anglo-American form has involved the names of even more concerns. The principal companies dealing either with manufacture or distribution of Edison phonographs, records and accessories are as follows:

1) Edison Speaking Phonograph Company (U.S.)   from April 24th 1878
   operated from January 1878 as The Phonograph Company (for promotion of the TINFOIL Phonograph)

2) Edison Phonograph Toy Manufacturing Company (U.S.)   from October 1887 to 1896
   for promotion of the Edison Talking Doll

3) Edison Phonograph Company (U.S.)   from October 28th 1887 to June 1888
   for promotion of Edison wax cylinder phonograph

4) Gilliland (Edison) Sales Company (U.S.)   June 1888
   sole agent for the 'Perfected' Phonograph

5) Edison Phonograph Works/ex Company (U.S.)   from May 12th 1888
   The manufacturing firm at West Orange supplying machines and cylinders to North American Phonograph Co. and Edison United Phonograph Company

6) <u>North American Phonograph Company</u> (U.S.) bought shares and patents of Edison Phonograph Company and became second sole distributing agent for Edison Phonograph Works in North America except for sales in District of Columbia, Virginia and Delaware where American Graphophone, also part of North American controlled. North American was started by Jesse Lippincott. After he died in early 1893, North American handled only American goods and was declared bankrupt in August 1894. North American had the first monopoly of the talking machine in the United States and the world

from July 14th 1888 to August 1894

7) <u>Edison Phonograph Company</u> (U.K.) formed with Col. Gouraud as proprietor and J. Lewis Young as general manager

mid 1888 to February 1890

8) <u>Edison Phonograph Company</u> (U.S. & U.K.) of Newark, New Jersey and owner of Edison overseas patents. Acquired British Edison patents that had been taken out by Colonel Gouraud, which were sold to Edison Bell Phonograph Corporation in 1892. Edison had no direct financial interest in this company after 1896.

from February 1890 to 1902/3

9) <u>United States Phonograph Company</u> (U.S.) George Tewksbury's company of Newark N.J. and an early Edison export distributing subsidiary, and was bought up by Edison's National Phonograph Company in 1897. Makers of records and accessories

from 1893 to 1897

10) <u>Edison Phonograph Toy and Automaton Co. Ltd.</u> (U.K.)

from 1890 to 1893

11) <u>Edison Bell Phonograph Corporation Ltd.</u> (U.K.) to exploit the Edison phonograph in Great Britain as well as Bell-Tainter Graphophones and office machines; it had acquired the U.K. monopoly to any developments and improvements made in the Edison laboratory also and all machines bought through Edison United.

from November 30th 1892 to 1898

12) <u>National Phonograph Company</u> (U.S.) was formed by Edison to market his goods in the United States, and the third sole sales agent of Edison phonograph products and new holder of Edison phonograph patents in North America

from January 28th 1896 to February 28th 1911

13) <u>Edisonia Limited</u> (U.K.) was licensed sales outlet of Edison Bell Phonograph Corporation Ltd. The first Company lawfully to make and sell Edison Bell machines and other makes in the U.K. from 1898. Proprietors: J. E. Hough and backers. Bought up by Edison Bell Phonograph Corporation Ltd. in 1898, and manufacturing only for second Edison Bell Consolidated Co. in 1902. Edisonia Ltd. originally reformed from London Phonograph Company. <u>The Edisonia Talking Machine Company</u> of Newark, N.J. was formed in 1898 by the three Petit brothers and had no connection with the above.

1897-1898

14) <u>Edison Bell Consolidated Phonograph Co.</u> (U.K.) procured sales of Edison and other makes of machines on the takeover of Edisonia Ltd. with the business of the Edison Bell Phonograph Corporation Ltd. A major shareholder was Edison United Phonograph Company

from 1898 to December 1901

15) <u>Edison Bell Consolidated Phonograph Company Ltd.</u> (U.K.) (The second company, all British) Edisonia manufactured only for this company in 1902. Bankrupt in 1909, then bought by J. E.. Hough to form part of J. E.. Hough Ltd., who bought Edison Bell assets from the receiver in the same year

from December 1901 to March/April 1909

16) (British) <u>National Phonograph Company Limited</u> (U.K.) was incorporated in March 1902 by two Englishmen, J. Lewis Young and Ernest Sinclair 'anticipating' Edison entry into the United Kingdom market, but re-organized by the American company in time for Edison trading to start in the spring of 1903

from 1902

425

17) <u>Thomas A. Edison Inc.</u> (U.S.) from March 1st 1911
was formed from the re-organization of several of Edison-controlled manufacturing enterprises that had existed in separate corporations, including National Phonograph Company. The phonograph department was now presented as 'The Phonograph Division' and 'The Ediphone Division'

18) <u>Thomas A. Edison Ltd.</u> (U.K.) from August 1912
absorbing the National Phonograph Company Limited and Edison Manufacturing Company in Great Britain. Withdraws from Phonograph marketing in Europe in 1914, but marketing other Edison goods, batteries, films, film projectors and office machines.

Index

A

ACME	250
Adams-Randall, Charles	252
Aerophone	21
Aiken, Edward L.	181
AJAX	261
ALVA	52, 161, 250
AMBEROLA	181
American Graphophone	45
Amet, Edward H.	71
Amet motor phonograph	71
Andem, James L.	253
Ansonia Clock Company	29
ARMY & NAVY Disc Phonograph	210
Arnold, William S.	238
Automatic Phonograph Exhibition Company	238, 239
Automatic Reginaphone	259
Automatic Telegraph	13
Automatic Vaudeville Company	276
Auxetophone	278
Aylsworth, Jonas W.	45, 181

B

Babson Brothers	179, 186, 209
Babson, Henry	335
Bacigalupi, Peter	20
Bahr and Proschild	33
Bailey, Charles	21
BALMORAL	52
Barraud, Francis	53
Batchelor, Charles 14, 20, 29, 35, 38, 40, 46, 67, 288, 315	
Batteries	367
Bell, Alexander Graham	14
Bell, Chichester	40
Bell-Tainter	29, 65
Bell-Tainter Graphophone	71
Bergmann, Sigmund	17
Bettini	111
BIJOU	264
Blackman, M.	310
Blue Amberol	35
Brady, Mathew	16
Brehmer Salon Phonograph	18
Briggs, Lowell C.	29
British Patent No. 10,970	252
British Patent No. 15,206	380
British Patent No. 15,245	287
British Patent No. 1644	70
British Patent No. 20,257	35
British Patent No. 2196	132
British Patent No. 2196/09	150
British Patent No. 28,759	320
British Patent No. 3,814	327
British Patent No. 6923	260
British Patent No. 7962	92
British Patent No. 9762	252
British Patent No. 9996	252
Broich, Joseph	72
Buehn Phonograph Company	211
BUSINESS Phonograph	375

C

Capps, Frank	74
Cheever, Charles	17, 238
Chicago Talking Machine Company	71
Chronophone	276
Cinephone	276
CLASS C	53
CLASS E	158
CLASS E CONCERT	261
CLASS H	53
CLASS M	158, 239
CLASS M CONCERT	261
CLASS S	113, 239
CLASS T	65, 66
CLASS W	67
CLIMAX	264
Columbia Phonograph	73
CONCERT	151, 244
CONCERT DUPLEX	404
CONCERT Electric Phonograph	158
CONCERT GRAND	404
CONCERT MAJESTIC	262

CONCERT WINDSOR	262
CONQUEROR	52
Consolidated Electric Storage Company	368
Constable, John P.	186, 211
Cortina Academy of Languages	328
Cortina, Count Rafael Diez de la	328
Cromelin, Paul	226
Cygnet Horn	357

D

Dickinson, Charles	335
Dickson, W. K. L.	46
Dictaphone	369
Dictating Cylinder Phonograph	21
Dolbeer, F. K.	226
Douglas Phonograph Company	341
Douglass, Leon F.	335
Dunton, John C.	255
Dyer, Frank L.	85, 226

E

E Electric	244
ECLIPSE	247, 250
Ediphone	369
Edison Automatic Coin-Slot Phonograph	244
Edison Bell	53
Edison Bell Consolidated Phonograph Co. Ltd.	54
Edison Phonograph Parlor	239
Edison Phonograph Toy Manufacturing Company	29, 33
Edison Phonograph Works	55
Edison Phonographic Toy and Automaton Company Ltd.	35
Edison Speaking Phonograph Company	17, 18, 21, 23, 238
Edison United Phonograph Company	35, 55, 74, 247
Edisonia	53
Edisonic	221
Edmunds, Henry	388
Electric Coin-Slot Phonograph	236, 261
Electrograph	326
EXCELSIOR	264

F

Fire of December 9, 1914	186, 196, 209, 283
FIRESIDE	175
Fitch, William	72
Ford, Henry	212

G

GEM	134
Georgia Phonograph Company	241
Gilliland, Ezra T.	42, 43, 339
Glass, Louis	73
Gouraud, Colonel George	35, 46, 65, 70, 72, 393
Graf, Thomas	349
Graphophone Grand	255
Greenhill, Joseph Exall	71
Gress, G. V.	256

H

Hawthorne and Sheble	51
Herzog Art Furniture Co.	183, 188
Heyerdahl & Co.	43
Hilton Speed Indicator	100
Holden, Delos	181
Holland Brothers	238
Hope-Jones, Robert	276
Hough, James	53
Howe	66
Hubbard, Gardiner G.	17

I

IDELIA	81, 165
IMPERIAL	244
Indestructible Record Company	312
International Correspondence School	146, 330
International Textbook Company	333

J

Jacques, William W.	29, 38
Julien Battery	368

K

Kämmer and Reinhart	35
Keller, Albert	238
Kentucky Phonograph Company	241
KINETOPHONE	275
Kinetophonograph	271
Kinetoscope	271
Kruesi, John	15
Kyoto horn	353

L

Lalande Battery	367
Ling Attachment	239
Ling, Jacob H.	239
Lippincott, Jesse	47, 65, 237
Little Menlo	393
Lombard, Thomas R.	253
London Records	52
London Stereoscope Company	70
London Stereoscopic and Photographic Company	391
London Stereoscopic Company	35, 70
Loriot and Ostrom	20

M

M Electric	244
Macdonald, Thomas	151
Manhattan Phonograph Company	263
Menlo Park	13, 22
Metropolitan Phonograph Company	238
Michigan Phonograph Company	239
MILITARY	49
Miller, Walter	244
Mobley, Edwin H.	313
Moore, George A.	244
Moore, George W.	256
Moore Talking Scale Company	244
Moore's Multiplex Attachment	256
Moriarty, S. F.	48
Moriarty, S.F.	113
Multiphone	255
Multiplex	255
Multiplex Automatic Phonographs	255
Multiplex Coin-Operated Phonographs	255
Multiplex Phonograph Co	256
Music Master	358

N

National Academy of Sciences	43
National Phonograph Company	72, 74
New Diamond Amberola Store	225
New Duplex	403
New Jersey Phonograph Company	241
New York Exhibition Company	238
New York Phonograph Company	52, 161, 241, 407
Nipper	53
North American Phonograph Company	47, 48, 56, 72, 291

O

Ohio Phonograph Company	236, 407
Ohio Phonograph Company of Cincinnati	73
Old Dominion Phonograph Company	241
OPERA	89, 228
ORATORIO	152
Ott, John	20

P

Pacific Phonograph Company	252
Pariophone	237
Parsons, Sir Charles	276
Peerless motor phonograph	71
Perfection coin-slot phonograph	270
PHONO-KINETOSCOPE	271
Phonogram	239
Phonoscope	256
Pierman, Alexander N.	276
Polyphone Attachment	335
Pooley Furniture Company	183, 188
PORTABLE	49
Premier Manufacturing Company Ltd.	132, 146
PREMIUM	226

R

REGAL	244
Regina Company	259
Regina Hexaphone	259
Reginaphone	259
Repeating Attachment	100
Rosenthal, Dr. Richard S.	329
Russell, Oliver D.	29

S

Schiffl, Charles	188
SCHOOL	233
Scribner, George	19
Searchlight Horn Company	353
Shavers	362
Sheip and Vandegrift, Inc.	358
Simon and Helbig	33
Skillin, James L.	255
Spokane Phonograph Company	252
SPRING MOTOR	52, 75
Spring-Driven Coin-Slot Phonograph	263
Spring-Driven Phonograph	70
STANDARD	113
Standard Metal Manufacturing Company	353

Standard Slot Machine	244	U.S. Patent No. 406,569	37
State Phonograph Company	253	U.S. Patent No. 406,570	366
Stevens, B.F.	35	U.S. Patent No. 406,571	366
Stollwerck, Ludwig	75	U.S. Patent No. 413,282	37
Swarf box	47	U.S. Patent No. 414,760	366

T

		U.S. Patent No. 423,039	37, 38
Tainter, Sumner	40	U.S. Patent No. 428,750	252, 342
Talking Doll	21, 28	U.S. Patent No. 428,751	252
Tea Tray Manufacturing Company	353	U.S. Patent No. 430,278	320, 321
Technical Supply Company	333	U.S. Patent No. 440,046	253
Tewksbury, George	74, 75	U.S. Patent No. 441,609	366
The New England Phonograph Company	241	U.S. Patent No. 443,507	380
Tone Tests	222	U.S. Patent No. 453,741	92, 320
Toppan, F. W.	253	U.S. Patent No. 454,941	320
TREADLE	65	U.S. Patent No. 456,301	37, 38
Treadle Phonograph	65	U.S. Patent No. 457,344	366
Triton Motor	74	U.S. Patent No. 460,338	380
TRIUMPH	52	U.S. Patent No. 462,228	92
		U.S. Patent No. 465,972	92, 320, 366

U

		U.S. Patent No. 472,684	260
U.S. Horn Company	353	U.S. Patent No. 484,583	321, 366
U.S. Patent No. 105,338	320	U.S. Patent No. 484,584	320
U.S. Patent No. 200,521	36	U.S. Patent No. 484,585	320
U.S. Patent No. 201,760	287	U.S. Patent No. 488,190	320
U.S. Patent No. 227,679	36, 379	U.S. Patent No. 488,191	380
U.S. Patent No. 341,214	40	U.S. Patent No. 494,633	92
U.S. Patent No. 375,579	69	U.S. Patent No. 495,557	253
U.S. Patent No. 382,414	366	U.S. Patent No. 495,869	260
U.S. Patent No. 382,416	36, 342	U.S. Patent No. 513,097	406
U.S. Patent No. 382,462	36	U.S. Patent No. 518,209	253
U.S. Patent No. 383,299	36	U.S. Patent No. 523,556	342
U.S. Patent No. 386,974	320, 342, 366	U.S. Patent No. 532,718	92
U.S. Patent No. 393,465	366	U.S. Patent No. 535,445	92
U.S. Patent No. 393,466	320	U.S. Patent No. 541,924	270, 342
U.S. Patent No. 393,640	36, 342	U.S. Patent No. 567,738	92
U.S. Patent No. 393,966	36, 320	U.S. Patent No. 568,116	260
U.S. Patent No. 393,967	320	U.S. Patent No. 570,378	92
U.S. Patent No. 393,968	320	U.S. Patent No. 604,740	112, 132
U.S. Patent No. 394,106	37, 320	U.S. Patent No. 605,667	320
U.S. Patent No. 397,280	37, 320	U.S. Patent No. 607,588	112
U.S. Patent No. 400,629	37	U.S. Patent No. 613,670	337
U.S. Patent No. 400,646	37, 320	U.S. Patent No. 634,025	260
U.S. Patent No. 400,647	37, 320	U.S. Patent No. 648,645	157
U.S. Patent No. 400,650	380	U.S. Patent No. 655,225	260
U.S. Patent No. 400,851	37	U.S. Patent No. 680,060	253, 260
U.S. Patent No. 406,568	380	U.S. Patent No. 690,069	320

U.S. Patent No. 702,985	253	U.S. Patent No. 978,014		260
U.S. Patent No. 744,266	320	U.S. Patent No. 996,625		320
U.S. Patent No. 744,267	342	U.S. Patent No. 998,218		361
U.S. Patent No. 771,441	361	U.S. Patent No. 1,002,479		112
U.S. Patent No. 771,851	342	U.S. Patent No. 1,010,333		361
U.S. Patent No. 772,485	380	U.S. Patent No. 1,024,839		321
U.S. Patent No. 772,938	287	U.S. Patent No. 1,041,922		112
U.S. Patent No. 796,857	366	U.S. Patent No. 1,046,188		92
U.S. Patent No. 797,102	260	U.S. Patent No. 1,049,216		320
U.S. Patent No. 797,725	361	U.S. Patent No. 1,050,355		187
U.S. Patent No. 798,087	342	U.S. Patent No. 1,055,621		327
U.S. Patent No. 798,478	92, 112, 132	U.S. Patent No. 1,058,284		361
U.S. Patent No. 800,890	321	U.S. Patent No. 1,167,500		380
U.S. Patent No. 802,212	321	U.S. Patent No. 1,187,115		194
U.S. Patent No. 811,010	92, 157	U.S. Patent No. 1,220,480		187, 232
U.S. Patent No. 816,608	260	U.S. Patent No. 1,229,749		380
U.S. Patent No. 820,158	361	U.S. Patent No. 1,265,179		187
U.S. Patent No. 821,071	92, 112, 174	U.S. Patent No. 1,297,466		380
U.S. Patent No. 829,123	287	U.S. Patent No. 1,359,966		187
U.S. Patent No. 831,455	342	U.S. Patent No. 1,420,317		380
U.S. Patent No. 831,987	93, 174, 232	U.S. Patent No. 1,425,177		187
U.S. Patent No. 832,249	93, 174, 232	U.S. Patent No. 1,465,764		380
U.S. Patent No. 842,042	150	U.S. Patent No. 1,821,621		380
U.S. Patent No. 847,631	380	U.S. Patent No. 2,010,717		380
U.S. Patent No. 855,622	380	United States Phonograph Company		72, 74, 247
U.S. Patent No. 864,686	260	Universal Shaving Machine		365
U.S. Patent No. 865,674	93, 174, 232	**V**		
U.S. Patent No. 867,597	287			
U.S. Patent No. 878,029	361	VICTOR		52
U.S. Patent No. 878,032	92, 112, 174	Victor Talking Machine Company		52
U.S. Patent No. 881,843	361	Vivaphone		276
U.S. Patent No. 883,971	260	Voicewriter Ediphone		378
U.S. Patent No. 889,480	361	VULCAN		261
U.S. Patent No. 905,033	320	**W**		
U.S. Patent No. 909,455	260	Walshaw, Arthur		146
U.S. Patent No. 911,491	342	Wangemann, Theodore		30
U.S. Patent No. 925,430	260	WATER		67
U.S. Patent No. 932,200	132	Water Motor Phonograph		65
U.S. Patent No. 936,264	150	Weber, Peter		183, 188, 195
U.S. Patent No. 942,475	92	West Coast Phonograph Company		252
U.S. Patent No. 948,675	260	West Point horn		360
U.S. Patent No. 951,496	320	WINDSOR		244, 249
U.S. Patent No. 955,424	93, 112, 174	Wolke, Herman		146
U.S. Patent No. 960,560	361	Wortley, Col. Stuart		16
U.S. Patent No. 964,221	349	**Y**		
U.S. Patent No. 975,377	320	Young, J. Lewis		66, 72